Fodor's 2010

NEW ORLEANS

Where to Stay and Eat for All Budgets

Must-See Sights and Local Secrets

Ratings You Can Trust

Fodor's Travel Publications New York, Toronto, London, Sydney, Auckland
www.fodors.com

FODOR'S NEW ORLEANS 2010

Editor: Molly Moker

Editorial Contributors: Michelle Delio, Jeanne Faucheux, Kandace Power Graves, Paul A. Greenberg, Molly Jahncke, David Parker Jr., Sue Strachan

Production Editor: Carrie Parker

Maps & Illustrations: David Lindroth and Mark Stroud, *cartographers*; Bob Blake, Rebecca Baer, *map editors*; William Wu, *information graphics*

Design: Fabrizio LaRocca, *creative director*; Guido Caroti, Siobhan O'Hare, *art directors*; Tina Malaney, Chie Ushio, Ann McBride, Jessica Walsh, *designers*; Melanie Marin, *senior picture editor*

Cover Photo: (French Quarter): Bill Heinsohn/Alamy

Production Manager: Amanda Bullock

ISBN 978–1–4000–0840–7

ISSN 0743–9385

SPECIAL SALES

This book is available at special discounts for bulk purchases for sales promotions or premiums. Special editions, including personalized covers, excerpts of existing books, and corporate imprints, can be created in large quantities for special needs. For more information, write to Special Markets/Premium Sales, 1745 Broadway, MD 6-2, New York, New York 10019, or e-mail specialmarkets@randomhouse.com.

AN IMPORTANT TIP & AN INVITATION

Although all prices, opening times, and other details in this book are based on information supplied to us at press time, changes occur all the time in the travel world, and Fodor's cannot accept responsibility for facts that become outdated or for inadvertent errors or omissions. So **always confirm information when it matters,** especially if you're making a detour to visit a specific place. Your experiences—positive and negative—matter to us. If we have missed or misstated something, **please write to us.** We follow up on all suggestions. Contact the New Orleans editor at editors@fodors.com or c/o Fodor's at 1745 Broadway, New York, NY 10019.

PRINTED IN THE UNITED STATES OF AMERICA

10 9 8 7 6 5 4 3 2 1

Be a Fodor's Correspondent

Your opinion matters. It matters to us. It matters to your fellow Fodor's travelers, too. And we'd like to hear it. In fact, we need to hear it.

When you share your experiences and opinions, you become an active member of the Fodor's community. That means we'll not only use your feedback to make our books better, but we'll publish your names and comments whenever possible. Throughout our guides, look for "Word of Mouth," excerpts of your unvarnished feedback.

Here's how you can help improve Fodor's for all of us.

Tell us when we're right. We rely on local writers to give you an insider's perspective. But our writers and staff editors—who are the best in the business—depend on you. Your positive feedback is a vote to renew our recommendations for the next edition.

Tell us when we're wrong. We're proud that we update most of our guides every year. But we're not perfect. Things change. Hotels cut services. Museums change hours. Charming cafés lose charm. If our writer didn't quite capture the essence of a place, tell us how you'd do it differently. If any of our descriptions are inaccurate or inadequate, we'll incorporate your changes in the next edition and will correct factual errors at fodors.com immediately.

Tell us what to include. You probably have had fantastic travel experiences that aren't yet in Fodor's. Why not share them with a community of like-minded travelers? Maybe you chanced upon a beach or bistro or B&B that you don't want to keep to yourself. Tell us why we should include it. And share your discoveries and experiences with everyone directly at fodors.com. Your input may lead us to add a new listing or highlight a place we cover with a "Highly Recommended" star or with our highest rating, "Fodor's Choice."

Give us your opinion instantly at our feedback center at www.fodors.com/feedback. You may also e-mail editors@fodors.com with the subject line "New Orleans Editor." Or send your nominations, comments, and complaints by mail to New Orleans Editor, Fodor's, 1745 Broadway, New York, NY 10019.

You and travelers like you are the heart of the Fodor's community. Make our community richer by sharing your experiences. Be a Fodor's correspondent.

Happy traveling!

Tim Jarrell, Publisher

CONTENTS

MAPS

Fodor's Features

ABOUT THIS BOOK

OUR RATINGS

Sometimes you find terrific travel experiences and sometimes they just find you. But usually the burden is on you to select the right combination of experiences. That's where our ratings come in.

As travelers we've all discovered a place so wonderful that its worthiness is obvious. And sometimes that place is so experiential that superlatives don't do it justice: you just have to be there to know. These sights, properties, and experiences get our highest rating, **Fodor's Choice,** indicated by orange stars throughout this book.

Black stars highlight sights and properties we deem **Highly Recommended,** places that our writers, editors, and readers praise again and again for consistency and excellence.

By default, there's another category: any place we include in this book is by definition worth your time, unless we say otherwise. And we will.

Disagree with any of our choices? Care to nominate a place or suggest that we rate one more highly? Visit our feedback center at www.fodors.com/feedback.

BUDGET WELL

Hotel and restaurant price categories from ¢ to $$$$ are defined in the opening pages of each chapter. For attractions, we always give standard adult admission fees; reductions are usually available for children, students, and senior citizens. Want to pay with plastic? **AE, D, DC, MC, V** following restaurant and hotel listings indicate if American Express, Discover, Diners Club, MasterCard, and Visa are accepted.

RESTAURANTS

Unless we state otherwise, restaurants are open for lunch and dinner daily. We mention dress only when there's a specific requirement and reservations only when they're essential or not accepted—it's always best to book ahead.

HOTELS

Hotels have private bath, phone, TV, and air-conditioning and operate on the European Plan (aka EP, meaning without meals), unless we specify that they use the Continental Plan (CP, with a continental breakfast), Breakfast Plan (BP, with a full breakfast), Modified American Plan (MAP, with breakfast and dinner), Full American Plan (FAP, with all meals), or are all-inclusive (AI, including all meals and most activities). We always list facilities but not whether you'll be charged an extra fee to use them, so when pricing accommodations, find out what's included.

Many Listings

- ★ Fodor's Choice
- ★ Highly recommended
- ✉ Physical address
- ✣ Directions
- 📫 Mailing address
- ☎ Telephone
- 📠 Fax
- 🌐 On the Web
- ✉ E-mail
- 🎟 Admission fee
- ⏲ Open/closed times
- Ⓜ Metro stations
- 💳 Credit cards

Hotels & Restaurants

- 🏨 Hotel
- 🛏 Number of rooms
- 👍 Facilities
- 🍽 Meal plans
- ✕ Restaurant
- ✍ Reservations
- 🚬 Smoking
- 🍷 BYOB
- ✕🏨 Hotel with restaurant that warrants a visit

Outdoors

- 🏌 Golf
- ⛺ Camping

Other

- 👶 Family-friendly
- ⇨ See also
- ✉ Branch address
- ☞ Take note

Experience New Orleans

WORD OF MOUTH

"NOLA is different things for different people, which is what made it so great. You can party, learn history, walk around and look at gorgeous buildings, see cemeteries and enjoy weather that is typically better than much of the country."

—cancankant

"The purpose of this trip was all about having fun and New Orleans did not disappoint! I knew we were heading to the right town when I surveyed our early morning flight and discovered the majority of people were already partaking in adult beverages. I hadn't seen boozing on a plane that early since my last trip to Las Vegas."

—shormk2

www.fodors.com/community

NEW ORLEANS TODAY

As much as people here would like to move on, there's no getting around Hurricane Katrina—which not only devastated New Orleans, but also reshaped the rest of the world's perception of the city. Four years after the disaster, many people think that New Orleans is either (A) still underwater or (B) completely fine. Neither impression is accurate. The water is gone, but heavily flooded neighborhoods are still rebuilding. The levees that guard the city from storms have been repaired and improved, and big conventions and sporting events have returned—but New Orleans still has a long way to go. The good news for visitors is that virtually all of the attractions that make it such a fun place to be, including the famous French Quarter, are intact. Downtown is buzzing during the day, music pours from clubs every night, and the indomitable spirit and easy manner of the city's residents still make even the most jaded visitor feel welcome.

Today's New Orleans

. . . is still in recovery mode. Four years after Katrina, the areas where tourists tend to wander—downtown, the riverfront, the French Quarter, Faubourg Marigny, the Warehouse District, and the Garden District/Uptown—all show little outward sign of the storm's devastating floods. Tourists visiting these areas could easily forget that an unthinkable national disaster happened here. But predominantly residential areas like East New Orleans, Lakeside, and the Ninth Ward are still visibly struggling to recover. It seems unlikely that New Orleans will ever regain its former population. The most recent statistics indicate that the December 2008 population was roughly two-thirds what it had been prestorm. But Katrina wasn't strong enough to kill New Orleans's soul and vibrant culture: its unique fusion of European, African, and American traditions is still healthy and strong.

. . . is proud of its traditions. Red beans and rice on Monday, St. Joseph's altars, jazz funerals, a Christmas visit to Mr. Bingle in City Park—this is a place steeped in tradition, one that guards its unique customs fiercely. Take Mardi Gras, for example: some of the parading organizations, known as krewes, have been around for more than 150 years, dutifully building elaborate floats each year and parading through the streets in masks. The Mardi Gras Indian tradition, likewise, is shrouded in secrecy and ritual: "tribes" of mostly African-American revelers spend months constructing fanciful, Native American–influenced costumes, in

WHAT WE'RE TALKING ABOUT

Much of the city is happily anticipating May 3, 2010, when Ray Nagin's stint as mayor will officially end after two terms. Nagin, who enjoyed a brief burst of popularity after Hurricane Katrina, is now suspected of running, or at least overseeing, a corrupt administration. (Antics included an all-expenses paid by a City Hall vendor vacation to Hawaii for the Nagin family, and the destruction of thousands of e-mails by his staff, information that Nagin's office is required by law to preserve.) Residents are looking for a different sort of mayor now, preferably a political outsider.

The success of grassroots recovery programs is a happy topic of conversation and a huge contrast to the deep skepticism locals feel about any project with government involvement. Success stories about locally led projects abound, including the Ninth

tribute to actual tribes that once helped escaped slaves find freedom.

. . . is one giant movie set. Or that's how it seems every spring, with multiple film projects going on at any given moment. The scenic backdrop is one reason for all the activity; generous tax credits and a growing local film industry are the other drivers behind what civic boosters have dubbed "Hollywood South." In 2008 there was a lot of buzz surrounding *The Curious Case of Benjamin Button* and its star (and part-time resident) Brad Pitt; in 2009, films made at least in part in New Orleans included action thriller *The Expendables*, comic-western *Jonah Hex*, comedy *I Love You Phillip Morris*, and the supernatural thriller *Dead of Night*.

. . . is like no other place in America. It sounds like a tourist brochure cliché, but it's true: New Orleans does feel like a place out of step with the rest of the country. Some of that is due to geography: this port city has seen an influx of many cultures over the course of its long history. It welcomes diversity and tolerates lifestyles that deviate from the norm—a big reason artists and other creative types have long put down roots here. The fact that the city lies mostly below sea level lends it a certain degree of fatalism and probably, if unconsciously, informs the New Orleans's live-for-today attitude. At times, all that quirkiness can make it a frustrating place to live—but fascinating nonetheless.

. . . is on the verge of ____. Fill in the blank; your guess is as good as anybody's. New Orleans has survived an insane amount of fires, floods, epidemics, and scandals since its founding in 1718, and there are many encouraging signs—new buildings, restorations, festivals (more than 250 events celebrating everything from catfish to hot sauce, swamp stomps to folk art, are listed in *The Times-Picayune* current guide)—that even the hellhound Katrina couldn't keep this amazing city down for long. But questions remain: will the repaired levees hold up against another (God forbid) big storm? Will New Orleans manage to move past its propensity to political scandals, crime, and all the ills of urban poverty? Despite the many fortune-tellers plying their trade in the Quarter, no one knows for sure what the future holds for New Orleans.

Ward's George Washington Carver High School sports program, Brad Pitt's Make it Right housing-renewal program, the New Orleans Hope and Heritage Project which aims to preserve the past and safeguard the future, and Tipitina's Foundation for musicians.

What's that strange smell in the French Quarter? Lately, it's been a citrus-scented spray that SDT, a local sanitation company, uses to clean the streets. The streets of the Quarter are indeed cleaner, and the spray's television commercials have made its owner, Sidney Torres IV, a New Orleans celebrity (his pal Lenny Kravitz stars in one, and Torres's movie-star good looks certainly don't hurt). So fond are locals of Torres's cleanup services that when Mayor Ray Nagin recently tried to cut back, citing budget woes, the city council threatened to file a law suit against him. Nagin backed down. All of this has led to speculation that the handsome Torres may make a run for mayor himself.

NEW ORLEANS PLANNER

Getting There

By air: Most major and a few regional airlines serve Louis Armstrong International Airport in Kenner, 15 mi east of downtown New Orleans. A taxi from the airport to the French Quarter costs a flat rate of $28 for two people; for more than two passengers the fixed rate is $12 per person. Shared-ride shuttles to hotels are available for about $15 per person. If you're traveling light and have a lot of extra time, you can take Jefferson Transit's airport bus, which runs between the main terminal entrance and the CBD. Fare is $1.60.

By train: Three Amtrak lines serve New Orleans: the *City of New Orleans* from Chicago; the *Sunset Limited* service between New Orleans and Los Angeles; and the *Crescent*, which connects New Orleans and New York by way of Atlanta. For tickets and schedules, call ☎ *800/872–7245* or visit 🌐 *www.amtrak.com*.

Getting Around

On public transportation: Streetcars are a great way to see the city. The St. Charles line runs from Canal Street to the intersection of Claiborne and Carrollton avenues; along the way it passes the Garden District, Audubon Park, and Tulane and Loyola universities. The Riverfront line skirts the French Quarter along the Mississippi, from Esplanade Avenue to the Ernest N. Morial Convention Center. Some Canal line streetcars make a straight shot from the Quarter to the cemeteries at City Park Avenue; others take a spur at Carrollton Avenue that goes to City Park and the New Orleans Museum of Art.

At present, bus travel in New Orleans is a pretty depressing experience (although the Regional Transit Authority has pledged to update its aging fleet in the coming months), but a few lines are of use. The Magazine bus runs the length of shopping mecca Magazine Street, from Canal and Camp streets to the Audubon Zoo entrance at the far edge of Audubon Park. The Esplanade bus serves City Park, and drops Jazz Fest passengers off a few blocks from the Fair Grounds.

Fares for streetcars and buses are $1.25 ($1.50 for express lines); VisiTour visitors' passes have one-day unlimited rides for $5 and a three-day unlimited pass for $12. For route maps, timetables, and more information, visit 🌐 *www.norta.com*.

By car: If you don't plan to drive outside the city limits, you probably won't need a car—you'll save money traveling by streetcar, cab, and on foot. If you do decide to drive, keep in mind that some streets are in ragged condition, traffic lights routinely malfunction, and parking in the Quarter is tight (and parking regulations vigorously enforced).

By Taxi: Taxis are often the most convenient way to move around, and drivers are used to short trips, so don't hesitate to grab a cab if you're leery about walking back to your hotel at night. Most locals will recommend United Cabs, Yellow Checker, and Veterans. Don't get into an unlicensed/unmarked "gypsy" cab. Rates are $1.60 per mi or 20¢ for every 40 seconds of waiting, plus a base of $2.50; each additional passenger is $1.

Safety

Much of the post-Katrina media coverage has focused on New Orleans's escalating crime rate. Sadly, this isn't just sensationalism—gangs operate in the city's underpopulated neighborhoods, there's a growing homelessness problem, the murder rate is among the highest in the nation, and armed robberies occur all too frequently. These grim statistics should not dissuade you from visiting, but you need to exercise caution if you venture outside the well-touristed areas—especially at night.

The French Quarter is generally safe, but pay attention to your surroundings and your possessions (especially expensive cameras and dangling shoulder bags). Use special caution in the areas near Rampart Street and below St. Philip Street at night, and be alert on all quiet quarter side streets.

The CBD and Warehouse District are safe, but take a cab at night if there aren't many other pedestrians around.

Do not walk around in the Bywater or the lower part of Faubourg Marigny at night, and avoid Garden District side streets after dark.

Algiers Point is reasonably safe to walk around in by day—but the neighborhoods surrounding it can get sketchy very quickly.

All that said, the New Orleans Police Department does take pains to keep violent crime out of the tourist zones, with many uniformed and plainclothes police stationed throughout the Quarter and at special events.

Helpful Web Sites

www.fodors.com: Log on to the Travel Talk Forums to get advice from New Orleanians and travelers who have recently visited the Crescent City.

www.neworleanscvb.com: Head here for up-to-date information from the New Orleans Convention & Visitors Bureau.

www.nola.com: Find out what's happening from the city's daily newspaper, the *New Orleans Times-Picayune*.

www.nolafugees.com: This Web site offers an irreverent (and frequently off-color) slice of post-Katrina life in New Orleans. Warning: not for the sensitive or easily offended.

www.offbeat.com: The Web site for the monthly magazine *Offbeat* has extensive club and live-music listings, along with features covering the local music scene.

When to Go

May through September is hot and humid—double 100 days (100°F and nearly 100% humidity) aren't uncommon. Just mustering the energy to raise a mint julep to your lips may cause exhaustion. These long, hot summers may explain why things are less hurried down here. If you visit during July and August, you'll find lower hotel prices.

June through November there are heavy rains and occasional hurricanes. These conditions occur mainly with quick changes in temperature that accompany cold fronts in the fall. Although winters are mild compared with those in northern climes, the high humidity can put a chill in the air December through February. Nevertheless, the holiday season is a great time to visit, with few conventions in town, a beautifully bedecked French Quarter, and "Papa Noel" discounted rates at many hotels.

Perhaps the best time to visit the city is early spring. Days are pleasant and nights are cool. The azaleas are in full bloom, the apricot scent of sweet olive trees wafts through the evening air, and the city bustles from one festival to the next. Below are New Orleans's average daily maximum and minimum temperatures.

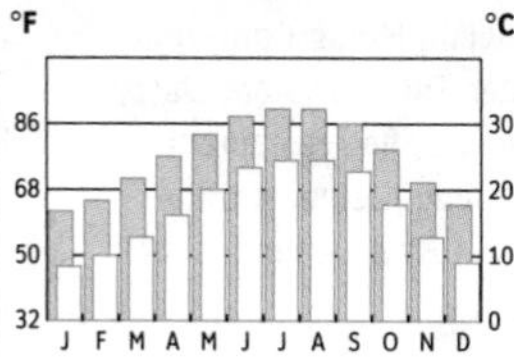

WHAT'S WHERE

1 The French Quarter. The geographic and cultural heart of the city since the early 1700s, the Quarter is a vibrant commercial and residential hodgepodge of wrought-iron balconies, beckoning courtyards, antiques shops—and, of course, tawdry Bourbon Street.

2 Faubourg Marigny and Bywater. The Marigny, New Orleans's first suburb, has nightclubs, cafés, and some lovingly restored Creole cottages; grittier Bywater, despite gentrification, retains its working-class credentials while accommodating a burgeoning arts scene.

3 Tremé. The cradle of jazz and second-line parades fell into decline when much of it was razed to make room for a freeway and public "improvements" like Armstrong Park. But a trip to the tiny Backstreet Cultural Museum conjures memories of the historically African-American neighborhood's heyday.

4 CBD and Warehouse District. Most of the city's newer hotels are clustered here, near Canal Street or the sprawling Morial Convention Center. There also are classy museums, fine restaurants, a bustling casino, and the city's most adventurous art galleries.

5 The Garden District. Stunning early-19th-century mansions make this a great neighborhood for walking, followed by an afternoon browsing the shops and cafés along bustling Magazine Street.

6 Uptown. Audubon Park and the campuses of Tulane and Loyola universities anchor oak-shaded Uptown; hop on the St. Charles streetcar to survey it in period style.

7 Bayou St. John and Mid-City. Rambling City Park and the New Orleans Museum of Art are the main draws here, but there are also some good, inexpensive restaurants and lively bars.

8 Metairie and the Lakefront. The south shore of Lake Pontchartrain is a good place for a bike ride or picnic; suburban Metairie hosts the Metairie Cemetery and Longue Vue House and Gardens.

9 Plantation Country. Hit the tour-bus trail up the Mississippi to see how Louisiana's wealthy planters once lived, and take time to explore some of the pretty small towns like St. Francisville.

10 Cajun Country. Awesome food, rockin' dance halls, more festivals than you can shake a crawfish net at—and in Lafayette, a surprisingly sophisticated cultural scene—await.

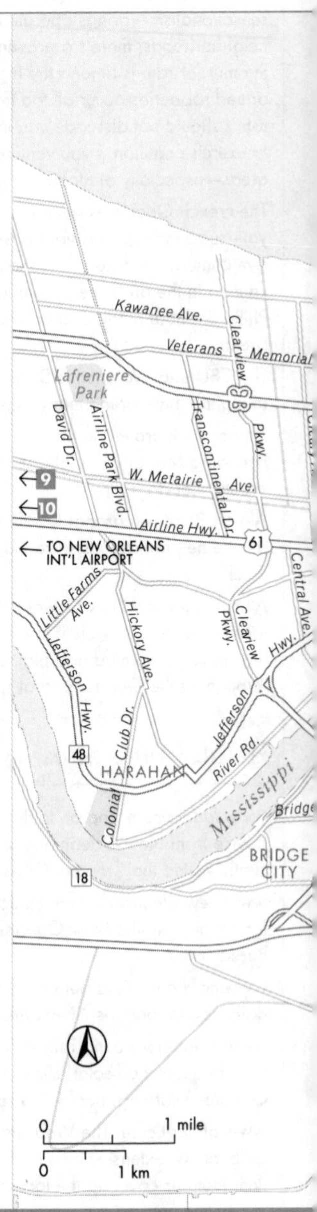

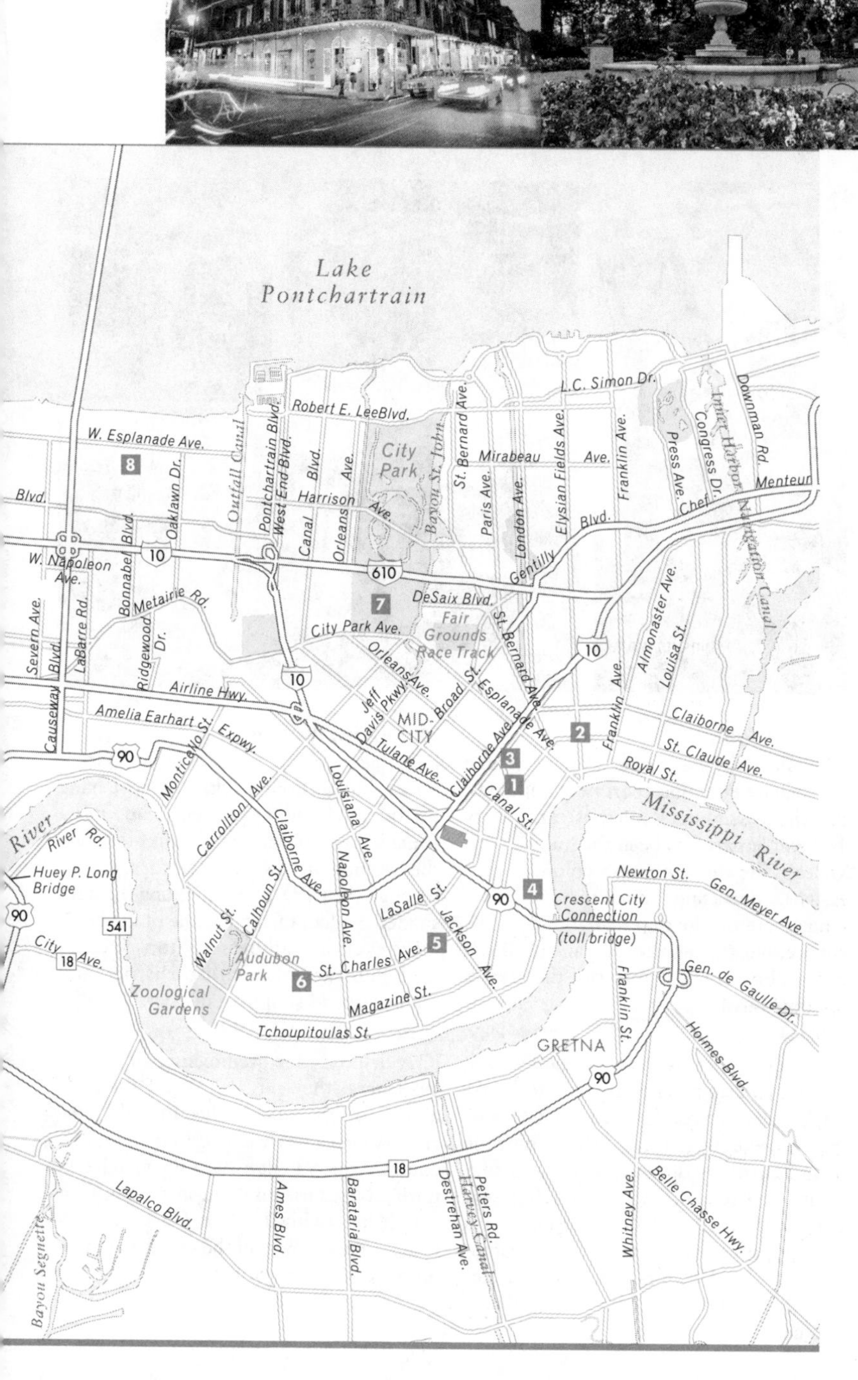
Lake Pontchartrain
City Park
Fair Grounds Race Track
MID-CITY
Mississippi River
Audubon Park
Zoological Gardens
GRETNA
Crescent City Connection (toll bridge)
Huey P. Long Bridge
Robert E. LeeBlvd.
L.C. Simon Dr.
W. Esplanade Ave.
Mirabeau Ave.
Harrison Ave.
Gentilly Blvd.
Chef Menteur
W. Napoleon Ave.
Metairie Rd.
DeSaix Blvd.
City Park Ave.
Airline Hwy.
Amelia Earhart Expwy.
Claiborne Ave.
St. Claude Ave.
Royal St.
Canal St.
Tulane Ave.
Esplanade Ave.
Newton St.
Gen. Meyer Ave.
Gen. de Gaulle Dr.
Holmes Blvd.
St. Charles Ave.
Magazine St.
Tchoupitoulas St.
Lapalco Blvd.
Belle Chasse Hwy.
Bayou Segnette
Harvey Canal
Inner Harbor Navigation Canal
Outfall Canal
Bayou St. John

NEW ORLEANS TOP ATTRACTIONS

Jackson Square

(B) Flanked by St. Louis Cathedral, the antebellum Pontalba apartment buildings, and the Mississippi River, postcard-pretty Jackson Square has been the hub of New Orleans life since the city's colonial start. Artists, musicians, and fortune-tellers congregate on the plaza surrounding the square, but the manicured park itself is a peaceful oasis in the midst of the French Quarter bustle.

Bourbon Street

(A) Crude and crass, New Orleans's most famous entertainment strip isn't to everyone's taste, but you have to see it at least once—preferably under the nighttime neon lights. Tawdry strip clubs and souvenir shops scream for attention, but look closer and you'll find local jazz musicians showing off their chops, elegant restaurants, and faded bars where luminaries like Mark Twain and Tennessee Williams imbibed.

St. Charles Avenue Streetcar

(D) Three streetcar lines converge on Canal Street, but this one packs the most bang for the buck-and-a-quarter. Following a route in use since a steam train first plied the avenue in 1835, streetcars clatter through the CBD, then roll along the oak-shaded median through some of the city's most exclusive addresses. Stops include Audubon Park, the Garden District, and the Riverbend shopping district.

Garden District

(C) A field day for architecture buffs and gardeners, the leafy Garden District is a remarkably intact collection of 19th-century Greek Revival mansions and raised cottages, many built by wealthy merchants during New Orleans's cotton heyday. Cap a visit here with lunch at Commander's Palace and a browse of the shops and cafés on busy Magazine Street.

The Parks

(E) New Orleans is home to two impressive urban parks, each with its own character and attractions. Audubon Park, across from the campuses of Tulane and Loyola universities, sports waterfowl–filled lagoons, a world-class zoo, and great views of the Mississippi River. Across town, City Park is home to the New Orleans Museum of Art and an adjacent sculpture garden, along with the New Orleans Botanical Gardens and a mini-amusement park for kids. Both parks can be reached by streetcar.

French Market

(F) French trappers, seafood vendors, and more than a few rowdy sailors traipsed through these open-air stalls once upon a time. Today the place more resembles a bazaar, and alongside vegetable stalls and charcuteries selling alligator-on-a-stick, crawfish, and Cajun sausages you'll find stands packed with jewelry, bags, cheap sunglasses, and antiques. The quality of the merchandise varies (it's a great place to pick up Mardi Gras beads and hot sauces), but the scene is a lot of fun—especially on weekends.

Plantation Country

(G) Tucked among the chemical plants and oil refineries that generate Louisiana's new money, remnants of the Old South aristocracy line the banks of the Mississippi River from New Orleans to Baton Rouge. Many stately old plantation homes have been carefully restored, filled with period furnishings and opened to the public. However brutal the history, there's no denying the beauty of the mansions and their accompanying gardens. Check out Oak Alley for its famous tree-lined entrance; massive Nottoway plantation house, near White Castle; and the relatively modest Oakley House outside St. Francisville, one of the prettiest towns in the region.

GREAT ITINERARIES

HIGHLIGHTS OF NEW ORLEANS

Including a Trip to Plantation Country

Day 1: The French Quarter

Start by getting to know the city's most famous neighborhood. Sure, it's a cliché, but the café au lait and beignets at Café du Monde are a good place to begin, followed by a stroll around Jackson Square and St. Louis Cathedral. Cross the seawall and take in the views of the Mississippi River from Woldenberg Riverfront Park. Wander along North Peters Street to the shops and market stalls in the French Market, followed by a stroll around the mostly residential Lower Quarter and Faubourg Marigny. After lunch, explore the antiques stores and art galleries on Royal and Chartres streets, winding it all up with a cocktail in a shady courtyard; try Napoleon House, an atmospheric bar and café that makes a mean Pimm's Cup, or the French Quarter mainstay Pat O'Brien's. Save Bourbon Street for after dinner at one of the Quarter's esteemed restaurants; like anything that's lived hard and been around as long, it's much more attractive in low light.

Day 2: Uptown and the Garden District

The St. Charles Avenue streetcar rumbles past some of the South's most-prized real estate; take a seat in one of the antique wooden seats, raise a window, and admire the scenery on the way to leafy Audubon Park. Follow the paved footpath to the Audubon Zoo, keeping an eye out for the zoo's white tigers, a pair of albino brothers named Rex and Zulu. Board an inbound Magazine Street bus near the zoo entrance and take it a couple of blocks past Louisiana Avenue, where a number of restaurants, some with sidewalk tables, are clustered. Continue on Magazine to Washington Avenue and head left through the Garden District. Prytania Street, just past Lafayette Cemetery No. 1 (Anne Rice fans, take note), is a good axis from which you can explore the neighborhood's elegant side streets. Catch a downtown-bound streetcar on St. Charles, or wrap up the afternoon shopping and dining on Magazine Street.

Day 3: Remembering Katrina

It may strike some as macabre, but touring neighborhoods that were devastated by Hurricane Katrina and its subsequent floods has become a ritual for many visitors, not unlike the hordes that have made Lower Manhattan's Ground Zero a pilgrimage site. You can opt for a guided bus tour, which takes you to Lakeview and the infamous 17th Street Canal levee breach; some companies also travel to the Ninth Ward and Chalmette. If you have your own transportation, follow a drive through Katrina's aftermath on page 28 in our Remembering Katrina feature. After a somber tour of Katrina's devastation, a good antidote is to look for signs of renewal and rebirth. City Park, which sustained extensive wind and flood damage, has reopened its stately botanical gardens; nearby stands the venerable New Orleans Museum of Art and the adjacent Sydney and Walda Besthoff Sculpture Garden. Wrap the day up with dinner and live music downtown at one of the clubs on Frenchmen Street, in the Faubourg Marigny neighborhood, where the city's diehard party spirit soldiers on.

Day 4: Art, History, and Culture

Dedicate one day to a deeper exploration of the city's cultural attractions. Art lovers shouldn't miss the Warehouse

District, where a pair of fine museums—the Ogden Museum of Southern Art and the Contemporary Arts Center—anchors a vibrant strip of contemporary art galleries, most of which feature local artists. History buffs will want to check out the National World War II Museum, also in the Warehouse District, and the Historical Collection of New Orleans in the French Quarter, which hosts changing exhibits in a beautifully restored town home. New Orleans music aficionados can browse the bins at the Louisiana Music Factory, which has a wide selection of CDs—and occasional in-store performances—by Louisiana musicians.

Day 5: Heading Out of Town

Consider a day trip out of town to visit one of the region's elegant plantation homes, explore Cajun Country, or take a guided swamp tour. Some tour companies offer a combination of these destinations, with lunch included. Many of the antebellum mansions between New Orleans and Baton Rouge have been painstakingly restored and filled with period furniture; nature lovers will want to set aside time to explore the grounds and lush flower gardens. Swamp tours may sound hokey, but they're actually a good way to see south Louisiana's cypress-studded wetlands (and get up close and personal with the alligators and other critters that live there). Continue the nautical theme in the evening with a ride to Algiers Point aboard the Canal Street ferry for lovely sunset views of the New Orleans skyline.

TIPS

If you're venturing out in your own vehicle, be aware that street conditions, which weren't great to begin with, are still in disrepair in some places. Many bridges and neighborhood streets may be closed for repairs. Traffic signals can be erratic, and in the worst of the flood-damaged neighborhoods, debris and roofing nails left behind by contractors can be hazardous to tires.

Summers in New Orleans arrive early and stick around longer than most people would like. If visiting in the hot months, stay hydrated, limit your midday outdoor activities, and be prepared for sudden, sometimes torrential downpours.

Bring a sweater or light jacket with you: air-conditioning in attractions and restaurants can be aggressive.

New Orleanians are friendly, but odd requests from people on the street who offer to tell you where you got your shoes ("You got them on your feet," followed by demanding that you pay for this information) and other overtures from chatty, rather dubious-looking types should be ignored (feel free to pretend you don't speak English, if you like). Trust your intuition; if something doesn't feel right, don't worry about coming across as mean, just continue along your way.

Before you book your trip, visit *www.neworleansonline.com*, click travel tools, and download the sheet of coupons for lodging, dining, attractions, tour, and shopping discounts. This site is owned by the New Orleans Tourism Marketing Corporation and is also a great source for event information. *www.neworleanscvb.com* also offers a selection of downloadable coupons.

LOCAL FOR A DAY

Tired of time-share hawkers and tap dancers? Want to spend some time enjoying New Orleans the way locals do? Step one: get out of the Quarter.

Get Some Exercise

Go for a jog along the St. Charles Avenue streetcar tracks. You'll have plenty of company anywhere between Jackson Avenue and the university area—just follow the well-worn trails along the wide median (to really pass for a local, refer to it as the "neutral ground"). Keep an eye out for streetcars (duh) as well as vehicles crossing the tracks. If that sounds too risky, hit the paths in City Park. Or rent a bicycle and head for Audubon Park, where you can get on a paved jogging and bike trail that runs along the Mississippi River levee well into Jefferson Parish.

Find a Market

The Crescent City Farmers Market sets up at the corner of Girod and Magazine streets in the CBD on Saturday mornings; on Tuesday from 9 AM to 1 PM, it's held Uptown at Tulane Square, on Leake Avenue at Broadway. While you may not want to lug a bag of broccoli back to your hotel, there's always some good prepared food for sale (and a guest-chef-created weekly Green Plate Special), local chefs foraging for ingredients, and an entertaining bunch of vendors. If you happen to be around the third Saturday of the month, check out the Bywater Art Market at Palmer Park (at Royal and Piety streets in the Bywater), where the merchandise is high quality and the crowd never less than colorful.

Queue Up for Breakfast

Contrary to the impression you may have gleaned from Hollywood's version of New Orleans, locals as a rule do not start the morning with café au lait and a plate of beignets—but they do have their favorite spots, where on weekends you'll find lines of hungry customers stretching onto the sidewalk. Both Bluebird Café for pecan waffles and cheese grits (☒*3625 Prytania St., Uptown* ☎*504/895–7166*) and Slim Goodies Diner for sweet potato pancakes (☒*3322 Magazine St., Uptown* ☎*504/891–3447*) are open weekdays, when there's less chance of a wait. Thanks to word-of-mouth advertising, Elizabeth's (☒*601 Gallier St., Bywater* ☎*504/944–9272*) gets its share of tourists, but the Saturday and Sunday brunch crowd still mostly consists of neighborhood denizens.

Hang Out by the River

Locals love Riverview Drive—better known as the Fly—the riverside stretch of Audubon Park behind the zoo, even if they have no idea how it got its nickname (probably from a butterfly-shaped building that used to stand here). There are a couple of baseball diamonds and a football/soccer field, but most people are content to spread out on a blanket, have a picnic, and watch the ships go by on the Mississippi. The nearby dog park, on the levee just upriver from the park, is another popular gathering spot, especially in late afternoon.

NEW ORLEANS WITH KIDS

Get Out and Play

City Park. There's plenty to do here for the younger set, including two free playgrounds: one with swings near the Peristyle, and a new playground for older kids, just off Marconi Drive, that has more challenging things to clamber on. Storyland, a fairy tale theme park, is open on weekends year-round, and features a number of sculptures created by Blaine Kern Studios, the maker of Mardi Gras floats. Adjacent Carousel Gardens Amusement Park has low-impact rides, a miniature train that tours the park, and a beautiful 100-year-old carousel as a centerpiece. It's open weekends from March through December.

Barataria Preserve. Let the kids burn off some excess energy on the trails in this swamp outpost of the Jean Lafitte National Historic Park, about 15 mi from the French Quarter. Come when it's warm and you'll see lots of creepy-crawlies, including alligators.

Animals Everywhere!

Audubon Zoo. A well-designed showcase for animals from all over the world, the zoo also has a hands-on area for kids—where young volunteers show off real live zoo residents—and a petting zoo with docile goats, among other beasts.

Aquarium of the Americas. Loads of exotic sea creatures, a penguin exhibit, and an interactive area where kids can get their hands wet make the aquarium a favorite family destination. There's a fun museum shop and an IMAX theater next door.

Kiddie Culture

Louisiana Children's Museum. The Warehouse District museum tries to sneak in a little education while giving kids a place to romp, role-play, and dabble in the arts.

Rivertown. This 16-block historic district is packed full of kid-friendly fun. It's a bit of a haul out to Kenner, near the airport, but worth the effort to catch a Saturday-afternoon performance in the Children's Castle or to visit the Louisiana Toy Train Museum.

Summer Stages Children's Theater. This drama school for young actors stages kid-friendly fare in summer and a holiday program.

For Kids of All Ages

Blaine Kern's Mardi Gras World at Kern Studios. The city's most famous float-building family offers tours of their company's vast studio, where kids can try on costumes and watch the artists at work. In March 2009, the studio moved to new digs in the Robin Street Wharf behind the Ernest N. Morial Convention Center. The new space is five times larger than the old Algiers site.

Streetcars. You can't leave New Orleans without taking the kids for a ride in a streetcar, which you can also use to get to several of the sites listed above, including City Park (on the Canal Street line) and Audubon Park (St. Charles Avenue).

FREE AND ALMOST FREE

Free Museums and Galleries

Unless you're a dues-paying member or a Louisiana resident, you won't get a break at most New Orleans museums—although you can buy a Power Pass (three days, $107 per person, *www.visiticket.com*) to save a significant amount on the admittance fees to the city's leading museums and attractions. It costs nothing, however, to browse the Warehouse District galleries on and around Julia Street, where you'll find works by established and up-and-coming artists. Make a detour through the lobby and mezzanine of the Renaissance Arts Hotel (⊠*700 Tchoupitoulas St.*), which has an impressive collection on display.

The Sydney and Walda Besthoff Sculpture Garden in City Park, next to the New Orleans Museum of Art, has major work by important 20th-century artists, including Henry Moore, Jacques Lipchitz, Barbara Hepworth, and Seymour Lipton, dramatically set among lagoons and moss-laden oak trees.

Uptown, on the Tulane University campus, the Newcomb Art Gallery hosts shows featuring work by internationally known artists—like the photographer Diane Arbus and master silversmith William Spratling, two recent examples—as well as themed exhibitions and work by Newcomb's art school alumni.

Free Music

Outdoor festivals like the Satchmo Summer Fest and French Quarter Festival are great places to hear live music for free. Street bands also serenade visitors daily in the French Quarter—although if you linger, you'll be asked to toss a few bucks into the hat.

Drop by the Jean Lafitte National Historic Park's French Quarter visitor center to get a schedule of upcoming shows; the park hosts concerts by Louisiana musicians in the courtyard. ⊠*419 Decatur St.* ☎*504/589–3882.*

The New Orleans Jazz National Historical Park sponsors live performances and lectures Tuesday–Saturday at its French Market office (⊠*916 N. Peters St.* ☎*504/589–4806*). The performers—who are invariably good—cover the jazz spectrum, from traditional brass band music to modern jazz.

If you happen to be in town on a Wednesday from early April to late June, check out the free Wednesday at the Square concert series at Lafayette Square in the CBD, across from Gallier Hall. Around 5 PM, a horde of downtown workers converges on the square to hear good local bands, dance, and socialize. There's plenty of food and drink available (not free, alas).

Free Ride

The Canal–Algiers ferry offers some of the best views of the city, and there's no charge if you're not in a car. It's a fun thing to do with kids, and a great way to get a sense of the Mississippi River's magnitude. The pedestrian entrance is on the plaza at the foot of Canal Street, across from Harrah's Casino; it docks on the West Bank at Algiers Point, a quaint historic neighborhood that makes for a good daytime stroll. At night, though, stay on board for the return trip.

A ride on one of the streetcars is a fun, cheap way to see the city. For just $1.25, you can take a ride Uptown, to the Riverfront, or to City Park, with stops at various attractions along the way. All three lines pick up on Canal Street. So pull the window down, sit back, and enjoy the sights.

OFFBEAT NEW ORLEANS

Cemeteries

It may sound odd, but the old cemeteries in and around New Orleans, where tombs have to be built above the boggy ground to keep the remains of loved ones from drifting away, are fascinating places to visit. Those near the French Quarter (St. Louis No. 2 and St. Roch, for example) aren't safe to visit alone, however; it's best to go on a tour or with a large group. Lake Lawn Metairie Cemetery (✉ *5100 Pontchartrain Blvd.* ☎ *504/486–6331*), on the other hand, is safe to tour; the office even offers audio guides to help motorists find their way around the stately cemetery, the final resting place of luminaries like Al Hirt, Louis Prima, and Civil War general P. G. T. Beauregard. Guided tours are available by appointment. One note: because it's a very busy cemetery, officials prefer that people visit between 8:30 and 10:30 AM or after 3:30 PM, when there's less chance of disrupting a funeral in progress.

Snoballs

Generations of New Orleanians who grew up in the days before air-conditioning developed a method for coping with stifling summers: the snoball, shaved ice served in a cup or Chinese take-out container and topped with everything from simple syrup to fat-laden condensed milk. Hansen's Sno-Blitz Sweet Shop (✉ *4801 Tchoupitoulas St.* ☎ *504/891–9788* ⏲ *May–Aug.*) has been dishing them out since 1934; another stalwart is Plum Street Snowball at 1300 Burdette Street (☎ *504/866–7996* ⏲ *Mar.–Oct.*). For visitors, the fun lies less in the actual product (although a snoball can be pretty darn refreshing on a hot summer day) than in being part of a local ritual.

Weird Museums

Home to a small but interesting collection of art and artifacts related to voodoo history and practice in the city, the New Orleans Historic Voodoo Museum (✉ *724 Dumaine St.* ☎ *504/680–0128*) offers insight into a spiritual tradition that persists to this day. It's worth a visit if only for the handcrafted voodoo dolls and gris-gris (magic talisman) bags sold in the small shop.

Louis Dufilho, America's first licensed pharmacist, operated an apothecary, La Pharmacie Francaise, in this 1823 town home. Today it holds the New Orleans Pharmacy Museum (✉ *514 Chartres St.* ☎ *504/565–8027*), an interesting collection of ancient medicine bottles, a huge leech jar, eyeglasses, and some truly unsettling surgical instruments. The house and spacious courtyard alone are worth the price of admission.

Tiny Abita Springs, north of Lake Pontchartrain, is notable for three things: artesian spring water, Abita Beer, and an oddball institution, the U. C. M. Museum (✉ *22275 Hwy. 36, at Grover St., Abita Springs* ☎ *985/892–2624*). Artist John Preble's strange vision—sort of a Louisiana version of Watts Towers—is an obsessive collection of found objects (combs, old musical instruments, paint-by-number art, taxidermy experiments gone horribly awry . . .) set in a series of ramshackle buildings, including one covered in broken tiles. Truly odd and entertaining, but not for the clutter-phobic.

BEST FESTS AND PARADES

New Year's Eve

You'd expect a party town to throw a big New Year's bash, right? Join the crowd on the Mississippi River near Jax Brewery for fireworks, live music, and the annual countdown to midnight (marked by "Baby Bacchus" dropping from the top of the brewery).

Mardi Gras, February or March

There's simply nothing quite like Mardi Gras. The biggest event in the city's busy festival calendar has been around for well over a century, and for a celebration of frivolity, people here take Carnival very seriously. There are almost daily parades—even one for dogs, the Krewe of Barkus—in the two weeks leading up to Fat Tuesday, when pretty much the entire city takes the day off, gets in costume, and hits the streets. *www.mardigrasneworleans.com.*

St. Patrick's Day, March

A couple of big parades roll on the weekend closest to March 17: one that starts at Molly's in the Market and winds through the French Quarter, and an Uptown parade that goes down Magazine Street. On St. Paddy's Day, the streets around Parasol's Restaurant & Bar, in the Irish Channel neighborhood, turn into one big, green block party. Two days later (March 19) the town celebrates Saint Joseph's Day with home-cooked food and goodie bags filled with cookies and lucky fava beans. Check the *Times-Picayune* classified ads for announcements of altars that you can visit, and be prepared to make a small contribution to cover costs—$5 a person or so.

Easter

Three fun parades hit the streets of the French Quarter on Easter Sunday: one led by local entertainer Chris Owens, another dedicated to the late socialite Germaine Wells, and a gay parade that takes the festive bonnet tradition to a whole new level.

Tennessee Williams/New Orleans Literary Festival, March

This annual tribute to the *Streetcar Named Desire* playwright, who spent much of his career in New Orleans, draws well-known and aspiring writers, lecturers, and a handful of Williams's acquaintances. It closes with contestants reenacting Stanley Kowalski's big "Stella-a-a!" moment. ☎*504/581–1144* *www.tennesseewilliams.net.*

French Quarter Festival, April

A lot of locals consider this the best festival. With stages set up throughout the Quarter and on the river at Woldenberg Park, the focus is on local entertainment—and, of course, food. ☎*504/522–5730* *www.fqfi.org.*

Louisiana Strawberry Festival, April (Ponchatoula, LA)

They grow 'em big and sweet north of Lake Pontchartrain, and this annual berry-theme bash draws big crowds. Expect rides, a parade, beauty contests, music, and lots of dessert. ☎*985/370–1889 or 800/917–7045* *www.lastrawberryfestival.com.*

Festival International de Louisiane, late April (Lafayette, LA)

Lafayette's pretty downtown becomes one big stage for musicians from Louisiana and throughout the French-speaking world. There's art, theater and dance, great food—and, best of all, the entertainment is free. ☎*337/232–8086* *www.festivalinternational.com.*

New Orleans Jazz & Heritage Festival, April–May

Top-notch local and international talent take to several stages the last weekend of April and first weekend of May. The

repertoire covers much more than jazz, with big-name pop stars in the mix, and there are dozens of lectures, quality arts and crafts, and awesome food to boot. Next to Mardi Gras, Jazz Fest is the city's biggest draw; book your hotel as far in advance as possible. ☎*504/410–4100* ⊕*www.nojazzfest.com.*

Breaux Bridge Crawfish Festival, early May (Breaux Bridge, LA)

The hard-partying Cajun may be a stereotype, but this festival in Breaux Bridge, 12 mi east of Lafayette, only reinforces it. There's lots of great Cajun and zydeco music to go with the mudbugs. ☎*337/332–6655* ⊕*www.bbcrawfest.com.*

New Orleans Wine & Food Experience, May

Winemakers and oenophiles from all over the world converge for five days of seminars, tastings, and fine food. The Royal Street Stroll, when shops and galleries host pourings and chefs set up tables on the street, is especially lively. ☎*504/529–9463* ⊕*www.nowfe.com.*

Essence Music Festival, July

Held around Independence Day, this three-day festival draws top names in R&B, pop, and hip-hop to the Louisiana Superdome. The event also includes talks by prominent African-American figures and empowerment seminars. ⊕*www.essence.com/essence/emf.*

Southern Decadence, early September

Labor Day means picnics, a long weekend, and—in New Orleans, at least—hundreds of drag queens–for-a-day parading through the Quarter. What began as a small party among friends has evolved into one of the South's biggest gay celebrations. The parade rolls (and as the day wears on, staggers) on Sunday, but Decadence parties and events start Thursday evening.

Art for Art's Sake, early October

Art lovers and people-watchers pack the Warehouse District and Magazine Street galleries for this annual Saturday-evening kickoff to the arts season. What's on the walls usually plays second fiddle to the party scene, which spills out into the streets.

Celebration in the Oaks, late November–early January

City Park's majestic oaks, Botanical Gardens, Carousel Garden, and Storyland amusement park are awash in holiday lights and decorations during this popular weeks-long event. There's food and rides, a miniature train decked out for Christmas, and entertainment by local school groups. ☎*504/482–4888* ⊕*neworleanscitypark.com.*

A New Orleans Christmas, December

The lighting of Canal Street kicks off this monthlong celebration. Royal Street shops and historic homes don holiday decorations, restaurants feature special *reveillon* menus, and thousands of carolers gather in Jackson Square for a candlelit sing-along. Around Christmas, bonfires are lighted on the levee at various points along the Mississippi, from below New Orleans up into Cajun Country. Legend says the bonfires were lighted by the early settlers to help Papa Noel (the Cajun Santa Claus) find his way up the river. Steamboat tour companies offer special cruises for the occasion.

GET OUTTA TOWN

Cajun Country

The land that gave the world one of its great cuisines—and a refuge for French-Canadian exiles in the 18th century—is worth at least one overnighter. Lafayette, with its attractive downtown and plentiful accommodations, makes a good hub for exploring the region. The Cajun kitsch can be a bit much at times, but there are some outstanding restaurants and museums, including the Paul and Lulu University Art Museum and Acadian Village, a re-creation of an early-19th-century Acadian settlement. Venture south to picturesque Abbeville, where restaurants serve up some mean oysters on the half shell, or to New Iberia and nearby Avery Island, home of the famous Tabasco hot sauce and a gorgeous 250-acre garden. Breaux Bridge, site of the annual Crawfish Festival, has antiques shops and some excellent Cajun restaurants, including Café des Amis and Mulate's. St. Martinville, south of Breaux Bridge, is an attractive small town and home of the Evangeline Oak, immortalized in Longfellow's classic poem "Evangeline."

To the north lie Grand Coteau, a quaint, historic village set on a natural bluff, and Opelousas, a hotbed of zydeco music; nearby Plaisance hosts the annual Southwest Louisiana Zydeco Music festival each Labor Day weekend. A bit farther afield, the normally quiet town of Mamou goes bonkers on Fat Tuesday, when the traditional Courir de Mardi Gras takes to the streets; Saturday mornings, little Fred's Lounge gets packed to the gills with locals and more than a few tourists two-stepping and waltzing to live Cajun music.

Plantation Country

For *Gone With the Wind* fans, the stretch of the Mississippi north of New Orleans is the ultimate Southern experience. Tour buses ply the highway on both sides of the river, but with a car and a map, it's easy to explore on your own. Fortunes were made here in the 18th and 19th centuries—on the backs of the slaves that worked these plantations—and vestiges of the Old South's wealthy heyday remain in the region's lavish homes, many lovingly restored and open to the public. Highlights include Oak Alley, with its procession of ancient oak trees that flank the entrance, and Nottoway, the largest extant plantation house. Several homes offer accommodations and dining for those who want to linger.

Many of the small towns that dot Plantation Country are fun to explore, but St. Francisville, about 25 mi north of Baton Rouge, deserves special mention. The historic town center is a well-preserved collection of antebellum homes and buildings, and the river landing there is one of the few places in south Louisiana where the Mississippi isn't hemmed in by levees. A cluster of fine plantation homes are nearby, including Rosedown Plantation and Gardens and the attractive Oakley House at Audubon State Historic Site, where John James Audubon taught drawing to the plantation owner's daughter while executing some of the works in his Birds of America series. Baton Rouge itself is worth a visit to see the Old State Capitol (and the new one, where Governor Huey P. Long met his untimely end) and its lively downtown.

REMEMBERING KATRINA

It took New Orleans nearly 300 years to etch its image on the public consciousness—a city known around the world for food and music, pageantry and debauchery, and an irreverent, *laissez-faire* culture more attuned to the Caribbean than the Heartland. But it took one great storm a matter of hours to sear a new picture.

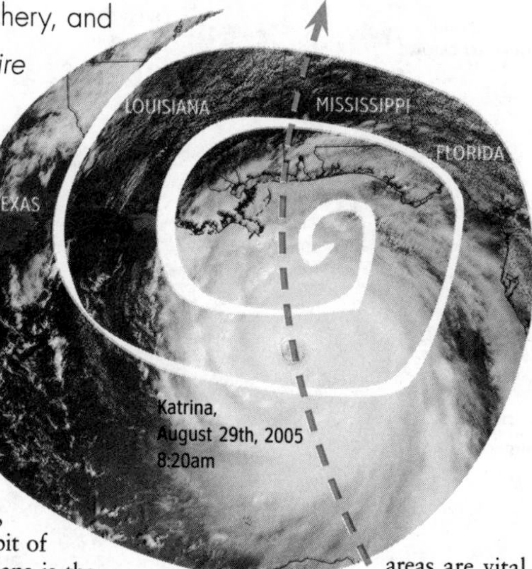

The site of the nation's worst natural disaster in more than a century and, for a few terrifying days, a pit of human suffering, New Orleans is the first major American city to be nearly drained of its population. Four years after Hurricane Katrina struck, the city has regained about ⅔ of its former population. Yet several New Orleans neighborhoods remain in a kind of limbo. Small businesses and some residents have trickled back into the heavily damaged areas, but many more are waiting for a number of factors to kick in—insurance settlements, federal and state assistance, and direction from city officials—before they return.

Visitors have come back, and they find that the city retains its sense of joy and hospitality. French Quarter and Morial Convention Center areas are vital. For many, however, it's important to see first-hand the places millions of people came to know through news reports and images: neighborhoods like the Lower Ninth Ward, where a torrent of water tossed houses and cars, and the 17th Street Canal, where brackish Lake Pontchartrain poured through a collapsed floodwall and inundated much of the city.

The following pages include a recap of the disaster, a self-guided driving tour of damaged neighborhoods, and information on how you can help rebuild the city.

Evacuee arrives at New Orleans airport

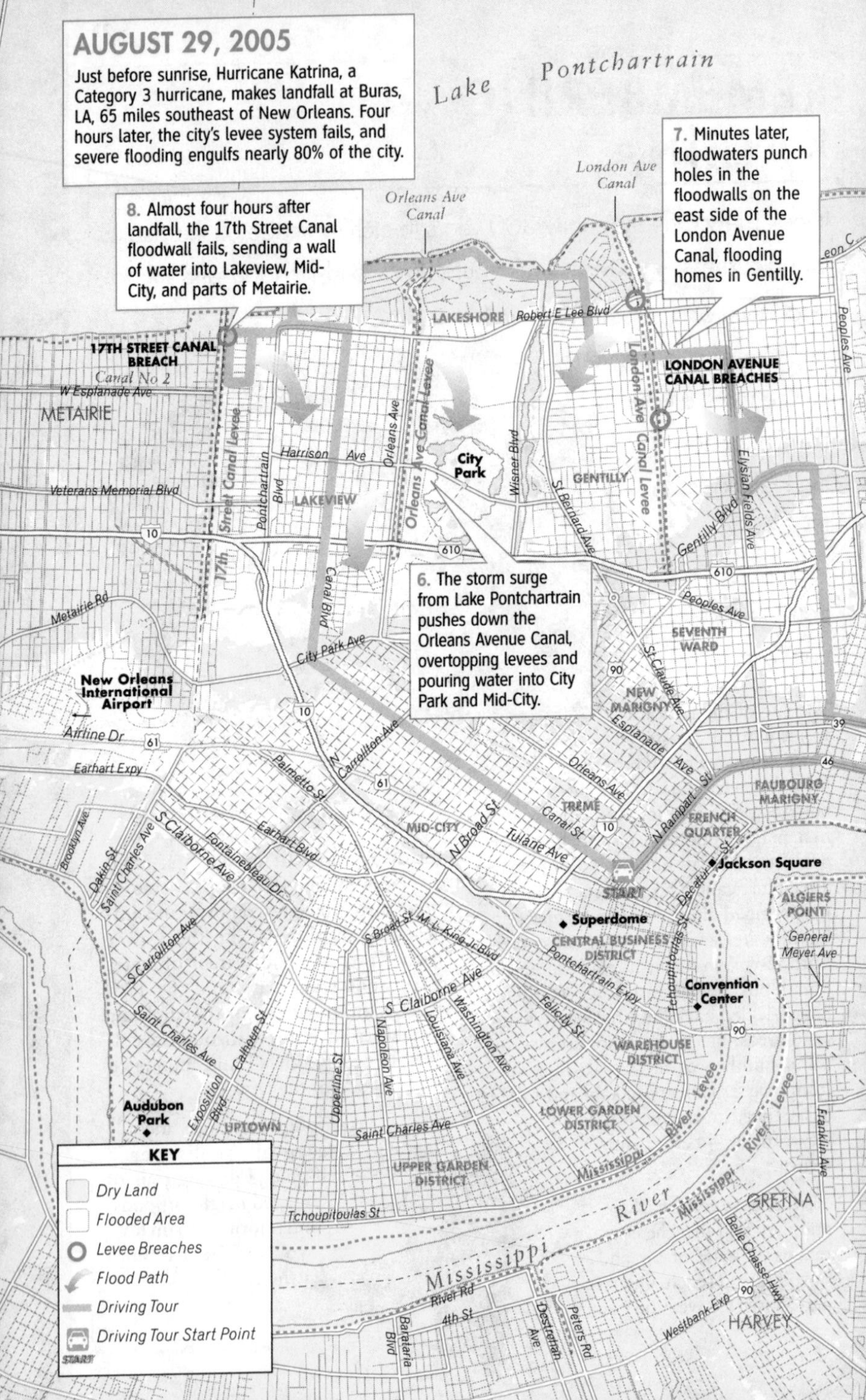
AUGUST 29, 2005
Just before sunrise, Hurricane Katrina, a Category 3 hurricane, makes landfall at Buras, LA, 65 miles southeast of New Orleans. Four hours later, the city's levee system fails, and severe flooding engulfs nearly 80% of the city.
Lake Pontchartrain
7. Minutes later, floodwaters punch holes in the floodwalls on the east side of the London Avenue Canal, flooding homes in Gentilly.
8. Almost four hours after landfall, the 17th Street Canal floodwall fails, sending a wall of water into Lakeview, Mid-City, and parts of Metairie.
6. The storm surge from Lake Pontchartrain pushes down the Orleans Avenue Canal, overtopping levees and pouring water into City Park and Mid-City.
17TH STREET CANAL BREACH
LONDON AVENUE CANAL BREACHES
Orleans Ave Canal
London Ave Canal
LAKESHORE
Robert E Lee Blvd
Canal No 2
W Esplanade Ave
METAIRIE
17th Street Canal Levee
Orleans Ave Canal Levee
London Ave Canal Levee
Harrison Ave
City Park
GENTILLY
LAKEVIEW
Veterans Memorial Blvd
Pontchartrain Blvd
Orleans Ave
Wisner Blvd
St Bernard Ave
Gentilly Blvd
Elysian Fields Ave
Peoples Ave
Canal Blvd
Metairie Rd
City Park Ave
SEVENTH WARD
NEW MARIGNY
St Claude Ave
Esplanade Ave
New Orleans International Airport
Airline Dr
Earhart Expy
Palmetto St
N Carrollton Ave
Orleans Ave
TREME
Canal St
MID-CITY
N Broad St
Tulane Ave
N Rampart St
FAUBOURG MARIGNY
FRENCH QUARTER
Jackson Square
START
Superdome
CENTRAL BUSINESS DISTRICT
ALGIERS POINT
General Meyer Ave
Brooklyn Ave
Dakin St
Saint Charles Ave
S Claiborne Ave
Fontainebleau Dr
Earhart Blvd
S Broad St
M L King Jr Blvd
Pontchartrain Expy
Decatur St
Tchoupitoulas St
Convention Center
S Carrollton Ave
S Claiborne Ave
Felicity St
WAREHOUSE DISTRICT
Saint Charles Ave
Calhoun St
Napoleon Ave
Louisiana Ave
Washington Ave
Uppertine St
Audubon Park
Exposition Blvd
UPTOWN
Saint Charles Ave
LOWER GARDEN DISTRICT
River Levee
UPPER GARDEN DISTRICT
Mississippi
Tchoupitoulas St
Mississippi River
GRETNA
Franklin Ave
Belle Chasse Hwy
River Rd
4th St
Barataria Blvd
Destrehan Ave
Peters Rd
Westbank Exp
HARVEY
KEY
Dry Land
Flooded Area
Levee Breaches
Flood Path
Driving Tour
Driving Tour Start Point
START

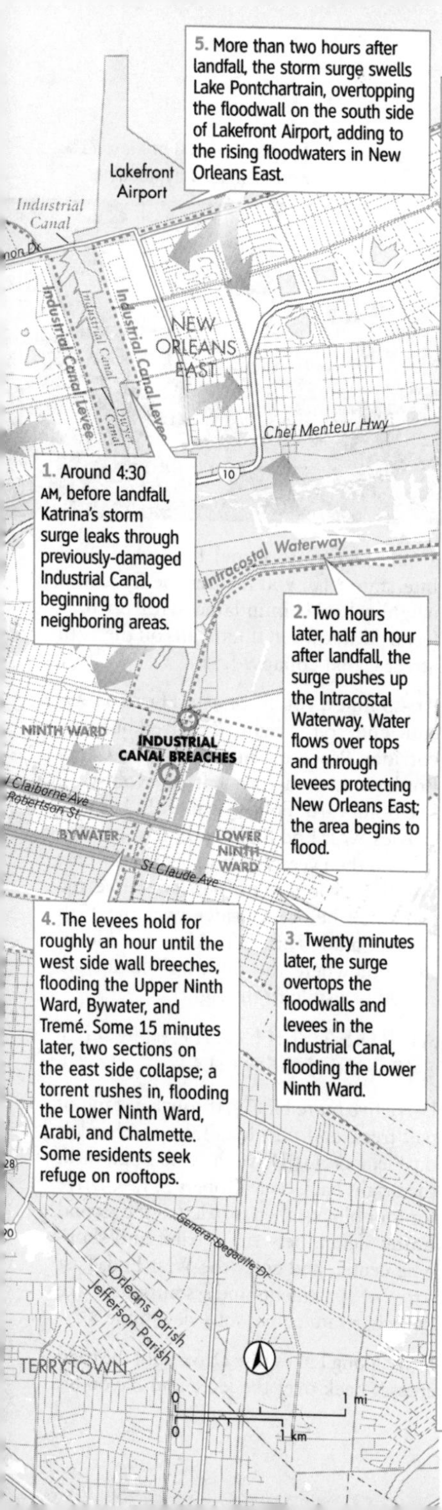

1. Around 4:30 AM, before landfall, Katrina's storm surge leaks through previously-damaged Industrial Canal, beginning to flood neighboring areas.

2. Two hours later, half an hour after landfall, the surge pushes up the Intracostal Waterway. Water flows over tops and through levees protecting New Orleans East; the area begins to flood.

3. Twenty minutes later, the surge overtops the floodwalls and levees in the Industrial Canal, flooding the Lower Ninth Ward.

4. The levees hold for roughly an hour until the west side wall breeches, flooding the Upper Ninth Ward, Bywater, and Tremé. Some 15 minutes later, two sections on the east side collapse; a torrent rushes in, flooding the Lower Ninth Ward, Arabi, and Chalmette. Some residents seek refuge on rooftops.

5. More than two hours after landfall, the storm surge swells Lake Pontchartrain, overtopping the floodwall on the south side of Lakefront Airport, adding to the rising floodwaters in New Orleans East.

Lakefront Airport
Industrial Canal
Industrial Canal Levee
NEW ORLEANS EAST
Chef Menteur Hwy
10
Intracostal Waterway
NINTH WARD
INDUSTRIAL CANAL BREACHES
Claiborne Ave
Robertson St
BYWATER
LOWER NINTH WARD
St Claude Ave
General Degaulle Dr
Orleans Parish
Jefferson Parish
TERRYTOWN
0 1 mi
0 1 km

The days that followed

August 30
The breach at the 17th Street Canal gets larger; Lakeview floodwaters rise to nine feet. Many people climb onto roofs to escape. Crowds build at the Superdome, seeking refuge. Rescuers in helicopters and boats pick up hundreds of stranded people, and reports of looting begin to emerge.

August 31
The first buses arrive at the Superdome to take refugees to the Astrodome in Houston.

September 1
National Guard arrives. Looting, carjacking, and other violence spreads. Crowds at the Superdome swell to 25,000, with another 20,000 at the New Orleans Convention Center.

September 2
Congress approves $10.5 billion for immediate rescue and relief efforts.

September 4
Superdome and Convention Center are fully evacuated. Nearly 45,000 refugees.

September 8
An additional $52 billion in aid approved by Congress.

September 17
Business owners are allowed back into Algiers, French Quarter, the CBD, and Uptown.

September 23
A storm surge from Hurricane Rita overtops an Industrial Canal levee, reflooding the Lower Ninth Ward; surge also tops the London Avenue Canal, reflooding Gentilly.

September 26
After suspending re-entry due to Hurricane Rita, the city allows residents to return.

February 18, 2006
The first official Mardi Gras parade (in Orleans Parish), Pontchartrain, rolls.

February 28
Amid controversey, thousands turn out to celebrate Mardi Gras.

April 28
First day of New Orleans Jazz and Heritage Festival.

May 20
C. Ray Nagin is re-elected Mayor of New Orleans.

June 24
Approximately 20,000 attend American Library Association meeting, the largest conference in the city post Katrina.

Hurricane Katrina was the **third-strongest landfalling U.S. hurricane** ever recorded.

Nearly 80% of the city was flooded.

Almost 200,000 homes, 71%, were damaged by flooding.

Car and levee in the Lower Ninth Ward.

A POST-KATRINA DRIVE

Now that New Orleans' tourist areas are completely repaired, to truly understand the devastation of Hurricane Katrina you need to see it at the neighborhood level. This tour will give you a sobering glimpse of the formidable challenges the city faces as it rebuilds its levees and neighborhoods and restores its population. As you tour the flood-destroyed areas, you may encounter debris, potholes, malfunctioning traffic signals, and construction. Bring a map, and be prepared to alter your route. Use appropriate caution; as some neighborhoods have repopulated, crime, unfortunately, has also returned. This tour is not for everyone: Heed warnings in the city and don't drive at night.

TO MID-CITY & 17TH ST. CANAL

Start at the intersection of Canal and North Rampart streets. Driving on Canal, away from the Mississippi River, alongside the streetcar tracks, you'll pass under the Interstate 10 elevated freeway at North Claiborne Avenue and into Mid-City. You will pass many buildings that are still boarded up, some bearing the ominous stain of the flood line. At just over 2 miles, you'll reach the intersection of Canal and South Carrollton Avenue, where a cluster of restaurants has reopened. Another 0.8 miles, at the end of the streetcar tracks, you'll reach City Park Avenue and a pair of historic cemeteries. Take a right, then a quick left onto Canal Boulevard. Past Interstate 610, you'll enter the Lakeview neighborhood, inundated with up to 9 feet of water when floodwalls on the 17th Street Canal collapsed.

At 4.5 miles, you'll come to Harrison Avenue and, to the right, a revived business corridor. Proceed 1 mile farther on Canal Boulevard, then turn left on Robert E. Lee Boulevard. Follow Robert E. Lee as it crosses West End Boulevard, first curving left and then veering right. Six blocks past West End, you'll come to Bellair Drive, the last street before a bridge over the 17th Street Canal. Turn left. After one block, the spot where the floodwall break occurred is visible to the right.

ACROSS THE LAKEFRONT THROUGH GENTILLY

Drive five more blocks, through a stand of oak trees, and turn left. Take another left on Fleur de Lis Drive, a wide boulevard, then right back on to Robert E. Lee. Drive for four blocks, then turn left at the second traffic signal, between a bank and shopping center, and enter the West End. Past a row of apartments and restaurants, Lake Pontchartrain comes into view (mile 8).

Drive along Lakeshore Drive until the road crosses back over the levee and Bayou St.

New Orleans population: 462,270 (August 2005), 295,450 (December 2007), 311,850 (July 2008).

There are now 888 restaurants open in the New Orleans metropolitan area.

Almost all New Orleans major hotels have reopened; 33,000 of 38,000 rooms are now available.

Above: Abandoned homes near the 17th St. Canal breach. Right: Scenes from Tennessee street, in the Lower Ninth Ward.

John. (Note that Lakeshore Drive can be closed to traffic for no apparent reason; Robert E. Lee can be used as an alternate route.) At the traffic circle, take a right on Paris Avenue; here, you'll pass through a neighborhood that escaped relatively unscathed. After Paris Avenue crosses Robert E. Lee, the damage quickly becomes apparent. Eight blocks past Robert E. Lee, pass Fillmore Avenue, make a U turn, turn right on Fillmore, and cross the London Avenue Canal. Storm surge from the canal was responsible for destroying much of the surrounding neighborhood. At 12.6 miles, turn right on Elysian Fields Avenue. Drive 1 mile, and continue through the large intersection at Gentilly Boulevard. Then, make a U-turn, and turn right on Gentilly Boulevard (a shady ridge that stayed mostly above water).

At mile 14, turn right on Franklin Avenue. The street passes under a freeway and through a hard-hit section of the 7th Ward before arriving at North Claiborne Avenue.

TO THE LOWER NINTH WARD

Cross North Claiborne, then North Robertson. Go one-half block, make a U-turn, then take a right on North Robertson. This street takes you into the Upper Ninth Ward and, in about 1.5 miles, over the Industrial Canal. To the left is the Lower Ninth Ward. One block past the foot of the bridge make a U turn, then turn right on Tennessee Street. To the left is the site of the levee breach that destroyed the neighborhood; it has since been repaired. Go seven blocks to North Tonti, turn right, then drive one block and take a right again on Reynes. Most of the houses and debris have long been cleared, so there are few reminders that this was once a densely populated neighborhood. Cross North Claiborne and, five blocks later, take a right on St. Claude Avenue, where you will cross another drawbridge.

St. Claude Avenue proceeds through the Upper Ninth Ward; Bywater, which did not flood, is on the left as you make your way back Downtown. A little over a mile past the Industrial Canal, you'll cross a series of railroad tracks. Just past Elysian Fields Avenue, St. Claude curves to the left and merges with North Rampart Street before arriving at Esplanade Avenue and the French Quarter's edge. From here, it's less than a mile on North Rampart to your Canal Street starting point.

VOLUNTOURISM

Tourism is the driving force behind New Orleans's economy, and visitors' dollars are helping the city rebuild. But if you want to have a more-direct impact on the Crescent City's reconstruction, get to work. The groups listed below help connect volunteers with all sorts of jobs—everything from gutting/rebuilding homes, landscaping, environmental and cultural preservation, to clerical assistance.

BAYOU REBIRTH

Bayou Rebirth matches volunteers to wetlands restoration projects in Southeast Louisiana. Healthy wetlands, like the ones that once surrounded the greater New Orleans area, lessen the impact of hurricane storm surges. In addition to helping renew precious environmental resources, volunteers get to experience the beautiful ecosystem of the Mississippi River delta. Full day and half day opportunities are available. ☎ *504/267–7500* 🌐 *bayourebirth.org*

BEACON OF HOPE

This grass roots organization is focused on rebuilding neighborhoods in the Lakeside, Gentilly, and Lower Ninth Ward neighborhoods—and actually getting the work done rather than sitting in meetings talking about it. Volunteer opportunities range from light office work to heavy cleanup. In general they work with groups of 10–200 volunteers. ☎ *504/322–2514* 🌐 *www.lakewoodbeacon.org*

CATHOLIC CHARITIES

Volunteer opportunities range from half day activities to two day opportunities, from assisting at Second Harvesters Food Bank to helping repaint and repair a person's home damaged from Katrina. ☎ *504/310–6962* 🌐 *www.ccano.org*

HABITAT FOR HUMANITY

Habitat's mission is to eliminate homelessness and make housing affordable. The organization is building new homes in Orleans and St. Bernard parishes; the most-prominent project is the almost-complete Musicians' Village in the Upper Ninth Ward.

Volunteers work from 7:15 AM to 2 PM and must be at least 16 years old. ☎ *504/861–2077* 🌐 *www.habitat-nola.org*

KATRINA CORPS

This grass-roots organization works with multiple groups and hosts a variety of different projects. Service opportunities include renovating/repairing schools and houses, house gutting, land preservation, and mentoring. Katrina Corps asks for contributions per volunteer (average $10–$20) and provides lunch, transportation, tools, and beverages. ☎ *413/627–4992* 🌐 *www.katrinacorps.org*

THE NEW ORLEANS HOPE AND HERITAGE PROJECT

This community-based organization puts local people in charge of city renewal efforts and disaster planning. Projects range from evacuation plans for humans and pets, community-based insurance plans, home rebuilding programs, internships in construction and community care, counseling for post-traumatic stress disorder, and developing neighborhood cultural centers. 🌐 *www.neworleanshealingcenter.org*

Exploring New Orleans

2

WORD OF MOUTH

"Get an all day streetcar ticket for $5 and take a ride up the St. Charles line to see all of the beautiful homes including the Wedding Cake house."

—writealiving

"Much of the fun of NOLA is exploring and you'll certainly stumble across several interesting places. Don't forget to visit Frenchmen St."

—SAnParis2

"Take a tour of the graveyards . . . but only on a tour, don't do it with just yourself or one more person. Also, take the ghost tour . . . we did the one that starts at the voodoo shop and it was great."

—BWBlakely

www.fodors.com/community

By Michelle Delio and Molly Jahncke

SOMETIME DURING YOUR VISIT TO NEW ORLEANS, find a wrought-iron balcony, an oak-shaded courtyard, or a columned front porch and sit quietly, favorite beverage in hand, at 6 AM. At this hour, when the moist air sits heavy on the streets, New Orleans is a city of mesmerizing tranquility. Treasure those rare minutes of calm in a city where there is so much to see, hear, eat, drink, and do.

The spiritual and cultural heart of New Orleans is the French Quarter, where the city was settled by the French in 1718. You can easily spend several days visiting museums, shops, and eateries in this area. Yet the rest of the city's neighborhoods, radiating out from this focal point, also make for rewarding rambling. The mansion-lined streets of the Garden District and Uptown, the aboveground cemeteries that dot the city, and the open air along Lake Pontchartrain provide a nice balance to the commercialization of the Quarter. Despite its sprawling size, New Orleans has a small-town vibe, perhaps due to locals' shared cultural habits and history. Families have lived in the same neighborhoods for generations; red beans and rice appears on almost every table on Monday; people visit cemeteries and whitewash the tombs of their departed on All Saints' Day; and from the smartest office to the most down-home local bar, New Orleanians are ready to celebrate anything at the drop of a hat.

To experience this fun-filled city, you can begin with the usual tourist attractions, but you must go beyond them to linger in a corner grocery store, sip a cold drink in a local joint, or chat with a stoop-sitter. New Orleanians, for all their gripes and grumbling, love their city. They treasure custom and tradition, take in stride the heat and humidity of a semitropical climate, and face life with a laid-back attitude and an undying sense of hope and faith that sometimes seems fatalistic to outsiders.

GETTING YOUR BEARINGS

The city occupies an 8-mi stretch between the Mississippi River and Lake Pontchartrain, covering roughly 365 square mi of flat, swamp-drained land. The heart of the city, downtown, includes the famous old area called the Vieux Carré (Old Square), or the French Quarter; the historic African-American district of Tremé; the Central Business District (CBD); and the Warehouse District. Across the river from downtown is an extension of New Orleans known as the Westbank, which includes the neighborhood of Algiers Point.

Downriver from the sights-packed French Quarter are the Faubourg Marigny and the Bywater districts, neighborhoods developed in the early 1800s. This mainly residential area is also home to eateries, cafés, music clubs, and collectibles shops. Across Rampart Street from the French Quarter lies Tremé. A couple of small museums add to the allure of this historic residential area. Although parts of this neighborhood saw significant flooding from Hurricane Katrina, most of the damage was caused by wind, rather than water. The museums have now returned, along with many residents.

Canal Street divides the French Quarter from the "American Sector," as it was designated in the early days following the Louisiana

Purchase. Americans built their homes in increasing extravagance as they began to make money in the city and moved farther upriver. Eventually, a business district overtook what had been the residential blocks just uptown from Canal, and now the lawyers and artists of the CBD and Warehouse District share the area, taking advantage of the bars, clubs, and loft apartment buildings in this burgeoning neighborhood. Since Katrina, the CBD has seen a faster recovery and more growth—including new music venues and bars—than practically any part of the city.

WHICH WAY?

Directions in a city that bases its compass on the curve of the river can be hopelessly confusing. Canal Street, a long avenue that runs from the river to the lake, divides the city roughly into uptown and downtown sections. Streets to the north of Canal are named North and run downtown; those to the south of Canal are named South and run uptown. Only the French Quarter is laid out in a grid pattern. Ask a New Orleanian for directions and you are likely to hear about so many blocks downtown or uptown and on the lake or river side. The best advice is to keep a map handy at all times.

Canal Street, which was undergoing a revival before the storm, has seen a slower recovery than other parts of the CBD. Although a handful of new stores have opened along the street, more than a few storefronts remain shuttered. Some new clothing stores have moved in, replacing businesses unable to recover from Katrina. The historic streetcar continues to run down the center of the street. The foot of Canal Street, where the French Quarter, the CBD, the Warehouse District, and the Mississippi River converge, is the site of major attractions such as the Aquarium of the Americas, Woldenberg Riverfront Park, Harrah's New Orleans Casino, and the Riverwalk shopping-and-entertainment complex.

The St. Charles Avenue streetcar parallels the Mississippi River on a route several blocks inland along St. Charles Avenue, home to antebellum mansions, the Garden District, and the university sector Uptown. It is usually the best way to get to these areas.

Metairie, hurricane-damaged Mid-City, and the lakefront are accessible primarily by automobile. City Park, within Mid-City, covers a vast area that includes the New Orleans Museum of Art, the Botanical Garden, and an outdoor sculpture garden, plus miles of lagoons, golf courses, and recreation areas. The park was significantly damaged by Katrina, but groups of volunteers have joined with park employees to make it once again a worthwhile place to while away the afternoon.

The Mississippi River dominates New Orleans, even passing through one corner of it. The point across the river from downtown, Algiers, was settled in the late 1800s and remained fairly isolated until a modern bridge and regularly scheduled ferries connected it with the east bank in the 1960s. Algiers continues to maintain a small-town flavor, with pocket parks surrounded by Victorian cottages and oak-canopied streets.

GETTING AROUND

Downtown, the Garden District, and Algiers are best explored on foot, because sites are near one another and should be experienced at a slow pace. For other areas, biking, driving, or riding the streetcar is recommended because of the long distances covered.

If you want to visit the areas damaged by Hurricane Katrina, you will have to do it by car. Many of these areas are still deserted and should not be toured on foot or at night.

TAKE CARE

Be alert to conditions around you, taking precautions not to wander alone on deserted streets or in questionable areas. New Orleans has a high crime rate. If in doubt about the safety of sights to visit, ask hotel personnel for advice, tour areas in groups when possible, and take a cab at night. (Areas requiring special precautions are noted throughout this chapter.)

THE FRENCH QUARTER

The French Quarter was largely spared Katrina's destruction. Although flooding and disorder touched its Canal Street edge, you'll have to look closely to find signs of damage elsewhere within its well-defined borders. In the weeks and months following Katrina, the French Quarter became a focal point of media coverage and recovery operations. In this center of New Orleans cuisine and culture, a great commissary for emergency personnel was erected beside the old Jackson Brewery.

Although the crowds have been lighter since the storm, the nightlife returned here almost immediately. Contractors and relief workers quickly found their way to the Bourbon Street clubs, reviving the raucous, bawdy spirit of that strip. Since Katrina, the French Quarter has resumed its role as a major center of tourism and entertainment, where music pours from the doorways of bars as freely as the drinks flow within them. On an ordinary evening, a stroll through the French Quarter is also a moving concert, where the strains of traditional jazz, blues, classic rock and roll, and electronic dance beats all commingle.

During the day, the Quarter offers several different faces to its visitors. The streets running parallel to the river all carry distinct personas: Decatur Street is a strip of tourist shops and hotels uptown from Jackson Square; downtown from the square, it becomes an alternative hangout for leather-clad regulars drawn to shadowy bars, vintage clothing resellers, and novelty shops. Chartres Street is a relatively calm stretch of inviting shops and eateries. Royal Street is the address of sophisticated antiques shops and many of the Quarter's finest homes. Bourbon Street claims the sex shops, extravagant cocktails, and music clubs filmmakers love to feature. Dauphine and Burgundy streets are more residential, with just a few restaurants and bars serving as retreats for locals.

The French Quarter is the only section of New Orleans in which you will find an easily navigable grid pattern to the streets, so take advantage of it. The city curves with the river, so locals generally describe locations based on relative proximity to the river or the lake and to uptown or downtown. Thus, "it's on the downtown, lakeside corner" of a given intersection indicates that a destination is more or less on the northeast corner. As local directions also often refer to the number block that a site is on (as in the 500 block of Royal Street), block numbers are included on the French Quarter and Faubourg Marigny map. The numbers across the top of the map are applicable to all the streets parallel to North Rampart Street. Those streets in the French Quarter that are perpendicular to North Rampart Street all start at 500 at Decatur Street and progress at increments of 100 at each block in the direction of North Rampart.

Numbers in the margin correspond to numbers on the French Quarter and Faubourg Marigny map.

JACKSON SQUARE AND THE RIVERFRONT

WHAT TO SEE

12 **Aquarium of the Americas.** Power failures during Katrina resulted in the major loss of the Aquarium's collection of more than 7,000 aquatic creatures. In a dramatic gesture of solidarity, aquariums around the country joined together with the Aquarium of the Americas in an effort to repopulate its stock. The museum, now fully reopened, has four major exhibit areas—the Amazon Rain Forest, the Caribbean Reef, the Mississippi River, and the Gulf Coast—all of which have fish and animals native to that environment. A special treat is the Seahorse Gallery, which showcases seemingly endless varieties of these beautiful creatures. The aquarium's spectacular design allows you to feel part of the watery worlds by providing close-up encounters with the inhabitants. A gift shop and café are on the premises.

Fodor's Choice ★

Woldenberg Riverfront Park, which surrounds the aquarium, is a tranquil spot with a view of the Mississippi. Package tickets for the aquarium and a river cruise are available outside the aquarium. You can also combine tickets for the aquarium and the **Entergy IMAX Theater,** a river cruise, and the **Audubon Zoo** in a package, or take the river cruise by itself. Note that the zoo cruise halts operation for several weeks around December each year for maintenance. ✉ *1 Canal St., French Quarter* ☎ *504/581–4629 or 800/774–7394* 🌐 *www.auduboninstitute.org* 🎟 *Aquarium $18; combination ticket with IMAX $23.50; combination ticket for aquarium, zoo, and round-trip cruise $41* ⏲ *Aquarium Tues.–Sun. 10–5.*

10 **Audubon Insectarium.** Shrink down to ant size and experience "Life Underground," explore the world's insect myth and lore, venture into a Louisiana swamp, and marvel at the hundreds of delicate denizens in the Japanese butterfly garden. Then tour the termite pavilion and other sections devoted to havoc insects in order to sample Cajun-fried crickets and other insect cuisine without a twinge of guilt. All this and more awaits you at the Audubon Insectarium, a $25 million facility that opened in the historic Customs House in June 2008. ✉ *423 Canal St., French Quarter* ☎ *800/774–7394* 🌐 *auduboninstitute.org* 🎟 *$15* ⏲ *Tues.–Sun. 10–6.*

16 **The Cabildo.** Dating from 1799, this Spanish colonial–style building is named for the Spanish council—or *cabildo*—that met there. The

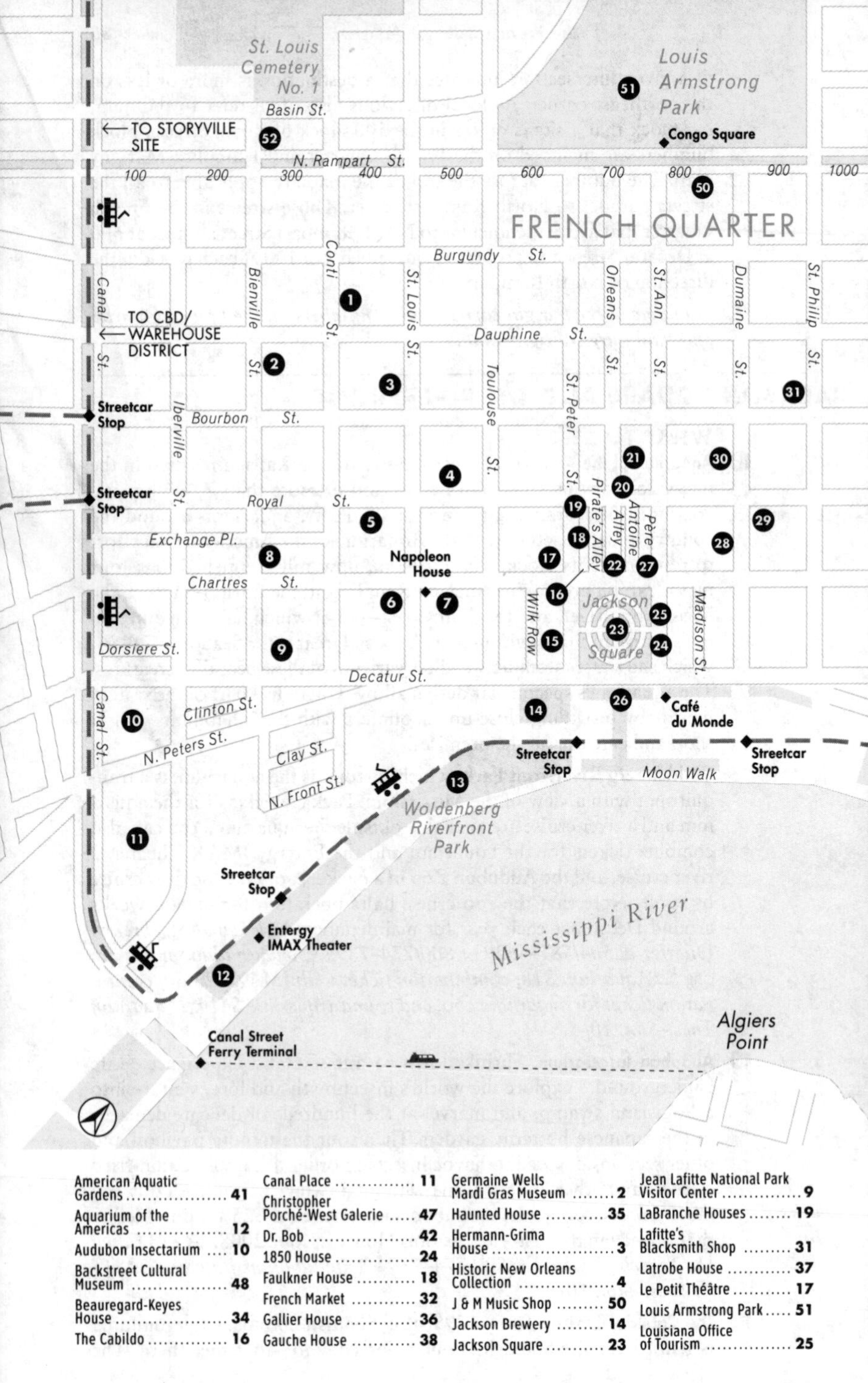
St. Louis Cemetery No. 1
Louis Armstrong Park
Congo Square
Basin St.
← TO STORYVILLE SITE
N. Rampart St.
100
200
300
400
500
600
700
800
900
1000
FRENCH QUARTER
Burgundy St.
Dauphine St.
Bourbon St.
Royal St.
Exchange Pl.
Chartres St.
Dorsiere St.
Decatur St.
Clinton St.
N. Peters St.
Clay St.
N. Front St.
Canal St.
Iberville St.
Bienville St.
Conti St.
St. Louis St.
Toulouse St.
St. Peter St.
Orleans St.
St. Ann St.
Dumaine St.
St. Philip St.
Pirate's Alley
Père Antoine Alley
Wilk Row
Madison St.
TO CBD/ WAREHOUSE DISTRICT
Streetcar Stop
Napoleon House
Jackson Square
Café du Monde
Moon Walk
Woldenberg Riverfront Park
Entergy IMAX Theater
Mississippi River
Canal Street Ferry Terminal
Algiers Point
American Aquatic Gardens 41
Aquarium of the Americas 12
Audubon Insectarium 10
Backstreet Cultural Museum 48
Beauregard-Keyes House 34
The Cabildo 16
Canal Place 11
Christopher Porché-West Galerie 47
Dr. Bob 42
1850 House 24
Faulkner House 18
French Market 32
Gallier House 36
Gauche House 38
Germaine Wells Mardi Gras Museum 2
Haunted House 35
Hermann-Grima House 3
Historic New Orleans Collection 4
J & M Music Shop 50
Jackson Brewery 14
Jackson Square 23
Jean Lafitte National Park Visitor Center 9
LaBranche Houses 19
Lafitte's Blacksmith Shop 31
Latrobe House 37
Le Petit Théâtre 17
Louis Armstrong Park 51
Louisiana Office of Tourism 25

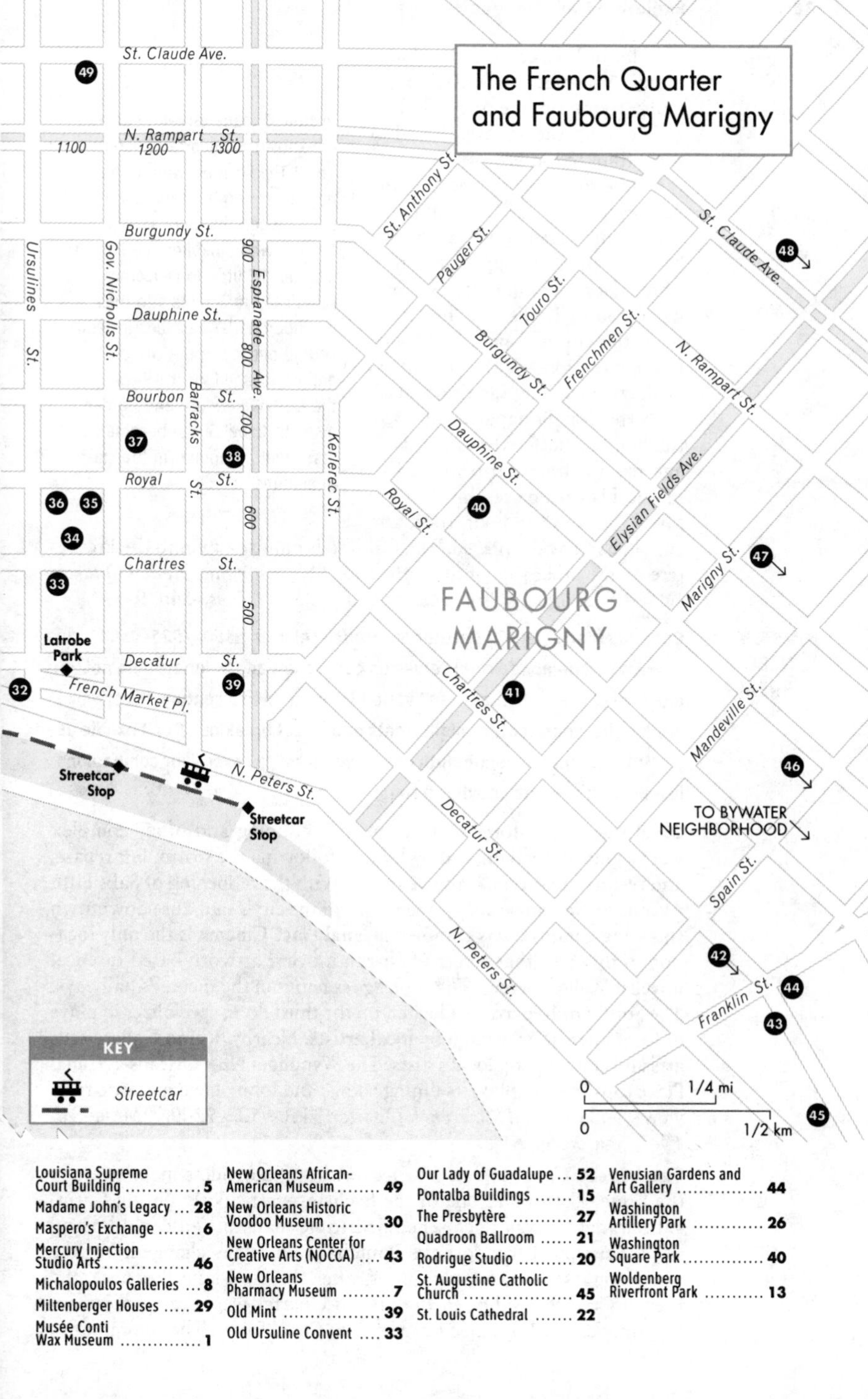

Louisiana Supreme Court Building **5**
Madame John's Legacy ... **28**
Maspero's Exchange **6**
Mercury Injection Studio Arts **46**
Michalopoulos Galleries ... **8**
Miltenberger Houses **29**
Musée Conti Wax Museum **1**
New Orleans African-American Museum **49**
New Orleans Historic Voodoo Museum **30**
New Orleans Center for Creative Arts (NOCCA) **43**
New Orleans Pharmacy Museum **7**
Old Mint **39**
Old Ursuline Convent **33**
Our Lady of Guadalupe ... **52**
Pontalba Buildings **15**
The Presbytère **27**
Quadroon Ballroom **21**
Rodrigue Studio **20**
St. Augustine Catholic Church **45**
St. Louis Cathedral **22**
Venusian Gardens and Art Gallery **44**
Washington Artillery Park **26**
Washington Square Park **40**
Woldenberg Riverfront Park **13**

transfer of Louisiana to the United States was made in 1803 in the front room on the second floor overlooking the square. This historic transaction was reenacted in the same room for the 200th anniversary of the purchase in 2003. The Cabildo later served as the city hall and then the Supreme Court. Three floors of multicultural exhibits recount Louisiana history—from the colonial period through Reconstruction—with countless artifacts, including the death mask of Napoléon Bonaparte. In 1988 the building suffered terrible damage from a four-alarm fire. Most of the historic pieces inside were saved, but the top floor, roof, and cupola had to be replaced. The Cabildo is almost a twin to the **Presbytère** on the other side of the cathedral. ✉ *Jackson Sq., French Quarter* ☎ *504/568–6968* 🌐 *lsm.crt.state.la.us* 🎫 *$6* ⏲ *Tues.–Sun. 9–5.*

BORDERLAND

In New Orleans, street medians are known as "neutral grounds." Why? The term evolved in the days following the Louisiana Purchase, when the Europeans and Creoles who inhabited the French Quarter did little to welcome American immigrants into their neighborhood. Americans instead settled outside of the city center and established what is now the CBD/Warehouse and Garden districts. Canal Street became the first "neutral ground" in the clash of cultures.

NEED A BREAK?

Café du Monde (✉ *800 Decatur St., French Quarter* ☎ *504/525–4544* 🌐 *www.cafedumonde.com*) serves up café au lait and beignets (and not much else) in a style that hasn't varied for more than a century. It's open around the clock, for late-night treats or a sweet breakfast. Don't exhale as you lift a beignet to your mouth unless you want to cover your companions in a dusting of white powdered sugar.

11 **Canal Place.** The stores of this upscale shopping and office complex were significantly damaged by looting following the storm, but repairs and restocking soon began in earnest. With the reopening of Saks Fifth Avenue in November 2006, the return of the city's signature downtown shopping complex was complete. **Canal Place Cinema** is the only location in this area that screens first-run movies; artwork based on local novelist Walker Percy's *The Moviegoer* hangs in the theater's hallways. The **Southern Repertory Theater,** on the third floor, specializes in plays of local interest or written by local artists. Nearby, **Rhino Gallery** sells arts and crafts by top local artists. The **Wyndham New Orleans at Canal Place** tops the complex; its dining rooms and lobby have fantastic river views. ✉ *333 Canal St., French Quarter* ☎ *504/522–9200* ⏲ *Mon.–Sat. 10–7, Sun. noon–6.*

Canal Street. Canal Street, 170 feet wide, is the widest main street in the United States and one of the liveliest—particularly during Carnival parades. It was once scheduled to be made into a canal linking the Mississippi River to Lake Pontchartrain; plans changed, but the name remains. In the early 1800s, after the Louisiana Purchase, the French Creoles residing in the French Quarter were segregated from the Americans who settled upriver from Canal Street. The communities had separate governments and police systems, and what is now Canal Street—and, most specifically, the central median running down Canal Street—was neutral ground between them. Today, animosities between these two groups are history, but the term "neutral ground" has survived as the name for all medians throughout the city.

Some of the grand buildings that once lined Canal Street remain, many of them former department stores and businesses now serving as hotels, restaurants, or souvenir shops. The Werlein Building (605 Canal Street), once a multilevel music store, is now the Palace Café restaurant. The former home of Maison Blanche (921 Canal Street), once the most elegant of the downtown department stores, is now a Ritz-Carlton hotel, with a ground floor devoted to an upscale mini-mall. One building still serving its original purpose is Adler's (722 Canal Street), the city's most elite jewelry and gift store. For the most part, these buildings are faithfully restored, so you can still appreciate the grandeur that once reigned on this fabled strip.

24 **1850 House.** A docent leads you through this well-preserved town house and courtyard, part of the **Pontalba Buildings** and furnished in the style of the mid-19th century, when the buildings were built as upscale residences and retail space. Notice the ornate ironwork on the balconies of the apartments: the original owner, Baroness Micaela Pontalba, introduced cast (or molded) iron with these buildings, and it eventually replaced much of the old hand-wrought ironwork in the French Quarter. The initials for her families, *A* and *P*—Almonester and Pontalba—are worked into the design. A gift shop and bookstore run by Friends of the Cabildo is downstairs. Call ahead to find out when the house is open for tours; operating hours vary. The Friends of the Cabildo offer an informative two-hour walking tour of the French Quarter that starts at this location. ✉ *523 St. Ann St., on Jackson Sq., French Quarter* ☎ *504/568–6968* 🎫 *$3, walking tour $12* ⏲ *Tues.–Sun. 9–5; tours Mon. at 1:30, Tues.–Sun. at 10 and 1:30.*

18 **Faulkner House.** The young novelist William Faulkner lived and wrote his first book, *Soldier's Pay,* here in the 1920s. He later returned to his native Oxford, Mississippi, and became a Pulitzer prize–winning writer. The house is not open for tours, but accommodates **Faulkner House Books** *(⇨ Shopping, French Quarter)* and the literary group **Pirate's Alley Faulkner Society,** which specializes in local and Southern writers. ✉ *624 Pirate's Alley, French Quarter* ☎ *504/524–2940* ⏲ *Daily 10–6.*

32 **French Market.** The sounds, colors, and smells here are alluring: street performers, ships' horns on the river, pralines, muffulettas, sugarcane, and Creole tomatoes. Originally a Native American trading post, later a bustling open-air market under the French and Spanish, the French Market historically began at Café du Monde and stretched along Decatur and North Peters streets all the way to the downtown edge of the Quarter. Today the market's graceful arcades have been mostly enclosed and filled with shops and eateries, and the fresh market has been pushed several blocks downriver, under sheds built in 1936 as part of a Works Progress Administration project. This area of the French Market, which

begins at Ursulines Street and contains a large **flea market** as well as a farmers' market area and its own praline and food stands, was slated for major renovation even before Katrina tore away its awnings and the 2005 hurricane season devastated the farming communities that provided its produce. The newly renovated French Market is a great place to shop for cheap souvenirs, sunglasses, or beads; it's also home to an expanded farmers' market.

Latrobe Park, a small recreational area at the uptown end of the French Market, honors Benjamin Latrobe, designer of the city's first waterworks. A modern fountain evoking a waterworks marks the spot where Latrobe's steam-powered pumps once stood. Sunken seating, fountains, and greenery make this a lovely place to relax with a drink from one of the nearby kiosks. ✉*Decatur St., French Quarter* ⏲*Daily 6–6; hrs may vary depending on season and weather.*

CHESS CHAMPIONS

Frances Parkinson Keyes's historical novel *The Chess Players* is based on the life of Paul Morphy, a New Orleanian considered one of the greatest modern chess masters. The Beauregard-Keyes House was originally built for Morphy's grandfather, and the present location of Brennan's restaurant was once Morphy's residence. If you're interested in challenging a living chess master, stop by Jude Acers' sidewalk table outside the Gazebo Café on Decatur Street. The two-time world-record holder for simultaneous games, Acers is at his table most days and takes on all challengers for a small fee.

14 **Jackson Brewery.** More commonly known as Jax Brewery, this former brew house was remodeled in the 1980s and is now home to a three-section shopping-and-entertainment complex. Outside are multilevel terraces facing the river, and inside are shops, a small museum preserving the history of the brewery, a food court, and the casual Lazy River restaurant. The New Orleans **Hard Rock Cafe** is here, too, housed in what was an old Jax brewery storehouse, right next door. ✉*600 Decatur St., French Quarter* ☎*504/566–7245* 🌐*www.jacksonbrewery.com* ⏲*Mon.–Sat. 10–6.*

23 ★ **Jackson Square.** Surrounded by historic buildings and plenty of the city's atmospheric street life, the heart of the French Quarter is this beautifully landscaped park. Originally called the Place d'Armes, the square was founded in 1718 as a military parade ground. It was also the site of public executions carried out in various styles, including burning at the stake, beheading, breaking on the wheel, and hanging. A **statue of Andrew Jackson,** victorious leader of the Battle of New Orleans in the War of 1812, commands the center of the square; the park was renamed for him in the 1850s. The words carved in the base on the cathedral side of the statue—THE UNION MUST AND SHALL BE PRESERVED—are a lasting reminder of the federal troops who occupied New Orleans during the Civil War and who inscribed them.

Among the notable buildings around the square are **St. Louis Cathedral** and **Faulkner House.** Two Spanish colonial–style buildings, the **Cabildo** and the **Presbytère,** flank the cathedral. The handsome rows of brick apartments on each side of the square are the **Pontalba Buildings.** The park is landscaped in a sun pattern, with walkways set like rays streaming out from the center, a popular garden design in the royal court of King Louis XIV, the Sun King. In the daytime, dozens of artists hang their paintings on the park fence and set up outdoor studios where they work on canvases or offer to draw portraits of passersby. These artists are easy to engage in conversation and are knowledgeable about many aspects of the Quarter and New Orleans. You can also be entertained by musicians, mimes, tarot-card readers, and magicians who perform on the flagstone pedestrian mall surrounding the square, many of them day and night. ⊠*French Quarter* ⏲*Park daily 8* AM*–dusk; flagstone paths on park's periphery open 24 hrs.*

25 **Louisiana Office of Tourism.** In addition to maps and hundreds (literally hundreds) of brochures about sights in the city and its environs, this information center has guides who can answer all of your questions. ⊠*529 St. Ann St., French Quarter* ☎*504/568–5661* ⏲*Tues.–Sat. 9–5.*

Mississippi River. When facing the river, you see to the right the **Crescent City Connection,** a twin-span bridge between downtown New Orleans and the Westbank, and a ferry that crosses the river every 30 minutes. The river flows to the left downstream for another 100 mi until it merges with the Gulf of Mexico. Directly across the river are the ferry landing and a ship-repair dry dock in a neighborhood called **Algiers Point.** Downriver, a row of burned wharves and warehouses is visible stretching along the Faubourg Marigny and Bywater neighborhoods to the Industrial Canal. These riverside structures were consumed in a massive fire occurring in the days following Hurricane Katrina. (The city has grand plans for redeveloping the area into parks and public areas, but no date has been set for the project, and the burned warehouses remain.) Much of the rescue-and-recovery operation was based around the river; for months after the storm, responders and other government employees were housed on cruise liners anchored here. Today, the river has returned to its normal activity of steamboats carrying tour groups, tugboats pushing enormous barges, and oceangoing ships. Sometimes a dredge is visible, dredging the river's bottom of silt to keep the channel open for large ships.

15 **Pontalba Buildings.** Baroness Micaela Pontalba built these twin sets of town houses, one on each side of Jackson Square, in the late 1840s; they are known for their ornate cast-iron balcony railings. Baroness Pontalba's father was Don Almonester, who sponsored the rebuilding of St. Louis Cathedral in 1788. The strong-willed Miss Almonester also helped fund the landscaping of the square and the erection of the Andrew Jackson statue in its center. She later moved to Paris, where she is buried. The Pontalba Buildings are publicly owned; the side to the right of the cathedral, on St. Ann Street, is owned by the state, and the other side, on St. Peter Street, by the city. In the state-owned side is the **1850 House,** and at 540-B St. Peter Street on the city-owned side is a plaque marking this apartment as that of Sherwood Anderson, writer and mentor to William Faulkner. ⊠*French Quarter.*

27 **The Presbytère.** One of twin Spanish colonial–style buildings flanking St. Louis Cathedral, this one, on the right, was designed to house the priests of the cathedral; instead, it served as a courthouse under the Spanish and later under the Americans. It is now a museum showcasing a spectacular collection of Mardi Gras memorabilia, and displays highlight both the little-known and popular traditions associated with New Orleans's most famous festival. The building's cupola, destroyed by a hurricane in 1915, was restored in 2005 to match the one atop its twin, the Cabildo. ✉*Jackson Sq., French Quarter* ☎*504/568–6968* 🌐*lsm.crt.state.la.us* 🎟*$5* ⏲*Tues.–Sun. 9–5.*

Fodor'sChoice ★

22 **St. Louis Cathedral.** The oldest active cathedral in the United States, this church at the heart of the Old City is named for the 13th-century French king who led two crusades. The current building, which replaced two structures destroyed by fire, dates from 1794 (although it was remodeled and enlarged in 1851). The austere interior is brightened by murals covering the ceiling and stained-glass windows along the first floor. Pope John Paul II held a prayer service for clergy here during his New Orleans visit in 1987; to honor the occasion, the pedestrian mall in front of the cathedral was renamed Place Jean Paul Deux. Nearly every evening in December brings a free concert held inside the cathedral. The statue of the Sacred Heart of Jesus dominates **St. Anthony's Garden,** which extends behind the rectory to Royal Street. The garden is also the site of a monument to 30 members of a French ship who died in a yellow-fever epidemic in 1857. ✉*615 Père Antoine Alley, French Quarter* ☎*504/525–9585* 🎟*Free.*

NEED A BREAK?

A great favorite among pensive French Quarter intellectuals, the tiny Pirates Alley Café (✉*622 Pirates Alley, French Quarter* ☎*504/524-9332*) is an ideal setting for espresso, wine, or a light salad or sandwich alongside St. Louis Cathedral.

26 **Washington Artillery Park.** This raised concrete area on the river side of Decatur Street, directly across from Jackson Square, is a great spot to photograph the square and the barges and paddle wheelers on the Mississippi. The cannon mounted in the center and pointing toward the river is a model 1861 Parrot Rifle used in the Civil War. This monument honors the local 141st Field Artillery of the Louisiana National Guard that saw action from the Civil War through World War II. Marble tablets at the base give the history of the group, represented today by the Washington Artillery Association. ✉*Decatur St. between St. Peter and St. Ann Sts., French Quarter.*

13 **Woldenberg Riverfront Park.** This stretch of green from Canal Street to Esplanade Avenue overlooks the Mississippi River as it curves around New Orleans, which inspired the Crescent City moniker. The wooden promenade section in front of Jackson Square is called **Moon Walk,** named for Mayor Moon Landrieu, under whose administration in the 1970s the riverfront beyond the flood wall was first opened to public view. Today, the French Quarter Festival main stages are located here. It's a great place for a rest (or a muffuletta sandwich picnic) after touring the Quarter, and you'll often be serenaded by musicians and amused by

street performers. The park is also home to art pieces including the modest **Holocaust Memorial**, with its spiral walkway clad in Jerusalem stone. At the center of the spiral are nine sculptural panels by Jewish artist Yaacov Agam. A statue of local businessman Malcolm Woldenberg, the park's benefactor, is located near *Ocean Song*, a large kinetic sculpture whose wind-powered movements are intended to evoke the patterns of New Orleans music. *Ocean Song* was created by recently deceased and much mourned local artist John T. Scott. ✉*French Quarter.*

2

INSIDE THE VIEUX CARRÉ

WHAT TO SEE

34 **Beauregard-Keyes House.** This stately 19th-century mansion with period furnishings was the temporary home of Confederate general P.G.T. Beauregard. The house and grounds had severely deteriorated by the 1940s, when the well-known novelist Frances Parkinson Keyes moved in and helped restore it. Her studio at the back of the large courtyard remains intact, complete with family photos, original manuscripts, and her doll, fan, and teapot collections. Keyes wrote 40 novels in this studio, all in longhand, among them the local favorite, *Dinner at Antoine's*. The house suffered some roof damage during Katrina, resulting in water stains along the dining room ceiling. Undaunted, the staff has reopened the site and continues its normal tour schedule. If you do not have time to tour the house, take a peek through the gates at the beautiful walled garden at the corner of Chartres and Ursulines streets. Landscaped in the same sun pattern as Jackson Square, the garden is in bloom throughout the year. ✉*1113 Chartres St., French Quarter* ☎*504/523–7257* 🎫*$5* ⏲*Mon.–Sat. 10–3, tours on the hr.*

Bourbon Street. Ignore your better judgment and take a stroll down Bourbon Street, past the bars, restaurants, music clubs, and novelty shops that have given this strip its reputation as the playground of the South. The bars of Bourbon Street were among the first businesses of the city to reopen after the storm; catering to the off-duty relief workers, they provided a different form of relief. On most nights, the crowds remain lighter here than in recent years, but the spirit of unbridled revelry is back in full swing. The noise, raucous crowds, and bawdy sights are not family fare; if you go with children, do so before sundown. Although the street is usually well patrolled, it is wise to stay alert to your surroundings. The street is blocked to make a pedestrian mall

OUT OF THE ASHES

The great fire of 1788, which destroyed most of the French Quarter, is said to have begun in the home of the Spanish army treasurer, Don Vincente, at 619 Chartres Street on the morning of Good Friday. Legend has it that Vincente, a good Catholic, was burning his Lenten candles for the holiday and either fell asleep or failed to notice when the curtains caught fire. This fire, along with a second great fire in 1794, fundamentally changed the architecture of the French Quarter: when rebuilt, the look was Spanish, rather than French, and brick and slate replaced wooden structures and shingles.

CLOSE UP

Micaela Pontalba

Every life has its little dramas, but how many of us can claim lives dramatic enough to inspire an opera? The Baroness Micaela Almonester de Pontalba is in that rarefied number, albeit posthumously. In 2003, on the 200th anniversary of the Louisiana Purchase, the New Orleans Opera Association commissioned an opera based on Pontalba and the mark she left on New Orleans—a legacy you can easily see even now in the Pontalba Buildings, the elegant brick apartments lining Jackson Square.

Micaela Almonester was of Spanish stock, the daughter of the wealthy entrepreneur and developer Don Andres Almonester, who was instrumental in the creation of the Cabildo and Presbytère on Jackson Square. Don Almonester died while Micaela was still young, but not before passing on to his daughter a passion for building and urban design. The rest of her life became a tale of the impact a single will can have upon an urban environment, as well as a tragedy-torn drama of international scope.

At the time of the Louisiana Purchase, in 1803, New Orleans was in cultural upheaval. Following a period under Spanish rule during the late 18th century, the French had reacquired the colony—and merrily sold it to the Americans. The often-complex blending of French and Spanish society was further complicated by the anticipated imposition of American laws and mores, so foreign to the population of New Orleans. Micaela Almonester was right in the middle of the confusion: daughter of Spanish gentry, she fell in love and married a Frenchman, who took her to Paris with his family to avoid coming under American rule in New Orleans.

The Pontalbas' marriage was particularly unhappy, and Micaela's relationship to her in-laws was poisoned by mistrust over family property. Control of her New Orleans inheritance became part of an increasingly bitter feud that included separation from her husband and, in its dramatic pinnacle, her attempted murder by her father-in-law. After the old baron inflicted four gunshot wounds on his daughter-in-law, he committed suicide, believing he had protected his son and his property. But Micaela, now Baroness de Pontalba following the old baron's death, survived her wounds. Within two years, she had recovered enough to conceive the plan for the buildings that bear her name, but a long series of delays, including a bitter divorce, halted the project. Micaela finally returned to New Orleans in the 1840s, in order to direct construction of the elegant apartment buildings that would complete the square her father had been so instrumental in developing during the previous century. The Pontalba Buildings, designed by James Gallier in the French style favored by Micaela, were dedicated in 1851 to great fanfare. Each building (one along each side of Jackson Square) contained 16 grand and lavishly detailed apartments.

Following the dedication of the buildings, Pontalba returned to France. She had been living in Paris for nearly 50 years by now, her children had grown up there, and it had become her home. Yet the pilgrimage she had made to New Orleans, in order to complete a dream in the name of her father's memory, hints that her heart had never really left her childhood home.

at night; often the area is shoulder to shoulder, especially during major sports events and Mardi Gras.

At Toulouse Street is the former site of the **French Opera House,** once one of New Orleans's most opulent public buildings, which burned down in 1919. There is probably a Lucky Dog vendor nearby, with a vending cart shaped like a hot dog. These carts were immortalized by John Kennedy Toole in his Pulitzer prize–winning novel about New Orleans, *A Confederacy of Dunces,* and their return after the storm was a welcome sight for visitors and locals alike. St. Ann Street marks the beginning of a short strip of gay bars, some of which retain links to the long history of gay culture in New Orleans.

> **GET A "GO CUP"**
>
> If you're on foot, you can get your beverage to go from any bar in the city. Open containers of alcohol are allowed on the streets, as long as they're not in glass containers. So when you're ready to leave, ask your bartender for a "go cup," pour your drink into the plastic cup, and head out the door to the next venue, drink in hand.

36 **Gallier House.** Famous New Orleans architect James Gallier designed this as his family home in 1857. Today it contains an excellent collection of early Victorian furnishings. The tour includes the house, servants' quarters, and a gift shop. ⊠*1132 Royal St., French Quarter* ☎*504/525–5661* 🎟*$10, combination ticket with Hermann-Grima House $18* ⏲*Tours Thurs.–Tues. 10, 11, noon, 2, 3.*

38 **Gauche House.** One of the most distinctive houses in the French Quarter, this mansion and its service buildings date from 1856. The cherub design of the effusive ironwork is the only one of its kind. It was once the estate of businessman John Gauche and is still privately owned. This house is not open to the public. ⊠*704 Esplanade Ave., French Quarter.*

2 **Germaine Wells Mardi Gras Museum.** During a 31-year period (1937–68), Germaine Cazenave Wells, daughter of Arnaud's restaurant founder Arnaud Cazenave, was queen of Carnival balls a record 22 times for 17 different krewes, or organizations. Many of her ball gowns, in addition to costumes worn by other family members, are on display in this dim, quirky, one-room museum above Arnaud's restaurant. ⊠*Arnaud's restaurant, 813 Bienville St., 2nd fl. (enter through restaurant), French Quarter* ☎*504/523–5433* 🎟*Free* ⏲*Daily during restaurant hrs.*

35 **Haunted House.** Locals agree that this is the most haunted house in a generally haunted neighborhood. Most blame the spooks on Madame Lalaurie, a wealthy but ill-fated socialite who lost both parents as a child, then two husbands before finding a third and moving with him into this mansion on Royal Street. Madame Lalaurie fell out with society when a fire in her attic exposed atrocious treatment of her slaves: according to newspaper reports, well-wishing neighbors who rushed into the house found seven mutilated slaves in one of the apartments. Madame Lalaurie fled town that night, but occupants of the house have told of hauntings ever since. One tour guide claims that when clients faint from the heat it is always by this house, and that cameras often mysteriously refuse to function when pointed at the house, which is not open to the public. ⊠*1140 Royal St., French Quarter.*

3 **Hermann-Grima House.** One of the largest and best-preserved examples of American architecture in the Quarter, this Georgian-style house has the only restored private stable and the only working 1830s Creole kitchen in the Quarter. American architect William Brand built the house in 1831. The house fortunately sustained only minor damage during Katrina and is open for visits and tours. Cooking demonstrations on the open hearth are held here all day Thursday from October through May. You'll want to check the gift shop, which has many local crafts and books. *820 St. Louis St., French Quarter 504/525–5661 $10, combination ticket with the Gallier House $18 Tours Thurs.–Tues. 10, 11, noon, 2, 3.*

Fodor's Choice ★

ARRRRGH!

Pirate's Alley takes its name, in part, from the popular myth that Jean Lafitte met here with General Andrew Jackson before the Battle of New Orleans. During this meeting, Lafitte supposedly made his offer to double-cross the British. The legend apparently has no historical foundation, but its romance was so appealing that the name of the alley (originally Orleans Alley) was officially changed. It's a picturesque way to get from Jackson Square to the shops and galleries of Royal Street.

4 ★ **Historic New Orleans Collection.** This private archive and exhibit complex, with thousands of historic photos, documents, and books, is one of the finest research centers in the South. It occupies the 19th-century town house of General Kemper Williams and the 1792 Merrieult House. Changing exhibits focus on aspects of local history. History tours and home tours of the houses, grounds, and archives are offered several times daily. A museum shop sells books, prints, and gifts. Children under 12 are not admitted. *533 Royal St., French Quarter 504/523–4662 www.hnoc.org Exhibit and research library (410 Chartres St.) free, tour of houses or archive galleries $5 Tues.–Sat. 9:30–3.*

9 ★ **Jean Lafitte National Park Visitor Center.** This center has free visual and sound exhibits on the customs of various communities throughout the state, as well as information-rich daily history tours of the French Quarter. The one-hour daily tour leaves at 9:30 AM; tickets are handed out one per person (you must be present to get a ticket), beginning at 9 AM, for that day's tours only. Arrive at least 15 minutes before tour time to be sure of a spot. The office also supervises and provides information on Jean Lafitte National Park Barataria Unit, a nature preserve (complete with alligators) across the river from New Orleans, and the Chalmette Battlefield, where the Battle of New Orleans was fought in the War of 1812. Each year in January, near the anniversary of the battle, a reenactment is staged at the Chalmette site. *419 Decatur St., French Quarter 504/589–2636 Daily 9–5.*

19 **LaBranche Houses.** This complex of lovely town houses, built in the 1830s by Widow LaBranche, fills the half block between Pirate's Alley and Royal and St. Peter streets behind the Cabildo. The house on the corner of Royal and St. Peter streets, with its elaborate, rounded cast-iron balconies, is the most-photographed residence in the French Quarter. *700 Royal St., French Quarter.*

31 **Lafitte's Blacksmith Shop.** The striking anvil no longer sounds in this ancient weathered building, the oldest bar in the Quarter. You'll hear only the clinking of glasses at this favorite local bar for patrons from all walks of life. Legend has it that the pirate Jean Lafitte and his cronies operated a blacksmith shop here as a front for their vast illicit trade in contraband. The building, dating from 1772 and thus a rare survivor of the 18th-century French Quarter fires, is interesting as one of the few surviving examples of soft bricks reinforced with timber, a construction form used by early settlers. A drink here just after sundown, when the place is lit only by candles, lets you slip back in time for an hour or so; it's far less appealing in broad daylight. ✉ *941 Bourbon St., French Quarter* ☎ *504/522–9377.*

37 **Latrobe House.** Architect Henry Latrobe designed this modest house with Arsene Latour in 1814. Its smooth lines and porticoes started a passion for Greek Revival architecture in Louisiana, evidenced later in many plantation houses upriver as well as in a significant number of buildings in New Orleans. This house, believed to be the earliest example of Greek Revival in the city, is not open to the public. ✉ *721 Governor Nicholls St., French Quarter.*

17 **Le Petit Théâtre.** Since 1916 this community-based theater group has entertained the Quarter with plays, musicals, and variety shows. The organization was originally housed in one of the Pontalba apartments on Jackson Square, but it quickly outgrew that space and moved to this building in 1922. Hosting the Tennessee Williams Festival every spring, Le Petit Théâtre attracts national attention. The flagstone patio with its fountain is postcard-perfect. The building next door is **Le Petit Salon** (✉ *620 St. Peter St., French Quarter*), headquarters of a ladies' literary club since 1925. The house was originally built for a pair of French newlyweds in 1838; the wrought-iron staircase leads to the formal, second-floor entrance. ✉ *616 St. Peter St., French Quarter* ☎ *504/522–2081* 🌐 *www.lepetittheatre.com.*

5 **Louisiana Supreme Court Building.** The imposing Victorian building that takes up the whole block of Royal Street between St. Louis and Conti streets is the Old New Orleans Court, erected in 1908. It was later the office of the Wildlife and Fisheries agency, and locals still most often refer to the building by that designation. After years of vacancy and neglect, this magnificent edifice was restored and reopened in 2004 and is now the elegant home of the Louisiana Supreme Court. ✉ *400 Royal St., French Quarter.*

28 ★ **Madame John's Legacy.** Now a state museum, this is the only example in the French Quarter of West Indies architecture and early Creole-colonial home design. The large, dark rooms of the main living space occupy the second story, and a porch (called a gallery) runs along the front and back of the house, providing ventilation during the steamy summers and protection from both sun and rain. The current building was constructed in 1789, following the 1788 fire that took out much of the Quarter. The house has a colorful past. The first owner, Jean Pascal, a French sea captain, was killed by Natchez Indians. The name "Madame John's Legacy" was adopted in the late 1800s from a short story by New Orleans writer

George Washington Cable. The popular tale was about Madame John, a "free woman of color" who, like many mulatto women at that time, became the mistress of a Frenchman. Having never married, the Frenchman, John (Jean), bequeathed his house and estate to her on his deathbed. ✉ *632 Dumaine St., French Quarter* ☎ *504/568–6968* 🎫 *$3* ⏲ *Tues.–Sun. 9–5.*

DON'T BET ON IT!

At some point during your visit to the French Quarter, you are bound to come across someone on the street who will offer you the following wager: "I bet you [insert dollar amount] I know where you got them shoes." It's a con, of course, and an old one at that. The answer is "You got them on your feet in New Orleans, Louisiana."

6 **Maspero's Exchange.** This restaurant, now known as Original Pierre Maspero's, was once a slave auction house and for many years thereafter the Exchange Coffeehouse, where the city's notable Creoles gathered. From the outside, the building appears to have only two floors, whereas inside, a middle floor, called an entresol, is in the area above the window arch. This low middle floor was used for storage. ✉ *440 Chartres St., French Quarter.*

8 **Michalopoulos Galleries.** One of New Orleans's most beloved artists, James Michalopoulos, exhibits his expressionistic visions of New Orleans architecture in this small gallery. Michalopoulos's palette-knife technique of applying thick waves of paint invariably brings van Gogh to mind—but his vision of New Orleans, where no line is truly straight and every building appears to have a soul, is uniquely his own. Michalopoulos was commissioned to create the official poster of the New Orleans Jazz and Heritage Festival in 1998, 2001, 2003, 2006, and 2009, bringing a new perspective to some of New Orleans's greatest musicians: Mahalia Jackson, Louis Armstrong, Dr. John, and Fats Domino. ✉ *617 Bienville St., French Quarter* ☎ *504/558–0505* 🌐 *www.michalopoulos.com* ⏲ *Mon.–Sat. 10–5:30, Sun. noon–5.*

29 **Miltenberger Houses.** The widow Amelie Miltenberger built this row of three brick town houses in the 1830s for her three sons. Two generations later, her daughter Alice Heine became famous for wedding Prince Albert of Monaco. Although the marriage ended childless and in divorce, Princess Alice was a sensation in New Orleans. ✉ *900, 906, and 910 Royal St., French Quarter.*

1 **Musée Conti Wax Museum.** The history of New Orleans and Louisiana unfolds in colorful vignettes in this kitschy but fun museum. Local legends are captured life size at seminal moments: Madame Lalaurie discovered torturing her slaves; Napoléon leaping out of the bathtub at news of the Louisiana Purchase; Marie Laveau selling gris-gris to downtown customers; the Duke and Duchess of Windsor attending a Mardi Gras ball. Written and audio explanations supplement the visual scenes. A miniature Mardi Gras parade fills one corridor. The museum is an enjoyable way to acquaint yourself and your children with New Orleans history, although the history depicted here tends toward the sensational and the occasionally unsubstantiated. ✉ *917 Conti St., French Quarter* ☎ *504/581–1993 or 800/233–5405* 🌐 *www.get-waxed.com* 🎫 *$7* ⏲ *Call for hours.*

2

NEED A BREAK?

Napoleon House Bar and Café (✉ *500 Chartres St., French Quarter* ☎ *504/524–9752* 🌐 *www.napoleonhouse.com*) is a favorite gathering place for local characters, who favor such romantic drinks as the Pimm's Cup (a refreshing mixture of lemonade and Pimm's, a light gin-based liquor) and the Sazerac (the original New Orleans cocktail, a mixture of rye whiskey, simple sugars, Herbsaint, and bitters). Snack on a muffuletta sandwich (ham, salami, mozzarella, and olive salad on seeded bread) in the lush courtyard or find respite from the heat in the cool, darkened interior. The building was the residence of Nicholas Girod, mayor of New Orleans from 1812 to 1815. Like many New Orleanians of the period, Girod was a staunch supporter of the French empire, and when he heard that Napoléon had escaped from his island exile, Girod declared his home ready to receive the emperor, should he make his way to America. Napoléon never crossed the Atlantic, but this bit of historical intrigue, amplified by legend, adds to the restaurant's allure.

30 **New Orleans Historic Voodoo Museum.** A large collection of artifacts and information on voodoo as it was—and still is—practiced in New Orleans is here in a two-room, rather homegrown museum. Items on display include portraits by and of voodoo legends, African artifacts believed to have influenced the development of the religion, and lots of gris-gris (bundles with magical ingredients). The gift shop sells customized gris-gris, potions, and handcrafted voodoo dolls. ✉ *724 Dumaine St., French Quarter* ☎ *504/680–0128* 🎫 *Museum $5* ⏲ *Mon.–Thurs. 10–6, Fri.–Sun. 10–7:30.*

7 **New Orleans Pharmacy Museum.** This building was the apothecary shop and residence of Louis J. Dufilho, America's first licensed pharmacist with his own shop, in the 1820s. His botanical and herbal gardens are still cultivated in the courtyard. To tour the musty shop is to step back into 19th-century medicine. Even the window display, with its enormous leech jar and other antiquated paraphernalia, is fascinating. Watch for free 19th-century seasonal health tips posted in the front window. ✉ *514 Chartres St., French Quarter* ☎ *504/565–8027* 🎫 *$5* ⏲ *Tues. and Thurs. 10–2; Wed., Fri., and Sat. 10–5.*

39 ★ **Old Mint.** Minting began in 1838 in this ambitious Ionic structure, a project of President Andrew Jackson. The New Orleans mint was to provide currency for the South and the West, which it did until the Confederacy began minting its own currency here in 1861. When supplies ran out, the building served as a barracks, then a prison, for

TALK OF THE TOWN

Although it's just two blocks away from Bourbon Street in the French Quarter, Burgundy Street is not pronounced like the wine (New Orleanians say "bur-GUN-dee" instead). And if you trot out your high school French to ask for directions to Chartres Street, a bemused local will probably ask if you mean "CHAW-tuhs." Farther uptown, the streets named for the muses offer more challenges: Calliope ("CAL-ee-ope") and Melpomene ("MELL-pa-meen").

Confederate soldiers; the production of U.S. coins recommenced only in 1879. It stopped again, for good, in 1909. After years of neglect, the federal government handed the Old Mint over to Louisiana in 1966; the state now uses the quarters to exhibit collections of the Louisiana State Museum. At the Barracks Street entrance, notice the one remaining sample of the mint's old walls—it'll give you an idea of the building's deterioration before its restoration. Hurricane Katrina ripped away a large section of the copper roof, and for months the twisted metal remained on the ground here, one of the most dramatic reminders of the storm in the French Quarter. After years of repairs, the museum reopened to the public in October 2007; its popular New Orleans Jazz Collection suffered significant water damage during the storm and is expected to go back on display in late 2009.

WHISTLING "DIXIE"

One popular theory for the origin of the term "Dixie" points back to Citizens Bank of New Orleans, which issued bilingual 10-dollar bank notes bearing the French word "dix" (10) on the reverse. The notes thus became known as "dixies," and the term eventually became synonymous with Louisiana, and then with the entire South. Historians are still debating this etymology . . . but it's a good story nonetheless.

At the foot of Esplanade Avenue, notice the memorial to the French rebels against early Spanish rule, the first instance of a New World rebellion against a European power. The rebel leaders were executed on this spot and give nearby Frenchmen Street its name. The principal exhibit here is the aforementioned **New Orleans Jazz Collection,** a brief but evocative tour through the history of traditional New Orleans jazz. In addition to informative written explanations, a wealth of artifacts movingly tells the story of the emergent art form. Among the gems are the soprano saxophone owned by Sidney Bechet, the trumpets of Pops Celestin and Dizzy Gillespie, and the cornet given to Louis Armstrong at the juvenile home where he spent much of his youth. Sheet music, biographies, personal effects, and photos round out the displays. Across the hall from the jazz exhibit are a few rooms filled with the beautiful and locally treasured Newcomb pottery. This school of pottery was developed by teachers and students at Newcomb Women's College in Uptown New Orleans during the late 19th and early 20th centuries, and it subtly reflects the art-nouveau movement. The **Louisiana Historical Center,** which holds the French and Spanish Louisiana archives, is open free to researchers by appointment. ☒*400 Esplanade Ave., French Quarter* ☎*504/568–6968* *Old US Mint $5.*

33 **Old Ursuline Convent.** The Ursulines were the first of many orders of religious women who came to New Orleans and founded schools, orphanages, and asylums and ministered to the needs of the poor. Their original convent was built in 1734 and is now the oldest French-colonial building in the Mississippi Valley, having survived the disastrous 18th-century fires that destroyed the rest of the Quarter. **St. Mary's Church,** adjoining the convent, was added in 1845. The original tract of land for a convent, school, and gardens covered several French Quarter

2

blocks. Now an archive for the archdiocese, the convent was used by the Ursulines for 90 years. The convent roof was significantly damaged by Katrina's winds, and a temporary patch is clearly visible on the Chartres Street side. The Ursuline Academy, the convent's girls' school founded in 1727, is now Uptown on State Street, where the newer convent and chapel were built. The academy is the oldest girls' school in the country. It's open to the public Tuesday through Sunday, but hours may be limited depending on the season; please call for more information. ✉*1100 Chartres St., French Quarter* ☎*504/529–2651* *$5.*

21 **Quadroon Ballroom.** In the early 1800s the wooden-rail balcony extending over Orleans Street was linked to a ballroom where free women of color met their French suitors, as Madame John of **Madame John's Legacy** is said to have done. The quadroons (technically, people whose racial makeup was one-quarter African) who met here were young unmarried women of legendary beauty. A gentleman would select a favorite beauty and, with her mother's approval, buy her a house and support her as his mistress. The sons of these unions, which were generally maintained in addition to legal marriages with French women, were often sent to France to be educated. This practice, known as plaçage, was unique to New Orleans at the time. The Quadroon Ballroom later became part of a convent and school for the Sisters of the Holy Family, a religious order founded in New Orleans in 1842 by the daughter of a quadroon to educate and care for African-American women. The ballroom itself is not open to visitors, but a view of the balcony from across the street is enough to set the historical stage. ✉*Bourbon Orleans Hotel, 717 Orleans St., 2nd fl., French Quarter.*

20 **Rodrigue Studio.** Cajun artist George Rodrigue started painting blue dogs in 1984, inspired by the spirit of his deceased pet Tiffany. Since then, the blue dog has found thousands of manifestations in various settings in the cult artist's paintings. Of late, Rodrigue has ventured a few non-blue-dog works, which after nearly two decades of singular focus seems like a radical move. Rodrigue's principal gallery, a single room rather eerily lined almost entirely with paintings of the blue dog (and her evil red twin), sits directly behind St. Louis Cathedral. Rodrigue has contributed a series of post-Katrina blue-dog prints as the George Rodrigue Art Campaign for Recovery, a fund-raising effort for the rebuilding process. Among the titles is *Throw Me Something F.E.M.A.*, a whimsical play on the cry of Mardi Gras–parade attendees: "Throw me something, mister!" ✉*721 Royal St., French Quarter* ☎*504/581–4244* 🌐*www.georgerodrigue.com* ⏲*Daily 10–6, hrs may vary; call ahead.*

FAUBOURG MARIGNY AND BYWATER

The Faubourg Marigny (pronounced FOE-berg MAR-ah-Nee), across Esplanade Avenue from the French Quarter, was developed in the early 1800s by wealthy planter Bernard de Marigny, the Creole bon vivant who made the dice game craps popular in America. Several of New Orleans's most distinctive street names owe their origin to de Marigny, and it is here that the visitor will find Desire Street just a block away from Piety Street. But some of the streets he named, such as Good

Children, Love, and Craps, no longer bear the evocative names de Marigny bestowed upon them.

With architectural styles ranging from classic Creole cottage to Victorian mansion, the Marigny is a residential extension of the Quarter. The streets are more peaceful and the residents more bohemian—what the French Quarter used to be like 20 years ago. Like the French Quarter, the Marigny rests on some of the city's highest ground, and it was mostly spared from Hurricane Katrina's flooding (with the exception of a few houses near the St. Claude Avenue border). Several of the old corner town houses were significantly damaged by Katrina's winds, and a few scars of the storm remain here. In addition, a number of fires following the storm consumed blocks of riverfront warehouses as well as several historic dwellings within the Marigny. Undeterred, Marigny dwellers have returned. Frenchmen Street, the Marigny's main strip, is lined with music clubs, coffee shops, and restaurants; music lovers spill into the streets on most weekend nights. Many of the streets intersect at odd angles; look for street names in inlaid tiles at corners.

HUBIG'S PIES

One local culinary delight that is almost unknown outside the city are the fried fruit turnovers made by Hubig's Pies on Dauphine Street in the Marigny. Simon Hubig founded the bakery in Fort Worth, Texas, and the New Orleans plant was just one of the chain. Forced by the Depression to close the other locations, Hubig held on to the New Orleans plant alone and brought on the current proprietors as partners. The pies are available in corner groceries around town.

The Bywater, a crumbling yet beautiful old neighborhood across the train tracks at Press Street, is a haven to those musicians and artists who find the Marigny too expensive and crowded. The New Orleans Center for Creative Arts (NOCCA) occupies a beautiful campus of renovated warehouses at its edge. The Mississippi runs the length of its boundary. The bars and coffee shops scattered around this neighborhood combine elements of its working-class roots and more recent hipster influx for a lively and distinctly local experience. Although you won't find the head-swiveling density of sights here that you will in the French Quarter, a tour through the Faubourg Marigny and especially the Bywater gives you a feel for New Orleans as it lives day to day, in a colorful, overgrown, slightly sleepy cityscape reminiscent of island communities and tinged with a sense of perpetual decay.

Numbers in the margin correspond to numbers on the French Quarter and Faubourg Marigny map.

WHAT TO SEE

41 **American Aquatic Gardens.** A commercial nursery and boutique gift shop, this small but wonderfully relaxing garden invites walks past grasses, reeds, flowers, and sculptures. Trees and fences that once shadowed some of the displays were lost during Katrina, but the sound of water still surrounds the visitor, and these grounds remain a tranquil retreat from the city for gardening enthusiasts and backyard snoozers alike.

✉621 Elysian Fields, Faubourg Marigny ☎504/944–0410 🌐www.americanaquaticgardens.com 🕑Daily 9–5.

47 **Christopher Porché-West Galerie.** This working studio and exhibit space holds the assemblages and other creations of Porché-West and, occasionally, other local artists. The atmosphere depends on the current vigor of Porché-West's activities: sometimes it is more work-oriented, sometimes more formally set up for exhibits. The gallery occupies an old pharmacy storefront, and it is open whenever the artist happens to be in, or by appointment. *✉3201 Burgundy St., Bywater ☎504/947–3880 🌐www.porche-west.com.*

42 **Dr. Bob.** This small compound of artists' and furniture-makers' studios includes the headquarters of Dr. Bob, beloved local folk artist. Dr. Bob remained in his shop during the storm until the riverfront fires across the street forced him out. The compound was damaged but has reopened, and his shop remains chock-full of original furniture, colorful signs (his "Be Nice or Leave" signs are all around town), and unidentifiable objects of artistic fancy. Prices start at $20 for a small "Be Nice" and most pieces are in the $200–$500 range. The sign outside advertises the open hours: BY CHANCE OR APPOINTMENT. *✉3027 Chartres St., Bywater ☎504/945–2225.*

OFF THE BEATEN PATH

Jelly Roll Morton House. Jazz enthusiasts will want to follow Frenchmen Street beyond the borders of the Marigny to pay homage to Jelly Roll Morton at the pianist and composer's modest former home, now a private residence with nary a plaque to suggest its import. Morton was a Creole of color (free African-American of mixed race), a clear distinction from darker blacks in those days; Morton himself always explained his roots as French. Though rather affluent when Morton lived here, the neighborhood has since declined. Although some neighbors have returned since Katrina, the streets remain sparsely populated and can be intimidating—plan to take a car or taxi here. *✉1443 Frenchmen St., Seventh Ward.*

46 **Mercury Injection Studio Arts.** Glassworks, mirrors, and paintings fill this tiny studio of artist Michael Cain. Don't be discouraged if the doors are closed: knock, and if Michael is around you're in for a show as he blows his fanciful pieces into existence. Visits by appointment are also available. *✉727 Louisa St., Bywater ☎504/723–6397 🌐www.michaelcainarts.com 🎫Free.*

43 **New Orleans Center for Creative Arts (NOCCA).** Many of New Orleans's most talented young musicians, artists, and writers pass through this high school arts program, where the faculty includes professional artists from around the country. Although the school covers all major artistic disciplines, the music program has been particularly successful: well-known alums include Donald Harrison, Terence Blanchard, Harry Connick Jr., and the Marsalis brothers. Following Hurricane Katrina, NOCCA became a combination National Guard barracks and command center for fire and rescue vehicles. Classes resumed in 2006, and the school is once again hosting its celebrated performing-arts events. *✉2800 Chartres St., Faubourg Marigny ☎504/940–2800 🌐www.nocca.com.*

Fodor's Choice ★

THE NINTH WARD

The Ninth Ward is the largest of New Orleans's wards, or legislative districts, traditionally one of the most colorful, and, since Hurricane Katrina, one of the most recognized. Few can forget the television news images in the days after the storm of rooftop rescues of Ninth Ward residents while the area sat under more than 9 feet of water. Sadly, today, little progress has been made in rebuilding and repopulating the Ninth Ward. A majority of homes and businesses still stand empty and in various stages of destruction; in some areas, entire neighborhoods have been cleared, leaving empty, eerie desolation. For this reason, many tourists want to visit the area to truly understand the damage Katrina wrought. Though it was always a low- to middle-income area, the Ninth Ward had the highest rate of home ownership in the city. It is now sparsely populated, and is not safe to visit alone, outside a car, or after dark. One bus tour, offered by **Grayline Tours** (☎ *504/569–1401 or 800/535–7786*), is a safe and informative way to learn about Hurricane Katrina's effect on the city, including the Ninth Ward. If you'd like to help make things better here and elsewhere in the city, go to the New Orleans tourism bureau's Web site (*www.neworleanscvb.com*) and click on the "voluntourism" link.

44 **Venusian Gardens and Art Gallery.** This former 19th-century historic church building now serves as Eric Ehlenberger's art studio and gallery, displaying his luminous sculptures and dioramas. ✉ *2601 Chartres St., Faubourg Marigny* ☎ *504/943–7446* 🌐 *venusiangardens.com* ⏲ *Weekdays 10–4; appointments preferred.*

NEED A BREAK?

Café Rose Nicaud (✉ *634 Frenchmen St., Faubourg Marigny* ☎ *504/949–3300* ⏲ *Daily 7–3*) is a neighborhood hangout that serves hot and iced coffee or tea, sandwiches, salads, and pastries. The café is named for the free woman of color who was the originator of the New Orleans coffee stands, and its walls often feature artwork celebrating African-American culture in New Orleans. The sidewalk tables are excellent vantage points for early-afternoon people-watching.

40 **Washington Square Park.** This park provides a large green space in which to play Frisbee or catch some sun. During the recovery period following the storm, relief groups created a campground here, offering free food and music. The far side of the park borders Elysian Fields, named for Paris's Champs-Élysées. Though it never achieved the grandeur of its French counterpart, Elysian Fields is a major thoroughfare. Small-scale festivals or events sometimes take place in Washington Square, which is the only city public space with a French-style double alley of oaks. ✉ *Bordered by Royal, Dauphine, and Frenchmen Sts. and Elysian Fields, Faubourg Marigny.*

TREMÉ

Across Rampart Street from the French Quarter, the neighborhood of Tremé (pronounced truh-MAY) claims to be the oldest African-American neighborhood in the country. Once the site of the Claude Tremé plantation, it became home to many free people of color during the late 18th and early 19th centuries. Although most of the neighborhood did not see significant flooding from Katrina, the winds wreaked havoc on its historic structures. A vibrant and developing area before the storm, Tremé has struggled to come back since Katrina. Residents are slowly trickling back, however, and more and more of these brightly colored historic homes are being repaired. Never a highly touristed area, the Tremé now offers an even more quiet and reflective experience (unless, of course, you happen upon a second-line parade!). **TIP→Like many New Orleans neighborhoods beyond the French Quarter, the Tremé has had problems with crime. Visit this area during the day, and enjoy having its rich, small museums to yourself.**

WHAT TO SEE

48 ★ **Backstreet Cultural Museum.** Local photographer and self-made historian Sylvester Francis is an enthusiastic guide through his own rich collection of Mardi Gras Indian costumes and other musical artifacts tied to the street traditions of New Orleans. Sylvester is also an excellent source for current musical goings-on in Tremé and throughout town. The museum has been renovated since Katrina and celebrated its grand reopening in early 2007. ⊠*1116 St. Claude St., Tremé* ☎*504/522–4806* *$5* *Tues.–Sat. 10–5.*

50 **J&M Music Shop.** A plaque on this 1835 building marks it as the former site of the recording studio that launched the rock-and-roll careers of such greats as Fats Domino, Jerry Lee Lewis, Little Richard, and Ray Charles. Although the patrons of the Laundromat that now resides in this space probably don't pay it much heed, this is one of the most significant musical landmarks in New Orleans. Owned by Cosimo Matassa, the studio operated from 1945 to 1955. ⊠*840 N. Rampart St., Tremé.*

51 **Louis Armstrong Park.** This large park with its grassy knolls and lagoons is named for native son and world-famous musician Louis Armstrong (1900–71), whose statue by Elizabeth Catlett is near the brightly lighted entrance on the outer boundary of the French Quarter. To the left inside the park is **Congo Square,** marked by an inlaid-stone space where slaves in the 18th and early 19th centuries gathered on Sundays, the only time they were permitted to play their music openly. The weekly meetings held here have been immortalized in the travelogues of visitors, leaving invaluable insight into the earliest stages of free musical practices by Africans in America and African-Americans. Neighborhood musicians still congregate here at times for percussion jams, and it is difficult not to think of the musical spirit of ancestors hovering over them. Marie Laveau, the greatly feared and respected voodoo queen of antebellum New Orleans, had her home a block away on St. Ann Street, and is reported to have held voodoo rituals here regularly.

Behind Congo Square is a large gray building, the **Morris F.X. Jeff Municipal Auditorium;** to the right, behind the auditorium, is the **Mahalia Jackson Center for the Performing Arts.** The St. Philip Street side of the park houses the **Jazz National Historical Park,** anchored by **Perseverance Hall,** the oldest Masonic temple in the state. Currently in the last stages of a $3 million restoration, the hall is scheduled to reopen in January 2010, and will house a jazz exhibit as well as host live performances of New Orleans Jazz. **TIP→Armstrong Park is patrolled by a security detail, but be very careful when wandering, and do not visit after dark.** ⊠*N. Rampart St. between St. Philip and St. Peter Sts., Tremé* ⏲*Auditorium and performing arts center open by event; check local newspapers for listings.*

49 **New Orleans African-American Museum.** Set in a historic villa surrounded by a lovely small park, this museum is a prime example of the West Indies–style, French-colonial architecture that used to fill much of the French Quarter. It was built in 1829 by Simon Meilleur, a prosperous brick maker: the main house was constructed with Meilleur's bricks, and the brick patio behind it bears imprints identifying the original manufacturer. Inside, temporary exhibits spotlight African and African-diaspora art and artists. The fence surrounding the complex was completely destroyed by Katrina, and some of the buildings within were damaged as well. The museum reopened in February 2008, and additional improvements are planned. ⊠*1418 Governor Nicholls St., Tremé* ☎*504/565–7497* ⊕*www.neworleansmuseums.com* *$5* ⏲*Tues.–Fri. 9–5, Sat. 10–4.*

52 **Our Lady of Guadalupe, International Shrine of St. Jude (Old Mortuary Chapel).** Constructed in 1826 to house funerals for victims of the city's yellow-fever epidemics, this chapel is the oldest church building in New Orleans. It was a house of worship for the city's Italian immigrant population in the late 19th and early 20th centuries. In 1935, parishioners began a devotion to St. Jude Thaddeus, patron saint of lost causes; today, the church serves as the International Shrine of St. Jude. The faithful make offerings and prayers at St. Jude's statue, which is set in a nook to the left of the altar. In the rear of the chapel, to the right of the entrance, stands the statue of St. Expedite, the only such statue in a North American Church, whose devotees claim he is the saint to petition for quick fixes for problems or cures against procrastination. An old (apocryphal) story holds that the nuns of the parish received a crate from Rome containing the statue—no identifying information for the saint it depicts. The word "expedite" was stamped on the shipping crate, so the sisters promptly erected the statue to St. Expedite. ⊠*311 N. Rampart St., Tremé* ☎*504/525–1551.*

45 **St. Augustine Catholic Church.** Ursuline nuns donated the land for this church in 1841. Upon its completion in 1842, St. Augustine's became an integrated place of worship; slaves were relegated to the side pews, but free blacks claimed just as much right to center pews as whites did. The architect, J. N. B. de Pouilly, attended the École des Beaux-Arts in Paris and was known for his idiosyncratic style, which borrowed freely from a variety of traditions and resisted classification. Some of the ornamentation in his original drawings was eliminated when money ran out,

CLOSE UP

A Music History Tour

The Birthplace of Jazz is a banner New Orleans wears with pride, and it's hard to visit the city without seeing and hearing signs of the rich musical heritage. The following list combines sights both on and off the beaten track.

Backstreet Cultural Museum. This tiny but fabulous museum brings together artifacts from the Mardi Gras Indian, brass band, and second-line traditions. ✉ *1116 St. Claude Ave., Tremé* ☎ *504/522–4806.*

Buddy Bolden's House. Cornetist Buddy Bolden is the legendary originator of the "hot" sound that came to be associated with jazz. He lived and played across St. Charles Avenue from the Garden District. ✉ *2309 and 2527 1st St., Uptown.*

Congo Square. Louis Armstrong Park, on the northern edge of the French Quarter, contains the original Congo Square site. During the 1700s and 1800s, the square was reserved on Sunday for slaves seeking entertainment on their day off. Sharing a common language of music, rhythm, and dance, they helped link African tribal drumming rituals to jazz. ✉ *N. Rampart St. between St. Philip and St. Peter Sts., Tremé.*

Danny Barker's Birthplace. Songwriter, vocalist, banjoist, guitarist, storyteller, and jazz historian Danny Barker performed from the 1930s all the way up to his death in 1994 and was a vital intergenerational link for New Orleans jazz musicians. Barker organized the Fairview Baptist Church Brass Band, whose alumni include Wynton and Branford Marsalis, Anthony "Tuba Fats" Lacen, and Charles and Kirk Joseph of the Dirty Dozen Brass Band. He worked through the 1970s as assistant curator of the New Orleans Jazz Museum and, leading his Onward Brass Band, encouraged younger players to keep Dixieland jazz alive. ✉ *1027–1029 Chartres St., French Quarter.*

George Vitale "Papa Jack" Laine's House. One of the most successful and influential bandleaders to emerge from the early period of jazz, Laine was also a pioneer drummer. He is credited with helping to popularize the music. ✉ *2405 and 2422–2424 Chartres St., Marigny.*

Jazz National Historical Park. Appointed guardians of New Orleans's jazz heritage, the uniformed rangers of this unique national park are also expert musicians, compelling teachers, and affable guides to the city's music. Look for the free guides to jazz history walking tours in the bookstore. ✉ *Armstrong Park, N. Rampart St. between St. Philip and St. Peter Sts.; visitor center: 916 N. Peters St., Tremé/French Quarter* ☎ *504/589–4841 or 504/589–4806.*

Jelly Roll Morton's House. The legendary pianist, who blurred the line between ragtime and jazz, lived in a mixed-race neighborhood. A "Creole of color," Morton always described his roots as French. ✉ *1443 Frenchmen St.*

Louis Armstrong's birthplace. The man who would bring jazz to the world was born in the poorest of circumstances, in a neighborhood now consumed by the Orleans Parish Prison and associated buildings. The house itself was demolished, but the legendary address still draws fans and historians to the area where it once stood. ✉ *723 Jane Alley, Mid-City.*

but effusive pink-and-gold paint inside brightens the austere structure. The church grounds now also house the Tomb of the Unknown Slave, a monument dedicated in 2004 to the slaves buried in unmarked graves in the church grounds and surrounding areas. Following Katrina, the Archdiocese of New Orleans planned to close seven churches in the city, including St. Augustine. Public outcry, the church's historical significance, and parishioners' dedication saved the parish, and its 10 AM Sunday gospel-jazz services continue. ✉ *1210 Governor Nicholls St., Tremé* ☎ *504/525–5934*.

Storyville. The busy red-light district that lasted from 1897 to 1917 has been destroyed, and in its place stands a public-housing project. Storyville spawned splendid Victorian homes that served as brothels and provided a venue for the raw sounds of ragtime and early jazz; an extremely young Louis Armstrong cut his teeth in some of the clubs here. The world's first electrically lighted saloon, Tom Anderson's House of Diamonds, was at the corner of Basin and Bienville streets, and the whole area has been the subject of many novels, songs, and films. In 1917, after several incidents involving naval officers, the government ordered the district shut down. Some buildings were razed almost overnight; the housing project was built in the 1930s. Only three structures from the Storyville area remain, the former sites of three saloons: Lulu White's Saloon (237 Basin Street), Joe Victor's Saloon (St. Louis and Villere streets), and "My Place" Saloon (1214 Bienville Street). Currently, a historical marker on the "neutral ground" (median) of Basin Street is the only visible connection to Alderman Sidney Story's experiment in legalized prostitution. ✉ *Basin St. next to St. Louis Cemetery No. 1, Tremé.*

CBD AND WAREHOUSE DISTRICT

Bordered by the river, St. Charles Avenue, Poydras Street, and the Interstate 10 expressway and filled with former factories and cotton warehouses, the Warehouse District began its renaissance when the city hosted the World's Fair here in 1984. Old abandoned buildings were renovated to host the fair and its events, setting the scene for future development. Structures that housed the international pavilions during the fair now make up the New Orleans Morial Convention Center and a number of hotels, restaurants, bars, and music clubs. New Orleanians will always remain sensitive to the plight of the many citizens who suffered in the days following Katrina as they sought refuge in and around the battered Convention Center. However, in the year following the hurricane, the center underwent an extensive renovation, and the surrounding neighborhood has since regained its former charm and vibrancy. Today, the Warehouse District remains one of the hottest residential and arts-and-nightlife areas of the city, dotted with modern renovations of historic buildings, upscale loft residences, excellent eateries, and a number of bars and music clubs. Part of Harrah's property, Fulton Street Mall is a pedestrian promenade lined with restaurants and clubs, and hosts outdoor events such as Miracle on Fulton Street during the Christmas holidays. Stretching from the river to Carrollton Avenue, Julia Street is lined with upscale contemporary art galleries and artist studios. The Warehouse District (also, appropriately, known as the Arts District) is a museum hub, home to the National World War II Museum, the Ogden Museum of Southern Art, the Contemporary Arts Center, the Louisiana Children's Museum, and the Memorial Hall Confederate Museum—all within a three-square-block radius.

2

The Central Business District (CBD) covers the ground between Canal Street and Poydras Avenue, with some spillover into the Warehouse District's official territory. The neighborhood includes many iconic buildings, including the Louisiana Superdome, the World Trade Center, and Harrah's Casino. There are also beautiful old government and office buildings, particularly around central Lafayette Square. Canal Street is the CBD's main artery and the official dividing line between the business district and the French Quarter; street names change from American to French as they cross Canal. Now served by the Canal Street streetcar, the palm tree-lined grand avenue is slowly beginning to regain some of its former elegance, particularly along Lower Canal Street as it nears the river.

Numbers in the margin correspond to numbers on the CBD and Warehouse District map.

WHAT TO SEE

11 **American-Italian Renaissance Foundation Museum and Library.** Italian–New Orleans customs are explained and artifacts exhibited in this small, thoughtful museum. The research library includes records of the large Southeastern Italian immigrant community. ✉ *537 S. Peters St., Warehouse District* ☎ *504/522–7294* 🌐 *www.airf.org* 🎫 *Free* 🕑 *Wed.–Fri. 10–4.*

6 **Arthur Roger Gallery.** A highlight among Julia Street galleries, this gallery showcases quality contemporary art, primarily by local and regional artists. There is also a satellite gallery at 730 Tchoupitoulas in the Renaissance Arts Hotel, two blocks from the main gallery. ✉ *432 Julia St., Warehouse District* ☎ *504/522–1999* 🕑 *Mon.–Sat. 10–5.*

16 **Blaine Kern's Mardi Gras World at Kern Studios.** Mardi Gras World's entertainment complex moved from Algiers Point to join Blaine Kern Studios and new private-event venues on the east bank of New Orleans in early 2009. Located just upriver of the New Orleans Convention Center, the massive 400,000-square-foot complex occupies the former Delta Queen Steamboat terminal and River City Casino sites right along the Mississippi River. The new Mardi Gras World brings the fun of its west bank predecessor closer to the city center with an enhanced guided tour through a maze of video presentations, decorative sculptures, and favorite megafloats from Mardi Gras parades such as Bacchus, Rex, and Endymion. Visitors enter through a plantation alley that is part Cajun swamp-shack village, part antebellum Disneyworld (Kern was a friend of, and inspired by, Walt Disney). If you're not here for the real thing, Mardi Gras World is a fun (and family friendly) backstage look at the history and artistry of Carnival. Admission includes cake and coffee. ✉ *1380 Port of New Orleans Pl., Warehouse Dis-*

Fodor's Choice ★

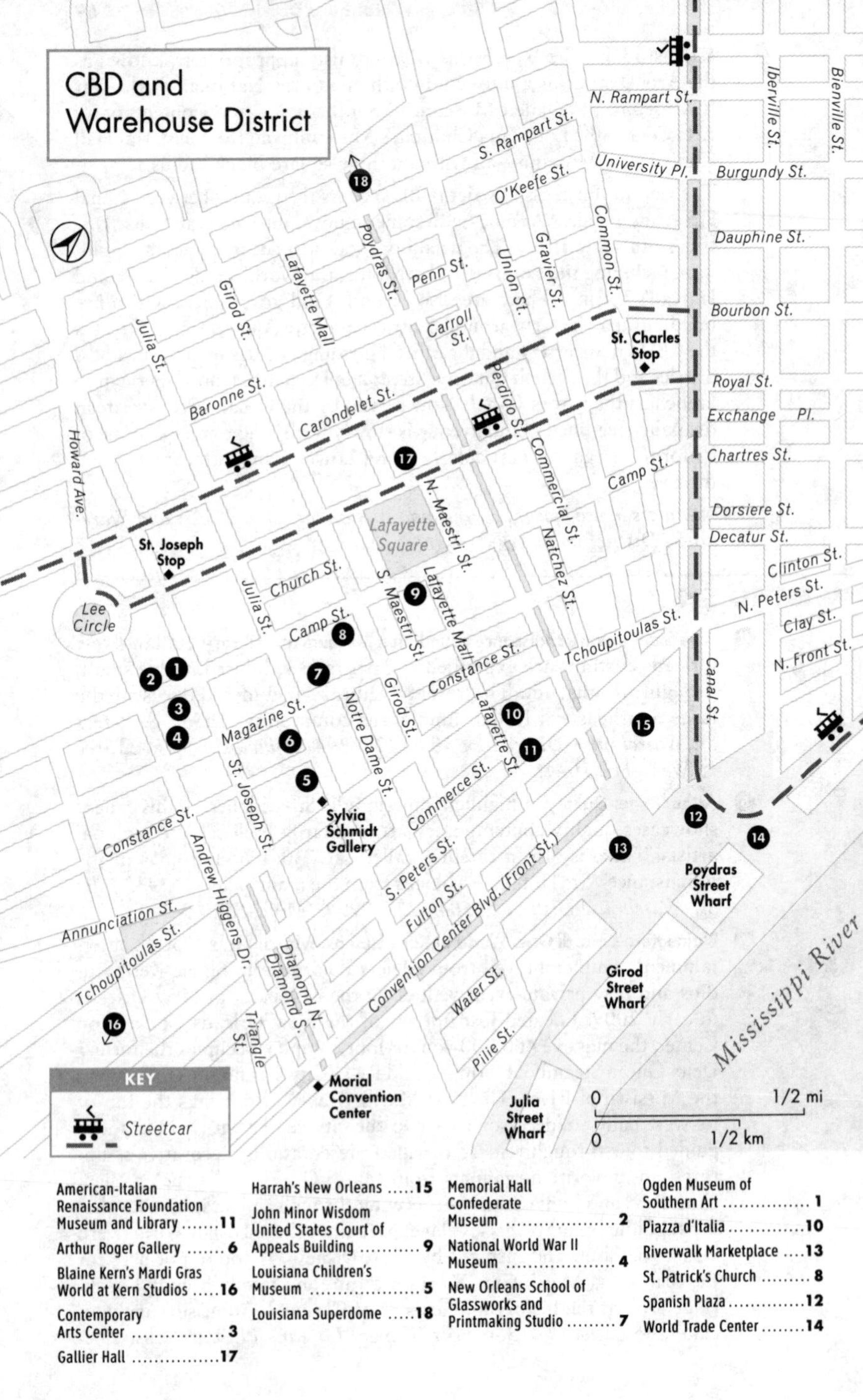
CBD and Warehouse District
N. Rampart St.
S. Rampart St.
University Pl.
O'Keefe St.
Iberville St.
Bienville St.
Burgundy St.
Dauphine St.
Bourbon St.
Royal St.
Exchange Pl.
Chartres St.
Dorsiere St.
Decatur St.
Clinton St.
N. Peters St.
Clay St.
N. Front St.
Canal St.
Poydras St.
Penn St.
Union St.
Gravier St.
Common St.
Lafayette Mall
Girod St.
Julia St.
Carroll St.
St. Charles Stop
Perdido St.
Baronne St.
Carondelet St.
Howard Ave.
Commercial St.
Camp St.
N. Maestri St.
Lafayette Square
Natchez St.
St. Joseph Stop
Church St.
Lee Circle
S. Maestri St.
Tchoupitoulas St.
Constance St.
Magazine St.
Notre Dame St.
Lafayette St.
St. Joseph St.
Commerce St.
Sylvia Schmidt Gallery
Constance St.
Andrew Higgens Dr.
S. Peters St.
Fulton St.
Convention Center Blvd. (Front St.)
Poydras Street Wharf
Annunciation St.
Tchoupitoulas St.
Diamond S.
Diamond N.
Water St.
Girod Street Wharf
Mississippi River
Triangle St.
Pilie St.
KEY
Streetcar
Morial Convention Center
Julia Street Wharf
0 1/2 mi
0 1/2 km
American-Italian Renaissance Foundation Museum and Library 11
Arthur Roger Gallery 6
Blaine Kern's Mardi Gras World at Kern Studios 16
Contemporary Arts Center 3
Gallier Hall 17
Harrah's New Orleans 15
John Minor Wisdom United States Court of Appeals Building 9
Louisiana Children's Museum 5
Louisiana Superdome 18
Memorial Hall Confederate Museum 2
National World War II Museum 4
New Orleans School of Glassworks and Printmaking Studio 7
Ogden Museum of Southern Art 1
Piazza d'Italia 10
Riverwalk Marketplace 13
St. Patrick's Church 8
Spanish Plaza 12
World Trade Center 14

trict ☎*504/361–7821 or 800/362–8213* 🌐*www.mardigrasworld.com* 🎟*$18* ⏲*Daily 9:30–5*

3 **Contemporary Arts Center.** Founded in 1976, the center endured long, hard years of economic and cultural stagnation to finally emerge as a keystone to the now vibrant Warehouse District arts scene. Today the center hosts cutting-edge exhibits, featuring both local artists and the work of national and international talent. Two theaters present jazz productions, films, dance, plays, lectures, and experimental and conventional concerts, including a New Orleans music series. Hours vary during concerts, performances, lectures, and special events; call or check the Web site for details. ✉*900 Camp St., Warehouse District* ☎*504/528–3805, 504/528–3800 theater box office* 🌐*www.cacno.org* 🎟*Gallery admission $5* ⏲*Thurs.–Sun. 11–4.*

17 **Gallier Hall.** This Greek Revival building, modeled on the Erectheum of Athens, was built in 1845 by architect James Gallier Sr. It served as City Hall in the mid-20th century. Today it hosts special events and is the mayor's official perch during Mardi Gras parades; the kings and queens of many parades stop here to be toasted by the mayor and dignitaries. The grand rooms inside the hall are adorned with portraits and decorative details ordered by Gallier from Paris. ✉*545 St. Charles Ave. (entrance on the side at 705 Lafayette St.), CBD* ☎*504/565–7457, 504/658–3623 for appointment* ⏲*Weekdays 9–5; visits by appointment.*

15 **Harrah's New Orleans.** The only land-based casino in the New Orleans area, Harrah's contains 115,000 square feet of gaming space divided into five areas, each with a New Orleans theme: Jazz Court, Court of Good Fortune, Smugglers Court, Mardi Gras Court, and Court of the Mansion. There are also 100 table games, 2,100-plus slots, and live entertainment at Masquerade, which includes an ice bar, lounge, video tower and dancing show. Check the Web site for seasonal productions, including music, theater, and comedy. Dining and libation choices include the extensive Harrah's buffet, Cafés on Canal food court, Besch Steak House, Bamboo Court, Gordon Biersch, Grand Isle, and Ruth's Chris Steak House (the last three are part of Harrah's newly developed Fulton Street Mall, a pedestrian promenade that attracts casual strollers, club goers, and diners). ✉*8 Canal St., CBD* ☎*504/533–6000 or 800/427–7247* 🌐*www.harrahs.com* ⏲*Daily 24 hrs.*

9 **John Minor Wisdom United States Court of Appeals Building.** New York architect James Gamble Rogers was summoned to design this three-story granite structure as a post office and court building in 1909. By the 1960s the post office had moved to larger digs, and McDonough No. 35 High School found refuge here after Hurricane Betsy in 1965. Today the Renaissance Revival building houses the Fifth Circuit Court of Appeals in an elaborately paneled and ornamented series of courtrooms. The dark, cool corridors of the ground floor have an arcaded, bronzed ceiling. As you enter the building and pass security, turn left and continue around the corner to find the library, where you can pick up information on the courthouse. Outside, a repeating sculpture of four women stands on each corner of the building: the four ladies represent History, Agriculture, Industry, and the Arts. The building is

named for Judge John Minor Wisdom, the New Orleans native who was instrumental in dismantling the segregation laws of the South. Judge Wisdom received the Presidential Medal of Freedom in 1993. ✉ *600 Camp St., CBD* ☎ *504/310–7777* ⏲ *Weekdays 8–5.*

Julia Street. Contemporary-art dealers have adopted this strip in the Warehouse District as their own. The street is lined with galleries, specialty shops, and modern apartment buildings, with the greatest concentration stretching from South Peters Street to Carrollton Avenue. The first Saturday evening of each month gallery owners throw open their doors to show off new exhibits, to the accompaniment of wine, music, and general merriment. White Linen Night in August and Art for Art's Sake in October also find the galleries welcoming visitors with artist receptions and live entertainment.

FREE FUN

From April to June, the Young Leadership Council, the Downtown Development District, and several corporate sponsors present Wednesdays at the square, weekly events that feature food, beer and soft drinks, and free concerts in Lafayette Square (bordered by St. Charles, Camp, and Lafayette streets). Bring a blanket and enjoy the music from 5 to 7:30.

Lee Circle. At the northern edge of the Warehouse District, a bronze statue of Civil War general Robert E. Lee stands high above the city on a white marble column in a traffic circle. Lee faces due north, as he has since 1884. New Orleanians say it's because you can never turn your back on a Yankee. Recent extensive renovation and new construction have greatly improved the area immediately around the circle, which now includes the **Contemporary Arts Center,** the **Ogden Museum of Southern Art,** the **National World War II Museum,** and the **Memorial Hall Confederate Museum.**

5 **Louisiana Children's Museum.** An invaluable resource for anyone traveling with kids, the top-notch Children's Museum is 30,000 square feet of hands-on educational fun. Favorite activities include a mini–grocery store (with both carts and registers manned by visitors), a role-play café, Mr. Rogers' Neighborhood, and a giant bubble station. A welcoming environment is provided for children with disabilities: most exhibits are accessible, and some are aimed directly at increasing children's awareness of disabilities. Art teachers lead classes daily; theatrical storytelling takes place every morning and afternoon; and special activities such as jewelry making, face painting, and scavenger hunts are held each week. An indoor playground is reserved for toddlers ages three and under, and Toddler Time activities are held at 10 AM on Tuesday and Thursday. There's also a mini–fitness center with a kid-size stationary bicycle and rock-climbing wall. ✉ *420 Julia St., Warehouse District* ☎ *504/523–1357* 🌐 *www.lcm.org* 🎫 *$7.50* ⏲ *Tues.–Sat. 9:30–4:30, Sun. noon–4:30 (last ticket sold at 4).*

18 **Louisiana Superdome.** Home to the NFL's New Orleans Saints, the Louisiana Superdome has been the site of many Sugar Bowls, several NCAA Final Four basketball tournaments, the BCS championship game, a record nine Super Bowls, and the 1998 Republican National Convention.

The Superdome was badly damaged during Katrina and in its aftermath, when it served as a refuge of last resort for evacuees; the stadium underwent extensive renovations in the year that followed. The Superdome reopened for football in September 2006, when the Saints beat the Atlanta Falcons in front of the largest audience in ESPN history.

Built in 1975, the Superdome seats up to 71,000 people, has a 166,000-square-foot main arena, and a roof that covers almost 10 acres at a height of 27 stories. The bronze statue on the Poydras Street side is the Vietnam Veterans Memorial. The **New Orleans Arena,** behind the Superdome, is home to the NBA New Orleans Hornets. Across from the Superdome on Poydras Street is a large abstract sculpture called the *Krewe of Poydras*. The sculptor, Ida Kohlmeyer, meant to evoke the frivolity and zany spirit of Mardi Gras. A couple of blocks down Poydras Street from the Superdome is the Bloch Cancer Survivors Monument, a block-long walkway of whimsical columns, figures, and a triumphal arch in the median of Loyola Avenue. **■TIP→The streets around the Superdome and Arena are usually busy during business hours, but at night and on weekends, except during a game, this area should not be explored alone.** ⊠*1 Sugar Bowl Dr., CBD* ☎*504/587–3663* 🌐*www.superdome.com.*

NEED A BREAK?

The brightly decorated bar and dining room inside Lucy's Retired Surfers Restaurant and Bar (⊠***701 Tchoupitoulas St., Warehouse District*** ☎***504/523–8995*** 🌐***www.lucysretiredsurfers.com*)**, **open from 11 AM until late (kitchen closes at 10 PM), provide a nice spot for a margarita, a cup of coffee, or a Southwestern-style snack. During happy hour the bar fills up with professionals who work in the area.**

2 **Memorial Hall Confederate Museum.** This ponderous stone building at Lee Circle was built in 1891 to house a collection of artifacts from the Civil War, making it the oldest museum in the state. The displays include uniforms, flags, and soldiers' personal effects, which thankfully survived Hurricane Katrina intact. ⊠*929 Camp St., Warehouse District* ☎*504/523–4522* 🌐*www.confederatemuseum.com* 🎟*$7* ⏲*Wed.–Sat. 10–4.*

4 **National World War II Museum.** Exhibits take visitors from the Normandy invasion to the sands of Pacific Islands and the Home Front. The brainchild of historian and writer Dr. Stephen Ambrose, who taught for many years at the University of New Orleans until his death in 2002, this moving, well-executed examination of World War II covers far more ground than simply D-Day. The seminal moments are re-created through propaganda posters and radio clips from the period; biographical sketches of the military personnel involved; a number of short documentary films (including one bitterly sad film on the Holocaust, featuring interviews with survivors); and collections of weapons, personal items, and other artifacts from the war. The exhibits occupy a series of galleries spread through the interior of a huge warehouse space. One spotlighted exhibit, in a large, open portion of the warehouse near the entrance, is a replica of the Higgins boat troop landing craft, which were manufactured in New Orleans. In 2005 the museum announced

Fodor's Choice ★

a $300 million expansion plan to quadruple the size of the facility in several phases. Across the street from the current facility, a 4-D theater experience produced by Tom Hanks and a canteen featuring live period entertainment are set to open in November. This is the first of six new pavilions proposed for the expanded campus, due to be completed in 2015. Check the Web site for updates on the expansion and a list of current movies, lectures, events, and programs. ✉ *925 Magazine St. (main entrance on Andrew Higgins Dr.), Warehouse District* ☎ *504/527–6012* 🌐 *www.nationalww2museum.org* 🎟 *$14* ⏲ *Oct.–June, daily 9–5; July–Sept., Tues.–Sun. 9–5.*

SECOND TO NONE

If you're lucky, you'll get swept up in a jazz street parade during your New Orleans visit. The parades themselves are often referred to as "second lines," a term that originated in the city's jazz funerals. Traditionally, a brass band accompanies a New Orleans funeral procession to the grave site, playing dirges along the way. On the return from the grave, however, the music becomes upbeat, celebrating the departed's passage to heaven. Behind the family, friends, and recognized mourners, a second group often gathers, taking part in the free entertainment and dancing—hence, the "second line."

7 **New Orleans School of Glassworks and Printmaking Studio.** With advanced reservation, the School of Glassworks gives demonstrations of all stages of glassmaking and design, printmaking, and silver alchemy in a large warehouse space. Special "make and take" exhibits for youngsters are popular, as are a variety of group and individual classes. Call at least several weeks in advance for reservations. A shop and gallery up front displays and sells the finished products. ✉ *727 Magazine St., Warehouse District* ☎ *504/529–7277* 🌐 *www.neworleansglassworks.com* ⏲ *June–Aug., weekdays 11–5; Sept.–May, Mon.–Sat. 10–5:30.*

1 ★ **Ogden Museum of Southern Art.** Art by Southerners, art made in the South, art about the South, artistic explorations into Southern themes, and more fill this Smithsonian affiliate's elegant building. More than 1,200 works collected by local developer Roger Ogden since the 1960s are on permanent display, along with pieces from Washington, D.C., and 15 Southern states spanning the 18th–21st centuries, plus featured exhibits. A central stair hall filters natural light through the series of galleries, and a rooftop patio affords lovely views of the surrounding area. The gift shop sells logo items, crafts by local artists, and books and movies celebrating the South. Thursday nights (6–8 PM) come alive with "Ogden After Hours," featuring live music, artist interviews, refreshments, children's activities, and special gallery exhibits. ✉ *925 Camp St., Warehouse District* ☎ *504/539–9600* 🌐 *www.ogdenmuseum.org* 🎟 *$10* ⏲ *Wed.–Sun. 11–5.*

10 **Piazza d'Italia.** This modern plaza by architect Charles Moore is a gathering place for the large Italian community on St. Joseph's Day and Columbus Day. Its postmodern style is reminiscent of a Roman ruin. On the South Peters Street side of the piazza is the **American-Italian Museum.**

13 **Riverwalk Marketplace.** Though tough economic times have shuttered some of its stores, this three-block-long center still contains several retail chains, local specialty shops, and a food court. New in 2008 is the Southern Food and Beverage Museum, complete with a cocktail exhibit, tasting room with chef demonstrations, and a food gift shop. Plaques along the river walkway relate bits of the Mississippi River's history and folklore. Nearby at the Poydras Street streetcar stop is a 200-foot-long mural in tropical motifs that was a gift to the city by Mexican artist Julio Quintanilla. Various cruise ships leave from the Julia Street Wharf slightly upriver; you can often see them from the front of the Riverwalk. ☒*1 Poydras St., Warehouse District* ☎*504/522–1555* 🌐*www.riverwalkmarketplace.com* ⏲*Mon.–Sat. 10–7, Sun. noon–6.*

8 **St. Patrick's Church.** A stark exterior gives way to a far more ornate, richly painted interior in this first church built in the American sector of New Orleans, intended to provide the city's Irish Catholics with a place of worship as distinguished as the French St. Louis Cathedral. The vaulted interior was completed in 1838 by local architect James Gallier, who moved here from Ireland in 1834 in order to work on the cathedral. High stained-glass windows and huge murals, painted in 1841, enrich the interior. ☒*724 Camp St., Warehouse District* ☎*504/525–4413.*

NEED A BREAK?

P. J.'s Coffee and Teas (☒*644 Camp St., CBD* ☎*504/529–3658* 🌐*www.pjscoffee.com*), a local chain serving delicious, cold-brewed iced coffee and a small selection of pastries and sandwiches, has a small but pleasant location just off Lafayette Square.

12 **Spanish Plaza.** For a terrific view of the river and a place to relax, go behind the **World Trade Center** at 2 Canal Street to Spanish Plaza, a large, sunken space with beautiful inlaid tiles and a fountain. The plaza was a gift from Spain in the mid-1970s; you can hear occasional live music played here and you can purchase tickets for riverboat cruises in the offices that face the river.

14 **World Trade Center.** Once occupied by foreign consulates and businesses involved in international trade, the World Trade Center has lost tenants over the past decade, sustained severe damage during Katrina, and now sits largely empty. Atop the center, the Plimsoll Club's spectacular views make it a popular venue for receptions and events. Walking around its outside, you can visit statues and plazas: Winston Churchill is memorialized in a bronze statue in **British Park Place,** also known as Winston's Circle, where the stone-inlaid street curves in front of the Riverfront Hilton to the right; and a bronze equestrian statue of Bernardo de Galvez, Spanish governor of Louisiana in the 1780s, guards the entrance of the **Spanish Plaza** behind the World Trade Center. ☒*2 Canal St., CBD* ☎*504/529–1601.*

GARDEN DISTRICT

With its beautifully landscaped gardens surrounding elegant antebellum homes, the Garden District lives up to its name. Although its homes aren't open to the public, outside of occasional special-event tours, enjoying the sights from outside the cast-iron fences is well worth the visit.

Originally the Livaudais Plantation, the Garden District was laid out in the late 1820s and remained part of the city of Lafayette until incorporated into New Orleans in 1852. The neighborhood attracted "new-moneyed" Americans who, looked down upon by the Creole residents of the French Quarter, constructed grand houses with large English-style gardens featuring lush azaleas, magnolias, and camellias. Three architecture styles were favored: the three-bay Greek Revival, center-hall Greek Revival, and raised cottage. Renovations and expansions to these designs through the years allowed owners to host bigger and more ostentatious parties, particularly during the social season between Christmas and Carnival. Today, many of the proud residents represent fourth- or fifth-generation New Orleanians.

CREOLE VS. CAJUN

The terms "Creole" and "Cajun" are used almost interchangeably outside Louisiana to refer to the region's cuisine, but a local would never confuse the two. Originally, the "Creole" was used to refer to people born in the colonies. In New Orleans today, it is often used to refer to people of mixed European and African heritage with long family traditions in the city. "Cajun," short for "Acadian," refers to the descendants of French residents of Nova Scotia, Canada, who sought refuge in Louisiana after being banished by the British in the 18th century.

The Garden District is divided into two sections by Jackson Avenue. Upriver from Jackson is the wealthy **Upper Garden District,** where the homes are meticulously kept. Below Jackson, the Lower Garden District is rougher in areas, though the homes here are often structurally just as beautiful and are increasingly being restored. Still, the streets are less well patrolled and best toured during the day. Magazine Street, lined with antiques shops, boutiques, restaurants, and cafés, serves as a southern border to the Garden District. St. Charles Avenue forms the northern border. Although the **Magazine Street bus** or **St. Charles Avenue bus** lines can get you here from downtown, take the historic streetcar if you can—it's a fun and leisurely way to see the sights along the avenue. A number of companies also offer walking tours *(⇨Day Tours and Guides in New Orleans Travel Smart)*.

Numbers in the margin correspond to numbers in the box and on the Garden District map.

UPPER GARDEN DISTRICT

WHAT TO SEE

10 **Adams House.** The curved gallery on the left side of this circa-1860 house is a twist on the raised-cottage theme. Greek Revival influence is evident in the columns and the windows. ✉*2423 Prytania St., Garden District.*

8 **Bradish-Johnson House.** A private girls' school since 1929, this regal building served as a residence when it was built in 1872. Though based on the common five-bay Garden District plan, this was the first house in

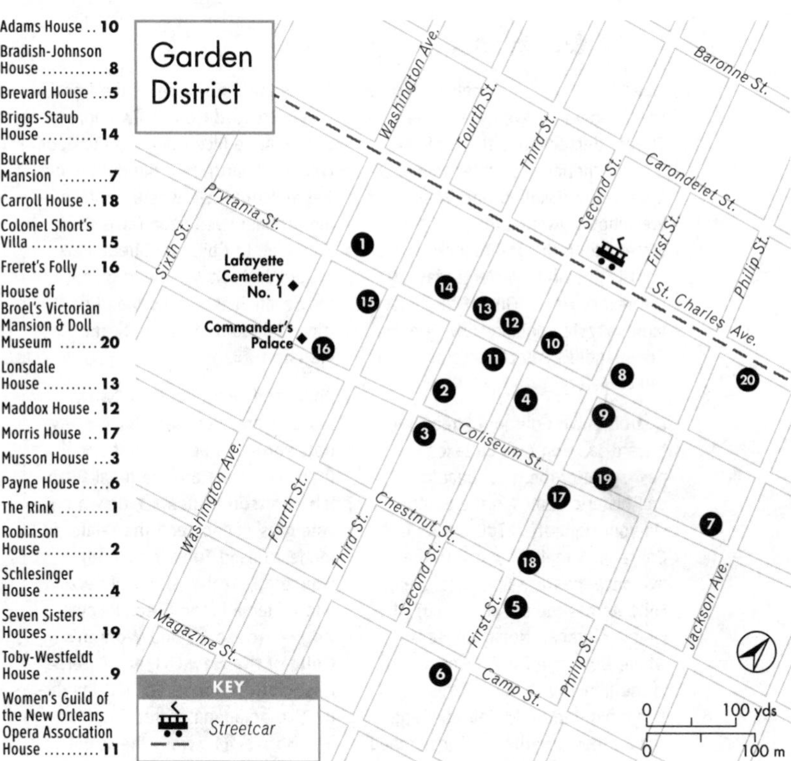

the district to embrace the French Second Empire style, visible in the mansard roof and ornamental details. ✉2343 *Prytania St., Garden District.*

5 **Brevard House.** Though Anne Rice moved out of the elegant Garden District home in 2004, the famous novelist's fans still flock to see the house that inspired the Mayfair Manor in her series *Lives of the Mayfair Witches.* The house is a three-bay Greek Revival, extended over a luxurious side yard and surrounded by a fence of cast-iron rosettes that earned the estate's historical name, Rosegate. ✉1239 *1st St., Garden District.*

14 **Briggs-Staub House.** The only Gothic Revival house in the district was built around 1849. Garden District Americans shunned the Gothic Revival style as linked to Creole-Catholic tradition, but Londoner Charles Briggs ignored decorum and had James Gallier Sr. design this anomaly, touted as a "Gothic cottage." The interior departed from a strict Gothic breakup of rooms to make it better suited for entertaining. ✉2605 *Prytania St., Garden District.*

7 **Buckner Mansion.** This 1856 home was built by cotton factor Henry S. Buckner in overt competition with the famous Stanton Hall in Natchez, built by Buckner's former partner. Among the luxurious details are 48 fluted cypress columns and a rare honeysuckle-design cast-iron fence.

A GOOD WALK

One block from the streetcar stop at the Washington Avenue and Prytania Street intersection is the **Rink ❶**, a small shopping complex that was once a roller-skating rink. Walk down Washington Avenue toward Coliseum Street: along the 1600 block on your right is the white-walled **Lafayette Cemetery No. 1.** One of the most famous restaurants in New Orleans, Commander's Palace, is across from the cemetery.

A stroll down Coliseum Street toward Jackson Avenue takes you past some of the most beautiful and historic homes in the South. On your right, the 2700 block of Coliseum Street is lined with the five once-identical houses of Freret's Folly. Across the street, at 2707, the white-columned Nolan House is where Benjamin Button was raised in the film *The Curious Case of Benjamin Button.* At Coliseum and Third streets are the white-columned **Robinson House ❷**, thought to be the first house in New Orleans with indoor plumbing, and the intricate iron-balconied **Musson House ❸**. Also featuring elaborate ironwork, the **Schlesinger House ❹**, to your left at Second Street, is a classic Greek Revival. Continuing along Coliseum, turn right and walk down First Street. The Italianate Morris House on the next corner and the Carroll House, where the classic *Toys In the Attic* was filmed, are on your left.

Across Chestnut Street is the transitional **Brevard House ❺**, home to author Anne Rice from 1989 to 2004. One block farther on the right is the **Payne House ❻**, where Confederate president Jefferson Davis died. Returning to Coliseum Street, look toward Jackson Avenue to glimpse the Seven Sisters Houses and the triple ballroom of the **Buckner Mansion ❼**.

Philip and First streets, between Prytania and Coliseum, have many noteworthy homes. At First and Prytania streets are the regal **Bradish-Johnson House ❽**, now a private girls' school, and the relatively modest raised **Toby-Westfeldt House ❾**. At the corner of Second and Prytania is the Greek Revival **Adams House ❿** and **Women's Guild of the New Orleans Opera Association House ⓫**, with its distinctive octagonal turret. The **Maddox House ⓬**, across the street, is an example of the five-bay Greek Revival expansion. Venture to your left down Prytania Street, the main artery of the district. No expense was spared in the construction of the **Lonsdale House ⓭**, at Prytania and Third streets. Across Third, the **Briggs-Staub House ⓮** is one of the few Gothic Revival houses in the city. Cross Prytania at the corner of Fourth Street to **Colonel Short's Villa ⓯**, known for its cornstalk fence.

The triple ballroom was used by debutantes practicing their walks and curtsies. Now privately owned, the house served as the campus of Soulé College from 1923 to 1975. ⊠*1410 Jackson Ave., Garden District.*

⓲ **Carroll House.** This grand Italianate home and its neighbor at 1331 First Street, both designed by Samuel Jamison, have identical ornate cast-iron galleries. An original carriage house still stands on the large property. ⊠*1315 First St., Garden District.*

2

15 **Colonel Short's Villa.** Occupied for a brief time by the Union governor of post–Civil War Louisiana, the house was stylistically influential in the district because the two-story galleries of its dining room wing had railings made of cast iron rather than wood. The fence, with a pattern of morning glories intertwining with cornstalks, is the most famous example of cast iron in the Garden District. Legend has it that Colonel Short purchased the fence for his wife, who was homesick for Kentucky. A similar cornstalk fence appears in the French Quarter at 915 Royal Street. ✉*1448 Fourth St., Garden District.*

STAR SEARCH

The two-story 1850 corner house at 2417 Coliseum Street is home to actor John Goodman and his wife, Annabeth Hartzog. They bought the 5,000-square-foot home in 2005 from Trent Reznor, founder of the rock group Nine Inch Rails. Annabeth also owns a children's store, Pippen Lane, on nearby Magazine Street.

16 **Freret's Folly.** These once-identical Greek Revival houses were built by the son of New Orleans Mayor William Freret as a speculative project. In the wake of the Civil War, the venture failed financially, earning its name. ✉*2700 Coliseum St., Garden District.*

20 **House of Broel's Victorian Mansion and Dollhouse Museum.** Antique furnishings fill this restored antebellum home. The dollhouse collection includes miniatures of Victorian, Tudor, and plantation-style houses. The home also houses a wedding store. Tours are available by appointment. ✉*2220 St. Charles Ave., Garden District* ☎*504/522–2220 or 800/827–4325* 🌐*www.houseofbroel.com* 🎫*Mansion and museum tour $10* ⏲*Mon.–Sat. 10–5.*

13 **Lonsdale House.** As a 16-year-old immigrant working in the New Orleans shipyards, Henry Lonsdale noticed how many damaged goods were arriving from upriver. Spotting a need for more-protective shipping materials, Lonsdale developed the burlap bag (clued in by his parents, who had picked up a sample in India). He made a fortune in burlap, only to lose it all in the 1837 depression. Lonsdale next turned to coffee importing, an industry that ran into problems during the Civil War: the Union blocked imports from Brazil, the major supplier of coffee to New Orleans. Lonsdale hit upon the fateful idea of cutting the limited coffee grinds with chicory, a bitter root, and New Orleanians have been drinking the blend ever since. The house, built with his entrepreneurial dollars, displays many fine details, including intricate cast-iron work on the galleries and a marble entrance hall. The statue of Our Mother of Perpetual Help in the front yard is a remnant of the house's more than 70 years as an active Catholic chapel, which ended with its controversial sale to novelist Anne Rice in 1996. Actor Nicholas Cage purchased the home in 2005, but at press time had it up for sale for $3.45 million. ✉*2523 Prytania St., Garden District.*

12 **Maddox House.** Built in 1852, this house exemplifies the five-bay, center-hall extension of the Greek Revival style—notice the Ionic and Corinthian columns that support the broadened galleries. Inside is a gold ballroom decorated by a Viennese artist for the original owners. ✉*2507 Prytania St., Garden District.*

17 **Morris House.** By the end of the 1850s, Garden District tastes began to evolve from the Greek Revival style to more fanciful designs. The Morris house is an excellent example of the Italianate style that became the new architectural vogue. ☒*1331 1st St., Garden District.*

3 **Musson House.** This Italianate house was built by impressionist painter Edgar Degas's maternal uncle, Michel Musson—a rare Creole inhabitant of the predominantly American Garden District. A later owner added the famous "lace" iron galleries. ☒*1331 Third St., Garden District.*

THE CURIOUS HOME OF BENJAMIN BUTTON

When director David Fincher saw the Garden District Nolan House, he told the location manager, "That's the one I want." The owner, Mary Nell Porter Nolan, had evacuated the city for Katrina and had yet to return. A housekeeper brought Fincher's note to a family member. Ms. Nolan refused the offer until Brad Pitt, the movie's star, called and convinced her that the film would be good for the city in the aftermath of the storm.

6 **Payne House.** Confederate president Jefferson Davis died here on December 6, 1889; a monument out front outlines his political and military careers. The two-story galleries overlook a side rose garden. Cast-iron ornaments the capitals of the Ionic columns, each embossed with the date (1848) and place (New York) of manufacture. ☒*1134 1st St., Garden District.*

1 **The Rink.** This small collection of specialty shops was once the location of the south's first roller-skating rink, built in the 1880s. Locals can be found here browsing in the **Garden District Book Shop,** which stocks regional, rare, and old books. ☒*Washington Ave. and Prytania St., Garden District.*

NEED A BREAK?

A pleasant place to relax is outdoors on the deck of Still Perkin' (☒*2727 Prytania St., Garden District* ☎*504/899–0335*) at the Rink. Gourmet coffees, teas, and baked goods are served.

2 **Robinson House.** Styled after an Italian villa, this home built in the late 1850s is one of the largest in the district. Doric and Corinthian columns support the rounded galleries. It is believed to be the first house in New Orleans with "waterworks," as indoor plumbing was called then. Years of extensive renovation based on the original plans culminated with a re-landscaping in 2005. ☒*1415 Third St., Garden District.*

4 **Schlesinger House.** This house's columns make it a classic example of the Greek Revival style popular in the 1850s, which was used in many plantation homes upriver, as well. The front gallery's ironwork was added in the 1930s. ☒*1427 Second St., Garden District.*

19 **Seven Sisters Houses.** Legend has it that the seven nearly identical shotgun houses occupying the 2300 block of Coliseum Street were built for seven sisters. In fact, they were the first speculation houses in the city, and some of the first in the United States. Though renovations have blurred the family resemblance, the homes are structurally distinguished only by the front galleries. ☒*2300 Coliseum St., Garden District.*

9 **Toby-Westfeldt House.** Dating from the 1830s, this unpretentious French-colonial home sits amid a large, plantation-like garden, surrounded by a copy of the original white-picket fence. Thomas Toby, a Philadelphia businessman, moved to New Orleans and had this house built well above the ground to protect it from flooding. The house is thought to be the oldest in this part of the Garden District. ✉*2340 Prytania St., Garden District.*

11 **Women's Guild of the New Orleans Opera Association House.** This fundamentally Greek Revival house, built in 1858, has a distinctive Italianate octagonal turret, added in the late 19th century. The last private owner, Nettie Seebold, willed the estate to the Guild in 1955. Furnished with period pieces, the house underwent extensive renovations in 2008 and is once again being used for receptions and private parties. ✉*2504 Prytania St., Garden District* ☎*504/899–1945.*

LOWER GARDEN DISTRICT

What largely appeals in the Lower Garden District is its recent gentrification. But even with many homes that are just as splendid as those in the Upper Garden District, the area is still less consistent than its upscale neighbor. A few crumbling houses still dot the area amid a larger proportion of spruced-up mansions and cottages, and a few empty storefronts sit alongside hip boutiques and antiques shops. Allot some time to explore the shops on Magazine Street between Jackson Avenue and Sophie Wright Park.

WHAT TO SEE

Derby Pottery. Fragments of wrought ironwork and other architectural details form the inspiration for many of Mark Derby's beautiful mugs, vases, and handmade Victorian reproduction tiles. His clocks and plaques, fashioned from reproductions of New Orleans's historic art-deco water-meter covers, have earned cult popularity. ✉*2029 Magazine St., Lower Garden District* ☎*504/586–9003* 🌐*www.derbypottery.com* ⏲*Mon.–Sat. 10–5.*

Eiffel Tower Building. Thirty years ago, engineers in Paris discovered hairline fractures in the Eiffel Tower supports. To lighten the load, they removed the restaurant on the second platform. New Orleans auto dealer McDonald Stephens bought the restaurant, which was disassembled into 11,000 pieces for shipping. Ever the romantic, Stephens hired New Orleans architect Steven Bingler to build a "jewel box" out of the pieces for his four beloved daughters. Bingler's vision, assembled on St. Charles Avenue in 1986, incorporated scattered pieces from the original restaurant into a contemporary outer structure meant to resemble the Eiffel Tower. The building went through many reincarnations, most unsuccessful, and fell into ruin until the New Orleans Culinary Institute signed a 20-year lease in 2004. Still owned by Stephens' daughters, it today houses the institute's Cricket Club, a supper club-style event venue. ✉*2040 St. Charles Ave., Lower Garden District* ☎*504/304–9467* 🌐*www.cricketclubevents.com.*

CLOSE UP

New Orleans Cemeteries

New Orleans's "cities of the dead," with rows of crypts like little houses and streets organized with signs, are some of the city's most enduring images. Of the metropolitan area's 42 cemeteries, 15 are examples of the aboveground burial practices of the French and Spanish. This method was adopted in New Orleans in the early 1800s because the high water table made it difficult to bury bodies underground without having the coffin float to the surface after the first hard rain. Wealthier families could afford to build ornate individual crypts, while a more economical option was burial inside the cemetery walls, in slots called "ovens." In the subtropical climate, bodies decomposed rapidly. After a year, the bones were swept out of the tomb, which was then ready for its next occupant. Modern-day burial methods permit underground interment, but many people prefer these ornate family tombs and vaults for their sanitation, efficiency, and mysterious beauty. The most notable of these cemeteries, listed below, are open to the public. The St. Louis cemeteries are in dangerous areas of the city, where organized group tours are the only rational way to visit. There are many good private tours, some more historical and others more theatrical. Good options are the detailed and accurate tours by nonprofit group **Save Our Cemeteries** (☎ *504/525–3377*).

Lafayette Cemetery No. 1. Begun around 1833, this was the first planned cemetery in the city, with symmetrical rows, roadways for funeral vehicles, and lavish aboveground vaults and tombs for the wealthy families who built the surrounding mansions. In 1852, 2,000 yellow-fever victims were buried here. Movies such as *Interview with the Vampire* and *Easy Rider* have used this walled cemetery for its eerie beauty. The cemetery is open to the public, and you can wander the grounds on your own or take an organized tour. ✉ *1400 block of Washington Ave., Garden District* 🎫 *Cemetery free, tour $6* ⏲ *Weekdays 7–2:30, Sat. 7–noon; Save Our Cemeteries tours Mon., Wed., Fri., and Sat. at 10:30.*

Lake Lawn Metairie Cemetery. The largest cemetery in the metropolitan area, known to locals simply as Metairie Cemetery, is the final resting place of nine Louisiana governors, seven New Orleans mayors, three Confederate generals, and musician Louis Prima. Many of New Orleans's noted families are also interred here in elaborate monuments ranging from Gothic crypts to Romanesque mausoleums to Egyptian pyramids. Walk the grounds or drive along named streets to see them. In the mid-1800s, this was the site of the Metairie Racetrack and Jockey Club. ✉ *5100 Pontchartain Blvd., Metairie* ⏲ *Daily 8–5.*

St. Louis Cemetery No. 1. Buried here, in the city's oldest cemetery, are such notables as Etienne Boré, father of the sugar industry; Daniel Clar, financial supporter of the American Revolution; Homer Plessy of the *Plessy vs. Ferguson* 1892 U.S. Supreme Court decision establishing the separate but equal "Jim Crow" laws; Paul Morphy, world-famous chess champion;

former mayor Ernest "Dutch" Morial; and Marie Laveau, voodoo queen. Her tomb is marked with Xs freshly chalked by those who still believe in her supernatural powers. St. Louis No. 1 abuts what used to be public housing projects, and the area can be unsafe if you venture too deep inside without a tour. Many group tours visit this cemetery, including one by Save Our Cemeteries and even a couple guided by local voodoo priestesses. ✉ *499 Basin St.,bounded by Basin, Conti, Tremé, and St. Louis Sts., Tremé* 🎫 *Cemetery free, tour $12* ⏲ *Mon.–Sat. 9–3, Sun. 9–noon; Save Our Cemeteries tours Sun. at 10.*

St. Louis Cemetery No. 2. St. Louis No. 2, established in 1823, includes the tomb of a second Marie Laveau, believed to be her daughter. A number of notable local musicians are buried here, including Danny Barker and Ernie K. Doe. Also entombed here are Dominique You, a notorious pirate, and Andre Cailloux, African-American hero of the American Civil War. On Claiborne Avenue four blocks beyond St. Louis Cemetery No. 1, it, too, is in a dangerous area of town—so only visit as part of a guided group tour. ✉ *N. Claiborne Ave. between Iberville and St. Louis Sts., Bayou St. John* ⏲ *Mon.–Sat. 9–3, Sun. 9–noon.*

St. Louis Cemetery No. 3. Established in 1854, the St. Louis No. 3 is one block from the entrance to City Park, at the end of Esplanade Avenue. It is lined with elaborate aboveground crypts, mausoleums, and carved stone angels. While crime is less of a concern than at St. Louis Nos. 1 and 2, a group tour is the more prudent alternative to exploring alone. ✉ *3428 Esplanade Ave., Bayou St. John* ⏲ *Mon.–Sat. 9–3, Sun. 9–noon.*

Goodrich-Stanley House. This restored Creole cottage is an excellent example of the modest prototype for much of the far more elaborate architecture of the surrounding Garden District. The scale, derived from the climate-conscious design prevalent in the West Indies, made it easily adaptable to the higher pretensions of the Greek Revival look, as well as the slightly more reserved Colonial Revival. Built in 1837, the house has had one famous occupant: Henry Morton Stanley, renowned explorer of Africa and founder of the Congo Free States who most notoriously uttered the phrase "Dr. Livingstone, I presume" upon encountering the long-lost Scottish missionary. ✉ *1729 Coliseum St., Lower Garden District.*

THE FLAIR TO SCARE

Popular New Orleans–born author Anne Rice used her hometown as the backdrop for dozens of novels, most dealing with the occult. The Garden District's Brevard House, which she occupied until 2004, was the inspiration for the haunted house of her Mayfair witches series. She also enjoyed the macabre beauty of Lafayette Cemetery No. 1; her most famous blood-sucking protagonist rose from its crypts in her best-selling novel The Vampire Lestat. Adding a touch of theater to a book signing at Garden District Book Shop, Rice was paraded from Brevard House to the cemetery in an ice-packed coffin.

New Orleans Metropolitan Convention and Visitors Bureau. The CVB is the main organization responsible for promoting, managing, and serving New Orleans's tourism industry. The lobby's visitor center has computer stations, brochure racks, and helpful staff to answer questions about area accommodations, restaurants, events, services, and attractions. ✉ *2020 St. Charles Ave., Lower Garden District* ☎ *504/566–5011 or 800/672–6124* 🌐 *www.neworleanscvb.com* ⏲ *Weekdays 8:30–5.*

St. Alphonsus Art and Cultural Center. No longer active, this mid-19th-century church was founded for Irish worshippers, while the church across the street served the German community, and a third one down the street (no longer standing) served the French. The frescoed, weathered interior has been preserved in its original form; admission includes a cassette tour. For an additional $2, you can take a guided tour (by appointment). A small museum displays artifacts and memorabilia from the area. A block toward the river from Magazine, St. Alphonsus is in a more sketchy area; use caution if you plan to walk here. ✉ *2045 Constance St., Lower Garden District* ☎ *504/524–8116* 🎫 *$3, $5 with guided tour* ⏲ *Tues., Thurs., and Sat. 10–2; guided tours by appointment.*

St. Vincent's Guesthouse. This large, brick structure was once an orphanage and home for unwed mothers. Today most of St. Vincent's has been converted into guest rooms, but you may be able to view the lobby and courtyard if you knock on the door. ✉ *1507 Magazine St., Lower Garden District* ☎ *504/523–3411.*

NEED A BREAK?

One block from Coliseum Square, at the corner of Magazine and Race streets, is Mojo Coffee House (✉ ***1500 Magazine St., Lower Garden District*** ☎ ***504/525–2244*** ⏲ ***Weekdays 6:30 AM–midnight, weekends 7 AM–midnight*)**, where you can have a seat, sip a cup of java, and relax before perusing the shops and galleries along lower Magazine.**

Thomas Mann Gallery I/O. Known for his imaginative jewelry and sculptural forays he calls "techno-romantic" design, Thomas Mann also showcases contemporary American crafts by other local artists. ✉ *1804 Magazine St., Lower Garden District* ☎ *504/581–2113* 🌐 *www.thomasmann.com* ⏲ *Mon.–Sat. 11–6.*

UPTOWN

Lying west of the Garden District, Uptown is the residential area on both sides of St. Charles Avenue along the streetcar route, upriver from Louisiana Avenue. It includes many mansions as sumptuous as those in the Garden District, as well as Loyola and Tulane universities and a large urban park named for John James Audubon. Traveling along the avenue from downtown to uptown provides something of a historical narrative: the city's development unfolded upriver, and the houses grow more modern the farther uptown you go.

Fodor's Choice ★ **The St. Charles Avenue streetcar,** which runs down the length of the avenue, from Canal Street to the Carrollton Riverbend, provides a wonderful way to take in the neighborhood. In the early 1900s streetcars were the most prominent mode of public transit and ran on many streets. Today, they operate along the riverfront, Canal Street, St. Charles Avenue, and Carrollton Avenue. **TIP→ Avoid rush hours—from 7 to 9 and 3 to 6—or you may have to stand still much of the way and will not be able to enjoy the scenery.**

Another main artery, Magazine Street, traverses the Uptown area with miles of antiques and home decor shops, boutiques, galleries, restaurants, and cafés. The Magazine Street bus can take you up and down the length of the street, which culminates at Audubon Park, a lush stretch of green that encompasses a track, fields, zoo, and golf course.

Numbers in the margin correspond to numbers on the St. Charles Avenue Uptown map.

TIMING St. Charles streetcar service runs every 10–15 minutes, with stops every few blocks, so expect the ride from Washington Avenue (in the center of the Garden District) or Louisiana Avenue to the Carrollton Riverbend to take about 45 minutes (considerably more during rush hour). Plan a half-day minimum for visiting the Audubon Zoo and enjoying the park that surrounds it.

WHAT TO SEE

7 **Anthemion.** A fashion for Colonial Revival architecture in the late 19th century indicated local weariness with the excesses of the Greek Revival craze that had dominated the midcentury. Anthemion, built in

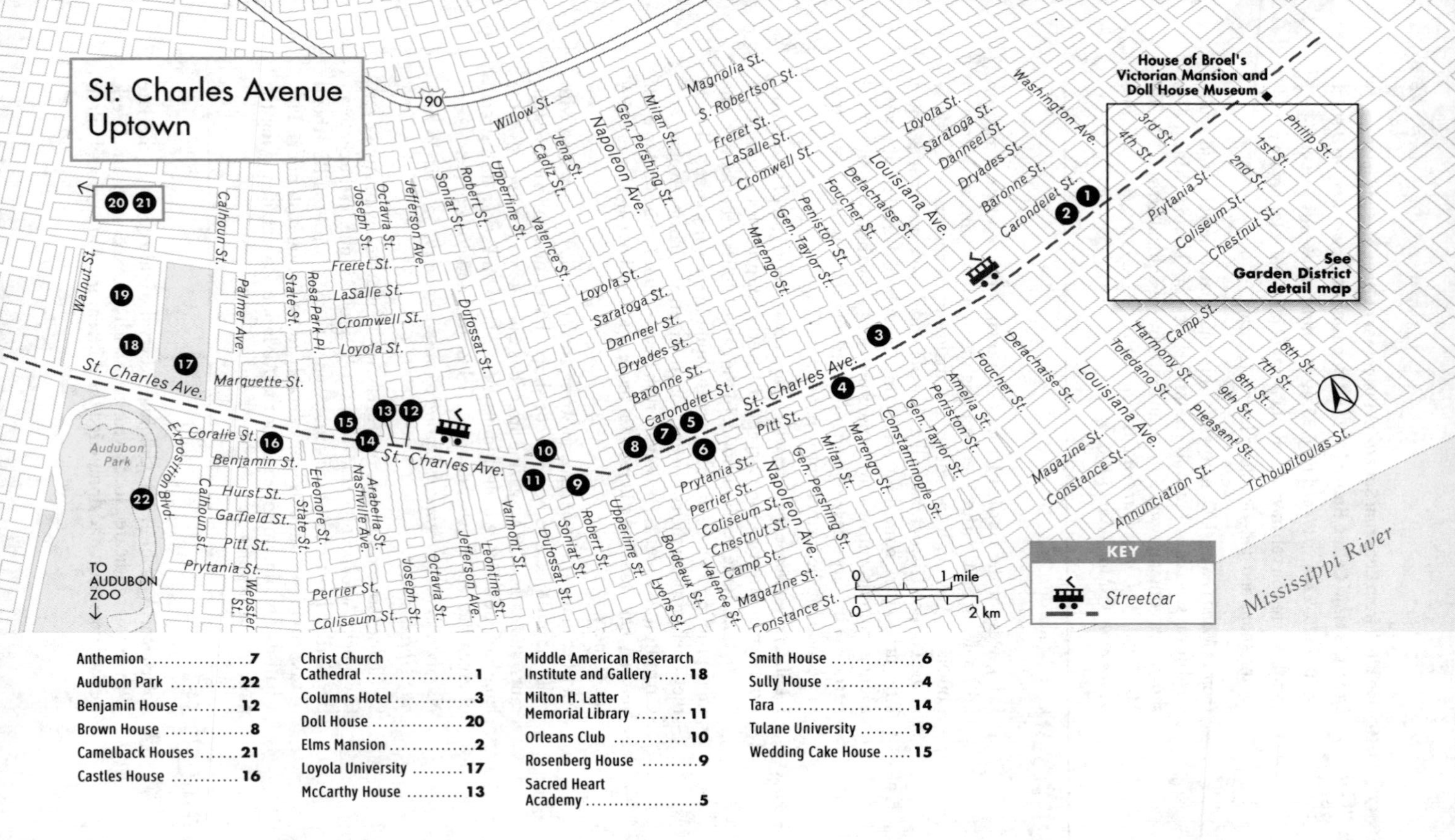
St. Charles Avenue
Uptown
House of Broel's Victorian Mansion and Doll House Museum
See Garden District detail map
KEY
Streetcar
0 1 mile
0 2 km
Mississippi River
TO AUDUBON ZOO
Audubon Park
St. Charles Ave.
Napoleon Ave.
Louisiana Ave.
Washington Ave.
Jefferson Ave.
Nashville Ave.
Exposition Blvd.
Rosa Park Pl.
Palmer Ave.
Walnut St.
Calhoun St.
Marquette St.
Willow St.
Magnolia St.
S. Robertson St.
Freret St.
LaSalle St.
Cromwell St.
Loyola St.
Saratoga St.
Danneel St.
Dryades St.
Baronne St.
Carondelet St.
Prytania St.
Coliseum St.
Chestnut St.
Camp St.
Magazine St.
Constance St.
Annunciation St.
Tchoupitoulas St.
Philip St.
1st St.
2nd St.
3rd St.
4th St.
6th St.
7th St.
8th St.
9th St.
Harmony St.
Toledano St.
Pleasant St.
Delachaise St.
Foucher St.
Amelia St.
Peniston St.
Gen. Taylor St.
Constantinople St.
Marengo St.
Milan St.
Gen. Pershing St.
Pitt St.
Perrier St.
Jena St.
Cadiz St.
Valence St.
Upperline St.
Robert St.
Soniat St.
Dufossat St.
Valmont St.
Leontine St.
Octavia St.
Joseph St.
Arabella St.
Eleonore St.
State St.
Coralie St.
Benjamin St.
Hurst St.
Garfield St.
Webster St.
Bordeaux St.
Lyons St.
90
Anthemion 7
Audubon Park 22
Benjamin House 12
Brown House 8
Camelback Houses 21
Castles House 16
Christ Church Cathedral 1
Columns Hotel 3
Doll House 20
Elms Mansion 2
Loyola University 17
McCarthy House 13
Middle American Reserarch Institute and Gallery 18
Milton H. Latter Memorial Library 11
Orleans Club 10
Rosenberg House 9
Sacred Heart Academy 5
Smith House 6
Sully House 4
Tara 14
Tulane University 19
Wedding Cake House 15

1896 and the headquarters of the Japanese consulate from 1938 to 1941, is an excellent example of this return to simplicity. ✉*4631 St. Charles Ave., Uptown.*

NEED A BREAK?

Stop for coffee and nosh at Refuel (✉*8123 Hampson St., Uptown* ☎*504/872–0187* 🌐*www.refuelcafe.com*). A shot of espresso and a snack in this fresh, modern café is the perfect energizer.

STATE (STREET) OF HARMONY

The homes along the first few blocks of State and Palmer streets off St. Charles Avenue are some of Uptown's loveliest and most exclusive. Residents prefer the privacy of living just off the thoroughfare. Here, old-guard socialite families live alongside limousine liberals in harmony. On Palmer, between St. Charles and Loyola avenues, James Carville, Democratic strategist and Tulane professor, lives with Republican strategist (and wife) Mary Matalin in a house they bought in 2008 for $2.2 million. Neighbors joke that the rooms are large enough to absorb arguments without bothering them.

22  ★ **Audubon Park.** Formerly the plantation of Etienne de Boré, the father of the granulated sugar industry in Louisiana, **Audubon Park** is a large, lush stretch of green between St. Charles Avenue and Magazine Street, continuing across Magazine Street to the river. Designed by John Charles Olmsted, nephew of Frederick Law Olmsted (who laid out New York City's Central Park), it contains the world-class **Audubon Zoo**; a 1.7-mi track for running, walking, or biking; picnic and play areas; Audubon Park Golf Course; a tennis court; horse stables; and a river view. Calm lagoons wind through the park, harboring egrets, catfish, and other indigenous species. The park and zoo were named for the famous ornithologist and painter John James Audubon, who spent many years working in and around New Orleans. None of the original buildings from its former plantation days remain; in fact, none of the buildings that housed the 1884–85 World's Industrial and Cotton Centennial Exposition have survived. The only reminder of the city's first World's Fair is Exposition Boulevard, the street address assigned to houses that front the park along the downtown side.

If time permits, you may want to venture beyond the zoo, cross the railroad tracks, and stroll along **Riverview Drive,** a long stretch of land behind the zoo that is part of Audubon Park, on the levee overlooking the Mississippi River. This area is referred to as "The Fly" by locals, after a butterfly-shaped building that was torn down here some years ago, and it is a popular place for picnics and pickup sports. ✉*Riverview Dr., off of Magazine St., Uptown* ☎*504/861–3527* 🌐*www.auduboninstitute.org* 🎫*Free.*

Overlooking the Audubon Park Golf Course is the **Audubon Park Clubhouse** (✉*Golf Club Dr., off of Magazine St., Uptown* ☎*504/212–5285*), where you can eat breakfast or lunch in the airy dining room, or relax with a refreshing drink on the oak-tree-shaded veranda. The clubhouse, designed to resemble an Acadian cottage, is on the interior end of the parking lot accessed from Magazine Street. The golf course is public and open seven days a week.

Audubon Park Golf Course (✉ *6500 Magazine St., Uptown* ☎ *504/212–5285, 504/212–5290 for course tee times* 🎫 *$30 weekdays, $40 weekends; green fees include cart and sales tax* ⏲ *Daily 7–dusk*) is a par-62, 4,220-yard Denis Griffiths–designed course among Tif Eagle greens, lagoons, and sprawling oaks at the center of the park.

NICE DIGS

Of all things, a Borders Book Store now occupies the former Bultman Funeral Home, a colossal mansion with an enclosed garden that was one of the most elegant funeral homes in the South. A balcony bears a wrought-iron motif of downward crossed arrows, a symbol of death. Tennessee Williams set his play *Suddenly Last Summer* here in the solarium. The building was bought by Borders in 2007, and today all that remains of the former mansion is its facade.

★ **Audubon Zoo.** Consistently ranked since its redevelopment as one of the top zoos in the nation, the Audubon Zoo presents a wide array of animals in exhibits that mimic their natural habitats. In the section of **Audubon Park** between Magazine Street and the river, the zoo is the perfect family attraction. Its Louisiana Swamp exhibit recreates the natural habitat of alligators, including rare albinos, nutria (large swamp rodents), and catfish; alligator-feeding time is always well attended. Other highlights include the reptile encounter and Komodo dragon exhibit, a Sumatran orangutan family, and white Bengal tigers. Several new attractions are available for additional ticket fees: a zoo train tour that departs every 30 minutes from the swamp exhibit; the children's zoo area; and the Safari Simulator Ride. You can walk here from the St. Charles Avenue streetcar or bus (No. 12), which stop across Audubon Park (allow a half hour). The Magazine Street bus also stops right at the zoo and can take you to and from Canal Street. ✉ *6500 Magazine St., Uptown* ☎ *504/581–4629* 🌐 *www.auduboninstitute.org* 🎫 *$12.50; combination ticket for zoo and Aquarium of the Americas $25.50; combination ticket for zoo, aquarium, and IMAX Theater $28.50* ⏲ *Tues.–Fri. 10–4, weekends 10–5.*

12 **Benjamin House.** This beaux arts beauty, built in 1912 for cotton factor Emanuel Benjamin, shares the block with Danneel Park. It was constructed of expensive limestone, leaving Benjamin with a bill of $30,000—an outrageous sum at the time. ✉ *5531 St. Charles Ave., Uptown.*

8 **Brown House.** Completed in 1904, the Brown House is the largest mansion on St. Charles Avenue. Its solid monumental look, Syrian arches, and steep gables make it a choice example of Romanesque Revival style. ✉ *4717 St. Charles Ave., Uptown.*

21 **Camelback Houses.** When these were built in the late 1800s, houses were taxed by the width and height of their facades: working-class homes were usually narrow and long. Sometimes a second floor was added to the back half of the house, giving it the architectural designation of "camelback." The camelback and the gingerbread-type decoration on porches were popular details at the turn of the 20th century. ✉ *7628–7630, 7632–7634, and 7820–7822 St. Charles Ave., Uptown.*

16 **Castles House.** Local architect Thomas Sully designed this 1896 Colonial Revival house after the Longfellow House in Cambridge, Massachusetts. The interior has often appeared in the pages of design magazines. ⊠*6000 St. Charles Ave., Uptown.*

1 **Christ Church Cathedral.** This Gothic Revival Episcopal church completed in 1887 has steeply pitched gables, an architectural detail that was a precursor to the New Orleans Victorian style. The cathedral is the oldest non–Roman Catholic church in the Louisiana Purchase: the congregation was established in 1805, and this is the third building erected on the same site. ⊠*2919 St. Charles Ave., Garden District.*

3 **Columns Hotel.** Built in 1884 as a private home, the Columns has been the scene of TV ads, movies, and plenty of weddings. The interior scenes of Louis Malle's *Pretty Baby* were filmed here. The Colonial Revival hotel has a popular bar and a grand veranda for sipping cocktails. The grand rooms of the first floor are open to the public; note the stained-glass skylight topping the mahogany stairwell. ⊠*3811 St. Charles Ave., Uptown* ☎*504/899–9308 or 800/445–9308* 🌐*www.thecolumns.com.*

20 **Doll House.** Designed in the same Tudor style as the main house beside it for the daughter of a former owner, this is the smallest house in New Orleans to have its own postal address. ⊠*7209 St. Charles Ave., Uptown.*

2 **Elms Mansion.** Built in 1869, this home saw the Confederate president Jefferson Davis as a frequent guest. The house, which has been meticulously maintained and furnished with period pieces, is the site of many receptions. Group tours of the interior are conducted on weekdays by appointment only. Highlights include a carved oak staircase and mantelpiece and 24-karat gilt moldings and sconces. ⊠*3029 St. Charles Ave., Garden District* ☎*504/895–9200* 🎟*Tours $5 per person* ⏲*Weekdays by appointment.*

17 **Loyola University.** The Jesuits built this complex facing the avenue in 1914. Today, it is known for its strong law, communications, and music programs. The modern Gothic-style building on the corner is the **Louis J. Roussel Building,** which houses the music department. The campus extends for two blocks behind the Gothic and Tudor edifice of the **Church of the Holy Name of Jesus.** The fourth floor of the neo-Gothic **library** holds the school's gallery. ⊠*6363 St. Charles Ave., Uptown.*

13 **McCarthy House.** A deep front lawn emphasizes the perfect symmetry of this classic Colonial Revival, constructed in 1903. The brick veneer and Ionic columns are emblematic of the style. ⊠*5603 St. Charles Ave., Uptown.*

18 **Middle American Research Institute and Gallery.** On the fourth floor of a musty old academic building, this research institute and gallery at **Tulane University** was established in 1924. There's an extensive range of pre-Columbian and Central and South American artifacts, complemented by an associated collection of books on Latin American culture housed in Tulane's main library. ⊠*Dinwiddie Hall, 4th fl., Tulane University, Uptown* ☎*504/865–5110* 🎟*Free* ⏲*Weekdays 8:30–5.*

11 **Milton H. Latter Memorial Library.** A former private home now serves as the most elegant public library in New Orleans. Built in 1907 and taking up an entire city block, this Italianate–beaux arts mansion was once the home of silent-screen star Marguerite Clark. It was then purchased by the Latter family and given to the city as a library in 1948 in memory of their son, who was killed in World War II. Sit and leaf through a copy of Walker Percy's *The Moviegoer* or John Kennedy Toole's *Confederacy of Dunces* (two popular novels set in New Orleans), or just relax in a wicker chair in the solarium. This is one of the few mansions on St. Charles Avenue open to the public. Local artisans contributed the murals and carved mantels. ✉*5120 St. Charles Ave., Uptown* ☎*504/596–2625* 🌐*www.nutrias.org* ⏲*Mon. and Wed. 9–8, Tues. and Thurs. 9–6, Sat. 10–5.*

> **PERFECT PICNIC**
>
> Spicy seafood to go makes for the perfect New Orleans picnic. For seasonal boiled specialties—crawfish, crabs, shrimp, andouille sausage, corn, potatoes, and garlic—stop by the Big Fisherman (3301 Magazine Street) on your way to Audubon Park. Ask if they have fresh crawfish pies available. And don't forget the paper towels at the supermarket next door.

10 **Orleans Club.** This sumptuous mansion was built in 1868 as a wedding gift from Colonel William Lewis Wynn to his daughter. The dormer windows, typical of French Empire style, were added during a remodeling in 1909. The side building, on the uptown side of the main building, is an auditorium added in the 1950s. The house is closed to the public but serves as headquarters to a ladies' social club and hosts many debutante teas and wedding receptions. ✉*5005 St. Charles Ave., Uptown.*

9 **Rosenberg House.** The brick facade and Corinthian columns on this stately 1911 house mark it as Colonial Revival, but a modern, Craftsman-style interior (not open to the public) suggests the progressive tastes of the Rosenbergs. The clean exterior and simple Doric columns of the Classical Revival–style Stirling House, next door at number 4930, are an interesting contrast. ✉*4920 St. Charles Ave., Uptown.*

5 **Sacred Heart Academy.** Unusual aspects of this building, a Catholic girls' school built in 1899, include wide, wraparound balconies (or galleries) and colonnades facing a large garden. The academy is exceptionally beautiful during the December holidays, when the galleries are decked with wreaths and garlands. ✉*4521 St. Charles Ave., Uptown.*

6 **Smith House.** This bucolic Mediterranean villa was built in 1906 for William Smith, president of the New Orleans Cotton Exchange. Smith planted the three live oak trees that have now grown to shade the expansive yard. The front porch is anchored by stone columns with capitals in the Greek honeysuckle-and-palmette pattern. ✉*4534 St. Charles Ave., Uptown.*

4 **Sully House.** This was the family home of local architect Thomas Sully, who designed it around 1890. Sully was known for his use of deep shades of color and varied textures. Similar gables, towers, and gingerbread appear on many other homes in the vicinity. ✉*4010 St. Charles Ave., Uptown.*

14 **Tara.** A replica built from the plans of the movie set of *Gone With the Wind,* Tara seems almost dwarfed here by far more sumptuous houses. ✉*5705 St. Charles Ave., Uptown.*

19 **Tulane University.** Next to Loyola University on St. Charles Avenue, the university's three original buildings face the avenue: **Tilton Hall** (1901) on the left, **Gibson Hall** (1894) in the middle, and **Dinwiddie Hall** (1936) on the right. The Romanesque style, with its massive stone look and arches, is repeated in the several buildings around a quad behind these. Modern campus buildings extend another three blocks to the rear. Tulane is known for its medical school, law school, and fine main library. The **Sophie H. Newcomb College for Women** was Tulane's coordinate women's college until it was dissolved as part of a post-Katrina renewal plan. The college's memorial institute maintains the **Newcomb College Center for Research on Women,** a women's resource center that brings in speakers, writers, and academics. Also on the Tulane campus is the **Middle American Research Institute.** ✉*6823 St. Charles Ave., Uptown.*

QUICK COOL DOWN

When the weather heats up in the spring and summer months, snoballs become the favorite way to cool down in New Orleans. Locals line up at seasonal stands tucked throughout Uptown for finely ground ice flavored with everything from chocolate to cherry to bubble-gum syrup. Some perennial favorites include **Hansen's Sno-Bliz** at 4801 Tchoupitoulas, **Plum Street Snowball** at 1300 Burdette, and **SnoWizard** at 4001 Magazine.

15 **Wedding Cake House.** A portico and decorative balconies help this house outshine most other mansions on the avenue. Its key beauty is the beveled leaded glass in its front door, one of the most beautiful entryways in the city. ✉*5809 St. Charles Ave., Uptown.*

BAYOU ST. JOHN AND MID-CITY

Above the French Quarter and below the lakefront, neither Uptown nor quite downtown, Mid-City is an amorphous yet proud territory embracing everything from the massive, lush City Park to gritty storefronts along Carrollton Avenue. It is a neighborhood of tremendous ethnic and economic diversity. Here you'll find great restaurants, cultural landmarks such as Rock and Bowl, restored former plantation homes, and crumbling inner-city neighborhoods. Actual sights are few and far between in Mid-City, and the neighborhood suffered heavily from flooding during Hurricane Katrina, but the area is recovering. The neighborhood around Bayou St. John near City Park is still one of the more picturesque in town and is fruitful for walks.

Numbers in the text correspond to numbers in the margin and on the Lakefront and City Park map.

WHAT TO SEE

8 **Alcee Fortier Park.** This tiny sliver of a park was named for philanthropist Alcee Fortier, who owned much of the surrounding area in the 19th century and founded a public school Uptown. It forms a focal point of

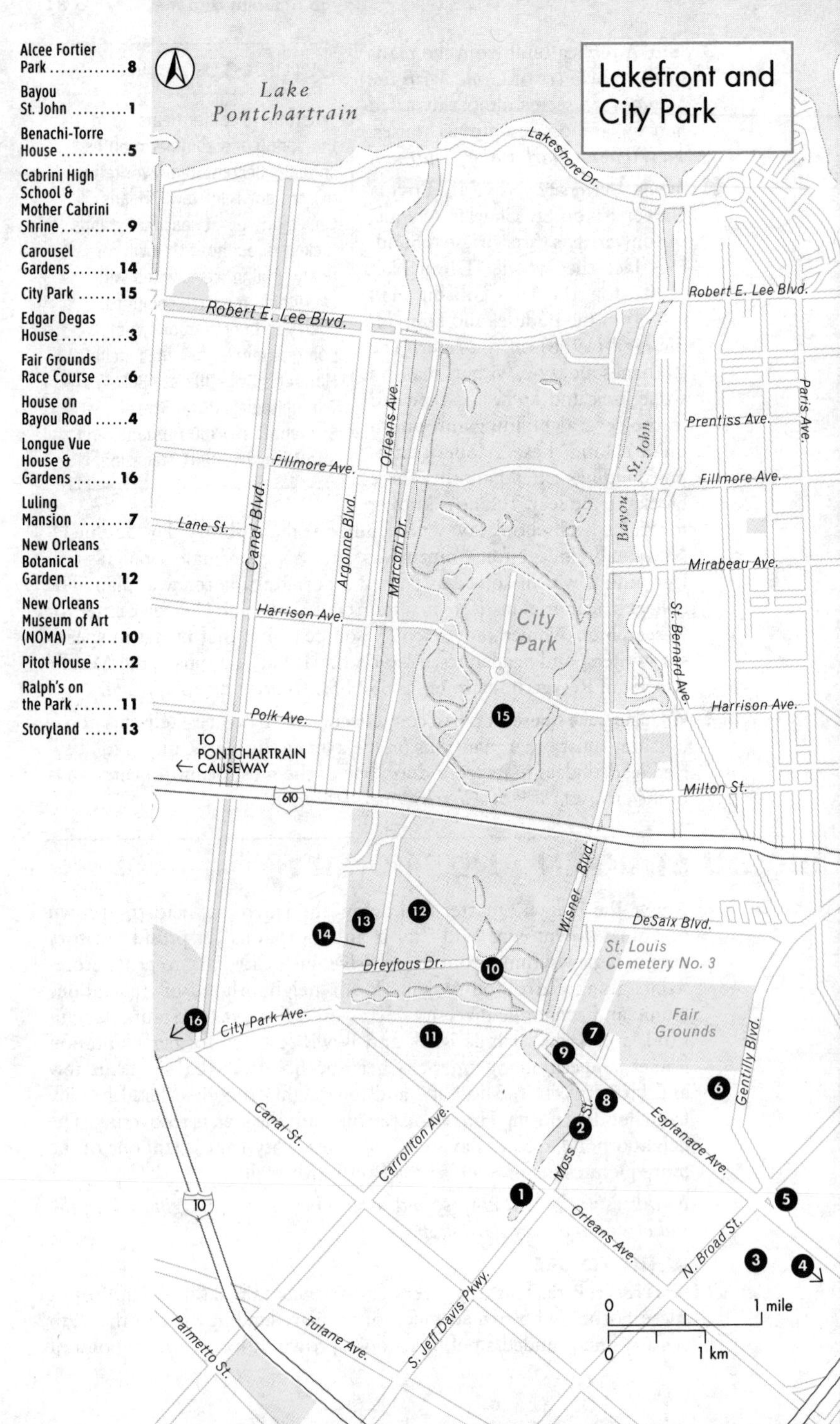

Lakefront and City Park
Alcee Fortier Park 8
Bayou St. John 1
Benachi-Torre House 5
Cabrini High School & Mother Cabrini Shrine 9
Carousel Gardens 14
City Park 15
Edgar Degas House 3
Fair Grounds Race Course 6
House on Bayou Road 4
Longue Vue House & Gardens 16
Luling Mansion 7
New Orleans Botanical Garden 12
New Orleans Museum of Art (NOMA) 10
Pitot House 2
Ralph's on the Park 11
Storyland 13
Lake Pontchartrain
Lakeshore Dr.
Robert E. Lee Blvd.
Robert E. Lee Blvd.
Orleans Ave.
Prentiss Ave.
Paris Ave.
Fillmore Ave.
Fillmore Ave.
Bayou St. John
Lane St.
Canal Blvd.
Argonne Blvd.
Marconi Dr.
Mirabeau Ave.
Harrison Ave.
City Park
St. Bernard Ave.
Harrison Ave.
Polk Ave.
TO PONTCHARTRAIN CAUSEWAY
610
Milton St.
Wisner Blvd.
DeSaix Blvd.
St. Louis Cemetery No. 3
Dreyfous Dr.
Fair Grounds
City Park Ave.
Gentilly Blvd.
Canal St.
Carrollton Ave.
Moss St.
Esplanade Ave.
10
Orleans Ave.
N. Broad St.
0
1 mile
0
1 km
S. Jeff Davis Pkwy.
Tulane Ave.
Palmetto St.

the Bayou St. John neighborhood, surrounded by hip restaurants and shops. ✉*Esplanade Ave. and Ponce de Leon Blvd., Bayou St. John.*

1 **Bayou St. John.** A bayou is an inlet: a still, narrow waterway that emerges from the swamp at one end and normally joins a larger body of water at the other. This bayou—the only remaining bayou in New Orleans—borders City Park on the east and extends about 7 mi from Lake Pontchartrain to just past Orleans Avenue. It is named for John the Baptist, whose nativity (St. John's Eve, June 23), the most important day in the year for voodoo practitioners, was notoriously celebrated on the bayou's banks in the 1800s. The first European settlers in the area, believed to have been trappers, coexisted with Native Americans here beginning in 1704. Graceful old homes join more-modern houses on picturesque Moss Street, along the section of the bayou nearest downtown.

5 **Benachi-Torre House.** This Greek Revival mansion was built in 1859 for the Greek consul in New Orleans. It earned the nickname "Rendezvous des Chasseurs" (meeting place of hunters) during the 19th century. The house is not open to the public. ✉*2257 Bayou Rd., at Tonti St., Bayou St. John.*

9 **Cabrini High School and Mother Cabrini Shrine.** Mother Frances Cabrini, the first American-citizen saint (she was canonized in 1946), purchased the land between Esplanade Avenue and Bayou St. John near City Park in 1905 and built the Sacred Heart Orphan Asylum here. She stayed in the Pitot House, which was on her property until she gave it to the city during construction of the orphanage. In 1959 the institution was converted to a girls' high school in St. Cabrini's name. Her bedroom has been preserved as it was when she lived here, filled with personal effects and maintained as a shrine. ✉*3400 Esplanade Ave., Bayou St. John* ☎*504/483–8690.*

14 **Carousel Gardens.** This small amusement park, open seasonally, has a New Orleans treasure as its centerpiece—a carousel from 1906 that is on the National Register of Historic Places. The rides here are geared to younger children, not thrill-seekers. But adults and kids alike enjoy the miniature train that takes passengers on a gentle sightseeing tour through City Park. ✉*Victory Ave., City Park, Bayou St. John* ☎*504/482–4888* 🌐*www.neworleanscitypark.com* *$3* *Mar.–Nov., weekends 11–4; Celebration in the Oaks: Nov. 27–29 and Dec. 4–30, Sun.–Thurs. 6–10, Fri. and Sat. 6–11.*

NEED A BREAK?

Just off Mystery Park, at the intersection of Mystery Street, Ponce de Leon Street, and Esplanade Avenue, is Fair Grinds Coffeehouse (✉***3133 Ponce de Leon St., Bayou St. John*** ☎***504/913–9072*** 🌐***www.fairgrinds.com Daily 6:30 AM–10 PM*****). Neighbors, musicians, and artists gather here for coffee, tea, and small snacks—including vegan treats—and a wide variety of community meetings, activities, and performances. Check the Web site for a calendar of events.**

15 **City Park.** City Park, a 150-year-old, 1,500-acre expanse of moss-draped oaks and gentle lagoons 2 mi from the French Quarter, suffered mightily in Hurricane Katrina's winds and flooding. The storm felled or damaged more than 1,000 trees, destroyed an 18-hole golf course, ravaged vegetation, and forced the park to lay off 90% of its staff. Nevertheless, the park has been rebuilt with the help of hundreds of local and visiting volunteers and is again a great place to walk or jog, play tennis, feed the ducks, visit one of its attractions, or simply relax. Just beyond the main entrance at the end of Esplanade Avenue stands the **New Orleans Museum of Art** and an adjacent sculpture garden; tucked elsewhere in the sprawling park are tennis courts, a sports stadium and running track, baseball diamonds and playgrounds, equestrian stable and golf course, along with miles of meandering walking paths and gentle lagoons rife with waterfowl. The park's art-deco benches, fountains, bridges, and ironwork are remnants of a 1930s Works Progress Administration refurbishment, and whimsical sculptures by renowned New Orleans artist Enrique Alferez dot the **New Orleans Botanical Garden**. The train garden here, operating on weekends only, is still a fun stop for the kids. Other children's favorites, Storyland and Carousel Gardens, are also open seasonally on weekends. Most attractions are clustered near the museum, but a stroll or picnic anywhere in the park is a wonderful way to relax. A popular drive-through Christmas holiday light display had to be scaled down after Katrina, but a walking tour and activities beginning annually after Thanksgiving pack in holiday revelers. Call ahead or check the park's Web site for revised hours and available activities. ✉ *Bordered by City Park Ave., Robert E. Lee Blvd., Marconi Dr., and Bayou St. John Mid-City* ☎ *504/482–4888* 🌐 *www.neworleanscitypark.com.*

Fodor's Choice ★

3 **Edgar Degas House.** Impressionist painter Edgar Degas, whose mother and grandmother were born in New Orleans, stayed with his Musson cousins in this house during an 1872 visit to New Orleans, producing more than 70 works while here. Today this is a B&B, though public tours, which include a film on Degas's family and their sojourn in New Orleans and a discussion of the historic neighborhood, are given by appointment. ✉ *2306 Esplanade Ave., Bayou St. John* ☎ *504/821–5009* 🌐 *www.degashouse.com* 🎟 *$10* 🕒 *Tours by appointment.*

6 **Fair Grounds Race Course and Slots.** The third-oldest racetrack in the country sits just off Esplanade Avenue, among the houses of Bayou St. John. Fire destroyed the historic old grandstand in the mid-1990s and Hurricane Katrina dealt the grounds a blow in 2005; but the newly renovated facility is modern and comfortable, complete with clubhouse restaurant, grandstand café, and concession-snack bars. This is a fun place to spend a sunny afternoon on the bleachers or a rainy afternoon inside the grandstand. Reservations are required and proper attire (collared shirts, closed shoes, no shorts) are required for the clubhouse. A slots facility was added in 2008. ✉ *1751 Gentilly Blvd., Bayou St. John* ☎ *504/943–2200 for box and restaurant reservations, 504/944–5515 for general information* 🌐 *www.fairgroundsracecourse.com* 🎟 *Grandstand free, clubhouse $6* 🕒 *Thanksgiving–Mar., check Web site for days and times.*

2

4 **House on Bayou Road.** This West Indies Creole–style house served as the main house to an indigo plantation. It was built in 1798 by Domingo Fleitas, who was originally from the Canary Islands. Today, it houses a B&B and the New Orleans Cooking Experience, a cooking school in residence. Call well in advance to book a cooking class. ✉*2275 Bayou Rd., Bayou St. John* ☎*504/945–0992* 🌐*www.houseonbayouroad.com.*

7 **Luling Mansion.** The massive three-story Italianate Luling Mansion was designed by architect James Gallier Jr., and built in 1865 for Florence A. Luling. When the Louisiana Jockey Club took over the Creole Race Course (now the Fair Grounds) in 1871, it purchased this nearby mansion. For the next 20-odd years, it served as the racing organization's clubhouse. It is not open to the public. ✉*1436–1438 Leda St., Bayou St. John.*

12 **New Orleans Botanical Garden.** The botanical garden has recovered dramatically from the Katrina floodwaters that damaged much of its indigenous flora. Though the garden is still recovering, you can stroll its peaceful 10 acres and enjoy statuary by noted local artist Enrique Alferez. In the Train Garden, open on weekends, baguette-size cars roll through a miniature New Orleans village. ✉*Victory Ave., City Park, Bayou St. John* ☎*504/483–9386* 🌐*www.neworleanscitypark.com* 🎫*$6* ⏲*Tues.–Sun. 10–4:30.*

10 ★ **New Orleans Museum of Art (NOMA).** Gracing the main entrance to City Park is this traditional fine arts museum, built in 1911. Modern wings, added to the original structure in the 1990s, bring light and space into the grand old building, which has an elegant central staircase and many formal rooms used as galleries. The jeweled treasures, particularly some of the famous eggs by Peter Carl Fabergé, are a favorite exhibit, along with European and American paintings, sculpture, drawings, prints, and photography. The museum holds one of the largest glass collections in the country and has developed a unique Art of the Americas collection that includes a range of Latin American and Native American works. Several period-room installations feature 18th- and 19th-century American furniture and decorative arts. The comprehensive Asian art wing includes a good selection of Japanese paintings of the Edo period; African, Oceanic, pre-Columbian, and Louisiana art are also represented. Temporary exhibits often favor local topics, such as Louis Armstrong or Edgar Degas (Degas's mother's family was from New Orleans, and Degas visited and painted here).

Henry Moore's handsome Reclining Mother and Child greets visitors at the entrance of the **Sydney and Walda Besthoff Sculpture Garden** (☎*504/658–4100* 🌐*www.noma.org* 🎫*Free* ⏲*Wed.–Sun. 10–4:45*). Most of the garden's 57 sculptures, representing some of the biggest names in modern art, were donated by local pharmacy magnate and avid collector Sydney Besthoff. After Katrina, the garden suspended its daily guided tours, but you don't really need one to enjoy the collection, which includes major pieces by Jacques Lipchitz, Barbara Hepworth, and Joel Shapiro, or a stroll along the indigenously landscaped bayou that meanders through the park. ✉*1 Collins Diboll Circle, City Park,*

Bayou St. John ☎*504/658–4100* 🌐*www.noma.org* 🎫*$8; free to Louisiana residents* ⏲*Thurs.–Sun. 10–5, Wed. noon–8.*

2 **Pitot House.** One of the few surviving houses that lined the bayou in the late 1700s, and the only Creole-colonial style house in the city open to the public, Pitot House is named for James Pitot, who bought the property in 1810 as a country home for his family. Pitot built one of the first cotton presses in New Orleans and served as the city's mayor from 1804 to 1805 and later as parish court judge. The Pitot House was restored and moved a block to its current location in the 1960s to make way for the expansion of Cabrini High School. It is noteworthy for its stucco-covered brick-between-post construction, an example of which is exposed on the second floor. The house is typical of the West Indies style brought to Louisiana by early planters, with galleries around the house that protect the interior from both rain and sunshine. There aren't any interior halls to stifle ventilation, and opposing doors encourage a cross breeze. The house is furnished with period antiques from the United States, and particularly Louisiana. ✉*1440 Moss St., Bayou St. John* ☎*504/482–0312* *www.louisianalandmarks.org* 🎫*$7* ⏲*Wed.–Sat. 10–3 or by appointment.*

Fodor's Choice ★

11 **Ralph's on the Park.** In 1860 Jean-Marie Saux opened a coffeehouse just outside the entrance to City Park, selling cold lemonades to the thirsty aristocrats who would venture out here from the French Quarter for the day. When Union troops set up camp in City Park during the Civil War, General Butler frequented Saux's establishment. Saux operated his coffee shop for 33 years before selling it to the Alciatore family, who also owned and operated Antoine's restaurant in the French Quarter (and still do). Since that time, the property has changed hands repeatedly, at one point serving as a favorite eatery among the prostitutes of Storyville. Now owned by famed local restaurateur Ralph Brennan, it is open for dinner daily, lunch on Friday, and Sunday brunch; a full dinner menu is also served at the bar. Sunset prix-fixe dinner menus are available from 5:30 to 7:30 on Monday, Wednesday, and Friday. ✉*900 City Park Ave., Bayou St. John* ☎*504/488–1000* 🌐*www.ralphsonthepark.com.*

13 **Storyland.** This whimsical park adjacent to the botanical garden has been a favorite romping ground for generations of New Orleans kids. The park's life-size figures, culled from children's literature, were created by some of the city's premiere Mardi Gras float builders and feature plenty of nooks and passageways for toddlers and young children to explore. ✉*Victory Ave., City Park, Bayou St. John* ☎*504/482–4888* 🌐*www.neworleanscitypark.com* 🎫*$3* ⏲*Weekends 11–6, Tues.–Fri. 10–3.*

METAIRIE AND THE LAKEFRONT

The neighborhood of Old Metairie is part of Orleans Parish and feels like much of Uptown. The historic **Longue Vue House and Gardens,** tucked along what seems like a country road, and the New Orleans Country Club are in the center of a particularly attractive area. Carving out several acres in the middle of Old Metairie, the elaborate tombs of the Lake Lawn Metairie

Cemetery, the city's largest, are visible from the Interstate 10 Expressway. Outside of old Metairie, however, the area has a more modern, suburban feel. The newer sections of Metairie extend to the lakefront, much of which was heavily damaged by Hurricane Katrina. Although renovation and rebuilding continue in various degrees in many pockets, some houses and buildings remain empty and untended, with high floodwater lines still marking their exteriors. Still, a stroll, drive, or picnic along Lakeshore Drive on a sunny day is a pleasant way to take in **Lake Pontchartrain.**

LOCAL LORE

At the front of Metairie Cemetery, one monument rises 85 feet above Interstate 10; Daniel Moriarty, an Irish immigrant and successful businessman, ordered the $185,000 structure built for his wife when she died in 1887. Four demure female statues today dubbed Faith, Hope, Charity, and Mrs. Moriarty, top the monument. The fabled reasons for Moriarty's extravagance: to make amends for his less attentive days as a husband and to thumb his nose at New Orleans society, which never fully accepted the couple.

WHAT TO SEE

Lake Pontchartrain. For over a century, this has been a popular spot for fishing and boating enthusiasts: in good weather you may see lots of sailboats and windsurfers. Swimming, once very common, is slowly coming back into fashion thanks to pollution cleanup efforts. Lakeshore Drive, a road along Lake Pontchartrain, has many park and picnic areas that are popular on warm weekends and holidays. The many parking bays encourage you to stop and take a walk or sit on the seawall, the cement steps bordering the lake. The wall is a 5½-mi levee-and-seawall protection system, built by the Orleans Levee Board in the 1930s and leased to the U.S. government for a hospital and for Army and Navy installations during and after World War II. A Navy air station at Elysian Fields and Lakeshore Drive once stood at the present site of the University of New Orleans. The land around the seawall area (Lake Vista) was turned into private residential districts in the 1930s. This area is relatively safe during the day because of frequent police patrols. It's best, however, not to linger after sunset.

16  ★ **Longue Vue House and Gardens.** Eight acres of gardens embellished with fountains surround this city estate fashioned in the 1940s after the great country houses of England. The villa-style mansion is decorated with its original furnishings of English and American antiques, priceless tapestries, modern art, porcelain, and pottery. The fine millwork, special-ordered from New York, is mahogany and birch. You must visit the house by tour (given hourly Wednesday–Sunday), but the gardens are open for independent exploration daily. They have various themes: the formal Spanish court, for instance, is modeled after a 14th-century Spanish garden, while a Discovery Garden introduces kids to the intricacies of horticulture. The gardens are in an ongoing state of restoration after Hurricane Katrina, which caused some tree and larger plant losses. ✉ *7 Bamboo Rd., Metairie* ☎ *504/488–5488* 🌐 *www.longuevue.com* 🎫 *$10* ⏲ *House and garden Mon.–Sat. 10–4:30, Sun. 1–5 or by appointment; shop daily 10–4.*

Mardi Gras and Jazz Fest

WORD OF MOUTH

"The food inside Jazz Fest is a huge attraction, and it's reasonably priced. $10 or less will get you meal-sized sandwiches (the cochon de lait po-boy, as well as the softshell crab po-boy, are standouts), not to mention dozens of regional specialties like crawfish in any manner, shape or form you might imagine, alligator, catfish, oysters, etc."

—Callaloo

"Not every krewe takes the same final route, though they generally follow St. Charles at least up to Lee Circle. While some people might pre-book their spot in the stands with Ticket Master (you can't pay your way in the day/night of), there's something to be said for the freedom to move from block to block."

—cdnatfodors

www.fodors.com/community

By Sue Strachan

IF YOU BELIEVE YOU'VE PARTIED WITH THE BEST, but you haven't experienced New Orleans's two major annual celebrations, Mardi Gras and Jazz Fest, it's time to expand your revelry repertoire. Just before Lent and again just before the summer heat, New Orleanians step out of their own reality and into the streets for the grandest parties of all. If it is your first trip to the Crescent City, plan carefully and do some research before you arrive. The city will welcome you, pamper you, and teach you the fine art of stepping lively.

So why is it that New Orleans is so comfortable in the party mode? Some have their theories: it's the port, the sub-sea-level elevation, or the mosquitoes that give them the fever. New Orleanians don't look for explanations or justifications—they just roll with it.

MARDI GRAS

Mardi Gras (French for "Fat Tuesday") is the final day of Carnival, an entire Christian holiday season that begins on the Twelfth Night of Christmas (January 6) and comes crashing to a halt on Ash Wednesday, the first day of Lent. Though Mardi Gras is technically merely one day within the season, the term is used interchangeably with Carnival, especially as the season builds toward the big day. As sometimes befalls the Christmas holiday, the religious associations of Carnival serve mainly as a pretext for weeks of indulgence. Also, like Christmas, Carnival claims elaborately developed traditions of food, drink, and music, as well as a blend of public celebration (the parades) and more-exclusive festivities, which take the form of elaborate private balls.

On Mardi Gras day, many New Orleanians don costumes, face paint, and masks, and then take to the streets for the last hurrah before Lent. It's an official city holiday, with just about everyone but the police and bartenders taking the day off. People roam the streets, drink Bloody Marys for breakfast and switch to beer in the afternoon, and admire one another's finery. Ragtag bands ramble about with horns and drums, Mardi Gras anthems pour from boom boxes, and king cakes (ring-shaped cakes topped with purple, green, and gold sugar) are everywhere. The Zulu, Rex, and the "trucks" parades roll Uptown to downtown with large floats carrying riders who throw plastic beads and trinkets to onlookers. They call it America's largest street party, and that seems about right.

Don't be smug: if you visit, you'll catch the fervor. After a few moments of astonished gaping, you'll yell for throws, too, draping layers of beads around your neck, sipping from a plastic "go-cup" as you prance along the street, bebopping with the marching bands, and having a grand old time.

It is never too early to begin planning your trip for Mardi Gras. Mark your calendar—the next Mardi Gras falls on February 16, 2010 (in 2011, Mardi Gras falls on March 8).

CLOSE UP

Mardi Gras Lingo

Carnival balls: Many krewes have black-tie balls to present debutantes. Alas, you can't buy a ticket—you have to be invited.

Coconuts: Usually decorated; a prized throw only given out by riders in the Zulu parade.

Debutante: Young women, usually college sophomores or juniors, who are presented into society at Carnival balls and parties.

King cake: An oval cake that has a plastic baby hidden inside. King cakes are eaten from January 6—"Twelfth Night"—until Mardi Gras; whoever gets the baby has to buy the next cake. King cakes are often decorated with purple, green, and gold sugar, with or without icing.

Krewe: A term used by Carnival organizations to describe themselves, as in Krewe of Iris.

Lundi Gras: French for "Fat Monday," the day before Mardi Gras; celebrated by the arrival of Rex, King of Carnival, via boat to the riverfront. Today, the event also includes the King of Zulu, who greets Rex, and a festival with bands and food.

Mardi Gras: "Fat Tuesday" in French; the day before Ash Wednesday and the culmination of the festivities surrounding Carnival season.

Mardi Gras Indians: Groups of black men who are dressed in elaborate costumes—or "suits"—to resemble Native Americans. Most men are in "tribes" that march on Mardi Gras, in addition to St. Joseph's day and Super Sunday. This custom started in the late 19th century in response to blacks being excluded from white Mardi Gras parades and organizations.

Purple, green, and gold: The official colors of Mardi Gras (purple represents justice, green signifies faith, and gold stands for power), chosen by the first Rex in 1872.

Rex, King of Carnival: There has to be a king, right? And this king and his krewe roll on Fat Tuesday.

"Show your . . .": What float riders may ask women to do to get beads. Not recommended unless you want to end up on the next installment of *Girls Gone Wild.*

Throw: Anything thrown off a float, such as beads, plastic cups, doubloons (fake metal coins), or stuffed animals.

"Throw me somethin', mister": Phrase shouted at float riders to get their attention so they will throw beads.

HISTORY

No one is absolutely sure how Mardi Gras celebrations started. The history of early Louisiana Carnival celebrations isn't really documented until the 1800s, when private balls were held by the descendants of French and Spanish settlers. There were also raucous street processions, where young men wore masks and costumes and sometimes dumped flour on passersby. Then on February 24, 1857, Mardi Gras changed. At 9 PM, 60 or so men dressed like demons paraded through the streets with two floats in a torch-lighted cavalcade. The group called itself the Mistick Krewe of Comus, after the Greek god of revelry. The krewe

CARNIVAL ROYALTY

So how do you become king or queen of a Mardi Gras parade or ball? It depends on the krewe. The hierarchy is a parody of royalty—there are a king, queen, dukes, knights, and captains, though this varies by krewe. In older-society krewes, the king is chosen by the members; other krewes rely on random drawings. Rex, King of Carnival, is chosen by the inner circle of the Rex krewe, called the School of Design; the honoree is always a prominent philanthropist and member of the New Orleans business community. Krewes like Bacchus and Endymion pick celebrity kings or grand marshals.

Becoming a queen also varies per krewe: a debutante has to find the golden bean in a faux king cake to become Queen of the Twelfth Night Revelers; other krewes put the matter to a vote. The queen and her court don't necessarily have to be debutantes—again, it depends on the krewe.

was started by men from both New Orleans and Mobile, Alabama, where Mardi Gras parades had begun a few years earlier. Wanting to observe the holiday more fully, these men formed a secret society and sent 3,000 invitations to a ball held at New Orleans's Gaiety Theater. As time passed (with lapses during the Civil War), invitations to the Comus ball became so coveted that one year the krewe captain advertised a $2,000 reward for two missing invitations. Comus crowned Robert E. Lee's daughter, Mildred Lee, its first queen in 1884. Though Comus no longer parades, the krewe still holds its annual ball, one of the city's most exclusive.

Through the years, other groups of men organized Carnival krewes, each with its own distinctive character. In 1872, 40 businessmen founded the School of Design, a new krewe whose ruler would be dubbed Rex, and sponsored a daytime parade for the Mardi Gras visit of His Imperial Highness the Grand Duke Alexis of Russia. They created a banner of green for faith, gold for power, and purple for justice—these remain the official Carnival colors. The first Rex parade was thrown together quickly with borrowed costumes, and there was no ball. The first reception was not until the next year, when a queen was chosen on the spot at a public ball. Eventually invitations and formal dress became required. Rex still parades on Mardi Gras morning, featuring some of the loveliest floats of Mardi Gras, and holds its lavish ball Mardi Gras night. Rex and his queen are considered the monarchs of the entire Carnival celebration. Their identities are kept secret until Mardi Gras morning, when their pictures claim the front page of the newspaper.

For many decades, krewes were strictly segregated by race; even Jews and Italians were banned from guest lists of the exclusive older balls (known as the old-line krewes). So other segments of society started clubs of their own. A black butler and dance instructor from Chicago started the Illinois Club in 1895. Though this club split into two krewes—the Original Illinois Club and the Young Men's Illinois Club—the debutantes who serve on the courts still perform the founder's dance, the Chicago Glide, in parallel galas. The Illinois clubs don't have parades, but the Zulu Social Aid and Pleasure Club, organized in 1909 by working-class black men, does. The Zulu parade precedes Rex down St. Charles Avenue on Mardi Gras day. Zulu was one of the first krewes to integrate, and today members span the racial and economic spectrums. These days, the elaborately decorated coconuts that Zulu float riders offer the crowd are among the most coveted of Mardi Gras throws.

SATCHMO'S REIGN

"There's a thing I've dreamed of all my life, and I'll be damned if it don't look like it's about to come true—to be King of the Zulu's parade. After that, I'll be ready to die."

—Louis Armstrong, *Time*, Feb. 21, 1949

After the Depression and World War II, Carnival krewes started popping up everywhere. Some were for doctors, others for businessmen, some for residents of certain neighborhoods, for women, for military men, or for gay men. The gay balls are splendid extravaganzas, with court members dressed in drag and bearing enormous, fantastical headdresses.

Parade standards changed in 1969, when a group of businessmen looking to entertain tourists the Sunday before Mardi Gras founded the Krewe of Bacchus, named after the god of wine. The sassy group stunned the city by setting new rules and strutting out with a stupendous show that dwarfed the old-line parades. The Bacchus floats (designed by Blaine Kern, who creates many other Carnival floats) were bigger than any seen before, and the king was Danny Kaye, not a homegrown humanitarian but a famous entertainer. The party following the parade was in the old Rivergate Convention Center, not in the Municipal Auditorium or a hotel ballroom, where the other balls were held. There was no queen and no court, and the party was called a rendezvous, not a ball. All guests could dance, not just members and their wives as was the custom in old-line balls, where nonmembers merely watched the proceedings. The floats rode right into the Rivergate, and you didn't have to be socially prominent—or even white—to join. The crowds have loved Bacchus from day one, and guessing which celebrities will follow the likes of Nicholas Cage, Elijah Wood, and James Gandolfini as monarch has become as popular as wondering about the identity of Rex. The arrival of Bacchus ushered in an era of new krewes with open memberships, including the Krewe of Endymion, and today many of the parades are held by these younger groups.

PARADES

Carnival parades begin in earnest two weekends before Mardi Gras, with parades day and night on weekends; there are parades each night starting the Wednesday before Mardi Gras. These parades are not the spectator activities that the term "parade" often signifies. The give-and-take between the riders on the floats and parade goers is what defines these events. The communication medium here is the "throws," or gifts the riders throw or hand to spectators. The most common throws are plastic beads, the most elaborate of which are worn like trophies by proud receivers. Other favorites include doubloons, or oversize aluminum coins, first introduced by Rex as His Majesty's official currency; plastic cups with the date and theme of the parade; medallion beads with the individual krewe's insignia; and stuffed animals.

Almost all Carnival krewes, or organizations, select a different theme each year for their parade. Themes range from whimsical to hard-edged political, though always with a tendency toward irreverence and satire. The politically incorrect is part and parcel of the subversiveness that characterizes Carnival, and stabs at government officials, racist or sexist jokes, and the glorification of gluttony are only a few of the offenses that all New Orleanians giggle at gleefully during Mardi Gras. The throws from a given float or parade will sometimes reflect that year's theme, one reason why locals dive for doubloons and plastic cups imprinted with the date and logo.

MUST-SEE PARADES

- **Bacchus:** Flashy. Be on the lookout for the immense Bacchagator and other oversize floats depicting jungle creatures.
- **Endymion:** Even flashier. Its members are known for generous throws.
- **Muses:** It's girls gone wild for this all-woman krewe.
- **Rex:** Living up to its name, this truly is the king of parades.
- **Tucks:** Like a rowdy little brother, Tucks is full of bawdy humor and mischief.
- **Zulu:** Unique for its decorated coconut throws.

The floats and bands make up the bulk of the parades, with the odd walking "club," dance troupe, or convertible car tossed in here and there. During night parades, an extra ingredient is the flambeaux, torch-bearing dancers who historically lighted the way for the parades. These days they provide little more than nostalgia and some fancy stepping to the bands, but they still earn tips along the route for their efforts.

Though parades used to roll through the French Quarter, these days the most popular ones start Uptown at Magazine Street and Napoleon Avenue, continuing down St. Charles Avenue to Canal Street, and following Canal to their finish. Though it's chaotic all along the route, heading downtown, parade goers become more numerous: Lee Circle is particularly lively. The real action, though, is along Canal Street itself, where raucous downtowners and tourists converge. Many of the marching bands save their best energy for the turn onto Canal, where the riders generously unload their throws.

In the weeks before Mardi Gras, two quirky parades run through the Quarter. The **Krewe du Vieux** hits the street two Saturdays before Mardi Gras. Nearly every brass band in town participates, and the small floats are decorated along satirical, often off-color themes, and are pulled by donkeys, not by tractors as in other parades. One week later, on the Sunday afternoon one week before Mardi Gras, the **Krewe of Barkus** rolls along a winding route through the Quarter in the vicinity of St.

Ann Street, featuring thousands of elaborately costumed canines and their proud owners, often in coordinated attire. This is one of the most fun afternoons of the entire year in New Orleans.

MARDI GRAS FOR EARLY BIRDS

While most revelers arrive in New Orleans the Friday before Mardi Gras, many major parades actually start that Wednesday. They go the traditional St. Charles Avenue to Canal Street route. Below is a list of parades and start times:

Wednesday:

- Ancient Druids, 6:30 PM

Thursday:

- Babylon, 5:45 PM
- Muses, 6:15 PM
- Chaos, 6:30 PM

MARDI GRAS WEEKEND

Although changes sometimes occur, the following parades are staples of Mardi Gras weekend.

Friday. Hermes, one of the oldest parading krewes, rolls first, in the early evening (usually around 6). They're followed by **Krewe d'Etat,** a krewe formed in 1996 by local business leaders with a taste for satire. The Krewe d'Etat has a Dictator in place of the usual king and a Revolution instead of a ball (the sort of revolution that is by invitation only). The krewe prides itself on new and imaginative throws, such as a small stuffed jester that changes outfits annually and, when squeezed, drops such pearls of wisdom as "Live to ride—ride to live!" "Hail to the Dictator!" and "Krewe d'Etat rules!" Following Krewe d'Etat is **Morpheus,** which was founded in 2000 by a group of Carnival veterans. Their love of tradition shows in their old-school floats, but the group is also cutting-edge since it is open to both men and women. New in 2009, Krewe d'Etat and Morpheus started at Jefferson Avenue and Magazine Street (instead of the traditional starting point of Napoleon Avenue and Magazine Street). The new start point was a success, so this could become a permanent route change.

Saturday. Saturday spotlights the largest women's krewe, **Iris,** which was formed in 1922 and began parading in 1959. Ordinarily demure members of Uptown garden clubs let loose from behind their long masks and white gloves, flirting with the men along the route and tossing flowers to young hunks. Iris starts at 11, and is immediately followed by **Tucks,** a young, fun parade founded some 38 years ago by Loyola University students who would tour through a few Uptown streets on the way to their favorite bar, Friar Tucks. The theme is always tongue-in-cheek, and the throws are beautifully coordinated with the decor of the individual floats. A Friar Tuck doll is a must-catch from this parade.

Following Tucks, there's a several-hour break before Mid-City **Endymion,** one of the blockbuster parades of the season. Many parade goers camp out in Mid-City instead of seeing the Uptown parades because the festivities—bands, food, and other entertainment—start at noon at the Orleans Avenue neutral ground. It's a good idea to secure a place to stand because spectators at this parade have a tendency to be territorial about their spots (some camp out several days beforehand). Endymion is notorious for delays; despite the afternoon starting time, it regularly reaches Canal Street late in the evening. Endymion finishes by rolling straight into the Superdome for the Extravaganza, a party attended by upwards of 14,000 people. The lineup for 2009 included REO Speedwagon and the Grand Marshal, musician Kid Rock.

Sunday. Thoth is a daytime parade with a heartwarming peculiarity: it has designed an anomalous route that passes numerous nursing homes and hospitals, including Children's Hospital, at Tchoupitoulas and Henry Clay Avenue, by Audubon Park. It eventually turns onto Napoleon Avenue and rejoins the usual St. Charles–Canal route. The other daytime Sunday parades are **Okeanos** and **Mid-City,** named for the neighborhood it originally rolled through.

SATIRICAL PARADES

Since the beginning of Mardi Gras in New Orleans, krewes have used satire as a safe way to poke fun at politicians and others. Here is a list of some of the most risqué performers:

- Krewe d'Etat
- Krewe de Vieux
- Morpheus
- Muses

Fodor's Choice ★ One of the great Mardi Gras parades, **Bacchus** takes the St. Charles–Canal route Sunday night. The floats are spectacular, including some regular favorites like the endless Bacchagator and the mammoth King Kong, as well as some new floats each year; the Budweiser Clydesdales are another crowd-pleaser. The monarch is always a celebrity (actor Val Kilmer reigned in 2009). Marching bands are at their horn-swinging best for Bacchus, and the throws pour plentifully from the floats.

★ **Monday.** There are no day parades Monday, but **Lundi Gras,** or the Monday before Mardi Gras, has become a major event downtown, especially at Spanish Plaza by the Riverwalk. King Zulu, then Rex, King of Carnival, arrive by boat along the Mississippi River and formally greet one another and their subjects at the Spanish Plaza dock. A large stage at Spanish Plaza hosts live music throughout the day. Monday night brings one of the oldest krewes and one of the youngest end to end. **Proteus,** formed in 1882, pays tribute to the sea god with beautiful floats in the old wagon style. **Orpheus,** founded in 1993, always has the latest in parade technology, such as confetti blowers and automatic plastic-cup dispensers. The krewe is Harry Connick Jr.'s project, and the charming crooner's own float is one of the highlights.

MARDI GRAS DAY

On Mardi Gras day it seems that every street in the city sees a piece of a procession at one point or another. One of the following krewes is sure to meet your styles and tastes.

Early on Mardi Gras morning, you can catch **Zulu,** the oldest African-American parade. If you are not prepared, the black-faced riders, some of them in mock African dress, can seem in shockingly bad taste, but these parodies of minstrelsy are the long-standing traditions of the krewe. Zulu rolls down Jackson Avenue, turning onto St. Charles ahead of Rex, and reaches Canal Street around 11 AM, though in keeping

> **REX'S ROYAL ROOTS**
>
> In 1872, Russian Grand Duke Alexis Romanoff visited New Orleans during Mardi Gras. Local businessmen wanted to entertain the duke, so they held a daytime parade—and Rex was born.

with their mischievous customs, this timing can vary dramatically. **Rex,** traditionally regarded as king of Carnival, greets his subjects following Zulu. His floats are intricate, old-fashioned affairs, one of the visual high points of Mardi Gras day. Behind Rex are the truck parades: more than 200 flatbed trucks, each rented and decorated by an independent group, carrying some 7,000 riders in all. The trucks roll one after another for hours, without bands or walking groups between them.

Mardi Gras day also brings the appearances of the **Mardi Gras Indians** and the **walking clubs.** The walking clubs zigzag all over town, stopping in bars and swapping paper flowers and beads for kisses. One of the more regular clubs, the **Krewe of St. Ann** was founded by a group of friends in 1969. The parade begins in the Bywater District and works its way through Faubourg Marigny before entering the Quarter. This is your best chance to see the Mardi Gras strutting of some of the city's most elaborately designed costumes. And since there is no formal membership, you can join the fun as long as you're in costume!

Predating most of the major parades, the **Mardi Gras Indians** hold their own rituals in the backstreets on Mardi Gras morning. The Indians are members of African-American organizations who dress in intricately beaded costumes that often take all year to create (traditional Indians do not wear the same suit two years in a row). The Indians parade through backstreets, chanting songs from the Mardi Gras Indian repertory. The Indian tribes fall into two major categories: Uptown and downtown. To seek out the Uptown tribes on Mardi Gras morning, venture into the streets across St. Charles Avenue from the Garden District, between Jackson and Washington avenues. The downtown tribes generally revolve around Tremé. To find them, head away from the French Quarter on Ursulines Street.

WHERE TO WATCH

Where to watch parades is an important decision. **Uptown** is more of a family zone, which is not to say it is not crowded and frenzied. Most activity, though, is focused around the parades; outside parade hours, the streets revert to relative normalcy. Particularly good places to catch the parades include the vicinity of the Columns Hotel (3811 St. Charles Avenue, between Peniston and General Taylor streets), which charges a fee for access to its bar and bathrooms. The expansive front porch provides a good vantage point for those who don't need to catch any more beads. The corner of Napoleon and St. Charles avenues is a crowded but exciting place to watch, as the floats and bands turn onto St. Charles Avenue. Going downtown, it is generally family friendly through to the Garden District, with more raucous crowds in front of bars. Between Jackson Avenue and Lee Circle is a more crowded and energetic (sometimes rowdy) place to watch, and a number of bars and stores on this strip can keep you lubricated and fed. On Mardi Gras day, costuming begins very early on St. Charles Avenue, and the street is fairly crowded by 8 AM. If you plan to spend time Uptown, it is worth getting up and out early (try to get there by 7) to share in the excitement of anticipation. The day begins with various walking clubs and makeshift bands strolling by, followed by the Zulu parade, with Rex close on its heels.

MARDI GRAS ROYALTY

In 1956, the Duke and Duchess of Windsor attended the balls for Rex and Comus—and actually bowed to the make-believe monarchs.

A week or so before Mardi Gras, things heat up **downtown** and along Bourbon Street and throughout the French Quarter. By Mardi Gras weekend the crowds are so thick it is difficult to walk down Bourbon. Drinking, exchanging beads, and exhibitionism are popular activities along Bourbon, where lines form to enter the bars and drink prices go through the roof. The side streets offer some degree of refuge while still sustaining a high party pitch. At some point, most parades roll down Canal Street, which marks one boundary of the French Quarter, and the crowds shift over accordingly to bounce to the marching bands and catch some beads before ducking back into the bars or the street scene. Unlike in Uptown, where parades are the focal point, downtown the parades seem merely a blip on the screen of general frenzy.

In deference to the religious pretext for this holiday, Mardi Gras "ends" with the arrival of Ash Wednesday and the Lenten season. At midnight on Tuesday night, downtown streets are cleared, and police officers on foot, in cars, and on horses cruise through the French Quarter blaring from their loudspeakers "Mardi Gras is over. Go home."

MARDI GRAS SAFETY

Whether you choose to watch the parades or to give yourself over to the madness of the mass party on Bourbon Street and throughout the Quarter, use common sense, dress comfortably, and leave your valuables safely locked up at home or in safe-deposit boxes at your hotel. Don't carry excessive amounts of cash and don't wear tempting jewelry. Travel with one or more people rather than alone if possible, and set a permanent meeting spot where your family or group will convene at preset times throughout the day.

The police increase surveillance during the chaotic Carnival season. It is legal to carry alcoholic beverages (but not glass bottles) in the streets, but excessive public drunkenness might draw the attention of the cops. Do not throw anything at the floats or bands of parades, a ticketable and truly hazardous act. On the other hand, throwing change to the flambeaux, or torch carriers, who historically light the way for night parades, is customary.

WOMEN AT MARDI GRAS

More women than you would imagine flash as barter for good beads; if you feel tempted to follow suit, be aware that the personal videos shot on Bourbon Street often wind up on the Internet or on DVDs like *Girls Gone Wild.* Also be aware that New Orleans police do crack down on public indecency during Carnival. And if you are groped or feel threatened in any way, be assured that a police officer will probably be in your sight range.

A FEST TO DIET FOR

It takes 4 tons of crawfish and 6 tons of both rotini pasta and Crawfish Monica Sauce to make enough Crawfish Monica to feed festival crowds. Chefs go through 3 tons of pork to make a fest's worth of cochon de lait po'boys, and 3 tons of crawfish and 6 tons of cheese for the ever-popular crawfish bread.

CHILDREN AT MARDI GRAS In many respects Mardi Gras seems designed for kids. Floats, parades, whimsical gifts, costumes, street vendors with tasty snacks and exciting toys mark the season and revelry carries the day. The daytime parades are most suitable for family-rated fun. If you want to bring children to the evening parades, stay along the St. Charles Avenue route, generally between General Pershing Street and Jackson Avenue, though no spot is immune from the raucous and the bawdy.

Children are especially vulnerable during Mardi Gras and must be carefully watched. ■ TIP→ **Each year accidents occur when children (or adults) venture too near the wheels of floats. If you have kids with you, pick a spot some way back from the rolling parade.** Keep a trained eye on little hands and running feet. Many parents take the added precaution of having children carry a note in their pockets with the parents' names, contact phone numbers, and local address.

JAZZ AND HERITAGE FESTIVAL

Don't let the four-letter word at the center of its name intimidate you—one need not be a jazz fanatic to love the New Orleans Jazz and Heritage Festival. This is no stuffy, high-toned event for music scholars; Jazz Fest, as it's known to locals, is a sprawling, rollicking celebration of Louisiana music, food, and culture held the last weekend in April and the first weekend in May. It takes place at the city's historic Fair Grounds Race Course, which reverberates with the sounds of rock, Cajun, zydeco, gospel, rhythm and blues, hip-hop, folk, world music, country, Latin, and, yes, traditional and modern jazz. Throw in world-class arts and crafts, exhibitions and lectures, and an astounding range of Louisiana-made food—reason enough alone for many Jazz Fest fans to make the trek—and you've got a festival worthy of America's premiere party town. Over the years, Jazz Fest lineups have come to include internationally known performers—Wynton Marsalis, Dave Matthews Band, the O'Jays, and Sugarland topped the bill in 2009—but at its heart the festival is about the hundreds of Louisiana musicians who live, work, and cut their chops in the Crescent City. A lot of New Orleans musicians are still recovering from Hurricane Katrina, and the Jazz and Heritage Festival is their chance to show a huge, international audience that the music survives—and the foundation that the festival benefits works to restore their lives and livelihoods.

HISTORY

Veterans of the first Jazz and Heritage Festival talk about that event, which took place in 1970 in what's now Armstrong Park, with the same awe and swagger of those who saw the Beatles' first U.S. tour or rolled in the mud at Woodstock in 1969. No wonder: the initial lineup included such legendary performers as Mahalia Jackson, Duke Ellington, Pete Fountain, Al Hirt, Fats Domino, The Meters, and the Olympia Brass Band, along with scores of other musicians and parading Mardi Gras Indian tribes. It was hardly an instant success; an oft-repeated anecdote has it that around 350 people attended the first Jazz Fest, about half the number of performers on hand.

> **LONG RUNS**
>
> The Meters, the Preservation Hall Jazz Band, Pete Fountain, the Dukes of Dixieland, the Original Tuxedo Jazz Band, Olympia Brass Band, and Lars Edegran & the New Orleans Ragtime Orchestra all performed at the first Jazz Fest in 1970—and were back at the fest in 2006.

Since then, Jazz Fest has grown in size and stature; in 2006, the first post-Katrina festival drew some 350,000 people over its two weekends and showcased the talents of some 6,000 performers, artisans, and chefs. Diehard fans travel from all over the country, even the world, to mix it up with locals, indulge in Creole and Cajun food, and take in as much music as time and stamina allow. At night, the party extends into the early-morning hours at bars and nightclubs throughout the city.

WHAT GOES ON

Most of the action takes place inside the track at the Fair Grounds Race Course in Mid-City, from 11 AM to sundown Friday through Sunday of the first weekend, and Thursday through Sunday of the second weekend. Three main stages evenly spaced around the track are reserved for the biggest draws, with a half dozen or so smaller performances and lecture spaces scattered across the grounds or in the horse-racing track's grandstand.

MUSIC AND HERITAGE

For an event dedicated to an improvisational genre of music, Jazz Fest is a remarkably structured affair, with performers granted somewhere between 45 and 75 minutes to strut their stuff. Even musicians notorious for starting late and playing long are expected to stick to the tight schedule. Some stages have a specific musical bent: the Congo Square stage, for example, hosts African and African diaspora music, and the Fais-Do-Do Stage specializes in Cajun and zydeco performers. Fans of traditional jazz head for the Heritage Stage, and just about everyone spends at least a few minutes in the Gospel Tent, seeking refuge from the relentless New Orleans sun while soaking up the exuberant testimony from the likes of the Unstoppable Gospel Singers and the Greater St. Stephen Mass Choir. In 2007 the Jazz and Heritage Festival reinstated a Thursday event, which had been missing since Hurricane Katrina,

CLOSE UP

The Second Line

One of the great joys of the Jazz Fest is the odd parade that occasionally takes over the pedestrian paths, bursting through the center of the fairgrounds with an explosion of color, sun-brellas, horns, feathers, and fancy footwork. This apparently chaotic event is called a second line.

The second line is a type of parade historically associated with jazz funerals; the term "second line" is often thought originally to have referred to the secondary group of participants in such a parade, behind the band and the family. "Second line" is also used to refer to the distinctive dance moves that can be glimpsed during New Orleans street parades of all sorts.

During the early 20th century, the New Orleans second line served an important community function. At that time, African-Americans were not allowed to buy insurance, so they formed mutual-aid societies—called Social Aid and Pleasure Clubs—to help members through tough times. When a member's house burned down, or when someone died and the family lacked the funds for a proper funeral, the club would step in to help. Live bands and second-lining become integral parts of the fund-raising efforts. Combined with the city's longstanding penchant for a parade, these activities led to the current second-line brass-band parade tradition.

Sylvester Francis has spent the better part of a lifetime documenting second-line parades and jazz funerals; his **Backstreet Cultural Museum** (✉ *1116 St. Claude Ave., Tremé* ☎ *504/303-9058* 🌐 *www.backstreetmuseum.org*) is a repository of Mardi Gras Indian costumes, second-line mementos, and tons of photographs. Francis also mans a Backstreet Museum booth at Jazz Fest, and will fill you in, cheerfully and at length, on the finer points of one of the city's most distinctive traditions. If you get wind of an authentic second line taking place in the city, go, but use caution. Stick to the safer-looking streets, and be prepared to make an exit if things start to get edgy.

to the second weekend lineup. Crowds tend to be lighter that day, but the talent is no less impressive. The crowd-averse should also consider arriving early on any given day, when it's easier to browse the handsome arts and crafts on display and mill about the grounds without having to jostle for space. Organizers tend to schedule each festival day with the marquee stars appearing last—and the crowds inevitably build as the afternoon goes on.

With its wealth of talent (and the constant lure of amazing food), Jazz Fest presents a logistical planning challenge to the attendee. A schedule and map are essential. Don't stress out trying to catch all the big names, however; inevitably, it's the obscure bluesman, anonymous gospel shouter, or up-and-coming brass band that provides the most indelible Jazz Fest memory.

Festival regulars make good use of the fairgrounds' stately grandstand, which hosts exhibits, panel discussions on New Orleans music and culture, cooking demonstrations (often with free samples) by local chefs, and interviews with musicians, artists, and writers. This multifloor, partially enclosed facility also provides an air-conditioned respite from the sun and heat, which can be intense in late spring. Most important, there are restrooms with hot water and actual plumbing on every floor for those who have an aversion to the portable toilets scattered around the racetrack's perimeter.

GOOD EATS

Vaucresson Sausage Company is the only original food vendor still at the Jazz Fest. Helmed by Vance Vaucresson, the company is based in New Orleans. It serves a hot sausage po'boy and a crawfish sausage po'boy.

Full schedules and ticket information are available on the Jazz Fest Web site (*www.nojazzfest.com*). The artist lineup for 2010 will be released at the end of 2009.

FOOD

Two words: arrive hungry. Jazz Fest's food is almost as revered as its music, and rightly so. Behind the food booths' delightfully low-tech plywood facades, which resemble stage sets in a cheap Western film, an army of cooks from all over Louisiana are hard at work, turning out dishes both familiar (shrimp po'boys and jambalaya) and exotic (alligator sausage, anyone?). It's all delicious, and not a bad deal, with even the most generous platters dished out for under $10. Some perennial favorites include gumbo, soft-shell-crab or cochon de lait po'boys, and Crawfish Monica, a creamy pasta dish. Vegetarians have plenty to choose from, too, especially at the food booths near Congo Square, where a plate of jama-jama (sautéed and seasoned spinach) and fried plantains provide fuel for a day of stage-hopping. Cool down with a tall cup of strawberry lemonade or chilled fruit salad dusted with shaved coconut. The festival, like the city itself, has broadened its culinary repertoire in recent years, and now includes sushi, Central American, and other international options. But the focus is still Creole-Cajun, as demonstrated by the sheer number of people chowing down on oyster po'boys and baskets of boiled crawfish. Keep in mind that outside food and beverages, other than bottled water, are not allowed inside the gates. Cold beer is widely available at tents on the festival grounds, but hard liquor is not served or permitted.

SHOPPING

The competition for crafts booths is nearly as fierce as that for food stalls. Unlike the cooks, however, the artists represented at Jazz Fest hail from not only Louisiana but from all over the United States. Craft areas include Contemporary Crafts, near the Gospel Tent, which sells wares from nationwide artists and artisans; the Louisiana Marketplace, near the Fais-Do-Do Stage and Louisiana Folklife Village, which showcases folk art from the city and the region; and a Native American Village, which spotlights performances and crafts related to Native American culture. Surrounding the Congo Square stage are stands with African and African-influenced artifacts, clothing, and accessories. TIP→ **Many of the artists have a spot for only one of the two weekends; ask about their schedule before putting off that purchase until the following week.** A tent not far from the main gate sells CDs by musicians playing the festival, as well as

CLOSE UP

French Quarter Festival: Where the Locals Go

The French Quarter Festival, usually the third weekend of April, has always been a favorite with locals (it was founded in 1983), but in the past couple years, the festival has grown to attract visitors from around the globe. Why? Well, first of all, it's free. Second? It's set throughout the scenic French Quarter: Woldenberg Park (which faces the Mississippi River), Jackson Square, the Old U.S. Mint, and the streets and clubs in this historic area. Should we keep going? The festival has always had a local flavor that the Jazz Fest often overlooks. Cajun, zydeco, funk, soul, rock 'n' roll, jazz (everything from traditional to Dixieland to bebop) and blues—you'll find it somewhere in the French Quarter. Local restaurants serve up seafood, po'boys, sausage, pasta, gumbo, burritos, barbecue, and much more—all with that distinct New Orleans flavor. Another bonus: April is one of the prettiest times of year in New Orleans—especially in the French Quarter. ☎ *504/522–5730* 🌐 *www.fqfi.org*.

music by other New Orleans and Louisiana artists; a nearby tent sports festival-approved shirts and accessories, along with the official, limited-edition Jazz Fest posters, which range in price from about $70 for a numbered silkscreen to several hundred dollars for a signed and numbered remarque print. ■TIP→ **It is not necessary to bring large amounts of cash to the festival. ATM machines are located throughout the site.**

FESTIVAL BASICS

PLANNING

Depending on the weather, Jazz Fest crowds tend to peak on Saturday and Sunday from midafternoon to closing, with the second weekend typically drawing the largest numbers. Thursday and Friday crowds are a little lighter.

Families and groups will often stake out a patch of ground near one stage, spread a blanket, and use it as a gathering spot for the day. Longtime fest goers bring plastic poles topped with a flag or silly hat to let friends know where they are encamped, or where the party has migrated, although festival security has lately become stricter about prohibiting such props. A traditional meeting place is the tall, conspicuous flagpole at the center of the track, but the area can become too crowded to navigate at peak times; consider arranging to meet at a quieter spot in or near the grandstand. Most important, try not to set too ambitious an agenda, and be ready to ditch plans when the mood strikes, or the mix of heat, food, swirling crowds—even rain—starts to overwhelm. Duck into a shady tent for a sit and a chance to regroup; odds are, you'll discover some

A BITE OF HEAVEN

If you come across a Jazz Fest vendor selling crawfish beignets (think conch fritters, but infinitely better), get an order immediately. Trust us. It may change your life.

little-known but incredibly talented musician playing to an intimate, enthusiastic audience.

You can purchase a full program once you arrive at the festival, which includes detailed schedules and maps, as well as feature pieces. Locals usually simply tear each day's schedule and a map of the fairgrounds from the *Gambit* weekly or *OffBeat* monthly magazine. The daily *Times-Picayune* also publishes maps and schedules in its Friday "Lagniappe" section.

APPRECIATING ART

The first official Jazz Fest poster, a three-color art nouveau image of a second-line parade marshal from 1975, sold for $3.95 at the fair. Today, it fetches around $2,000.

For advance listings of artists to be featured and other information about the Jazz Fest, you can contact the **New Orleans Jazz & Heritage Foundation** (☎*504/522–4786* 🌐*www.nojazzfest.com*), which sponsors the festival.

TICKETS Tickets are no longer available by mail order; instead, you can purchase them in advance at any Ticketmaster outlet (☎*800/488–5252* 🌐*www.ticketmaster.com*). If you are in town a few days before the festival, you'll get the best price by picking them up yourself at the Jazz Fest box office in the New Orleans Arena (1501 Girod Street) or at the adjacent Louisiana Superdome's box office (1500 Poydras Street), which is open weekdays from 9 to 4:30. In 2009, advance tickets good for one day's admission were $40 (plus a few dollars for service fees). Expect to pay $10 more (and possibly endure long lines) if you wait to pay at the festival entrance. Children 2–11 pay $5 in advance or at the gate. Tickets are nonrefundable, and are sold by the weekend—in other words, a ticket purchased for the first weekend will get you in the first Friday, Saturday, or Sunday of the festival, but is not valid the second weekend. The festival also offers a pair of luxury packages called the Big Chief VIP Experience and the Grand Marshal VIP Pass; the premium passes, which range from $550 to $1,000, include admission (and reentry privileges) good for an entire weekend, access to shaded and strategically placed viewing stands at the three main stages, refreshments served in a private hospitality lounge, and other perks. The most expensive options include reserved, on-site parking.

WHAT TO WEAR AND BRING

Jazz Fest is no place to fret about fashion; although there are tents, the grandstand, and a few trees for shade, you'll likely spend most of the day in full sun, so cool and breathable fabrics, along with a wide-brim hat, are your best bets. The quintessential Jazz Fest outfit is shorts and a well-worn concert T-shirt for men, light cotton sundress for women, with a good number of festival goers stripping down to much less. If rain threatens, bring a cap and poncho. Sunscreen and sunglasses are crucial, and pack some hand sanitizer to wash up before—and after—that mayo-oozing po'boy. Wear comfortable shoes, and ones that can get dirty. It's a racetrack, after all, and no matter how groomed it looks at the outset, by the end of Jazz Fest the ground cover is a mix of dust, straw, mud, and crawfish shells. Cameras, tarps, and blankets are allowed, but not recording equipment or video cameras. Hard-shell coolers are prohibited, but empty collapsible coolers are allowed.

KNOW THE RULES

Jazz Fest security can be tight; read the rules before you arrive (available on the Jazz Fest Web site), and don't try to sneak any booze through the gates. Same goes for video cameras: still photos are allowed, but no filming or audio recording.

CHILDREN AT JAZZ FEST

Locals grew up going to Jazz Fest; you'll see many of them carrying on the family tradition, pushing strollers and herding young ones of their own. An area just inside the infield from the grandstand is devoted to children, with music, crafts, and storytelling geared toward kids. A bulletin board in the same area posts schedules and general advice for negotiating the festival with children; nearby, it is possible to "register" your children and create identification tags for them to wear at the festival. The lawn in this kids' area is generally less populated than elsewhere on the fairgrounds, making it easier to keep an eye on children as they run about. The Kids' Tent, meanwhile, provides shade with your music. The grandstand is another great place for a cool-off, and the generally relaxed atmosphere creates a kid-friendly zone.

SAFETY

Jazz Fest itself is safe, but the neighborhood around the fairgrounds can be dodgy, especially after dark. If you are walking to a car or bus stop after the festival ends, try to go in a group and be aware of your surroundings.

MARDI GRAS AND JAZZ FEST ESSENTIALS

To research prices, get advice from other travelers, and book travel arrangements, visit www.fodors.com.

BIKE TRAVEL

Renting bicycles (and locks) is a good way to sidestep the heavy street traffic and parking difficulties that Mardi Gras and Jazz Fest bring. New Orleans is small and flat, and the bike ride from the Garden District to the French Quarter takes about 15 minutes.

If you're biking to Jazz Fest from the French Quarter, just follow Esplanade Avenue away from the river, and veer right onto Bayou Road (where everyone else is headed) just before Broad Street. There are supervised bike lots near each festival entrance, though you must bring your own lock.

However, biking from Uptown to the festival grounds is not recommended, as you will have to get on major streets that can be dangerous for bikers.

BUS TRAVEL

Gray Line Tours offers continuous Jazz Fest Express shuttle service, starting at 10:30 AM, between the fairgrounds and three pickup points: the Sheraton Hotel at 500 Canal Street; the "lighthouse" at the Toulouse Street Wharf, next to Jax Brewery; and the parking area at Marconi

Meadows in City Park. Round-trip fare is $16 ($14, including parking, from the City Park location). Also check with hotel concierges for shuttle ticket availability.

A budget option is to take a Regional Transit Authority bus ($1.25 one way, $1.50 with a transfer). The Jackson–Esplanade bus (Number 91) stops along North Rampart Street before turning onto Esplanade Avenue; ask the driver where you should get off, or just follow the Jazz Fest crowd. It's a four-block walk from the bus stop to the fairgrounds. You can also buy an RTA VisiTour pass, which gives you unlimited rides for three days for $12.

GET INTO THE SPIRIT

If you're hanging out in the Gospel Tent—and you should—don't be too alarmed if you see overzealous performers being led offstage by a group of attendants in white. Choir members who get a little overcome with the spirit are led to a grassy area behind the tent, where they can recover.

INFORMATION **Festival shuttles Gray Line Tours** (☎ *504/569–1401 or 800/535–7786* 🌐 *www.graylineneworleans.com/jazzfest.html*). **Regional Transit Authority** (☎ *504/248–3900, 504/242–2600 automated information* 🌐 *www.norta.com*).

CAR TRAVEL

PARKING Parking is at a premium during Mardi Gras and Jazz Fest seasons. It's best to use your hotel's facilities, even if it means extra walking to the parade route. During the final weekend of Carnival the French Quarter is closed to automobile traffic; scope out a lot or a spot in the CBD. It is also impossible to cross the parade route at any point in a car, and many bus routes are disrupted. If possible, leave the car behind and take a taxi, the streetcar, or a bike—or just walk.

At Jazz Fest, parking at the fairgrounds is expensive and extremely limited; it is best to find another way to get here. If you must drive, you will have to come early for the privilege of paying $50 for a spot at the fairgrounds; otherwise, join the rest of the caravan making ever-wider circles beyond the fest in search of street parking, which is free (but zoned for two-hour maximum parking for nonresidents in many places). Parking-control officers can be aggressive about ticketing, or in some cases towing, cars that exceed the time limit or are parked too close to corners, driveways, or fire hydrants.

DISABILITIES AND ACCESSIBILITY

Because Mardi Gras is a street party, visitors with disabilities will be able to access almost all areas; only the private grandstands are not wheelchair accessible. That being said, be aware that street and sidewalk quality can vary, and some street curbs do not have ramps. Be sure to map out accessible restrooms ahead of time.

At Jazz Fest, the festival does its best to assist visitors with disabilities, from providing wheelchairs and special viewing locations and convenient restrooms to doing snack runs to a favorite food booth. However, this is a huge event held mainly on a dirt-and-grass field, and disabled visitors must be ready for a challenge. Service information for people with disabilities is available at the Access Center in front of the grandstand. People with mobility limitations should use the Gentilly Boulevard Vehicular Gate for accessible parking or the Gentilly Boulevard Pedestrian Gate when arriving or leaving by taxi. Reinforced surfaces crossing the track and paved pathways on the infield facilitate wheelchair passage. Telephones are mounted at wheelchair height. The Paralyzed Vets of America operates a booth located next to the Access Center in front of the Grandstand where you can borrow a conventional wheelchair.

COOL TALKING HEADS

Check out the exhibits, lectures, and interviews in the fairgrounds grandstand. They're often quite interesting, and the air-conditioned building provides welcome relief from the hot New Orleans sun.

Wheelchair-accessible shuttle-bus service is available at New Orleans Tours' designated pickup and drop-off points. All grandstand stages have reserved wheelchair spaces and accessible restrooms, and there are wheelchair-accessible portable toilets spaced throughout the fairgrounds; the Access Center has passkeys. Access assistance is available at food booths, and the Access Center can help arrange text-telephone service and assistive-listening devices for the hearing impaired. Braille and large-print programming information is available at all information booths and the Access Center, which also has recorded program information.

INFORMATION The **Jazz and Heritage Festival Web site** (*www.nojazzfest.com*) has information for people with disabilities. **Advocacy Center for the Elderly and Disabled** (*1010 Common St., Suite 2600* *504/522–2337 [also TTY], 800/960–7705 [also TTY] www.advocacyla.org*). **Jazz Fest Access Center** (*504/522–4786*). **New Orleans Tours** (*504/410–6104* *www.notours.com*). **RTA Paratransit** (*504/827–7433*).

EMERGENCIES

During Mardi Gras, the police are out in full force. If there's a problem, there should be police or paramedics somewhere along the parade route, especially near major intersections. For medical problems, familiarize yourself with local hospitals—not all have reopened since Hurricane Katrina. The nearest hospital to the parade route is Touro Infirmary, which is just off the parade route on Prytania Street, between Louisiana Avenue and Delachaise Street.

At Jazz Fest, two first-aid stations located near the Acura and Gentilly stages stock bandages, salves, and other basic medical needs. In case of problems more serious than a sunburn or a scrape, full medical facilities are available.

LODGING

Mardi Gras and Jazz Fest draw millions of people from the world over. Make room reservations as soon as possible—a year in advance is not too early. Space can become available off and on as reservations are released leading up to the event. A hotel may have no rooms available one day but 10 the next. Keep trying. Minimum-stay requirements are often in effect at area hotels. Many area hotels have special four-night-stay package rates. Consider bed-and-breakfasts Uptown or on Esplanade Avenue.

WORD OF MOUTH

"My biggest JazzFest tip is that there are flush toilets and sinks in the grandstand building. I think they even had plenty of toilet paper." —cocontom

MARDI GRAS LINKS

You'll find parade routes, schedules, and all things Mardi Gras on the following sites.

INFORMATION **Arthur Hardy's Mardi Gras Guide** (*www. mardigrasguide.com*). **MardiGras.com** (*www.mardigras.com*). **New Orleans Convention and Visitors Bureau** (*www.neworleanscvb.com*). **New Orleans Times-Picayune** (*www.nola.com*).

RESTROOMS

It can be tricky to gain access to a bathroom during Mardi Gras, so you may find yourself using a Port-o-Let most of the time. If you are staying at a hotel, it should give you a pass so you can come and go at your leisure. Most grandstands have portable toilets, and most restaurants and bars allow patrons to use their facilities. At certain intersections, such as Napoleon and St. Charles avenues, there are public Port-o-Lets—however, these are far and few between. Public urination is against the law and the police department will not hesitate to arrest someone for doing just that.

At Jazz Fest, the best bathroom spots are on the upper floors of the grandstand. This is well worth the walk; the bathrooms are air-conditioned and clean, and you can wash your hands. Otherwise, portable toilets are clustered in several locations outside the racetrack perimeter.

TAXIS

Cabs cruise the French Quarter and CBD but rarely beyond. Reliable companies with 24-hour service are United Cabs and Yellow-Checker Cabs. The metered fare is $3.50 at the flag drop, $1.60 per mi, and $1 for each additional passenger. During special events such as Jazz Fest and Mardi Gras, many cabbies charge a flat fee of $4 or $5 per passenger or the metered rate, whichever is higher. A metered taxi fare from the French Quarter to Jazz Fest should run about $10 to $12.

INFORMATION **United Cabs** (*504/522-9771 or 524-9606*). **Yellow-Checker Cabs** (*504/525-3311*).

VISITOR INFORMATION

INFORMATION **New Orleans Convention and Visitors Bureau** (*2020 St. Charles Ave., Garden District 504/566-5011 or 800/672-6124 www.visitneworleans.info*). **New Orleans Welcome Center** (*529 St. Ann St., on Jackson Sq., French Quarter 504/568-5661*).

Where to Eat

4

WORD OF MOUTH

"So off I went to Acme Oyster Bar. Yes at noon there was already a line on the sidewalk but being a single I only waited a few minutes for a spot at the bar . . . I ordered a half dozen chargrilled oysters—drizzled with a highly seasoned garlic butter. Delicious. But watching them opening all those beautiful, plump oysters won me over. I ordered a dozen on the half shell—still the BEST way to eat oysters."

—NeoPatrick

"In general, NO is one of the rare cities where locals and tourists eat well at the same places. The Central Grocery and Acme and Galatoire's are all full of locals and tourists, and for good reason."

—Ackislander

www.fodors.com/community

WHERE TO EAT PLANNER

Eating Out Strategy

Where should we eat? With hundreds of eateries competing for your attention, it may seem like a daunting question. But fret not—our expert writers and editors have done most of the legwork. The nearly 100 restaurants here represent the best the city has to offer, from Southern breakfasts and French patisseries to traditional Creole restaurants.

Tipping

The standard for tipping in New Orleans is no different from that in the rest of the country—at least 15% or 20%. Sales taxes for restaurants are 9.5%, which means that doubling the tax is a widespread practice. Most menus contain a notice when a service charge is automatically added to the bill for groups of eight or more.

What to Wear

Unless otherwise noted, restaurants listed in this book allow casual dress. Reviews mention dress only when men are required to wear a jacket. In a luxury restaurant or in one of the old-line, conservative Creole places, dress appropriately.

Reservations

Most restaurants in New Orleans accept reservations, and many popular places are booked quickly, especially on weekend nights. Reservations are always a good idea: we mention them only when they're essential or not accepted. Reserve as soon as you decide where and when you'd like to go; several weeks ahead of time is not too far in advance for trips during Mardi Gras, Jazz Fest, or other special events. Reservations for many restaurants can be made online at *www.neworleansrestaurants.com*.

Prices

The cost of a meal in the city's more upscale restaurants is about what you'd expect to pay in other U.S. cities. The bargains are found in the more casual, full-service restaurants, where a simple lunch or dinner can frequently be had for less than $25. However, even the more expensive restaurants offer fixed-price menus of three or four courses for substantially less than what an à la carte meal costs.

If you are watching your budget, be sure to ask the price of recited daily specials. The charge for specials at some restaurants is noticeably out of line with the other prices on the menu.

As a rule, serving sizes are more than generous—some would say unmanageable for the average eater—so many diners order two appetizers rather than a starter and a main course, which can make ordering dessert more practical. Some restaurants now offer small- or large-plate options.

Our restaurant reviews indicate what credit cards are accepted at each establishment, but if you plan to use a credit card it is a good idea to double-check its acceptability when making reservations or before sitting down to eat.

WHAT IT COSTS

	¢	$	$$	$$$	$$$$
AT DINNER	under $9	$9–$16	$17–$25	$26–$35	over $35

Restaurant prices are for a main course at dinner, excluding sales tax of 9.5%.

BEST BETS FOR NEW ORLEANS DINING

Fodor's writers and editors have selected their favorite restaurants by price, cuisine, and experience in the lists below. In the first column, Fodor's Choice properties represent the "best of the best" in every price category.

Fodor's Choice★

Arnaud's, $$$ p. 113
August, $$$ p. 124
Bistro at Maison de Ville, $$$ p. 113
Brigtsen's, $$$ p. 130
Commander's Palace, $$$ p. 132
Cuvée, $$$ p. 124
Galatoire's, $$$ p. 116
The Grill Room, $$$ p. 127
Irene's Cuisine, $$ p. 116
Mosca's, $$ p. 138
ONE, $$ p. 134
Stella!, $$$ p 119

By Price

¢

Café du Monde, p. 114
Croissant d'Or Patisserie, p. 115

$

Acme Oyster and Seafood Restaurant, p. 112
El Gato Negro, p. 115
Fiorella's Café, p. 116
Praline Connection, p. 120

$$

Irene's Cuisine, p. 116
Iris, p. 117
Mosca's, p. 138
ONE, p. 134

$$$

Arnaud's, p. 113
August, p. 124
Bistro at Maison de Ville, p. 113
Brigtsen's, p. 130
Commander's Palace, p. 132
Cuvée, p. 124
Galatoire's, p. 116
The Grill Room, p. 127
Stella!, p. 119

$$$$

Antoine's, p. 112
Broussard's, p. 114

By Cuisine

AMERICAN

Emeril's, p. 125
The Grill Room, p. 127
Iris, p. 117
Wolfe's in the Warehouse, p. 130

ASIAN

Kyoto, p. 133
Tan Dinh, p. 139
Wasabi, p. 120

CAJUN

Bon Ton Café, p. 124
Jacques-Imo's Café, p. 132
K-Paul's Louisiana Kitchen, p. 117

CREOLE

Arnaud's, p. 113
Bistro at Maison de Ville, p. 113
Brigtsen's, p. 130
Commander's Palace, p. 132
Galatoire's, p. 116

ITALIAN

Irene's Cuisine, p. 116
Mosca's, p. 138
Tommy's Cuisine, p. 129

SEAFOOD

Acme Oyster and Seafood Restaurant, p. 112
Casamento's, p. 130
GW Fins, p. 116

By Experience

BRUNCH

Brennan's, p. 114
Commander's Palace, p. 132
Mr. B's Bistro, p. 118
Palace Café, p. 129

CHILD-FRIENDLY

Acme Oyster and Seafood Restaurant, p. 112
Angelo Brocato's, p. 135
Crabby Jack's, p. 137
Johnny's Po-Boys, p. 117

GOOD FOR GROUPS

Antoine's, p. 112
Arnaud's, p. 113
Grand Isle, p. 125
Nola, p. 118

LATE-NIGHT DINING

Port of Call, p. 119
Rémoulade, p. 119

MOST ROMANTIC

Bistro at Maison de Ville, p. 113
Cuvée, p. 124
Martinique, p. 134
Stella!, p. 119

By Paul A. Greenberg

NEW ORLEANS IS KNOWN AS MUCH FOR ITS SENSORY expression as it is for its joie de vivre, and nowhere is this more evident than in the stellar cuisine offered at local restaurants. Traditional Louisiana dishes, such as jambalaya, red beans and rice, gumbo, and étouffée are readily available, but the delectable surprise of dining in New Orleans is the diversity of dishes and cuisines that are available, not to mention the culinary ingenuity on display.

Old or new, the menus at New Orleans's restaurants reflect three centuries of multiple cultures constantly contributing to the always-simmering culinary gumbo pot. What influences can you expect to taste? The list is long, but it's easy to find dashes of Spanish, French, Italian, German, African, Caribbean, and Croatian flavor—and increasingly, Asian and Latin influences.

Menus are often works in progress, constantly evolving. At ONE, Chef Scott Snodgrass's Uptown restaurant, the menu changes seasonally. Come in on a cold winter night, and you're likely to find ale-braised rabbit with stone-ground grits. Downtown at 7 on Fulton, you might opt for seared scallops with smoked tomatoes and almonds with hollandaise sauce. Or go traditional at the world-renowned Commander's Palace with chef Tory McPhail's crispy soft-shell crab with pinched herbs and shaved sweet onions. Still, if you have any lingering doubts about the imaginative spirit of New Orleans's culinary wizards, take a bite of the sweetbreads with capers and souffléed potatoes at Arnaud's. Case closed.

FRENCH QUARTER

$ SEAFOOD ✕ **Acme Oyster and Seafood Restaurant.** A rough-edge classic in every way, this no-nonsense eatery at the entrance to the French Quarter is a prime source for cool and salty raw oysters on the half shell; shrimp, oyster, and roast-beef po'boys; and tender, expertly seasoned red beans and rice. Table service, once confined to the main dining room out front, is now provided in the rear room as well. Expect lengthy lines outside, often a half-block long (trust us though, it's worth it). Crowds lighten in the late afternoon. ✉ *724 Iberville St., French Quarter* ☎ *504/525–1160* 🌐 *www.acmeoyster.com* ✍ *Reservations not accepted* 💳 *AE, D, DC, MC, V.*

$$$$ CREOLE ✕ **Antoine's.** If Antoine's wasn't already a culinary deity, Frances Parkinson Keyes made it one with her 1948 novel *Dinner at Antoine's.* Though some people believe Antoine's heyday passed before the turn of the 20th century, others wouldn't leave New Orleans without at least one order of oysters Rockefeller, a dish invented here. Other notables on the bilingual menu include *pommes de terre soufflées* (fried potato puffs), pompano *en papillote* (baked in parchment paper), and baked Alaska. Tourists generally sit in the front room, but walking through the grand labyrinth is a must. Be prepared for lackluster service. A jacket is required. ✉ *713 St. Louis St., French Quarter* ☎ *504/581–4422* 🌐 *www.antoines.com* ✍ *Reservations essential* 💳 *AE, DC, MC, V* ⏲ *No dinner Sun.*

$$$ CREOLE Fodor's Choice ★ ✕ **Arnaud's.** This grande dame of classic Creole restaurants still sparkles. In the main dining room, ornate etched glass reflects light from charming old chandeliers while the late founder, Arnaud Cazenave, gazes from an oil portrait. The adjoining jazz bistro offers the same food but is a more casual and music-filled dining experience. The ambitious menu includes classic dishes as well as more contemporary ones. Always reliable are Shrimp Arnaud—cold shrimp in a superb rémoulade—and Oysters Bienville, Petit Filet Lafitte, and praline crepes. Jackets are requested in the main dining room. Be sure to visit the Mardi Gras museum upstairs. ✉ *813 Bienville St., French Quarter* ☎ *504/523–5433* 🌐 *www.arnauds.com* *Reservations essential* 💳 *AE, D, DC, MC, V* ⏲ *No lunch Sat.*

$$$ SOUTHERN ✕ **Bayona.** "New World" is the label Louisiana native Susan Spicer applies to her cooking style, which results in such signature dishes as the Caribbean pumpkin soup with coconut, and Niman ranch pork chop with a spicy adobo glaze. The lunch omelet of andouille, smoked cheddar, and fried oysters is about as authentic as Louisiana cooking can be. These and other imaginative dishes are served in an early-19th-century Creole cottage that glows with flower arrangements, elegant photographs, and trompe l'oeil murals suggesting Mediterranean landscapes. Don't skip pastry chef Christy Phebus's sweets, such as a dark chocolate banana torte with espresso crème caramel. ✉ *430 Dauphine St., French Quarter* ☎ *504/525–4455* 🌐 *www.bayona.com* *Reservations essential* 💳 *AE, DC, MC, V* ⏲ *Closed Sun. No lunch Mon. or Tues.*

$ AFRICAN ✕ **Bennachin.** New Orleans's Creole cuisine borrows ingredients and techniques from the African diaspora, but Bennachin, which highlights the cooking of Gambia and Cameroon, is one of the city's few truly African restaurants. Beef stews are superb here, specifically one with a tart, gingery, ground-melon-seed sauce. All stews come with rice or mashed yams, which you traditionally eat with your hands. Vegetarian options include black-eyed-pea fritters, and spicy sautéed spinach served with plantains and coconut rice. Exposed-brick walls and African wall hangings surround about a dozen tables and a small open kitchen. Service is adequate. ✉ *1212 Royal St., French Quarter* ☎ *504/522–1230* 💳 *AE, D, MC, V* *BYOB.*

$$$ CREOLE Fodor's Choice ★ ✕ **Bistro at Maison de Ville.** Forget everything you thought you knew about hotel restaurants. "The Bistro," as locals refer to it, defies convention with its charming, European-inspired decor, intimate dining room that seats 44, and a kitchen so tiny it would fit in the average utility closet. Still, chef Greg Picolo's dishes, like fine sautéed Louisiana gulf fish, osso buco, bouillabaisse, and bacon-wrapped filet mignon, are so well conceived that one might picture an operation much larger and more sophisticated. The wine list is legendary in these parts, and the ambience is as well suited to a marriage proposal as it is to a power lunch. The Bistro may just be the best-kept secret in the French Quarter. ✉ *727 Toulouse St., French Quarter* ☎ *504/528–9206* 🌐 *www.hotelmaisondeville.com/dining* 💳 *AE, D, DC, MC, V.*

$$ CREOLE ✕ **Bourbon House.** Perched on one of the French Quarter's busiest corners, this is Dickie Brennan's biggest and flashiest restaurant yet (he also owns Palace Café and Dickie Brennan's Steakhouse); it's a solid hit with

seafood aficionados. If it weren't for the noisy adjacent sports bar, the raw bar would be prime real estate, with its sterling oysters on the half shell; chilled seafood platters; and antique, decorative oyster plates. Glistening beneath the golden glow of bulbous hanging lamps, the main dining room is a more appropriate place for digging into the Creole catalog—andouille sausage stuffed crab, oysters Bienville, and gulf fish pecan. Take your frozen bourbon-milk punch in a go-cup. Why? Because you can. ✉ *144 Bourbon St., French Quarter* ☎ *504/522–0111* 🌐 *www.bourbonhouse.com* ▭ *AE, D, DC, MC, V.*

$$$ CREOLE ✕ **Brennan's.** Lavish breakfasts are what first put Brennan's on the map. They're still a big draw from morning to night on two floors of luxuriously appointed dining rooms in a gorgeous 19th-century building. The best seats include views of the lush courtyard and fountain. For breakfast, eye-opening cocktails flow freely, followed by poached eggs sandwiched between such treats as hollandaise, creamed spinach, artichoke bottoms, and Canadian bacon; all are listed with suggested wines. Headliners at lunch or dinner include textbook versions of oysters Rockefeller and seafood gumbo, and bananas Foster, which was created here. Looking for consistency? Chef Lazone Randolph has been creating culinary delights in Brennan's kitchen for more than 40 years. The wine list is a stunner, both in quantity and quality. ✉ *417 Royal St., French Quarter* ☎ *504/525–9711* 🌐 *www.brennansneworleans.com* *Reservations essential* ▭ *AE, D, MC, V.*

$$$$ CREOLE ✕ **Broussard's.** If local restaurants were judged solely by the beauty of their courtyards, Broussard's would be a standout—but if you have the pleasure of dining here, you'll also enjoy consistently outstanding cuisine. From the chef's crab cakes with olive muffuletta relish and caper shallot mayonnaise; to a hearty corn, shrimp, and sweet potato bisque; to tender, grilled, pork-fillet medallions with horseradish, molasses, and mustard glaze, Brousard's provides a meal you won't forget anytime soon. Fight the good fight for an outdoor table, and ask about the selection of savory sauces to accompany your entrée. The praline crème brûlée is perfection. ✉ *819 Conti St., French Quarter* ☎ *504/581–3866* ▭ *AE, D, DC, MC, V* ⊗ *No lunch.*

¢ CAFE ✕ **Café du Monde.** No trip to New Orleans is complete without a cup of chicory-laced café au lait and addictive sugar-dusted beignets in this venerable Creole institution. The tables under the green-and-white-striped awning are jammed at every hour with locals and tourists feasting on powdery doughnuts and views of Jackson Square. ■ TIP→ **If there's a line for table service, head around back to the takeout window and get your coffee and beignets to go. Enjoy them overlooking the river right next door, or in Jackson Square.** The magical time to go is just before dawn, when the bustle subsides and you can hear the birds in the crepe myrtles across the way. Five satellite locations (Riverwalk Marketplace in the CBD, Lakeside Shopping Center in Metairie, Esplanade Mall in Kenner, Oakwood Mall in Gretna, and Veterans Blvd. in Metairie) are convenient but lack the character of the original. ✉ *800 Decatur St., French Quarter* ☎ *504/525–4544* 🌐 *www.cafedumonde.com* ▭ *No credit cards.*

4

$ CAFE **Café Maspero.** The low prices, big portions, and neighborhood camaraderie at the bar keep people coming back. Pastrami and corned beef are local favorites; the half-pound hamburger (with cheese, chili, or both) is long on bulk but short on taste. Arched doors and windows give the vast brick dining room a little character. Service is perfunctory, and, most days, be prepared to wait outside in line for up to half an hour. *601 Decatur St., French Quarter 504/523–6250 Reservations not accepted No credit cards.*

$ CAFE **Central Grocery.** This old-fashioned Italian grocery store produces authentic muffulettas, one of the gastronomic gifts of the city's Italian immigrants. Good enough to challenge the po'boy as the local sandwich champ, it's made by filling round loaves of seeded bread with ham, salami, mozzarella, and a salad of marinated green olives. Sandwiches, about 10 inches in diameter, are sold in wholes and halves. TIP→ **The muffulettas are huge! Unless you're starving, you'll do fine with a half.** You can eat your muffuletta at a counter, or get it to go and dine on a bench on Jackson Square or the Moon Walk along the Mississippi riverfront. The Grocery closes at 5:30 PM. *923 Decatur St., French Quarter 504/523–1620 D, MC, V No dinner.*

¢ CAFE **Croissant d'Or Patisserie.** Locals compete with visitors for a table in this colorful, pristine pastry shop, which serves excellent and authentic French croissants, pies, tarts, and custards, as well as an imaginative selection of soups, salads, and sandwiches. Wash them down with real French breakfast coffee, cappuccino, or espresso. Grab a table during breakfast hours for great people-watching. Hours are 7 AM to 2. *617 Ursulines St., French Quarter 504/524–4663 AE, MC, V Closed Tues. No dinner.*

$$$ STEAKHOUSE **Dickie Brennan's Steakhouse.** "Straightforward steaks with a New Orleans touch" is the axiom at this clubby and luxurious red-meat specialist, the creation of a younger member of the Brennan family of restaurateurs. After stellar martinis in the dark cherrywood-lined lounge, walk the drugstore-tile floor to the cavernous dining room and dig into classic, expensive cuts of top-quality beef and seafood. The standard beefsteak treatment is light seasoning and a brush of butter. Among the several other toppers are five buttery sauces. The expansive oyster bar has become a classic corner gathering place for tourists and locals. *716 Iberville St., French Quarter 504/522–2467 www.dickiebrennanssteakhouse.com AE, D, DC, MC, V No lunch Sat.–Tues.*

$ MEXICAN **El Gato Negro.** In the past few years a wave of new Mexican restaurants has opened in New Orleans, but this one stands out. Situated directly across from the famed French Quarter Flea Market, diners can enjoy pineapple or tangerine margaritas alfresco, and dig into huevos rancheros for breakfast, homemade pulled-pork tamales for lunch, and the best lamb chops in the French Quarter for dinner. On the high end of the menu, the bronzed grouper, scallops, and jumbo shrimp in diablo sauce is a sure winner. The burrito stuffed with filet mignon is truly distinctive, and the chef excels with sauces. *81 French Market Pl., French Quarter 504/525–9752 www.elgatonegronola.com Reservations not accepted AE, D, DC, MC, V Closed Mon.*

$ CAFE **Fiorella's Café.** Steps away from the hubbub of the French Quarter's flea market is this casual and friendly bar and eatery, which specializes in classic po'boys, New Orleans–style plate lunches, and some of the best fried chicken in town. Red beans and rice show up on Monday, meat loaf takes the spotlight on Tuesday, and Thursday is butter-bean day; hearty breakfasts are an everyday feature. Space is tight, but the food and the prices are easy to swallow. ✉ *45 French Market Pl. (another entrance at 1136 Decatur St.), French Quarter* ☎ *504/528–9566* ▭ *AE, D, MC, V.*

$$$ CREOLE Fodor's Choice ★ **Galatoire's.** Galatoire's has always epitomized the old-style French-Creole bistro. Many of the recipes date to 1905. Fried oysters and bacon en brochette are worth every calorie, and the brick-red rémoulade sauce sets a high standard. Other winners include veal chops in béarnaise sauce, and seafood-stuffed eggplant. The setting downstairs is a single, narrow dining room lighted with glistening brass chandeliers; bentwood chairs and white tablecloths add to its timelessness. You may reserve a table in the renovated upstairs rooms, though the action is on the first floor, where partying regulars inhibit conversation but add good people-watching entertainment value. Friday lunch starts early and continues well into early evening. A jacket is required. ✉ *209 Bourbon St., French Quarter* ☎ *504/525–2021* 🌐 *www.galatoires.com* ▭ *AE, D, DC, MC, V* ⊙ *Closed Mon.*

$ CREOLE **Gumbo Shop.** Even given a few modern touches—like the vegetarian gumbo offered daily—this place evokes a sense of old New Orleans. The menu is chock-full of regional culinary anchors: jambalaya, shrimp creole and rémoulade, red beans and rice, bread pudding, and seafood and chicken-and-sausage gumbos, heavily flavored with tradition but easy on your wallet. The patina on the ancient painting covering one wall seems to deepen by the week, and the red-and-white-check tablecloths and bentwood chairs are taking on the aspect of museum pieces. ✉ *630 St. Peter St., French Quarter* ☎ *504/525–1486* 🌐 *www.gumboshop.com* ⚠ *Reservations not accepted* ▭ *AE, D, DC, MC, V.*

$$ SEAFOOD **GW Fins.** Seafood is the quarry of many a New Orleans visitor, and GW Fins meets the demand with variety and quality, ranging from gumbos to New Bedford sea scallops. A bounty of fish species from around the world is among the menu's lures. Chef Tenney Flynn's menu changes daily, depending on what fresh seafood is delivered, but typical dishes have included a luscious Canadian sea bass, Hawaiian big-eye tuna, and sautéed rainbow trout with spinach, oysters, and shiitake mushrooms, fired up with tasso. For dessert, try the baked-to-order deep-dish apple pie. The spacious dining room's attractive modern decor and the enthusiastic service make this a relaxing refuge from the French Quarter's crowds. ✉ *808 Bienville St., French Quarter* ☎ *504/581–3467* 🌐 *www.gwfins.com* ▭ *AE, D, DC, MC, V* ⊙ *No lunch.*

$$ ITALIAN Fodor's Choice ★ **Irene's Cuisine.** Its walls are festooned with enough snapshots, garlic braids, and crockery for at least two more restaurants, but it all just adds to the charm of this cozy Italian-Creole eatery. From Irene DiPietro's kitchen come succulent roasted chicken brushed with olive oil, rosemary, and garlic; original, velvety soups; and fresh shrimp, aggressively seasoned and grilled before joining linguine glistening with herbed

olive oil. Waits here can stretch to the 60-minute mark during peak dinner hours, which is just enough time for a bottle of wine in the convivial little piano bar. It easily has the friendliest service personnel in the French Quarter. ☒ *539 St. Philip St., French Quarter* ☎ *504/529–8811* *Reservations not accepted* *AE, MC, V* *No lunch.*

$$ AMERICAN ✕ **Iris.** Once situated in a tiny, Uptown, clapboard house, Iris moved to fancier digs in the French Quarter at the end of 2008. Chef Ian Schnoenbelen's contemporary American cuisine plays out nicely in the sunchoke-and-cauliflower soup, octopus salad, and especially in the black-pepper-rubbed lamb T-bone steak. The braised beef short ribs with potato gnocchi is hearty fare, and unforgettable. The thoughtful balance between meat and seafood entrées, the array of salads, and the generously portioned appetizers are all reasons to stop and smell the irises. ☒ *321 N. Peters St., French Quarter* ☎ *504/299–3944* *www.irisneworleans.com* *AE, D, DC, MC, V* *No lunch Mon. and Wed. Closed Sun. and Tues.*

4

$ CAFE ✕ **Johnny's Po-boys.** Strangely enough, good po'boys are hard to find in the French Quarter. Johnny's compensates for the scarcity with a cornucopia of them, even though the quality is anything but consistent, and the prices are somewhat inflated for the tourist trade. Inside the soft-crust French bread come the classic fillings, including lean boiled ham, well-done roast beef in garlicky gravy, and crisply fried oysters or shrimp. The chili may not cut it in San Antonio, but the red beans and rice are the real deal. The surroundings are rudimentary. ☒ *511 St. Louis St., French Quarter* ☎ *504/524–8129* *www.johnnyspoboy.com* *No credit cards* *No dinner.*

$$$ CAJUN ✕ **K-Paul's Louisiana Kitchen.** In this comfortable French Quarter café of glossy wooden floors and exposed brick, chef Paul Prudhomme started the blackening craze and added "Cajun" to America's culinary vocabulary. Two decades later, thousands still consider a visit to New Orleans partly wasted without a visit to K-Paul's for his inventive gumbos, fried crawfish tails, blackened tuna, roast duck with rice dressing, and sweet potato–pecan pie. Prices are steep, but servings are generous. And although you can make reservations these days, it's still tradition to line up along Chartres Street before the doors open. ☒ *416 Chartres St., French Quarter* ☎ *504/524–7394* *www.kpauls.com* *Reservations essential* *AE, D, DC, MC, V* *Closed Sun. No lunch Mon.–Wed.*

$$ CREOLE ✕ **Le Meritage.** The way to attract more clientele when the economy goes south is as easy as portion size. Le Meritage offers distinctive menu options in small- and large-plate portions. Where else could you find a seared duck breast with fig compote, foie gras, and potatoes for $15? The dining room is contemporary chic, but the dinner check is surprisingly more akin to a casual lunch spot. Fresh, regional foods with ingredients indigenous to Louisiana populate the menu, and the wine list is well conceived and also affordable. And if all of that were not reason enough to dine here, the rotating exhibits of local artists' works is the perfect accompaniment. ☒ *1001 Toulouse St., French Quarter* ☎ *504/586–8000* *www.lemeritage.com* *AE, D, DC, MC, V.*

$ ITALIAN ✕ **Mona Lisa.** Ask a New Orleanian where to find the best pizza in the city, and you'll probably be directed to Mona Lisa, where the food has remained consistently mouthwatering for decades. The salads and sandwiches are outstanding, but you'll rarely see a table without a pizza on it. All of the usual ingredients are available, but there's also an imaginative selection of specialty pizzas, most notably the Hawaiian and the Mediterranean. The wine list has steadily improved over the years, and the tiramisu is one of the French Quarter's best-kept sweet secrets. Hundreds of versions of the Mona Lisa adorn the walls (Mona with a cigar? Check.) in a relaxed setting. ✉*1212 Royal St., French Quarter* ☎*504/522–6746* ✍*Reservations not accepted* ▭*AE, MC, V.*

$$$ CREOLE ✕ **Mr. B's Bistro.** Those who wonder if there really is a New Orleans restaurant that can properly cater to both tourists and locals need look no further than Mr. B's. Situated on one of the busiest French Quarter corners, this bistro never disappoints when it comes to consistency, culinary innovation, and full flavors. Using as many ingredients and products indigenous to Louisiana as possible, the chef offers a standout orange-and-black-pepper-crusted duck breast, an irresistible cider-cured pork chop, and one of the best barbecued shrimp dishes in the city. First-timers must try the "Gumbo Ya-Ya," and no meal here can end without the hot buttered pecan pie. Upscale yet accessible, Mr. B's is still on the map because of its just-right seasonings, its windows on the French Quarter world, and its dedication to service. ✉*201 Royal St., French Quarter* ☎*504/523–2078* 🌐*www.mrbsbistro.com* ▭*AE, D, DC, MC, V.*

$$$ CREOLE ✕ **Muriel's Jackson Square.** Among Jackson Square's many dining spots, Muriel's is easily the most ambitious, in both atmosphere and menu. In the large downstairs rooms, quaint prints and architectural relics evoke the city's colorful past, while diners in comfy chairs indulge in hearty updated renderings of old Creole favorites. Occasionally, the faint sounds of freelance jazz waft inside. The menu is diverse to say the least: from the seafood and andouille-sausage-stuffed mirliton at lunch, to the pecan-crusted puppy drum with Louisiana crab relish. Be sure to wait for a balcony table with a panoramic view of Jackson Square. ✉*801 Chartres St., French Quarter* ☎*504/568–1885* 🌐*www.muriels.com* ▭*AE, DC, MC, V.*

$$$ CREOLE ✕ **Nola.** Fans of Emeril Lagasse will want to grab a seat at the food bar overlooking the open kitchen in the chef's French Quarter restaurant. One of the few see-and-be-seen spots in the Quarter, Nola has freewheeling appetizers, the standout being "Miss Hay's stuffed chicken wings" with hoisin dipping sauce. Entrées, like the grilled pork porterhouse with sugar-glazed sweet potatoes, are heavy but delicious. Be warned, after a few bites of the buttermilk fried chicken with bourbon mashed sweet potatoes, you may start looking for property here. Leave room in your tummy, and heart, for the white-chocolate bananas Foster bread pudding. The space is arty and bright, but too many hard surfaces makes the noise bounce around, which can create a loud environment. ✉*534 St. Louis St., French Quarter* ☎*504/522–6652* 🌐*www.emerils.com* ✍*Reservations essential* ▭*AE, D, DC, MC, V* ⊗*No lunch Sun.–Thurs.*

$$$ ECLECTIC ✕ **Pelican Club.** Chef Richard Hughes's chic restaurant was once called "understated hip with a festive flip." Sassy New York flourishes

permeate the menu of this smartly decorated but eminently comfortable place in the heart of the French Quarter. Still, evidence of Hughes's Louisiana origins keeps popping up. He turns out what may be the best crab cakes in the city (infused with fresh gulf shrimp) but with the surprise addition of pineapple-jalapeño chutney, served over fried green tomatoes. Try to tackle the whole crispy fish with diver scallops, if you dare, and the Australian rack of lamb with rosemary-pesto crust is almost a spiritual experience. ✉ *312 Exchange Pl., French Quarter* ☎ *504/523–1504* 🌐 *www.pelicanclub.com* 💳 *AE, D, DC, MC, V* ⏲ *Closed Mon. No lunch.*

$ AMERICAN

✕ **Port of Call.** People wait for more than an hour outside Port of Call every night, in the heavy heat of July and the downpours of September, for fist-thick burgers made from freshly ground beef, grilled to order and served with baked potatoes (no fries here) that are always perfectly fluffy. For the definitive experience, drink a Monsoon while you wait (Port of Call's mind-bending take on the Hurricane), and order your potato "loaded" (with mushrooms, cheddar cheese, sour cream, butter, chives, and bacon bits). A juicy filet mignon is also available. The dark, smoky barroom isn't suitable for small children. ✉ *838 Esplanade Ave., French Quarter* ☎ *504/523–0120* 🌐 *www.portofcallneworleans.com* ✍ *Reservations not accepted* 💳 *AE, MC, V.*

$ CREOLE

✕ **Rémoulade.** Operated by the owners of the posh Arnaud's, Rémoulade is more laid-back and less pricey. It serves the same Caesar salad and pecan pie, as well as a few of the signature starters: shrimp Arnaud in rémoulade sauce, baked oysters, turtle soup, and shrimp bisque. The marble-counter oyster bar and mahogany cocktail bar date from the 1870s; a dozen oysters shucked here, paired with a cold beer, can easily turn into two dozen, maybe three. Tile floors, mirrors, a pressed-tin ceiling, and brass lights create an old-time New Orleans environment. It's open daily until midnight. ✉ *309 Bourbon St., French Quarter* ☎ *504/523–0377* 🌐 *www.remoulade.com* 💳 *AE, D, DC, MC, V.*

$$$ ECLECTIC

Fodor's Choice ★

✕ **Stella!** Chef Scott Boswell has evolved into one of the city's most innovative and daring culinarians. Try Louisiana gulf shrimp and chanterelle and lobster mushroom risotto. The porcini-crusted rack of Australian lamb and lamb rib eye is strictly upscale comfort food, the perfect prelude to chocolate cake with hot buttered pink lemonade. Stella! now sits comfortably among New Orleans's best fine-dining restaurants. ✉ *1032 Chartres St., French Quarter* ☎ *504/587–0091* 🌐 *www.restaurantstella.com* 💳 *AE, D, DC, MC, V* ⏲ *No lunch.*

$$$ AMERICAN

✕ **Wolfe's.** Chef Tom Wolfe has taken this venerable French Quarter eatery to new heights since assuming ownership in 2004. An excellent starter is the grilled sweetbreads brûlée, followed by a heirloom tomato and Vidalia onion salad and a grilled lamb T-bone, served over a candied-pecan shiitake mushroom salad. The main dining room is lined with sleek tufted banquettes, exhibiting the laid-back elegance of a fine French bistro. ✉ *1041 Dumaine St., French Quarter* ☎ *504/593–9535* 💳 *AE, D, MC, V* ⏲ *Closed Sun. and Mon. No lunch Tues.–Thurs. and Sat.*

FAUBOURG MARIGNY

$ MIDDLE EASTERN ✕ **Mona's Café & Deli.** The modest and spotless spaces at Mona's are not the most colorful in town. But inside this rather bare and simple place you'll find some of the best, basic, eastern Mediterranean cooking. Cut open a ball of crunchy fried *kibbe* and the reward is superbly seasoned beef and lamb. The tabbouleh here, made with lots of parsley and mint, is more than just seasoned bulgur wheat. Gyro sandwiches are meaty, and the falafel are flavorful, too. The Lebanese iced tea is eminently refreshing, as is the friendly laid-back service. ✉ *504 Frenchmen St., Faubourg Marigny* ☎ *504/949–4115* ▭ *AE, MC, V.*

$ CREOLE ✕ **Praline Connection.** Down-home cooking in the southern-Creole style is the forte of this very Southern restaurant a couple of blocks from the French Quarter. The fried or stewed chicken, smothered pork chops, fried chicken livers, and collard greens are definitively done, and the soulful filé gumbo, peas with okra, and sweet-potato pie are welcome in a neighborhood otherwise in short supply of soul food. Add a congenial staff and a comfortable dining room, and the result is a fine place to enjoy a relaxing mealtime. The adjacent sweetshop holds such delights as sweet-potato cookies and Creole pralines. ✉ *542 Frenchmen St., Faubourg Marigny* ☎ *504/943–3934* 🌐 *www.pralineconnection.com* ▭ *AE, D, DC, MC, V.*

$$ THAI ✕ **Sukho Thai.** Certainly the most extensive Thai restaurant in the area, Sukho Thai fits snugly into its arty neighborhood with servers wearing all black, an art gallery approach to decorating, and brightly colored dishes. Dry and wet curries are so vibrant that the pastes seem made-to-order. Whole steamed fish brushed with spicy chili sauce gains a citrusy perfume from lemongrass and Kaffir lime leaf. Creative house-made desserts take the form of barely sweetened coconut custard and black-rice pudding. The most imaginative and extensive tea menu in the area compensates for the lack of a liquor license. ✉ *1913 Royal St., Faubourg Marigny* ☎ *504/948–9309* 🌐 *www.sukhothai-nola.com* ▭ *AE, D, MC, V* *BYOB* *Closed Mon. No lunch weekends.*

$$ JAPANESE ✕ **Wasabi.** If it weren't for the smidgen of a sign jutting from the side of Wasabi's windowless building, you'd never guess at the bright, clean goings-on inside. The restaurant splits into two rooms; you wait in the neighborhoody bar area if the dining space is crowded (it usually is). The fish and rice are fresh as can be, with sushi chefs working in their open kitchen at all times, and a Japanese kitchen turns out succulent beef dishes and great udon noodle soups. The wasabi-honey-shrimp entrée combines three unlikely ingredients, but so many approve that it has become a signature. ✉ *900 Frenchmen St., Faubourg Marigny* ☎ *504/943–9433* 🌐 *www.wasabinola.com* *Reservations not accepted* ▭ *AE, D, DC, MC, V* *Closed Sun.*

CBD AND WAREHOUSE DISTRICT

$$$ ECLECTIC ✕ **7 on Fulton.** Restaurateur Vicky Bayley wowed the masses in the '90s with Mike's on the Avenue. Now she's back with this chic, sleek eatery just down the street from the Morial Convention Center. Rich entrées, such as the Cajun-fried rabbit with tasso cream and braised vegetables

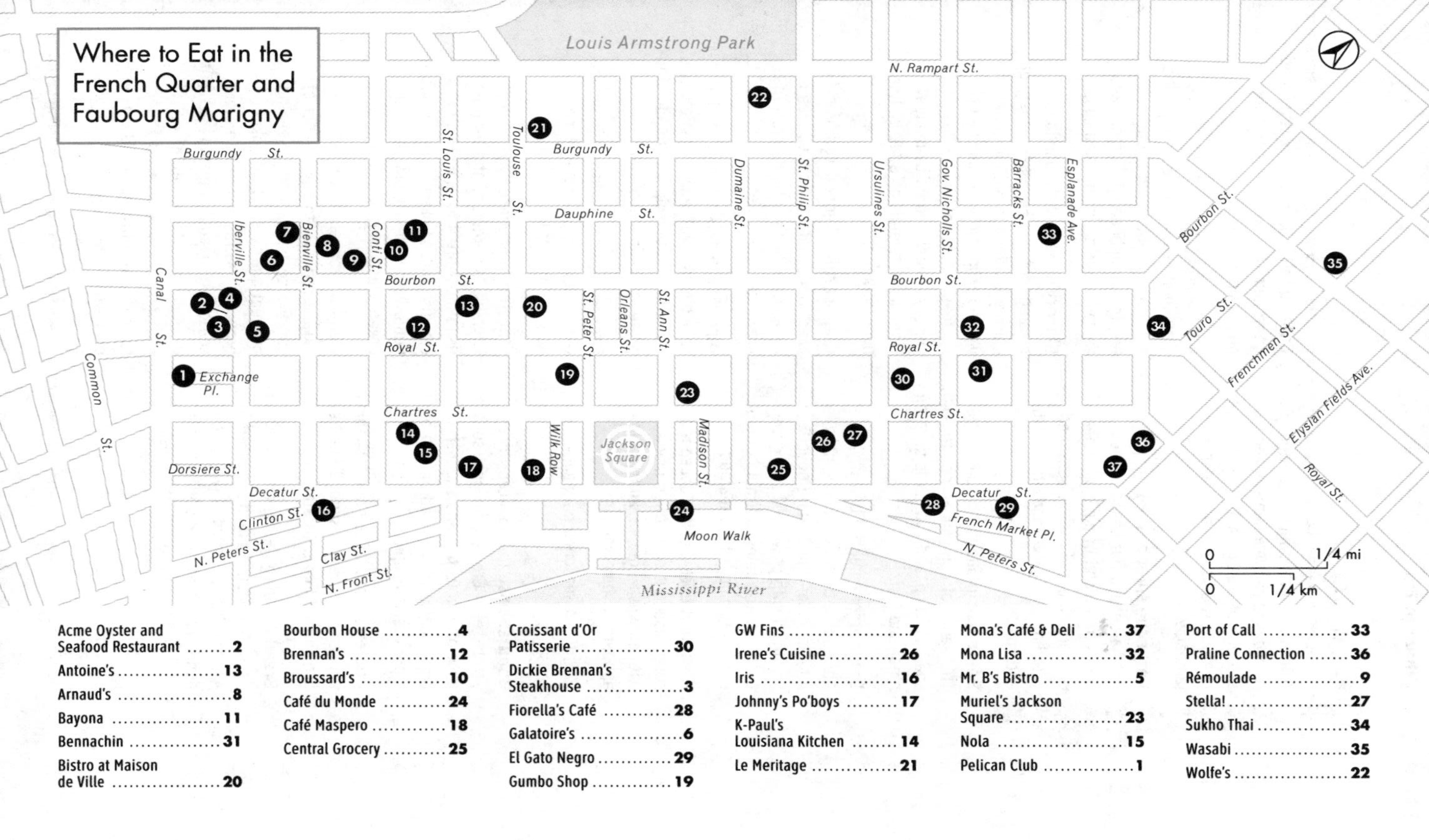

Acme Oyster and Seafood Restaurant 2
Antoine's 13
Arnaud's 8
Bayona 11
Bennachin 31
Bistro at Maison de Ville 20
Bourbon House 4
Brennan's 12
Broussard's 10
Café du Monde 24
Café Maspero 18
Central Grocery 25
Croissant d'Or Patisserie 30
Dickie Brennan's Steakhouse 3
Fiorella's Café 28
Galatoire's 6
El Gato Negro 29
Gumbo Shop 19
GW Fins 7
Irene's Cuisine 26
Iris 16
Johnny's Po'boys 17
K-Paul's Louisiana Kitchen 14
Le Meritage 21
Mona's Café & Deli 37
Mona Lisa 32
Mr. B's Bistro 5
Muriel's Jackson Square 23
Nola 15
Pelican Club 1
Port of Call 33
Praline Connection 36
Rémoulade 9
Stella! 27
Sukho Thai 34
Wasabi 35
Wolfe's 22

CLOSE UP

Food Glossary

Andouille (pronounced ahn-*dooey*). A mildly spiced Acadian smoked sausage of lean pork, it often flavors gumbos, red beans and rice, and jambalayas.

Barbecue shrimp. The shrimp are not barbecued but baked in their shells in a blend of olive oil, butter, or margarine and usually seasoned with bay leaf, garlic, and other herbs and spices.

Béarnaise (pronounced bare-*nayz*). This sauce of egg yolk and butter with shallots, wine, and vinegar is used on meat and fish.

Beignet (pronounced ben-*yay*). Although a beignet was originally a rectangular puff of fried dough sprinkled with powdered sugar, the term can also refer to fritters or crullers containing fish or seafood.

Bisque. A thick, heartily seasoned soup, bisque is most often made with crawfish, crab, or shrimp. Cream appears in some versions.

Boudin. A seasoned pork-and-rice sausage.

Bouillabaisse (pronounced *booey*-yah-base). A Creole bouillabaisse is a stew of various fish and shellfish in a broth seasoned with saffron and often more-assertive spices.

Boulette (pronounced *boo*-let). This is minced, chopped, or pureed meat or fish shaped into balls and fried.

Bread pudding. In the traditional version, stale French bread is soaked in a custard mix, combined with raisins, and baked, then served with a hot sugary sauce flavored with whiskey or rum.

Café au lait. This hot drink is a blend, often half and half, of strong coffee and scalded milk.

Café brûlot (pronounced broo-*loh*). Cinnamon, lemon, clove, orange, and sugar are steeped with strong coffee, then flambéed with brandy and served in special pedestaled cups.

Chicory coffee. The ground and roasted root of a European variety of chicory is added to ground coffee in varying proportions. Originally used for reasons of economy, coffee with chicory is now favored by many New Orleanians. It lends an added bitterness to the taste.

Crème brûlée (pronounced broo-*lay*). Literally, this means "burned cream." It's a custard with a brittle crust of browned sugar.

Dirty rice. In this cousin of jambalaya, bits of meat, such as giblets or sausage, and seasonings are added to white rice before cooking.

Dressed. A po'boy "dressed" contains lettuce, tomato, pickles, and mayonnaise or mustard.

Étouffée (pronounced ay-too-*fay*). Literally, "smothered," the term is used most often for a thick stew of crawfish tails cooked in a roux-based liquid with crawfish, fat, garlic, and green seasonings.

Gumbo. From an African word for okra, it can refer to any number of stewlike soups made with seafood or meat and flavored with okra or ground sassafras and myriad other seasonings. Frequent main ingredients are combinations of shrimp, oysters, crab, chicken, andouille, duck, and turkey. A definitive gumbo is served over white rice.

Jambalaya (pronounced jam-buh-*lie*-uh). Rice is the indispensable ingredient in this relative of Spain's paella. The rice is cooked with a mix of diced meat and seafood in tomato and other seasonings. Shrimp and ham make frequent appearances, as do sausage, green pepper, and celery.

Meunière (pronounced muhn-*yehr*). This method of preparing fish or soft-shell crab entails dusting it with seasoned flour, sautéing it in brown butter, and using the butter with lemon juice as a sauce. Some restaurants add a dash of Worcestershire sauce.

Mirliton (pronounced merl-i-*tawn*). A pale-green member of the squash family, a mirliton is usually identified as a vegetable pear or chayote. The standard preparation is to scrape the pulp from halved mirlitons, fill them with shrimp and seasoned bread crumbs, and bake them.

Muffuletta. The city's southern Italian grocers created this round-loaf sandwich traditionally filled with ham, salami, mozzarella, and a layer of chopped, marinated green olives. Muffulettas are sold whole and in halves or quarters.

Oysters Bienville (pronounced byen-*veel*). In this dish, oysters are lightly baked in their shells under a cream sauce flavored with bits of shrimp, mushroom, and green seasonings. Some chefs also use garlic or mustard.

Oysters en brochette (pronounced awn-bro-*shet*). Whole oysters and bits of bacon are dusted with seasoned flour, skewered, and deep-fried. Traditionally, they're served on toast with lemon and brown butter.

Oysters Rockefeller. This dish, baked oysters on the half shell in a sauce of pureed aromatic greens laced with anise liqueur, was created at Antoine's, which keeps its recipe a secret. Most other restaurants make do with spinach.

Panéed veal (pronounced pan-*aid*). Breaded veal cutlets are sautéed in butter.

Po'boy. A hefty sandwich, the po'boy is made with the local French bread and any number of fillings: roast beef, fried shrimp, oysters, ham, meatballs in tomato sauce, and cheese are common. A po'boy "dressed" contains lettuce, tomato, pickles, and mayonnaise or mustard.

Praline (pronounced *prah*-leen). A sweet patty-shaped confection made of pecans, brown sugar, butter, and vanilla.

Ravigote (pronounced rah-vee-*gote*). In Creole usage, this is a piquant mayonnaise—usually made with capers—used to moisten blue crabmeat.

Rémoulade (pronounced ray-moo-*lahd*). The classic Creole rémoulade is a brick-red whipped mixture of olive oil with mustard, scallions, cayenne, lemon, paprika, and parsley. It's served on cold peeled shrimp or lumps of back-fin crabmeat.

Souffléed potatoes. These thin, hollow puffs of deep-fried potato are produced by two fryings at different temperatures.

Tasso (pronounced *tah*-so). Acadian cooks developed this lean, intensely seasoned ham. It's used sparingly to flavor sauces and gumbos.

and the flame-grilled swordfish, win over even the most skeptical diners. The bar menu is reason enough to check this place out. The favorite dessert, chocolate doberge, will brighten your whole day, and don't miss the bacon-smoked foie gras pan perdu appetizer. ✉ *701 Convention Center Blvd., CBD* ☎ *504/525–7555* 🌐 *www.7onfulton.com* ✍ *Reservations essential* ▭ *AE, MC, V.*

$$$ SOUTHERN Fodor's Choice ★ **August.** If the Gilded Age is long gone, someone forgot to tell the folks at August, whose main dining room shimmers with masses of chandelier prisms, thick brocade fabrics, and glossy woods. Service is anything but stuffy, however, and chef John Besh's modern technique adorns every plate. Nothing is mundane here: handmade gnocchi with blue crab and winter truffle shares menu space with slow-cooked pork belly and butter-poached main lobster with black truffles. Expect the unexpected—like slow-roasted Kobe beef short ribs with Jerusalem artichokes. The sommelier is happy to confer with you on the surprisingly affordable wine list. ✉ *301 Tchoupitoulas St., CBD* ☎ *504/299–9777* 🌐 *www.restaurantaugust.com* ✍ *Reservations essential* ▭ *AE, MC, V* ⏲ *No lunch Sat.–Thurs.*

$$ CAJUN **Bon Ton Café.** The Bon Ton's opening in 1953 marked the first appearance of a significant Cajun restaurant in New Orleans, and its crawfish dishes, gumbo, jambalaya, and oyster omelet have retained their strong following ever since. The bustle in the dining room peaks at lunchtime on weekdays, when businesspeople from nearby offices come in droves for baked eggplant with shrimp, fried catfish, turtle soup, and warm, sugary bread pudding. If you can sacrifice the afternoon for pleasure, try a Rum Ramsey cocktail. The veteran servers are knowledgeable and fleet-footed. ✉ *401 Magazine St., CBD* ☎ *504/524–3386* 🌐 *www.thebontoncafe.com* ▭ *AE, DC, MC, V* ⏲ *Closed weekends.*

$$ CAJUN **Cochon.** Chef-owned restaurants are common in New Orleans, but this one builds on the owner's family heritage. Chef Donald Link prepares Cajun dishes he learned to cook at his grandfather's knee. The interior may be a bit too rustic and noisy for some patrons, but the food will make up for it. Try the fried boudin with pickled peppers—trust us on this one. Then move on to black-eyed pea and pork gumbo, and a hearty Louisiana cochon (pork) with turnips, cracklings, and cabbage. If you want to experience true regional cuisine, this is the place. ✉ *930 Tchoupitoulas St., Warehouse* ☎ *504/588–2123* 🌐 *www.cochon.com* ✍ *Reservations not accepted* ▭ *AE, MC, V.*

$$$ SOUTHERN Fodor's Choice ★ **Cuvée.** With a name that refers to a blend of wines, this restaurant divides its inspirations between France's Champagne region and south Louisiana. The menu rests on a firm French foundation, but the flavors are often distinctively New Orleans. Talented chef Robert Iacovone sometimes seems unstoppable, like when he fashions the city's most elegant cane syrup and smoked duck breast paired with walnut and blue cheese risotto, or when he presents his pork tenderloin with juniper and Gruyère apple strudel. Main courses are gutsy and inspired, as is the wine list. The space is defined by exposed brick and gilt-framed paintings. ✉ *322 Magazine St., CBD* ☎ *504/587–9001* 🌐 *www.restaurantcuvee.com* ✍ *Reservations essential* ▭ *AE, DC, MC, V* ⏲ *Closed Sun. No lunch Mon., Tues., and Fri.*

$$$ ITALIAN ✕ **Drago's.** For 40 years the Cvitanovich family restaurant has been a fixture in Metairie, just a short drive from downtown New Orleans. When it was revealed the family would open a second location inside the Hilton Riverside hotel, locals knew to expect good things. The Italian dishes and oyster-heavy menu that has satisfied the masses for decades are duplicated at the hotel, but on a larger scale. Best known for its charbroiled oysters, authentic Italian pasta recipes, live Maine lobster dishes, and fried seafood entrées, Drago's is a true local institution. Families love the place—especially because of the kids' menu—and the warm apple cobbler is the sweet stuff legends are made of. ✉ *2 Poydras St., CBD* ☎ *504/584–3911* 🌐 *www.dragosrestaurant.com* ▭ *AE, D, DC, MC, V* ⊙ *Closed Sun.*

$$$ ITALIAN ✕ **Eleven 79.** If the Rat Pack boys were alive today, they'd grab a corner table in this tiny, softly lighted Italian eatery, where garlic rules and red wine is revered. Dean Martin music adds a soft ambience, while candlelit tables serve as the perfect platform for tender pastas bathed in perfectly seasoned sauces. Start every meal with the house Italian salad, and be good to yourself with *panéed* (breaded) veal with asparagus, buffalo mozzarella, roasted red peppers, and lemon sauce. Every dish is full of flavor, and the chef has an even hand with seasonings. There is no such thing as a bad meal at Eleven 79. ✉ *1179 Annunciation St., Warehouse District* ☎ *504/229–1179* ✍ *Reservations essential* ▭ *AE, D, DC, MC, V* ⊙ *No lunch.*

$$$ AMERICAN ✕ **Emeril's.** Celebrity-chef Emeril Lagasse's urban-chic flagship restaurant is always jammed. A wood ceiling in a basket-weave pattern muffles much of the clatter and chatter. The ambitious menu gives equal emphasis to Creole and modern American cooking—try the barbecue shrimp here for one of the darkest, richest versions of the local specialty. Desserts, such as the renowned banana cream pie, verge on the gargantuan. Service is meticulous, and the wine list's depth and range should soothe even the most persnickety imbiber. ✉ *800 Tchoupitoulas St., Warehouse District* ☎ *504/528–9393* 🌐 *www.emerils.com* ✍ *Reservations essential* ▭ *AE, D, DC, MC, V* ⊙ *No lunch weekends.*

$$$ CREOLE ✕ **Emeril's Delmonico.** Chef Emeril Lagasse bought the traditional, unpretentious, century-old Delmonico and converted it into a large, extravagantly appointed restaurant with the most ambitious revamping of classic Creole dishes in town. The high-ceiling dining spaces are swathed in upholstered walls and superthick window fabrics. Local oyster preparations are a reliable option, as are New Orleans–style barbecue shrimp, crab cakes, and sautéed fish meunière. Prime dry-aged steaks with traditional sauces have emerged as a specialty in recent years, but the menu gets more ambitious by the month. Plush and polish are the bywords here, and the service can be exemplary. ✉ *1300 St. Charles Ave., CBD* ☎ *504/525–4937* 🌐 *www.emerils.com* ✍ *Reservations essential* ▭ *AE, D, DC, MC, V* ⊙ *No lunch.*

$$ SOUTHERN ✕ **Grand Isle.** This Louisiana fish camp–theme restaurant gave a significant boost to the emerging entertainment district surrounding the Fulton Street corridor and Harrah's Casino. All of the seafood served here comes directly off the coast of Grand Isle, Louisiana, and everything is fresh (never frozen). The rustic interior, reminiscent of 1920s and '30s

CLOSE UP

10 Places to Eat for Under $10

Angeli on Decatur. The huge windows are perfect for watching the parade of Decatur Street's pierced, tattooed, and woozy nightlife while you nosh on pizza, burgers, or Middle Eastern appetizers. The kitchen stays open late on weekends. ✉ *1141 Decatur St., French Quarter* ☎ *504/566-0077.*

Balcony Bar & Café. The kitchen at this popular Uptown bar stays open late—sometimes until 4 AM on weekends. The menu includes burgers, pizza, and various fried objects; a stiff margarita washes it down. ✉ *3201 Magazine St., Uptown* ☎ *504/895-1600.*

Café du Monde. At the end of some nights, only a mouthful of sugary fried dough will do. Café du Monde is ready with beignets and coffee or hot chocolate. It prides itself on never closing. ✉ *800 Decatur St., French Quarter* ☎ *504/525-4544.*

Clover Grill. As much a scene as a restaurant, this classic diner in the heart of the Quarter's gay section serves up waffles, omelets, and hamburgers grilled under abandoned hubcaps to devoted locals and the post-disco set. ✉ *900 Bourbon St., French Quarter* ☎ *504/598-1010.*

The Joint. While you may be hard-pressed to find good barbecue in New Orleans, the tiny nondescript "joint" is the exception to the rule. The only item higher than $10 is a rack of ribs for $10.95. Try the signature beer or lemonade with hot sauce. Really. ✉ *801 Poland Ave., Bywater* ☎ *504/949-3232.*

Juan's Flying Burrito. You may have to wait a half hour for a table, but the jerk chicken burritos and spicy shrimp quesadillas are worth it. The margaritas are powerful. ✉ *4724 S. Carrollton Ave., Mid-City* ☎ *504/486-9950* ✉ *2018 Magazine St., Uptown* ☎ *504/569-0000..*

La Peniche. A cult classic and a short stroll from the music clubs of Frenchmen Street, La Peniche is the post-party kitchen of choice among musicians and various hipsters. Pancakes, omelets, and burgers, along with local specialties like red beans and rice, are the standard fare. It's closed Tuesday night through Thursday morning. ✉ *1940 Dauphine St., Faubourg Marigny* ☎ *504/943-1460.*

Mimi's. This hip, friendly bar serves up a delicious menu of hot and cold tapas such as mushroom Manchego toast, grilled pork tenderloin with guava sauce, and salmon with saffron aioli. Nosh on a cheese and olive plate or serrano ham and chorizo plate until 2 AM on weekdays and 4 AM on weekends. ✉ *2601 Royal St., Bywater* ☎ *504/942-0690.*

Parkway Bakery & Tavern. Whether it's a sloppy, fully dressed roast beef po'boy; a thick, oversize burger; or a hot dog with perfectly seasoned chili, it all comes in under 10 bucks. Half of the fun here is perusing the 20th-century New Orleans memorabilia on the walls. ✉ *538 N. Hagan St., Mid-City* ☎ *504/482-3047.*

Trolley Stop Cafe. The exterior of this former gas station has been artfully transformed into a replica of a New Orleans streetcar. Inside, the lengthy menu features every conceivable breakfast dish and a full selection of sandwiches, salads, and soups. ✉ *1923 St. Charles Ave., Garden District* ☎ *504/523-0090.*

Louisiana, is the perfect backdrop for turtle stew, spicy boiled shrimp, lobster with roasted shrimp sauce, fresh gulf fish, and a lemon icebox pie that will make you fall in love with New Orleans all over again. The place is generally packed, but it's worth the wait (which also gives you an excuse to spend some time at the elegant mahogany bar). ✉*575 Convention Center Blvd., CBD* ☎*504/520–8530* 🌐*www.grandislerestaurant.com* ✍*Reservations not accepted* ▭*AE, D, DC, MC, V.*

$$$ AMERICAN Fodor's Choice ★ ✕**The Grill Room.** The British furnishings span several centuries in these dazzling dining spaces, with body-hugging chairs and canvases depicting aspects of upper-class England. The equally dazzling menus change frequently, and are filled with a smart combination of Louisiana specialties and Continental delicacies. The international flavors are exemplified by a grilled foie gras and lobster appetizer that precedes a panko-crusted veal chop or a wild Maryland striped bass. Just when you think the best is behind, out comes the city's best cheese plate, followed by soothing cordials. The wine cellar, with its collection of vintage Bordeaux reds, remains awesome. A jacket is required. ✉ *Windsor Court Hotel, 2nd level, 300 Gravier St., CBD* ☎*504/522–1992* 🌐*www.windsorcourthotel.com* ✍*Reservations essential* ▭*AE, D, DC, MC, V.*

$$ SOUTHERN ✕**Herbsaint.** Upscale food and moderate prices are among Herbsaint's assets. Chef Donald Link turns out food that sparkles with robust flavors and top-grade ingredients. Small plates and side dishes such as charcuterie, a knock-'em-dead shrimp bisque, house-made pasta, and cheese- or nut-studded salads are mainstays. Don't overlook the rich and flavorful Louisiana cochon with turnips, cabbage, and cracklins. Also irresistible: smoked beef brisket with horseradish potato salad. For dessert, the layered spice cake with figs and pecans will ensure future return trips. The plates provide most of the color in the lighthearted, often noisy, rooms. The wine list is expertly compiled and reasonably priced. ✉*701 St. Charles Ave., CBD* ☎*504/524–4114* 🌐*www.herbsaint.com* ✍*Reservations essential* ▭*AE, D, DC, MC, V* ⏲*Closed Sun. No lunch Sat.*

$$ SOUTHERN ✕**Lüke.** Chef John Besh's Lüke is a love letter to the old brasseries that once reigned in New Orleans; dine here, and you'll feel as if you've traveled back to a time when rattan bistro chairs, blackboard specials, and newspaper racks were de rigueur. Start your meal with a Sazerac (a local cocktail of whiskey, bitters, and absinthe) or mint julep, and work your way into rabbit and duck liver pâté, followed by a fried oyster, bacon, and avocado salad. French and Louisiana influences produce distinctive entrées including jumbo Louisiana shrimp, vanilla-scented duck with lavender honey, and a pressed sandwich of whole roast cochon de lait that will remind you why New Orleans is so revered as a culinary destination. ✉*333 St. Charles Ave., CBD* ☎*504/378–2840* 🌐*www.lukeneworleans.com* ▭*AE, D, DC, MC, V.*

$$$ SOUTHERN ✕**MiLa.** Chefs Slade Rushing and Allison Vines-Rushing, from Mississippi and Louisiana, respectively, merged the names and cuisines of their home states to produce MiLa. The restaurant defines a new Southern elegance with its comfy-chic atmosphere and its culinary tributes to each chef's childhood memories of Southern cooking. The results are dishes like sweet tea–brined rotisserie duck and hickory-smoked lamb

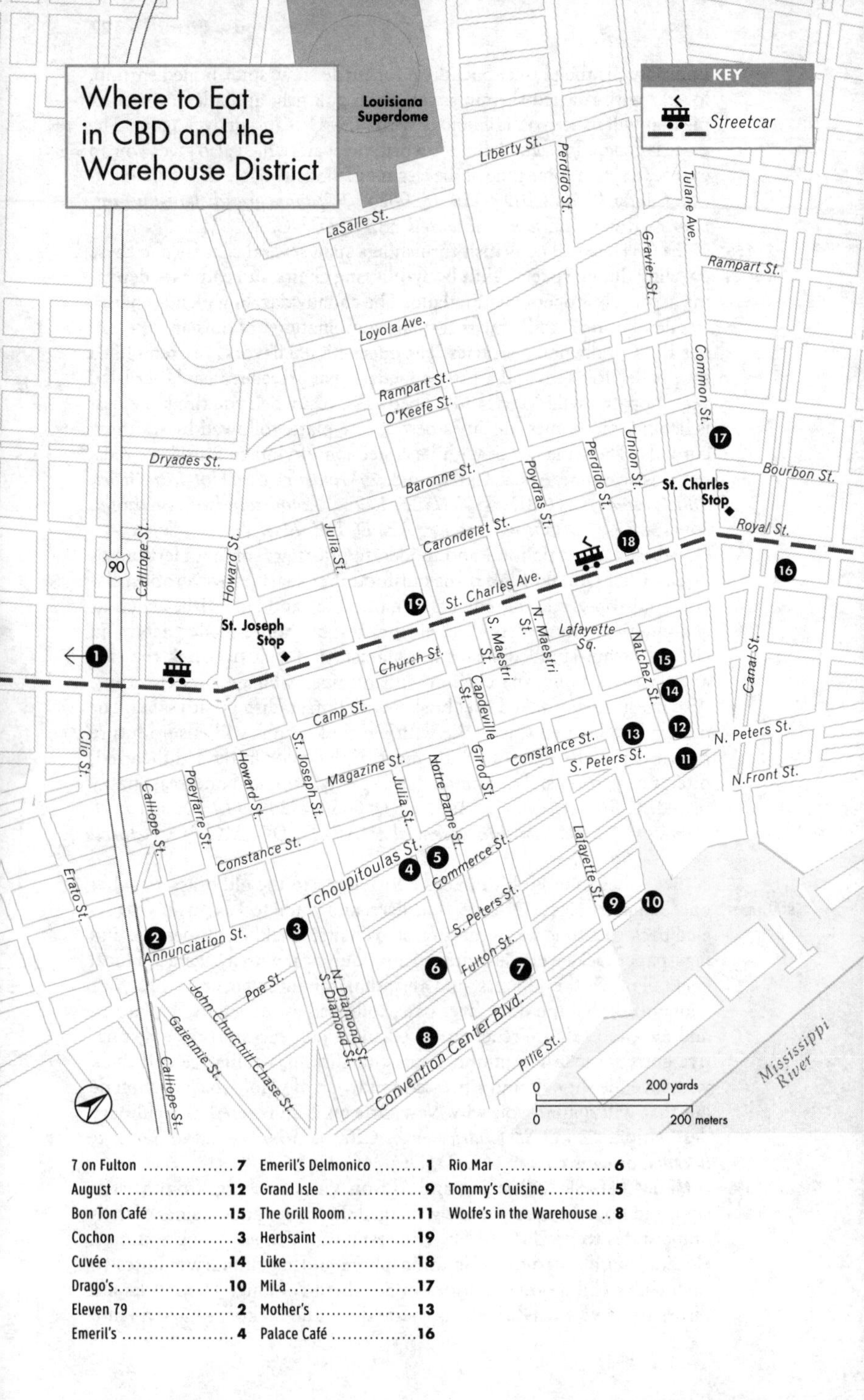

Where to Eat in CBD and the Warehouse District
KEY
Streetcar
Louisiana Superdome
St. Charles Stop
St. Joseph Stop
Liberty St.
Perdido St.
Tulane Ave.
LaSalle St.
Gravier St.
Rampart St.
Loyola Ave.
Common St.
Rampart St.
O'Keefe St.
Dryades St.
Baronne St.
Poydras St.
Perdido St.
Union St.
Bourbon St.
Royal St.
Carondelet St.
Julia St.
Howard St.
Calliope St.
90
St. Charles Ave.
S. Maestri St.
N. Maestri St.
Lafayette Sq.
Natchez St.
Canal St.
Church St.
Capdeville St.
Camp St.
N. Peters St.
N.Front St.
S. Peters St.
Constance St.
Girod St.
Notre Dame St.
Magazine St.
St. Joseph St.
Julia St.
Howard St.
Poeyfarre St.
Calliope St.
Clio St.
Erato St.
Constance St.
Tchoupitoulas St.
Commerce St.
Lafayette St.
S. Peters St.
Annunciation St.
Fulton St.
Poe St.
John Churchill Chase St.
Gaiennie St.
N. Diamond St.
S. Diamond St.
Convention Center Blvd.
Pilie St.
Calliope St.
Mississippi River
0
200 yards
0
200 meters
7 on Fulton 7
August 12
Bon Ton Café 15
Cochon 3
Cuvée 14
Drago's 10
Eleven 79 2
Emeril's 4
Emeril's Delmonico 1
Grand Isle 9
The Grill Room 11
Herbsaint 19
Lüke 18
MiLa 17
Mother's 13
Palace Café 16
Rio Mar 6
Tommy's Cuisine 5
Wolfe's in the Warehouse .. 8

rack. For the true insider experience, take a seat at the bar and try the hot deer sausage and cheddar biscuits. All of the restaurant's produce comes from a working farm in Mount Hermon, Louisiana. ✉*817 Common St., CBD* ☎*504/412–2580* 🌐*www.milaneworleans.com* ▭*AE, D, DC, MC, V* ⊙*No lunch weekends.*

$ CAFE ✕**Mother's.** Tourists line up for down-home eats at this island of blue-collar sincerity amid downtown's glittery hotels. Mother's dispenses delicious baked ham and roast beef po'boys (ask for "debris" on the beef sandwich and the bread will be slathered with meat juices and shreds of meat), home-style biscuits and jambalaya, and a very good chicken gumbo in a couple of bare-bones—yet charming—dining rooms. Breakfast service is a bit slow, but that doesn't seem to repel the hordes fighting for seats at peak mealtimes. Service is cafeteria style, with a counter or two augmenting the tables. ✉*401 Poydras St., CBD* ☎*504/523–9656* 🌐*www.mothersrestaurant.net* ✍*Reservations not accepted* ▭*AE, MC, V.*

$$ CREOLE ✕**Palace Café.** Crafted from what used to be New Orleans's oldest music store, this Dickie Brennan stalwart is a convivial spot to try some of the more imaginative contemporary Creole dishes, such as crabmeat cheesecake, stuffed rabbit, and seafood pastas. Desserts, especially the white-chocolate bread pudding and the house-made ice creams, are luscious. Drugstore-tile floors, stained cherrywood booths, and soothing beige walls set the mood. The wraparound mezzanine is lined with a large mural, populated by the city's famous musicians. Take a seat at the outdoor sidewalk café for small plates and wine. The Sunday jazz brunch is New Orleans all the way. ✉*605 Canal St., CBD* ☎*504/523–1661* 🌐*www.palacecafe.com* ✍*Reservations essential* ▭*AE, D, DC, MC, V.*

$$ SEAFOOD ✕**Rio Mar.** Chef Adolfo Garcia's largely seafood menu reflects his Spanish style and Panamanian heritage. Each of his several ceviches has its own distinct marinade and combination of superfresh seafood. For entrées, try the stewlike zarzuela of seafood, with chunks of fish and shellfish in a peppery red broth. It's all tapas at lunch, when you tick off your selections on a small menu card: salty Spanish ham, roasted peppers, Manchego cheese, marinated seafood. The dining room's low ceiling and tiled floor don't make for great acoustics, but the gold-hue walls with their rustic iron ornamentation would not be out of place in Barcelona. ✉*800 S. Peters St., Warehouse District* ☎*504/525–3474* 🌐*www.riomarseafood.com* ▭*AE, D, DC, MC, V* ⊙*Closed Sun. No lunch Sat.*

$$ ITALIAN ✕**Tommy's Cuisine.** The dining rooms here are clubby and festive, and the crowd is always interesting. Don't overlook the *panéed* oysters and grilled shrimp appetizer; the lamb chops blanketed with a rosemary port wine demi-glace; or the roasted half chicken saturated with rosemary and garlic. Service is gentlemanly, the chef's dinner specials are imaginative, and the wines span all of Italy. After dinner, head next door to the cushy Tommy's Wine Bar. ✉*746 Tchoupitoulas St., Warehouse District* ☎*504/581–1103* 🌐*www.tommysneworleans.com* ✍*Reservations essential* ▭*AE, D, DC, MC, V* ⊙*No lunch.*

4

$$ AMERICAN ✕ **Wolfe's in the Warehouse.** Chef Tom Wolfe is one of those diligent culinarians whose work is always infused with quality, and whose steady hand with seasonings is apparent in everything he prepares. Wolfe's is located in the Marriott Hotel and serves breakfast, lunch, and dinner. It's a lively spot, with a menu that supports the enthusiastic atmosphere. The best start to any meal are the Parmesan-crusted Louisiana oysters. If you want to know what true Louisiana cooking is about, try the apple wood-smoked bacon–wrapped duck roulade stuffed with roasted sweet pepper, spinach, and house-made Italian duck sausage Oh, and about the vanilla-bean cheesecake with strawberries and fresh cream: just do it. ✉ *859 Convention Center Blvd., Warehouse District* ☎ *504/613–2888* ▭ *AE, D, DC, MC, V.*

GARDEN DISTRICT/UPTOWN

$ THAI ✕ **Basil Leaf.** Familiar Thai standbys—spring rolls, pad thai, chicken-and-coconut soup, and the like—get a new lease on life in the kitchen of chef-proprietor Siam Tiparwat. These expertly prepared traditional dishes are backed up by a slew of thoroughly original creations served in the crisp, simple dining room, which is enlivened by a mural depicting a Buddhist temple. Gently flavored green and red Thai curries, especially those with chicken or shrimp, are prepared with the instinctual talent of a Thai native, as are the firm yet tender dumplings filled with bits of scallop. The sautéed calamari in basil–red curry sauce is addictive. ✉ *1438 S. Carrollton Ave., Uptown* ☎ *504/862–9001* ▭ *AE, D, MC, V* ⊙ *No lunch weekends.*

$$$ CREOLE Fodor's Choice ★ ✕ **Brigtsen's.** Chef Frank Brigtsen's fusion of Creole refinement and Acadian earthiness reflects his years as a Paul Prudhomme protégé. His dishes represent some of the best south Louisiana cooking you'll find anywhere. Everything is fresh and filled with deep, complex tastes. The butternut shrimp bisque defines comfort food. Rabbit and chicken dishes, usually presented in rich sauces and gravies, are full of robust flavor. The roux-based gumbos are thick and intense, and the warm bread pudding is worth every calorie. Trompe l'oeil murals add whimsy to the intimate spaces of this turn-of-the-20th-century frame cottage. Ask for a table on the enclosed front sun porch. ✉ *723 Dante St., Uptown* ☎ *504/861–7610* 🌐 *www.brigtsens.com* ✍ *Reservations essential* ▭ *AE, DC, MC, V* ⊙ *Closed Sun. and Mon. No lunch.*

$ SEAFOOD ✕ **Casamento's.** Tiled in gleaming white and cream-color ceramic, Casamento's has been a haven for Uptown seafood lovers since 1919. Family members still wait tables and staff the immaculate kitchen out back, while a reliable handful of oyster shuckers ensure that plenty of cold ones are available for the standing-room-only oyster bar. Specialties from the diminutive menu include oysters lightly poached in seasoned milk; fried shrimp, trout, and soft-shell-crab platters; and fried oysters, impeccably fresh and greaseless, served between thick slices of white toast. Everything is clean, and nothing is superfluous. Even the houseplants have a just-polished look. ✉ *4330 Magazine St., Uptown* ☎ *504/895–9761* 🌐 *www.casamentosrestaurant.com* ✍ *Reservations not accepted* ▭ *No credit cards* ⊙ *Closed Sun., Mon., and early June–late Aug.*

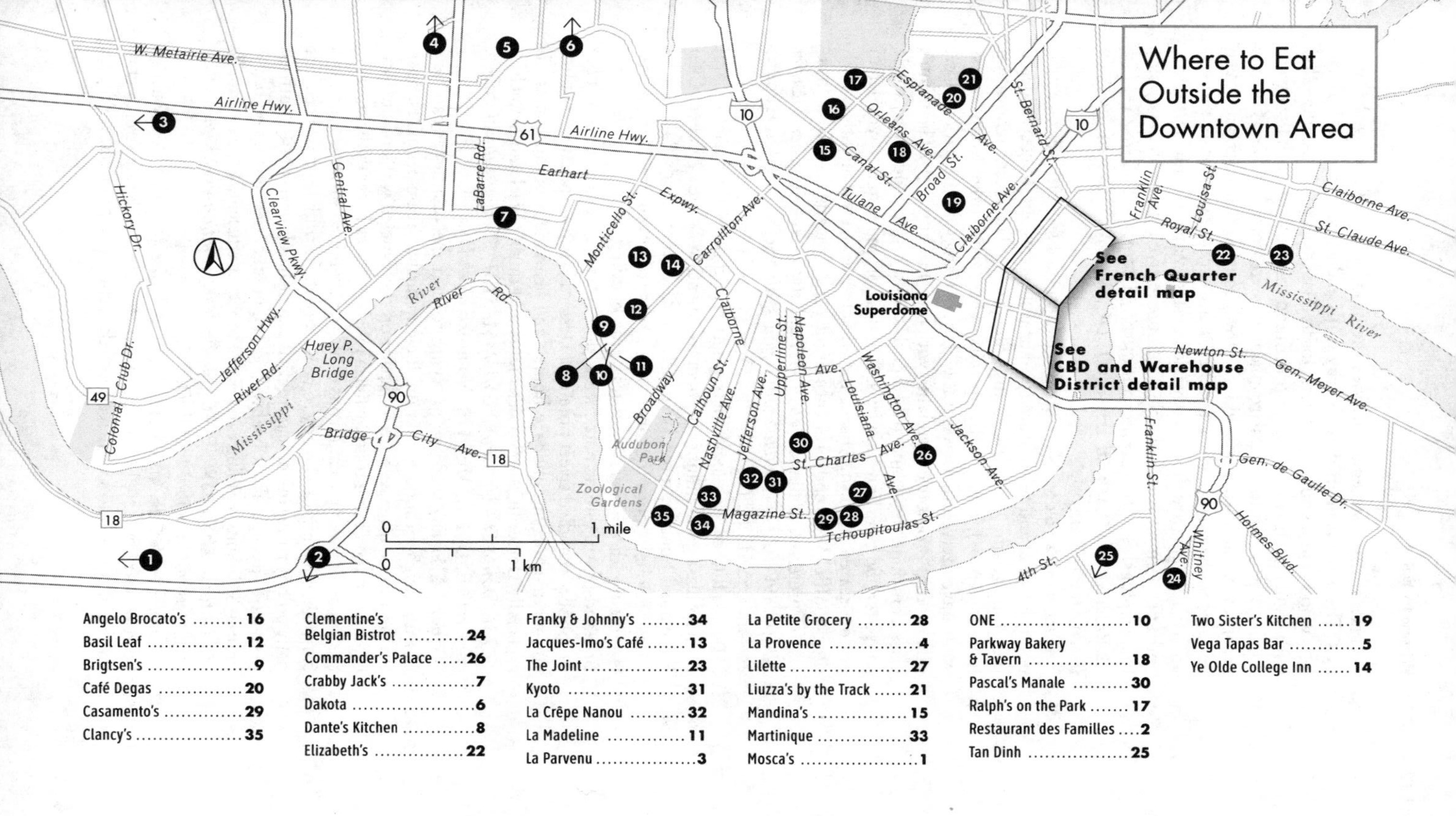

Angelo Brocato's **16**	Clementine's Belgian Bistrot **24**	Franky & Johnny's **34**	La Petite Grocery **28**	ONE **10**	Two Sister's Kitchen **19**
Basil Leaf **12**	Commander's Palace **26**	Jacques-Imo's Café **13**	La Provence **4**	Parkway Bakery & Tavern **18**	Vega Tapas Bar **5**
Brigtsen's **9**	Crabby Jack's **7**	The Joint **23**	Lilette **27**	Pascal's Manale **30**	Ye Olde College Inn **14**
Café Degas **20**	Dakota **6**	Kyoto **31**	Liuzza's by the Track **21**	Ralph's on the Park **17**	
Casamento's **29**	Dante's Kitchen **8**	La Crêpe Nanou **32**	Mandina's **15**	Restaurant des Familles **2**	
Clancy's **35**	Elizabeth's **22**	La Madeline **11**	Martinique **33**	Tan Dinh **25**	
		La Parvenu **3**	Mosca's **1**		

$$ SOUTHERN ✕ **Clancy's.** Understatement defines the mood at locally beloved Clancy's. The decor is neutral, with gray walls and a few ceiling fans above bentwood chairs and white linen cloths. The small bar is usually filled with regulars who know one another (and tourists who wish they were regulars). Most of the dishes are imaginative treatments of New Orleans favorites. Some specialties, like the fresh sautéed fish in cream sauce flavored with crawfish stock and herbs, are exceptional. Other signs of an inventive chef are the expertly fried oysters matched with warm Brie, and a peppermint-ice-cream pie. On more festive nights you may yearn for earplugs. ✉ *6100 Annunciation St., Uptown* ☎ *504/895–1111* *Reservations essential* *AE, D, DC, MC, V* *Closed Sun. No lunch Mon.–Wed.*

$$$ CREOLE Fodor's Choice ★ ✕ **Commander's Palace.** No restaurant captures New Orleans's gastronomic heritage and celebratory spirit as well as this one, long considered the grande dame of New Orleans's fine dining. The recent renovation has added new life, especially upstairs, where the Garden Room's glass walls have marvelous views of the giant oak trees on the patio below; other rooms promote conviviality with their bright pastels. The menu's classics include sugarcane-grilled pork chops; a spicy and meaty turtle soup; terrific bourbon-lacquered Mississippi quail; and a wonderful griddle-seared gulf fish. Among the addictive desserts is the bread-pudding soufflé. Weekend brunches are a New Orleans tradition. Jackets are preferred at dinner. ✉ *1403 Washington Ave., Garden District* ☎ *504/899–8221* *www.commanderspalace.com* *Reservations essential* *AE, D, DC, MC, V.*

$$ SOUTHERN ✕ **Dante's Kitchen.** Ask local chefs where they dine on their day off, and chances are a good number of them will mention Dante's Kitchen. Chef Emmanuel Loubier, a nine-year veteran of Commander's Palace, prepares seasonal menus for those with a sense of adventure. Duck breast is served with cranberry and foie gras pudding, pork is paired with Brie-and-pastrami mac and cheese, and every visit demands a helping of root beer candied sweet potatoes. Desserts, such as the sweet-potato-and-white-chocolate pie, are homey and hearty. An outdoor patio is especially welcoming on cooler nights and during weekend brunches. ✉ *736 Dante St., Uptown* ☎ *504/861–3121* *www.danteskitchen.com* *AE, D, DC, MC, V* *No lunch weekdays.*

$ SEAFOOD ✕ **Franky & Johnny's.** If you're trying to find the quintessential New Orleans neighborhood restaurant, look no further. Team pennants, posters, and football jerseys vie for space on the paneled walls of the low-ceiling bar and dining room, while a jukebox blares beneath them. From the kitchen's steaming cauldrons come freshly boiled shrimp, crabs, and crawfish, piled high and ready to be washed down with ice-cold beer. The daily po'boy roster might feature fried crawfish tails or oysters, meatballs in tomato sauce, or roast beef with gravy, but the fried-shrimp po'boy is Franky & Johnny's calling card. Table service is efficient. ✉ *321 Arabella St., Uptown* ☎ *504/899–9146* *www.frankyandjohnnys.com* *Reservations not accepted* *AE, D, MC, V.*

$$ CAJUN ✕ **Jacques-Imo's Cafe.** Oak Street might look like any other sleepy urban thoroughfare by day, but once the sun sets, the half-block stretch containing Jacques-Imo's Cafe feels like the center of the universe. Prepare

for lengthy, but festive waits in the crowded bar for a table in the boisterous, swamp-theme dining rooms (fortunately, the bartenders are skilled). The modest-looking but innovative food is worth it: deep-fried roast beef po'boys, alligator sausage cheesecake, Cajun bouillabaisse, and smothered rabbit over grits are among the excellent only-at-Jacques-Imo's specialties. All main courses come with salad and corn muffins. Reservations are accepted for parties of five or more. ✉*8324 Oak St., Uptown* ☎*504/861–0886* ▭*AE, D, DC, MC, V* ⊗*Closed Sun. No lunch.*

$ JAPANESE ✕ **Kyoto.** Part of a three-block commercial pocket of residential Uptown, Kyoto is as much a neighborhood restaurant as it is a destination for fresh fish and slightly Americanized sushi preparations. Behind the sushi bar in the front room, sushi chefs oversee the creation of off-menu rolls (the Steve Roll contains tuna, snow crab, salmon, and avocado); ask the chefs what special rolls are available. The tuna *tataki,* perhaps Kyoto's most frequently ordered item, is a masterpiece of ruby-red tuna, avocado, and a soy sauce tarted up with lime juice. Full of wooden tables and college students, the two dining rooms are bright and relaxed. ✉*4920 Prytania St., Uptown* ☎*504/891–3644* ▭*AE, D, MC, V* ⊗*Closed Sun.*

4

$ FRENCH ✕ **La Crêpe Nanou.** French chic for the budget-minded is the style in this welcoming little neighborhood bistro, where, during peak hours, there might be a half-hour wait for a table. Left Bank Paris is evoked by the woven café chairs out on the sidewalk and awnings that resemble metro-station architecture. The Gallic focus is evident in the filet mignon, which is served with one of several classic French sauces. Other reliable standbys are the pâté maison, Louisiana crawfish crepes in lobster sauce, and lavish dessert crepes. The best are the coffee ice cream crepes with chestnut cream, flamed with rum. Space is a little tight in the oddly configured dining areas, but the whimsical paintings and profuse greenery combine to create an inviting room. ✉*1410 Robert St., Uptown* ☎*504/899–2670* 🌐*www.lacrepenanou.com* *Reservations not accepted* ▭*AE, DC, MC, V* ⊗*No lunch. Closed Sun.*

$ CAFE ✕ **La Madeleine.** The lines are ever present in this French-theme bakery-café, which is part of a chain. The huge selection of pastries includes napoleons, cheesecakes, and éclairs, as well as brioches and breads from the wood-burning oven. Salads, hearty soups (the tomato basil is fantastic), overstuffed sandwiches, and light entrées are also available. Surprisingly, the kitchen excels with pasta dishes. It closes at 9 PM daily. ✉*601 S. Carrollton Ave., Uptown* ☎*504/861–8662* 🌐*www.lamadeleine.com* ▭*AE, D, MC, V.*

$$ AMERICAN ✕ **La Petite Grocery.** Flower shops often morph into intimate fine-dining establishments in New Orleans. This one, in soft creams and reds with just-bright-enough lighting and a sturdy, mahogany bar, has caught on in a big way with the locals. Chef-owner Anton Schulte draws on contemporary American tastes, using Louisiana raw materials when he can. A seemingly ordinary pan-roasted chicken is enlivened with mushroom bread pudding, while a braised lamb shank is served over stone-ground grits with grilled red onions and roasted peppers. Rich, sticky sauces in the French tradition are a major specialty—few dishes

are without one. ✉4238 *Magazine St., Uptown* ☎*504/891–3377* 🌐*www.lapetitegrocery.com* *Reservations essential* ▭*AE, MC, V* ⏲*Closed Sun. and Mon.*

$$ AMERICAN ✕ **Lilette.** Proprietor-chef John Harris uses New Orleans and French culinary traditions as springboards for Lilette's inspired dishes. Look for pan-roasted Alaskan cod with mushrooms and roasted potatoes, or roasted Muscovy breast of duck with creamed potatoes and fennel. For dessert, the goat cheese quenelles with lavender honey are as light as sorbet but more satisfying. The thoughtful wine list is boutique oriented, and the unique cocktail selection holds even more surprises. Framed mirrors hang along the maroon walls of the intimate front dining room–cum–bar. A few more tables fill out a second room and patio. ✉*3637 Magazine St., Uptown* ☎*504/895–1636* 🌐*www.liletterestaurant.com* *Reservations essential* ▭*AE, D, DC, MC, V* ⏲*Closed Sun. and Mon.*

$$ CARIBBEAN ✕ **Martinique.** The name suggests more Caribbean influence than is actually present in this one-room restaurant and its tropical courtyard. The French emphasis is Martinique's calling card, shining through in such items as butternut squash bisque, escargot with exotic mushrooms, oven-roasted cane-syrup infused duck breast, braised meat, chèvre, and demi-glace–based sauces. Budget for wine; the irresistible list is continually updated. Dinner menus change every eight weeks. The corner table in Martinique's courtyard is now a legendary marriage-proposal spot. ✉*5908 Magazine St., Uptown* ☎*504/891–8495* 🌐*www.martiniquebistro.com* *Reservations essential* ▭*AE, MC, V* ⏲*Closed Mon. No lunch Tues.–Thurs.*

$$ SOUTHERN Fodor'sChoice ★ ✕ **ONE.** Intimate, neighborhoody, and chic all at once, ONE proves that fine dining and casual elegance are not mutually exclusive. The interior is sleek and sophisticated, while the kitchen is wide open. Even though located as far uptown as you can go, this place is more than worth the trip. Guests can even request a seat at the food bar, where the chef cooks the food before your eyes. Chef Scott Snodgrass and co-owner Lee McCullough are the perfect hosts, and seem to love every minute of it. Typical of Snodgrass's creations are stewed country ribs in a red wine demi-glace, or a grilled beef tenderloin with warm beef shoulder rillettes and Stilton cheese. This is a place to dine slowly and linger over a good brandy. ✉ *8132 Hampson St., Uptown* ☎*504/301–9061* 🌐*www.one-sl.com* ▭*AE, D, DC, MC, V* ⏲*Closed Sun. No lunch Mon.–Wed. and Sat.*

$$ ITALIAN ✕ **Pascal's Manale.** This restaurant is closely identified with a regional anomaly: barbecue shrimp (which involves neither a barbecue nor barbecue sauce, but is strangely addictive). The original recipe, introduced a half century ago, remains unchanged: jumbo shrimp, still in the shell, are cooked in a buttery pool enhanced with just the right amount of Creole spice and pepper. The rest of the menu is populated mostly by regional seafood and Italian-style creations. Turtle soup, fried eggplant, and raw oysters are good starters. The atmospheric old bar and the two dining rooms were recently restored and refreshed, breathing new life into the venerable eatery. This is true New Orleans dining. Best of all, bartenders mix proper Sazeracs. ✉*1838 Napoleon Ave., Uptown* ☎*504/895–4877*

www.neworleansrestaurants.com/pascalsmanale *Reservations essential* *AE, D, DC, MC, V* *Closed Sun. No lunch Sat.*

MID-CITY

$ CAFE **Angelo Brocato's.** Traditional Sicilian fruit sherbets, spumoni, cannoli, pastries, and candies are the attractions at this quaint little sweetshop, now over a century old. The biscotti, traditional Sicilian desserts, and the lemon and strawberry ices haven't lost their status as local favorites. The shop closes at 10 PM weekdays (except Monday), 10:30 PM weekends. Plan to stand in line and chat with mostly locals. *214 N. Carrollton Ave., Mid-City* *504/488–1465* *www.angelobrocatoicecream.com* *D, MC, V* *Closed Mon.*

4

$ FRENCH **Café Degas.** Dining at Café Degas is like dining at a sidewalk café in Paris, even though the restaurant is completely covered. There's a tree growing through the center of the dining room, and the front windows overlook picturesque Esplanade Avenue. Employees are matter-of-fact, in a relaxing, European way. The regular fare here—pâté, onion soup, steamed mussels, duck in orange sauce, steaks, dessert crepes—is a mixture of French-bistro cooking and what you might find at a countryside inn. Daily specials, such as a perfectly chilled, creamy vichyssoise, are always creative and ingenious. *3127 Esplanade Ave., Mid-City* *504/945–5635* *www.cafedegas.com* *AE, D, DC, MC, V* *Closed Mon. and Tues.*

$ SOUTHERN **Liuzza's by the Track.** Fried-oyster po'boys drenched in garlic butter, milky bowls of sweet-corn-and-crawfish bisque, and grilled Reuben sandwiches with succulent corned beef are some of the reasons you might decide to tolerate the poor ventilation in this barroom near the racetrack and Jazz Fest grounds. The seafood gumbo is always different and always good—thin on body, but heavy on spice. The pièce de résistance here is a barbecue-shrimp po'boy, for which the shrimp are cooked in a bracing lemon-pepper butter with enough garlic to cure a cold. *1518 N. Lopez St., Mid-City* *504/943–8667* *Reservations not accepted* *AE, D, MC, V* *Closed Sun.*

$$ CREOLE **Mandina's.** Although New Orleans boasts many nationally known restaurants, locals here are most attracted to the city's neighborhood corner restaurant. Mandina's has been a fixture on Canal Street for decades, serving just the right combination of expected favorites, including étouffée, jambalaya, po'boys, fried seafood, and perfect pastas. A recent full renovation and expansion have done nothing to dampen locals' love for this place, nor have they diminished the full flavors of the house shrimp rémoulade, crawfish cakes, turtle soup, or tender red beans with Italian sausage. If you are looking for the ideal bar and restaurant to spend a football Sunday, this is your place, complete with flat-screen TVs and the iciest brewskis in town. *3900 Canal St., Mid-City* *504/482–9179* *www.mandinasrestaurant.com* *AE, D, DC, MC, V.*

$ CAFE **Parkway Bakery & Tavern.** Contractor-by-trade Jay Nix resurrected more than just a dilapidated building when he reopened Parkway: he also brought back to life a dormant community spirit. You can find neighbors and regulars from other parts of the city sinking into

Parkway's roast beef and grilled-ham po'boys; some simply wander in for a hot dog and beer at the bar, and to glance around at the New Orleans nostalgia decorating the walls. Local favorite Hubig's fried pies are the only desserts—you can chart the seasons by the available flavors. As it's near the fairgrounds, Parkway jumps during Jazz Fest. ✉*538 Hagan Ave., Mid-City* ☎*504/482–3047* 🌐*www.parkwaybakeryandtavernnola.com* *Reservations not accepted* *AE, D, MC, V* *Closed Tues.*

$$ CREOLE ✕**Ralph's on the Park.** Seasoned restaurateur Ralph Brennan conceived this beautifully renovated historic building to provide a menu that mixes contemporary Creole standbys with innovative twists. The culinary staff excels with full-flavored seafood dishes like crispy skin-on redfish with crab butter sauce, or pecan-crusted puppy drum with Creole mustard and caper meunière sauce. By all means, try the wild mushroom ravioli appetizer with Boursin cheese. For Sunday brunch, the veal grillades and thyme stone-ground grits will remind you that you are way down South. Vegetarians and produce-lovers are treated to an entire vegetarian menu, and the solid wine list is always evolving. ✉*900 City Park Ave., Mid-City* ☎*504/488–1000* 🌐*www.ralphsonthepark.com* *Reservations essential* *AE, MC, V* *Closed Mon. No dinner Sun.*

$ SOUTHERN ✕**Two Sister's Kitchen.** A bona fide Creole soul experience awaits at this family-owned eatery. Think fried chicken with macaroni and cheese; shrimp-and-okra stew; and deep, dark, oily, kitchen-sink gumbo. Chitterlings, smothered rabbit, and stewed hen also roll out of the kitchen in record time, as steam tables keep most of the prepared food warm during the hectic lunch rushes. As you dine, you're likely to overhear musicians recapping the previous evening's jazz performance. With its vinyl-topped tables and television, the dining room is far from spotless—but it's the epitome of homey. The kitchen closes by 4 PM. ✉*223 N. Derbigny St., Mid-City* ☎*504/524–0056* *Reservations not accepted* *No credit cards* *Closed Sun. No dinner.*

$ SOUTHERN ✕**Ye Olde College Inn.** A stalwart neighborhood joint, the age-old College Inn now occupies a new building, after decades in the older structure next door. Although the menu remains largely untouched, it is a bit more limited. The flat, greasy burgers are still among the best in town, particularly when ordered with fresh-cut french fries and a hot-pink nectar cream soda. The fried-green-tomato-and-shrimp rémoulade po'boy is one of the most delightfully indulgent sandwiches in town. A seat at the horseshoe-shaped oyster bar is arguably one of the best in town. Oh, and about the chocolate pecan caramel cluster cake? To die for. ✉*3016 S. Carrollton Ave., Mid-City* ☎*504/866–3683* 🌐*www.collegeinn1933.com* *AE, D, MC, V* *No dinner Sun. and Mon.*

BYWATER

$ SOUTHERN ✕**Elizabeth's.** "Real food, done real good" is the motto at Elizabeth's, a real down-home Southern joint where the vinyl-print tablecloths look just like grandma's, and where breakfast is the most important meal of the day. The menu offers everything from traditional po'boys (try the "Big Ass Hamburger") to a stellar braised lamb shank with roasted garlic, to crispy fried chicken livers with pepper jelly. The fried seafood platters are huge and moderately priced, and the fried-oyster po'boy is irresistible. Work off your breakfast upstairs with a game of pool. The staff is spunky, and so is the Bywater neighborhood clientele. This is a great place for a traditional Sunday breakfast. ☒*601 Gallier St., Bywater* ☎*504/944–9272* ✍*Reservations not accepted* ▭*MC, V* ⊗*Closed Mon. and Tues. No dinner Sun.*

$ SOUTHERN ✕**The Joint.** The owners couldn't have chosen a more appropriate name for this canary-yellow cinder-block building pressed up against the railroad tracks. If the color doesn't draw you in, the smell of meat—pork shoulder, pork ribs, beef brisket—cooking in the custom-made smoker out back will. Side dishes go above and beyond in concept and execution, particularly the sweet-and-sour baked beans, and the crispy-on-the-outside mac and cheese. Lemon pound cake is a fitting country dessert. Order takeout if comfort is a priority, as picnic tables and a jukebox set a spartan stage in the cool dining room. In a town not really known for great barbecue, this place is the exception. ☒*801 Poland Ave., Bywater* ☎*504/949–3232* ✍*Reservations not accepted* ▭*MC, V* ⊗*Closed Tues. and Wed.*

OUTSIDE CITY LIMITS

$ BELGIAN ✕**Clementine's Belgian Bistrot.** Affordable Belgian home cooking, more pleasing to the palate than to the eye, is in great abundance at this tucked-away suburban bistro. Beef stew made with Belgian ale, veal meatballs in red sauce, and mussels steamed in variously seasoned white-wine broths all come with freshly cut Belgian fries. Only the most disciplined diners can keep to just one order. Savory and sweet crepes, made-to-order and thicker than the French variety, are the greatest bargains. A fine selection of Belgian beers encourages lingering in the lodgelike environs. Call for directions. ☒*2505 Whitney Ave., Gretna* ☎*504/366–3995* ▭*D, MC, V* ⊗*Closed Sun. and Mon.*

$ SOUTHERN ✕**Crabby Jack's.** Panéed rabbit po'boys, fried-green-tomato-and-shrimp rémoulade salads, and fried chicken draw legions of urban New Orleanians out to Jefferson. Crabby Jack's is a down-home, boxy joint; it's not exactly comfortable, but since the food is too good to wait for, most people eat here. Smoky red beans, muffulettas, and jambalaya are all first-rate and cheap, though the creative fresh-fish specials provide a more definitive experience. This is also the site of a seafood wholesaler, and the seasonal boiled seafood couldn't get any fresher. If you want to eat "real" New Orleans food, eat here. ☒*428 Jefferson Hwy., Jefferson* ☎*504/833–2722* ▭*AE, D, MC, V* ⊗*Closed Sun. No dinner.*

$$$ CREOLE ✕**Dakota.** Warm colors, lustrous woods, and floral accents set the scene at Dakota, one of the most reliable and consistent fine dining experiences on the north shore. Owner-chef Kim Kringlie's inspirations may be multicultural, but his seasonal menus are solidly grounded in south Louisiana. A crackly soft-shell crab is stuffed with a variety of expertly seasoned shellfish. Corn-fired oysters are wrapped in bacon and served over crispy fried spinach. Veal medallions are served with three sauces and topped with jumbo lump crabmeat. The wine list is among the most complex and well-planned in the area. ☒*629 U.S. 190, Coving-*

ton ☎*985/892–3712* 🌐*www.restaurantcuvee.com/dakota* 💳*AE, DC, MC, V* ⊗*Closed Sun. No lunch Sat.*

$$$ ECLECTIC ✕**La Provence.** It's almost an hour's drive from central New Orleans, but the glorious French provincial food and relaxing atmosphere of this exceptional restaurant are well worth the trip. Now among the chef John Besh group of restaurants, La Provence has taken on even richer and more creative culinary stylings. The Berkshire pork loin is tender and savory, while the blue crab bisque is thickened and flavored with tapioca and crème fraîche. Separating the two dining rooms, hung with pleasant Provençal landscape paintings, is a hearth that welcomes you on damp winter days. In warmer seasons, the tree-shaded deck is almost as congenial. Best of all, most of the vegetables are grown on the property right near the massive herb garden. ✉*U.S. 190, 7 mi from the Lake Pontchartrain Causeway, Lacombe* ☎*985/626–7662* 🌐*www.laprovencerestaurant.com* ✍*Reservations essential* 💳*AE, MC, V* ⊗*Closed Mon. and Tues. No lunch Wed., Thurs., and Sat.*

$$ FRENCH ✕**Le Parvenu.** Inside a cozy little cottage, Le Parvenu's homey mood is reinforced by pastel-hue dining rooms lined with flouncy drapery and unobtrusive prints. "Classic" is the word that comes to mind time and again with the authentic French-Creole menus. Breaded lobster tails join lumps of first-quality crabmeat, crawfish, and shrimp in a sauce tinged with cognac. Braised and broiled veal flank steak is sliced thin and served under crunchy stir-fried onions. Cream soups are a specialty, and the best may be a bisque of mirliton dotted with bits of shrimp and crab. ✉*509 Williams Blvd., Kenner* ☎*504/471–0534* ✍*Reservations essential* 💳*AE, DC, MC, V* ⊗*No dinner Sun. No lunch Mon.–Thurs. and Sat.*

$$ ITALIAN Fodor'sChoice ★ ✕**Mosca's.** The food here—combining Louisiana ingredients and Italian ingenuity—is good enough to lure city folk to isolation about 30 minutes from the city. Baked oysters with bread crumbs, olive oil, garlic, and herbs approach the summit of Italian-Creole cuisine. The Italian shrimp are cooked in an herbed mix of olive oil and spices, the roasted chicken with rosemary is luscious, and the house-made Italian sausage is full of peppery goodness. Getting a table usually means waiting at the bar, even if you have made reservations (not accepted Saturday). "Worth the wait" would be an understatement. ✉*4137 U.S. Hwy. 90, Avondale* ☎*504/436–9942* ✍*Reservations essential* 💳*No credit cards* ⊗*Closed Sun. and Mon. No lunch.*

$$ CAJUN ✕**Restaurant des Familles.** No time for a trip to Cajun country? This restaurant, about a half-hour's drive from central New Orleans, is the next-best thing (although you'd better ask for directions when reserving a table). Just a few yards from the vast windows are the slow-moving waters of Bayou des Familles, providing a dramatic vista. Elegantly illuminated at night, the huge Acadian-style raised cottage has a kitchen that produces familiar, and locally beloved, seafood in the Creole style—shrimp rémoulade, crawfish étouffée, turtle soup, crawfish-stuffed rainbow trout, and fried oysters and bacon en brochette. The oyster-and-artichoke soup is one of the best around. ✉*Rte. 3134, north of the intersection with Rte. 45, Crown Point* ☎*504/689–7834* 🌐*www.restaurantdesfamilles.com* ✍*Reservations essential* 💳*AE, D, MC, V* ⊗*Closed Mon. and Tues.*

$ VIETNAMESE ✕**Tan Dinh.** Serving arguably the best Vietnamese food in the area, Tan Dinh is a 20-minute drive from downtown New Orleans, but a world away in flavor. Goat stew with bean curd, roasted quail with sticky-rice cakes, steamed flour cakes topped with dried shrimp, and jellyfish salad are among the more exotic menu items. Spring rolls, noodle soups, and sandwiches, all equally good, might be safer bets for Vietnamese newcomers. With cherrywood chairs and faux-marble tabletops, the restaurant exhibits a convincing polish. ✉*1705 Lafayette St., Gretna* ☎*504/361–8008* ✍*Reservations not accepted* 💳*No credit cards* ⏲*Closed Tues.*

$$ MEDITERRANEAN ✕**Vega Tapas Café.** The word *tapas* in the name is deceptive, since the serving sizes at Vega are closer to those of appetizers, with prices correspondingly lower. The high success rate of the dishes, mostly Mediterranean-inspired, enhances the adventure. If there is a calling card here, it's the chef's "Eggplant Napoleon," layered with fresh mozzarella, arugula, and oven-dried tomatoes. There is an educated selection of wines, many of them Spanish, and specialty cocktails. Everything is served in a large, minimally decorated room lined with hard surfaces, which ups the noise level a couple of notches. Rotating art exhibits feature local and regional artists. ✉*2051 Metairie Rd., Metairie* ☎*504/836–2007* 💳*AE, D, DC, MC, V* ⏲*No lunch weekends.*

4

Where to Stay

WORD OF MOUTH

"If you've not been to NOLA before you probably should stay in the Qtr. Although there are some 'cookie-cutter' type hotels, most are not."

—SAnParis2

"A couple years ago, we planned to go to NO in mid-May, but had to push our trip back a couple weeks. The difference in hotel rates between mid-May and early June was significant. It seems like the low season starts just after Memorial Day weekend."

—november_moon

"We stayed at the Royal Sonesta . . . I chose an interior room facing the pool courtyard rather than Bourbon Street, and was rewarded with (mostly) quiet nights."

—Callaloo

www.fodors.com/community

WHERE TO STAY PLANNER

Stay Strategy

Where should we stay? With hundreds of New Orleans hotels, it may seem like a daunting question. But fret not—our expert writers and editors have done most of the legwork. The 70-plus selections here represent the finest this city has to offer—from the best budget motels to the sleekest designer hotels. Scan "Best Bets" on the following page for top recommendations by price and experience. Or find a review quickly in the listings. Search by neighborhood, then alphabetically. Happy hunting!

Reservations

Book your room as far in advance as possible—up to a year ahead for Mardi Gras, Jazz Fest, or other special events.

In This Chapter

Services

Most hotels have private baths, central heating, air-conditioning, and private phones. More and more major hotels have added Wi-Fi or in-room broadband Internet service. Smaller B&Bs and hotels may not have all of these amenities; ask before you book your room.

Hotels that do not have pools may have agreements with nearby health clubs or other facilities to allow guests to use club facilities for a nominal fee.

Most hotels have parking available, but this can run you as much as $30 a day. Valet parking is usually available at the major hotels. If you park on the street, keep in mind that New Orleans meter attendants are relentless, and ticketing is imminent for illegally parked vehicles. The minimum fee for a parking ticket is $20.

Prices

Properties are assigned price categories based on a range from least expensive standard double rooms at high season (excluding holidays) to most expensive. We list all facilities available, but we do not specify whether they cost extra. When making accommodation inquiries, always ask what is included in the rate.

The lodgings we list are the most desirable in each price category, but rates are subject to change. Use Fodors.com to shop around for rooms before booking. Many major hotels occasionally offer Internet special rates. Be aware that room rates may be higher in October (considered peak convention season) and during the July 4 weekend (due to the annual Essence Music Festival). Rates are also high at the end of April and beginning of May during Jazz Fest. If you book for Mardi Gras, the major hotels will require either a three- or four-night stay.

WHAT IT COSTS

	¢	$	$$	$$$	$$$$
TWO PEOPLE	under $100	$100–$149	$150–$199	$200–$275	over $275

Prices are for two people in a standard double room in high season, excluding 13% city and state taxes.

BEST BETS FOR NEW ORLEANS LODGING

Here are our top hotel recommendations by price and experience. The very best properties—in other words, those that provide a particularly remarkable experience in their price range—are designated in the listings with the Fodor's Choice logo.

Fodor's Choice★

Chimes Bed and Breakfast, $ p. 165
Edgar Degas House, ¢ p. 167
Grand Victorian Bed and Breakfast, $$ p. 166
Harrah's New Orleans Hotel, $$ p. 157
Hotel Maison de Ville, $$ p. 149
Loews New Orleans Hotel, $$$ p. 159
Melrose Mansion, $ p. 151
Monteleone Hotel, $$$$ p. 152
Ritz-Carlton New Orleans, $$$$ p. 153
Royal Sonesta Hotel, $$$$ p. 153
Soniat House, $$$$ p. 154
Windsor Court Hotel, $$$ p. 163

By Price

¢

Bon Maison Guest House, p. 145
Edgar Degas House, p. 167
Lafayette Hotel, p. 159

$

Chimes Bed and Breakfast, p. 165
Hotel Provincial, p. 150
Melrose Mansion, p. 151
St. James Hotel, p. 162

$$

Grand Victorian Bed and Breakfast, p. 166
Harrah's New Orleans Hotel, p. 157
Hotel Maison de Ville, p. 149
International House, p. 158

$$$

Bourbon Orleans Hotel, p. 145
Loews New Orleans Hotel, p. 159
Omni Royal Orleans Hotel, p. 152
Windsor Court Hotel, p. 163

$$$$

Monteleone Hotel, p. 152
Ritz-Carlton New Orleans, p. 153
Royal Sonesta Hotel, p. 153
Soniat House, p. 154

By Experience

BEST FOR KIDS

Courtyard by Marriott, p. 155
Embassy Suites, p. 156
Homewood Suites by Hilton, p. 158
New Orleans Hilton Riverside, p. 160

BEST FOR ROMANCE

Claiborne Mansion, p. 148
Hotel Maison de Ville, p. 149
Loft 523, p. 160
W Hotel New Orleans, p. 163

BEST B&BS

Chimes Bed and Breakfast, p. 165
Grand Victorian Bed and Breakfast, p. 166
Lion's Inn, p. 151
Sully Mansion, p. 167

BEST GRANDE DAME HOTELS

Monteleone Hotel, p. 152
Roosevelt Hotel New Orleans, p. 162
Royal Sonesta Hotel, p. 153

BEST HOTEL BARS

International House, p. 158
Loews New Orleans Hotel, p. 159
Monteleone Hotel, p. 152
Westin Canal Place, p. 155

BEST POOLS

Loews New Orleans Hotel, p. 159
Monteleone Hotel, p. 152
Omni Royal Orleans, p. 152
Westin Canal Place, p. 155

BEST-KEPT SECRETS

Claiborne Mansion, p. 148
Hotel Maison de Ville, p. 149
St. James Hotel, p. 162
Soniat House, p. 154

By Paul A. Greenberg

DECIDING WHERE TO STAY IN NEW ORLEANS has everything to do with what you want from your visit. To be in the center of the action and to experience the city's rich culture, a French Quarter accommodation is your best choice. For a quieter, more serene experience in close proximity to major attractions, head to comfortable properties Uptown, in the Garden District, and in surrounding areas like the Faubourg Marigny. Business travelers will find the elegant, well-appointed Central Business District (CBD) hotels convenient and comfortable. And if you appreciate the contemporary-chic ambience of historic warehouses and commercial buildings that have been refashioned into elegant hotels, head to the Warehouse District, where massive spaces with exposed-brick walls add distinctive atmosphere to both moderately priced and upscale hotels.

New Orleans, much like New York, is a walking city. If you are visiting for the first time, book a hotel that is centrally located downtown and within walking distance of major attractions. Many hotels are located near the city's streetcar lines, which run the entire length of the city. If you plan to visit the city more than once, try to create a different lodging experience each time. For your next visit, perhaps a romantic getaway in an outlying guesthouse, where old-world charm and atmosphere are so proudly preserved.

FRENCH QUARTER/FAUBOURG MARIGNY

$$ **Astor Crowne Plaza.** Located on the edge of the French Quarter on bustling Canal Street, this property features a rooftop pool with spectacular city views. Dickie Brennan's Bourbon House Restaurant, with the best raw-seafood bar in the city, is on the lobby level. All guest rooms have large televisions and elegant, comfy furniture. The hotel is in an artfully restored downtown office building, within walking distance of everything that counts in the Quarter and downtown. **Pros:** convenient location; large guest rooms. **Cons:** unimaginative decor; main entrance opens to the busiest corner in the city. ✉ *739 Canal St., French Quarter* ☎ *504/962–0500 or 800/684–1127* 🌐 *www.astorcrowneplaza.com* *707 rooms, 25 suites* *In-room: Wi-Fi. In-hotel: restaurant, room service, bar, pool* *AE, D, DC, MC, V.*

$$ **Bienville House Hotel.** Small and intimate, the Monteleone sister hotel is the place for travelers searching for gracious old New Orleans ambience. The property finished a total renovation in 2008 and is in an exciting area of the Quarter, with colorful shops, restaurants, and entertainment venues nearby. Lovely guest rooms are furnished with antiques and reproduction pieces; some have balconies overlooking one of the most beautiful courtyards in the city. Top floor rooms all have access to a gorgeous sundeck. In late 2008, Uptown restaurant Iris relocated to the hotel. **Pros:** close to French Quarter attractions yet not in the middle of it. **Cons:** a bit pricey; noise carries inside at night from the street. ✉ *320 Decatur St., French Quarter* ☎ *504/529–2345* 🌐 *www.bienvillehouse.com* *80 rooms, 3 suites* *In-room: Wi-Fi. In-hotel: restaurant, bar, pool, laundry service, parking (paid)* *AE, D, MC, V.*

WHERE TO STAY			
Neighborhood	Vibe	Pros	Cons
French Quarter	The tourist-focused main event is action packed, yet charming. Lodging runs the gamut from small inns to luxury hotels.	Lots of visitor attractions and nationally acclaimed restaurants. Everything is within walking distance of your hotel.	Crowded, high-traffic area. If you're sound sensitive, request a room that does not face a main street.
Faubourg Marigny	More neighborhoody than the adjacent French Quarter, stay here if you want to be close to the action but not in the middle of it. Many nice bed-and-breakfast options.	Balanced residential/ commercial community. Close to French Quarter nightlife, but a more peaceful alternative.	Can be confusing to navigate for newcomers. Don't forget your map!
CBD and Warehouse District	The Warehouse District is also known as New Orleans's arts district. It's a great area for visitors who prefer accommodations in luxurious high-rise hotels or smaller boutique properties.	Good retail and restaurants, and some of the best galleries and museums in the city. Within walking distance of the French Quarter.	Crowded. Street vendors can be annoying.
Garden District/ Uptown	Residential, upscale, and fashionable, this neighborhood is a slower-paced alternative to staying downtown.	Beautiful and right on the historic St. Charles Ave. streetcar line. Traffic here is not as heavy as downtown.	Far from the French Quarter and tourist attractions; must drive or take public transportation.
Mid-City	This is primarily an urban/residential area, with few lodging options.	Many local businesses and mid-price restaurants. Home to City Park, the largest urban park in the country.	Not easy for tourists to navigate—far from tourist attractions. Will need car, and public transportation is not convenient.

5

¢ **Bon Maison Guest House.** Quaint accommodations lie within the gates of this 1833 town house, on the relatively quiet end of Bourbon Street. Rooms in the former slave quarters, off the lush brick patio with tropical plants, are pleasantly (if not elaborately) furnished and have ceiling fans. Two large suites with kitchenettes are in the main house. Be prepared for lots of stair climbing if your room is on one of the upper floors (the house doesn't have an elevator). All rooms have private entrances, kitchenettes, and baths. The quiet ambience will make you feel like you're staying in a private home. **Pros:** within walking distance of all French Quarter attractions; just a block or two from several major restaurants. **Cons:** uninspired room decor. ✉*835 Bourbon St., French Quarter* ☎*504/561–8498* 🌐*www.bonmaison.com* *3 rooms, 2 suites* *In-room: Wi-Fi, refrigerator* 💳*MC, V.*

$$$ **Bourbon Orleans Hotel.** Located in the absolute center of the French Quarter, this property has been exquisitely renovated. The lobby level exudes turn-of-the-20th-century New Orleans glamour, and includes

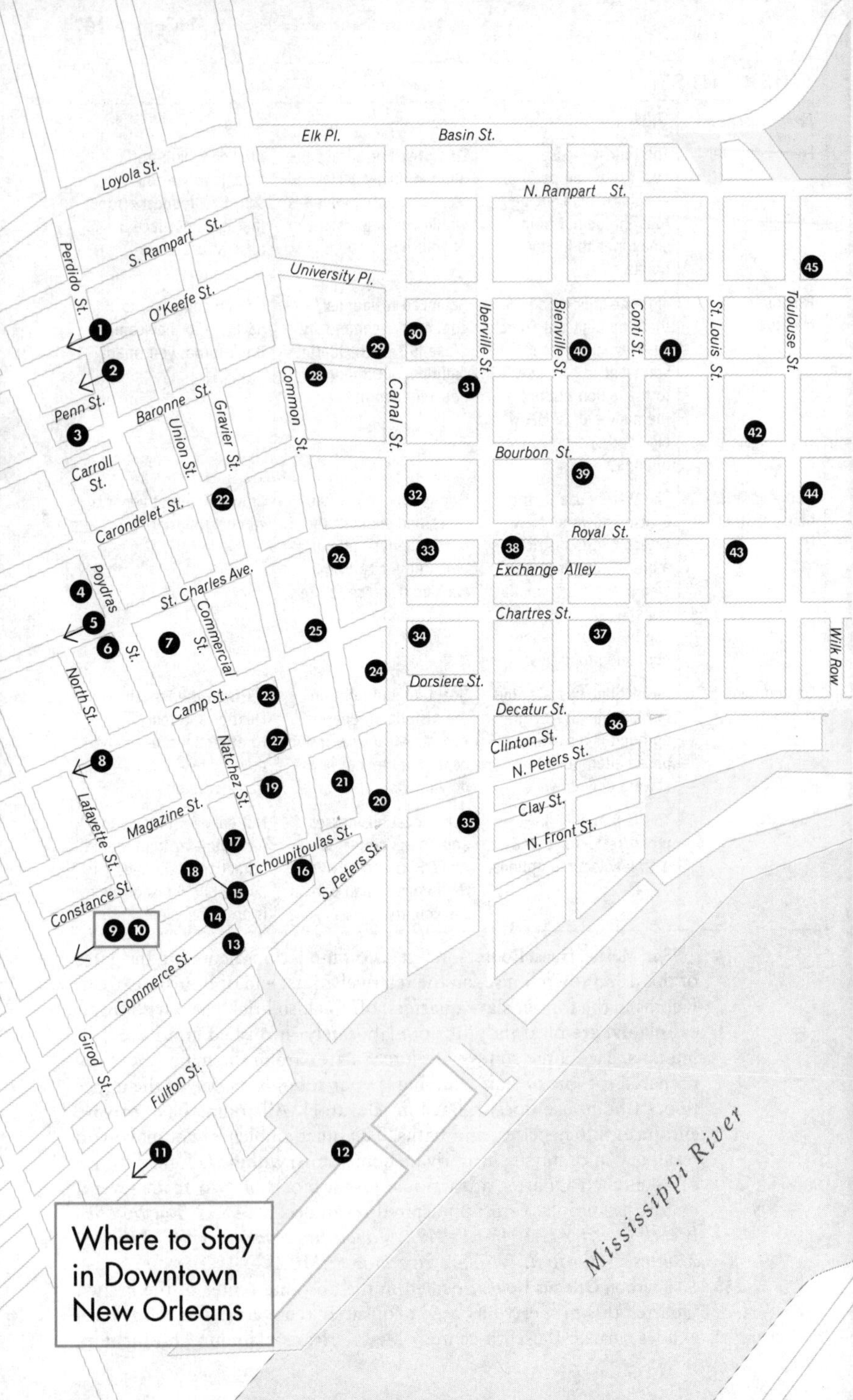
Where to Stay in Downtown New Orleans
Elk Pl.
Basin St.
Loyola St.
N. Rampart St.
S. Rampart St.
Perdido St.
University Pl.
O'Keefe St.
Iberville St.
Bienville St.
Conti St.
St. Louis St.
Toulouse St.
Common St.
Canal St.
Penn St.
Baronne St.
Union St.
Gravier St.
Carroll St.
Bourbon St.
Carondelet St.
Royal St.
Exchange Alley
Poydras St.
St. Charles Ave.
Commercial St.
Chartres St.
Wilk Row
North St.
Dorsiere St.
Camp St.
Decatur St.
Clinton St.
Natchez St.
N. Peters St.
Lafayette St.
Magazine St.
Clay St.
N. Front St.
Tchoupitoulas St.
S. Peters St.
Constance St.
Commerce St.
Girod St.
Fulton St.
Mississippi River

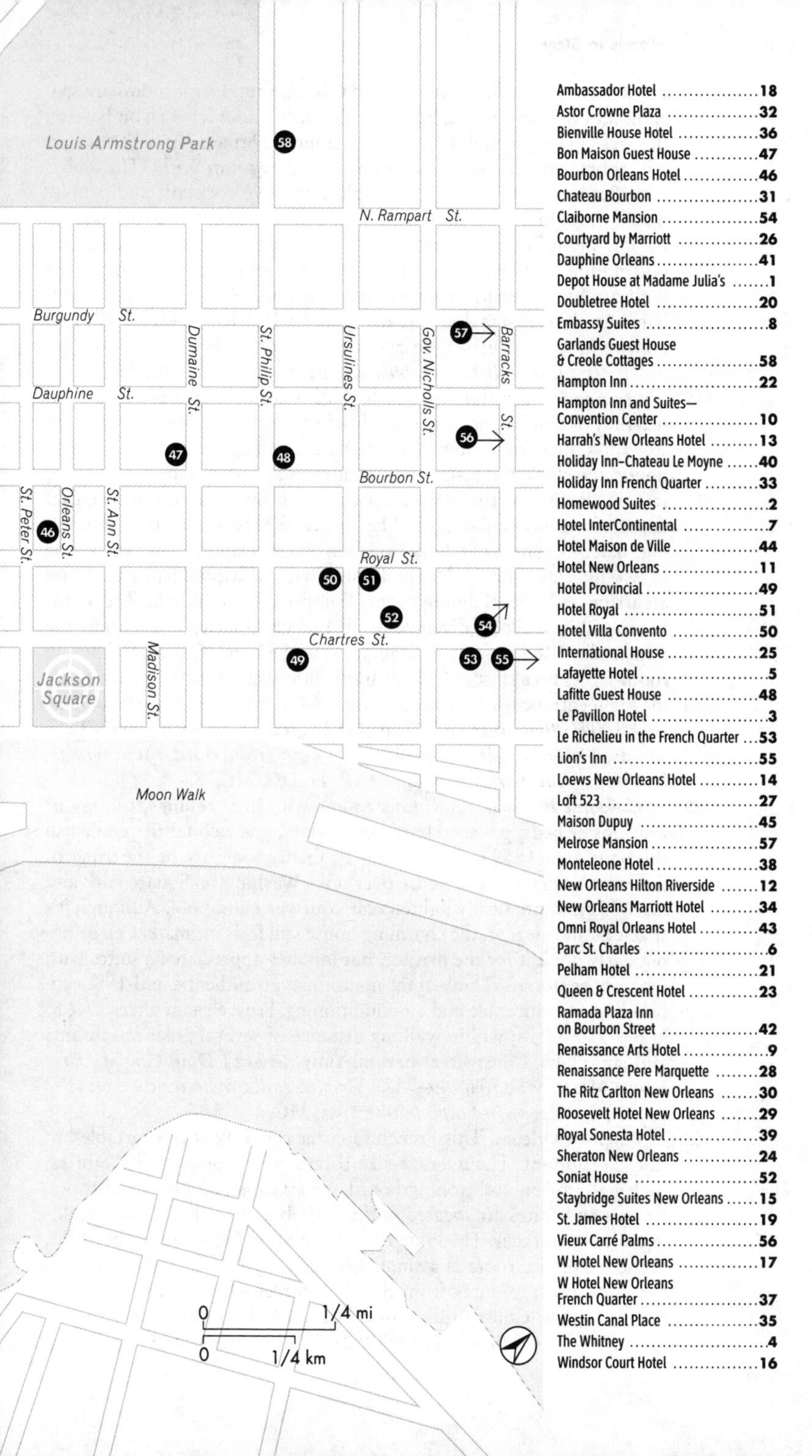

Louis Armstrong Park
58
N. Rampart St.
Burgundy St.
Dauphine St.
Dumaine St.
St. Philip St.
Ursulines St.
Gov. Nicholls St.
Barracks St.
57
56
47
48
Bourbon St.
St. Peter St.
Orleans St.
St. Ann St.
46
Royal St.
50
51
52
54
Chartres St.
49
53
55
Jackson Square
Madison St.
Moon Walk
0
1/4 mi
0
1/4 km
Ambassador Hotel 18
Astor Crowne Plaza 32
Bienville House Hotel 36
Bon Maison Guest House 47
Bourbon Orleans Hotel 46
Chateau Bourbon 31
Claiborne Mansion 54
Courtyard by Marriott 26
Dauphine Orleans 41
Depot House at Madame Julia's 1
Doubletree Hotel 20
Embassy Suites 8
Garlands Guest House & Creole Cottages 58
Hampton Inn 22
Hampton Inn and Suites—Convention Center 10
Harrah's New Orleans Hotel 13
Holiday Inn–Chateau Le Moyne 40
Holiday Inn French Quarter 33
Homewood Suites 2
Hotel InterContinental 7
Hotel Maison de Ville 44
Hotel New Orleans 11
Hotel Provincial 49
Hotel Royal 51
Hotel Villa Convento 50
International House 25
Lafayette Hotel 5
Lafitte Guest House 48
Le Pavillon Hotel 3
Le Richelieu in the French Quarter 53
Lion's Inn 55
Loews New Orleans Hotel 14
Loft 523 27
Maison Dupuy 45
Melrose Mansion 57
Monteleone Hotel 38
New Orleans Hilton Riverside 12
New Orleans Marriott Hotel 34
Omni Royal Orleans Hotel 43
Parc St. Charles 6
Pelham Hotel 21
Queen & Crescent Hotel 23
Ramada Plaza Inn on Bourbon Street 42
Renaissance Arts Hotel 9
Renaissance Pere Marquette 28
The Ritz Carlton New Orleans 30
Roosevelt Hotel New Orleans 29
Royal Sonesta Hotel 39
Sheraton New Orleans 24
Soniat House 52
Staybridge Suites New Orleans 15
St. James Hotel 19
Vieux Carré Palms 56
W Hotel New Orleans 17
W Hotel New Orleans French Quarter 37
Westin Canal Place 35
The Whitney 4
Windsor Court Hotel 16

the consistently outstanding Paillard's Restaurant. Guest rooms are spacious and well-appointed, but those that face the street are a bit hard on the ears, due to the nightly activity on Bourbon Street. Business travelers will appreciate ergonomic office chairs and in-room Wi-Fi. The lobby-level Bourbon Oh! bar is a quiet place to have cocktails and people-watch through wall-to-wall windows, and Napoleon's Itch bar is great for late-night Bourbon Street fun. **Pros:** recent meticulous renovation; outstanding restaurant. **Cons:** lobby level is often crowded and noisy with curious passersby; hotel is steps from loud, 24-hour Bourbon Street bars. ✉*717 Orleans Ave., French Quarter* ☎*504/523–2222* 🌐*www.bourbonorleans.com* *346 rooms, 16 suites* *In-room: Wi-Fi. In-hotel: restaurant, bars, gym, parking (paid)* ▭*AE, D, DC, MC.*

$$$$ **Chateau Bourbon.** John Kennedy Toole's comic masterpiece, *A Confederacy of Dunces,* begins under the clock of D.H. Holmes department store on Canal Street, now this well-maintained upscale hotel. In Toole's honor, the clock and a statue of the novel's antihero, Ignatius J. Reilly, remain. Rooms at the hotel are large, with high ceilings and neutral decor; some have columns and beams, remnants of the original building. Balcony rooms overlook Bourbon Street, Dauphine Street, or one of two interior courtyards. Three suites with whirlpool baths surround an atrium. The hotel dining room, Tiempo, is open only for breakfast. **Pros:** within walking distance of all French Quarter attractions; the outstanding Red Fish Grille is adjacent to the hotel. **Cons:** hotel dining room serves breakfast only; high-traffic intersection located just outside the main entrance; lots of street noise. ✉*800 Iberville St., French Quarter* ☎*504/586–0800 or 800/766–3782* 🌐*www.wyndham.com* *251 rooms, 11 suites* *In-room: Wi-Fi. In-hotel: restaurant, room service, bar, pool, gym, parking (paid)* ▭*AE, D, DC, MC, V.*

$$ **Claiborne Mansion.** Enormous rooms with high ceilings, canopy or four-poster beds, polished hardwood floors, and rich fabrics embellish this handsome 1859 mansion in the Faubourg Marigny, on the fringe of the French Quarter. The house overlooks Washington Square Park and has a lush, dramatically lighted rear courtyard and pool. Although it's spacious and elegant, the charming house still feels intimate. Celebrities regularly book it for the privacy, but families appreciate its suites with separate bedrooms. Think of the mansion as an authentic mid-19th-century home—with cable and air-conditioning. **Pros:** elegant alternative to hotels and B&Bs; within walking distance of several great restaurants and jazz clubs. **Cons:** street parking only. ✉*2111 Dauphine St., Faubourg Marigny* ☎*504/949–7327* 🌐*www.clairbornemansion.com* *2 rooms, 5 suites* *In-hotel: pool* ▭*AE, MC, V* *BP.*

$$ **Dauphine Orleans.** This French Quarter property is comfortable but not exceptional. The average-size rooms have good-quality fabrics; each has an iron and ironing board, a hair dryer, and two bathrobes. Rooms and suites are located in the main building, in a smaller building, and in cottages. The lounge is an erstwhile 19th-century bordello, and the exercise room is a small 19th-century Creole cottage just off the pool. **Pros:** minutes from Bourbon Street—but far enough away that it's quiet. **Cons:** utilitarian decor. ✉*415 Dauphine St., French Quarter* ☎*504/586–1800 or 800/521–7111* 🌐*www.dauphineorleans.*

com 104 *rooms, 7 suites* *In-room: Wi-Fi. In-hotel: bar, pool, gym, Wi-Fi, parking (paid)* *AE, D, DC, MC, V.*

$$ **Garlands Guest House & Creole Cottages.** This charming 1926 guesthouse is located in historic Tremé, within walking distance of the French Quarter (although walking here at night is not recommended). Freestanding Creole cottages and elegant suites are decorated with antiques and reproductions, and the gardens are meticulously maintained. The daily breakfast is exquisite, featuring local favorites like stuffed French toast and homemade biscuits with Southern gravy. The property has a secure, secluded feel; it's a quiet alternative to the French Quarter. **Pros:** not widely known, even among frequent New Orleans visitors; quaint, intimate surroundings. **Cons:** the neighborhood is a bit dicey—not a good place to walk around after dark. *1129 St. Phillip St., Tremé* *504/523–1372 or 800/523–1060* *www.historicgarlands.com* *10 rooms* *In-room: refrigerator, Internet* *AE, MC, V.*

5

$ **Holiday Inn–Chateau Le Moyne.** This quiet hotel one block off Bourbon Street exudes old-world atmosphere with its traditional New Orleans architecture and period furnishings. Eight suites are in Creole cottages off a tropical courtyard; all rooms are furnished with antiques and reproductions and have coffeemakers, hair dryers, and irons and ironing boards. Rooms are surprisingly large and those with courtyard views are peaceful respites from the hustle and bustle of the French Quarter. **Pros:** great location within walking distance of all French Quarter attractions; affordable rates; the moderately priced hotel restaurant serves authentic Southern breakfast. **Cons:** chain property. *301 Dauphine St., French Quarter* *504/581–1303 or 800/465–4329* *www.holiday-inn.com* *160 rooms, 11 suites* *In-room: Wi-Fi. In-hotel: restaurant, bar, pool, parking (paid)* *AE, D, DC, MC, V.*

$ **Holiday Inn French Quarter.** Although this could be a Holiday Inn in Anytown, USA, the advantage here is the location. This clean, busy, centrally located property is within walking distance of all the major French Quarter restaurants and the Central Business District. It's a good place to stay with kids (there are on-site laundry facilities). A nice indoor pool makes up for the lack of luxury. **Pros:** moderately priced by French Quarter standards; adjacent to popular bars and restaurants; kitschy "Key West" decor. **Cons:** utilitarian accommodations; slow elevators. *124 Royal St., French Quarter* *504/529–7211 or 800/448–2296* *www.holiday-inn.com* *374 rooms* *In-room: Internet. In-hotel: restaurant, room service, bar, pool* *AE, D, DC, MC, V.*

$$ Fodor'sChoice ★ **Hotel Maison de Ville.** Delightfully secluded amid the hustle and bustle of the French Quarter, this property oozes refined elegance and romance. Tapestry-covered chairs, a gas fire burning in the sitting room, and antiques-furnished rooms all contribute to a 19th-century atmosphere. Some rooms are in former slave quarters in the courtyard; others are on the upper floors of the main house. Breakfast is served on a silver tray, and port and sherry are available in the afternoon. For a special hideaway, book one of the hotel's Audubon Cottages. The Bistro at Maison de Ville is one of the best-kept culinary secrets in the French Quarter. **Pros:** unique rooms; personal and consistently above-average service. **Cons:** tough to get a reservation. *727 Toulouse St., French Quarter*

☎504/561–5858 or 800/634–1600 🌐www.maisondeville.com ⇨14 rooms, 2 suites, 7 cottages ♿In-room: Wi-Fi. In-hotel: pool, parking (paid), no kids under 12 ▭AE, D, DC, MC, V 🍽CP.

$ **Hotel Provincial.** The next time you want to stay in a "real New Orleans hotel," consider this one. The interiors have 19th-century touches, with exposed-brick walls, a lush courtyard with iron grillwork, and buildings that date back to the French Quarter's earliest years. The bright rooms are a good size, and many overlook the courtyard. It's like stepping back in time—but with all the modern conveniences. A big plus at this hotel is Stella!, chef Scott Boswell's fine-dining restaurant. **Pros:** quaint atmosphere; quiet surroundings (in a residential section of the French Quarter). **Cons:** suite rates are on the pricey side. *✉1024 Chartres St., French Quarter ☎504/581–4995 or 800/535–7922 🌐www.hotelprovincial.com ⇨93 rooms, 6 suites ♿In-room: Wi-Fi. In-hotel: restaurant, bar, pool, parking (paid) ▭AE, D, DC, MC, V.*

$$ **Hotel Royal.** Think of the coolest SoHo boutique hotel, mix in some authentic New Orleans traditional elegance, and this is your place. Many rooms in this circa-1830 home are pleasantly oversize; four have wet bars and balconies overlooking Royal Street, and two have hot tubs. Distinctly modern amenities complement high ceilings and antebellum furnishings. A recent renovation yielded comfortable and attractive updates, including classic modern lobby furnishings and elegantly constructed marble bathrooms. The complimentary Continental breakfast comes from the nearby Croissant d'Or, the favorite bakery of French Quarter residents. **Pros:** centralized French Quarter location; recent renovation. **Cons:** no in-room or in-hotel Wi-Fi; no elevator. *✉1006 Royal St., French Quarter ☎504/524–3900 or 800/776–3901 🌐www.melrosegroup.com ⇨30 rooms ♿In-room: Internet. In-hotel: parking (paid) ▭AE, D, DC, MC, V 🍽CP.*

$ **Hotel Villa Convento.** The Campo family provides around-the-clock service in this four-story 1848 Creole town house. Although it's just blocks from the Quarter's tourist attractions, shopping, and great restaurants, this guesthouse is on a surprisingly quaint, quiet street, close to the Old Ursuline Convent. Each morning you can have croissants and fresh-brewed coffee on the lush patio, or just step across the street to the charming Croissant d'Or. Rooms, which are furnished with reproductions of antiques, vary in price; some have balconies, chandeliers, or ceiling fans. **Pros:** located in the quieter residential section of the French Quarter; local legend says the hotel was once a high-traffic bordello. **Cons:** room decor and linens need updating. *✉616 Ursulines St., French Quarter ☎504/522–1793 🌐www.villaconvento.com ⇨25 rooms ♿In-room: Wi-Fi ▭AE, D, DC, MC, V 🍽CP.*

$$ **Lafitte Guest House.** A four-story 1849 French-style manor house, the Lafitte is meticulously restored, with rooms decorated with period furnishings. Room 40 takes up the entire fourth floor and overlooks French Quarter rooftops. Room 5, the loft apartment, overlooks the beautiful courtyard. Breakfast can be brought to your room, served in the Victorian parlor, or enjoyed in the courtyard; wine and hors d'oeuvres are served each evening. **Pros:** feels like a historic mansion; "Mansion rooms" with balcony are spectacular; new furnishings. **Cons:** located

on a high-traffic corner of Bourbon Street. ✉*1003 Bourbon St., French Quarter* ☎*504/581–2678 or 800/331–7971* 🌐*www.lafitteguesthouse.com* *14 rooms, 2 suites* *In-room: Wi-Fi. In-hotel: no-smoking rooms* *AE, D, DC, MC, V* *CP.*

$ **Le Richelieu in the French Quarter.** Close to the Old Ursuline Convent and the French Market, Le Richelieu combines the friendly personal charm of a small hotel with luxe touches (upscale toiletries, hair dryers)—at a moderate rate. Some rooms have mirrored walls and large walk-in closets, and all have brass ceiling fans, irons, and ironing boards. Balcony rooms have the same rates as standard rooms (you can request a balcony when you reserve, but the hotel will not guarantee one). An intimate bar and café is off the courtyard, with tables on the terrace by the pool. Many regular customers wouldn't stay anywhere else. **Pros:** great value; excellent service; some rooms have balconies. **Cons:** bathrooms are small and could use some updating. ✉*1234 Chartres St., French Quarter* ☎*504/529–2492 or 800/535–9653* 🌐*www.lerichelieuhotel.com* *69 rooms, 17 suites* *In-room: refrigerator, Wi-Fi. In-hotel: restaurant, bar, pool, parking (free)* *AE, D, DC, MC, V.*

5

$ **Lion's Inn.** As B&Bs go, this one is truly unique. From the swimming pool and hot tub in the private garden, to the multilingual (English, French, and Italian) staff to the singularly elegant, Old South room decor, the Inn is much like a traditional Louisiana mansion. The leisurely Continental breakfast in the courtyard is the perfect way to start the day, and the wine hour at dusk is relaxing and sociable. The two owners are as hospitable as they come. They even provide bicycles to get around town. **Pros:** gracious owners; private courtyard. **Cons:** may not be advisable to walk in the area late at night. *2517 Chartres St., Fauburg Marigny* ☎*504/945–2339* 🌐*www.lionsinn.com* *10 rooms* *In-hotel: pool, bicycles, Wi-Fi* *AE, D, DC, MC, V.*

$ **Maison Dupuy.** Seven restored 19th-century town houses surround one of the Quarter's prettiest courtyards, anchored by a spectacular fountain. Lush tropical greenery and palm trees provide a serene setting for meals and cocktails, and soft lighting and comfortable seating add to the courtyard's attraction. Most rooms are fairly large, and some have balconies. For casual dining, the French Quarter Bistro serves breakfast, lunch, and dinner. When you reserve, ask about the "Personal Service Concierge" feature. The hotel is two blocks from Bourbon Street. **Pros:** close to the heart of the French Quarter; excellent hotel restaurant. **Cons:** guests should exercise caution when walking in the area late at night. ✉*1001 Toulouse St., French Quarter* ☎*504/586–8000 or 800/535–9177* 🌐*www.maisondupuy.com* *187 rooms, 13 suites* *In-room: Wi-Fi. In-hotel: restaurant, pool, gym, parking (paid)* *AE, D, DC, MC, V.*

$ **Melrose Mansion.** Down pillows and fine-milled soaps; a full breakfast served poolside, in a formal dining room, or in your room; and rooms filled with 19th-century Louisiana antiques are among the attractions of this handsome 1884 Victorian mansion. Rooms and suites are spacious, with high ceilings and polished hardwood floors. Cocktails are served each evening in the formal drawing room. Baths are sumptuous affairs; those in suites have hot tubs. All but one of the rooms have a

Fodor's Choice ★

wet bar, and one has a private patio. **Pros:** pure luxury; very private; lots of pampering. **Cons:** unreasonable refund policy on reservations—and full room charges must be paid in advance. ✉*937 Esplanade Ave., French Quarter* ☎*504/944–2255* 🌐*www.melrosegroup.com* *8 rooms, 4 suites* *In-room: Wi-Fi. In-hotel: bar, pool* *AE, D, MC, V* *BP.*

$$$$ **Monteleone Hotel.** The grande dame of French Quarter hotels—with its ornate baroque facade, liveried doormen, and shimmering lobby chandeliers—was built in 1886 and renovated in 2004. A stellar addition is the full-service Spa Aria. Rooms are extra large and luxurious, with rich fabrics and a mix of four-poster beds, brass beds, and beds with traditional headboards. Junior suites are spacious; sumptuous VIP suites come with extra pampering. The slowly revolving Carousel piano bar in the lobby is a local landmark, and the first-rate dinner in the hotel's Hunt Room Grill is one of the city's best-kept secrets. There's live jazz every night in the lounge. **Pros:** ideal central location offering access to French Quarter and downtown locations; civilized, old New Orleans feel; recently renovated. **Cons:** while the Hunt Room Grill is nice, the hotel's more casual restaurant offers mediocre food and poor service. ✉*214 Royal St., French Quarter* ☎*504/523–3341 or 800/535–9595* 🌐*www.hotelmonteleone.com* *600 rooms, 55 suites* *In-room: Wi-Fi. In-hotel: 2 restaurants, bar, pool, gym, spa, Wi-Fi* *AE, D, DC, MC, V.*

Fodor's Choice ★

HAUNTED HOTEL

Generations of guests at the Monteleone have experienced paranormal events. A locked restaurant door opens and closes almost every evening, and an elevator occasionally stops on the wrong floor—leading guests down a hallway that grows chilly; some claim to have seen ghostly images of children playing. In March 2003, the International Society of Paranormal Research investigated and made contact with more than a dozen earthbound entities. Among them were several former employees and a man who died inside the hotel. If you'd like an experience with the otherworld, request haunted room 1462.

$$$ **New Orleans Marriott Hotel.** The Marriott has a fabulous view of the Quarter, the CBD, and the river. It's an easy walk from the Canal Place mall, the Riverwalk, and the Convention Center. Rooms are comfortable, service is friendly (if uneven), and nightly jazz enlivens the lobby—but the hotel lacks New Orleans charm. The Canal Street streetcar line provides convenient access to most parts of the city. Keep in mind that this high-rise convention hotel is located on Canal Street, the busiest street in the downtown area. **Pros:** good location; very clean; stunning city and river views. **Cons:** typical chain hotel; inconsistent service. ✉*555 Canal St., French Quarter* ☎*504/581–1000 or 800/228–9290* 🌐*www.neworleansmarriott.com* *1,290 rooms, 54 suites* *In-room: Internet. In-hotel: restaurant, bar, pool, gym, Wi-Fi, parking (paid)* *AE, D, DC, MC, V.*

$$$ **Omni Royal Orleans Hotel.** This elegant white-marble hotel built in 1960 is a replica of the grand St. Louis Hotel of the 1800s. Sconce-enhanced columns, gilt mirrors, fan windows, and three magnificent

chandeliers re-create the atmosphere of old New Orleans. All rooms have marble baths; some have balconies. The lobby level Rib Room has been one of the city's culinary showpieces for more than 40 years. The rooftop pool has the city's best overhead view of the French Quarter. **Pros:** old-world elegance; sparkling cleanliness throughout; central location; one of the best restaurants in the French Quarter. **Cons:** some rooms need updating, but a hotel-wide renovation is in progress; pool area can get crowded. ✉ *621 St. Louis St., French Quarter* ☎ *504/529–5333 or 800/843–6664* 🌐 *www.omnihotels.com* *346 rooms, 16 suites* *In-room: Wi-Fi. In-hotel: restaurant, pool, gym, parking (paid)* 💳 *AE, D, DC, MC.*

$$$$ **Ramada Plaza Inn on Bourbon Street.** Located on the site of New Orleans's original French opera house, this property is not one of the city's most elegant lodgings—but it is well kept and affordable. Rooms facing the courtyard are quieter, but the 32 with Bourbon Street balconies are coveted during Mardi Gras. The hotel is on one of the busiest blocks of Bourbon Street, so be prepared for 24-hour activity—both outside and in. **Pros:** ideal for those who want to be in the heart of the French Quarter. **Cons:** lackluster decor; utilitarian accommodations; slow service; high rates. ✉ *541 Bourbon St., French Quarter* ☎ *504/524–7611 or 800/535–7891* 🌐 *www.innonbourbon.com* *186 rooms, 2 suites* *In-room: Wi-Fi. In-hotel: pool, parking (paid)* 💳 *AE, DC, MC, V.*

5

$$$$ Fodor's Choice ★ **Ritz-Carlton New Orleans.** The Ritz occupies the artfully converted, historic Maison Blanche department store building with a luxurious hotel reminiscent of old New Orleans. Rooms are furnished with local antiques, and feature oversize marble bathrooms and plush linens. The Club Floor has 75 rooms, including one suite, with a concierge and a private lounge. The expansive lobby, adorned in carefully selected fine art and upscale furnishings found in traditional New Orleans homes, opens onto a luxurious courtyard. The hotel's dining room, Mélange, offers re-creations of signature dishes from high-profile restaurants throughout the city (though the quality of the food is inconsistent). The hotel, within walking distance of most attractions and minutes from the Convention Center, borders the French Quarter and faces the CBD. **Pros:** luxurious rooms and suites; excellent live evening entertainment; world-class spa; the afternoon tea in On Trois (the lobby lounge) is one of the most civilized traditions in the city. **Cons:** service is inconsistent; property has a chain-hotel feel. ✉ *921 Canal St., French Quarter* ☎ *504/524–1331* 🌐 *www.ritzcarlton.com* *527 rooms, 38 suites* *In-room: Wi-Fi. In-hotel: restaurant, bars, spa, parking (paid)* 💳 *AE, D, DC, MC, V.*

$$$$ Fodor's Choice ★ **Royal Sonesta Hotel.** Step from the revelry of Bourbon Street into the marble elegance of this renowned hotel's lobby, where lush plants enhance a cool, serene atmosphere. Most guest rooms are of average size, furnished with light-color reproduction antiques: many have French doors that open onto balconies or patios. Rooms facing Bourbon Street are noisy, but most are sufficiently soundproof. Begue's Restaurant is locally beloved and presents one of the city's best Sunday buffet brunches; the charming Desire Oyster Bar, on the lobby level,

faces Bourbon Street and serves local seafood delicacies. **Pros:** outstanding service; bustling, cavernous lobby; great balcony views of the Quarter. **Cons:** consistent high occupancy can lead to slow elevator service; rooms facing Bourbon street are noisy. ✉*300 Bourbon St., French Quarter* ☎*504/586–0300 or 800/766–3782* 🌐*www.royalsonestano.com* *500 rooms, 32 suites* *In-room: Wi-Fi. In-hotel: 2 restaurants, bar, pool, gym, parking (paid)* *AE, D, DC, MC, V.*

CLIMBERS BEWARE!

One of the best Mardi Gras parade–viewing spots in town is the Royal Sonesta Hotel balcony. To keep revelers from climbing up from the street below, the staff greases all the support poles with petroleum jelly. The media turns out in droves, and the hotel turns the event into a party. For many New Orleanians, this odd event signifies the true beginning to Mardi Gras weekend. Festivities start at 10 AM the Friday before Mardi Gras; after the poles are greased, many attendees flood into the hotel for a lavish seafood buffet.

$$$$ Fodor'sChoice ★ **Soniat House.** This singularly handsome property comprises three meticulously restored town houses built in the 1830s. Polished hardwood floors, Oriental rugs, and American and European antiques are complemented by contemporary artwork. Amenities include Annick Goutal toiletries, goose-down pillows, and Egyptian cotton sheets. Some rooms and suites have hot tubs. Exotic plants fill two secluded courtyards, where afternoon cocktails and an unforgettable breakfast ($12.50 extra) of homemade biscuits and strawberry jam, fresh-squeezed orange juice, and café au lait can be enjoyed, weather permitting. An on-site antiques shop carries exquisite European furnishings. Many regular New Orleans visitors consider this the city's finest hotel. **Pros:** sheer refined elegance; incomparable privacy; expert service; afternoon wine service that is as civilized as it gets. **Cons:** while the breakfast is delicious, portions and menu options are limited. ✉*1133 Chartres St., French Quarter* ☎*504/522–0570 or 800/544–8808* 🌐*www.soniathouse.com* *20 rooms, 13 suites* *In-room: Wi-Fi. In-hotel: parking (paid)* *AE, MC, V.*

$$ **Vieux Carré Palms.** In a residential neighborhood on the edge of the French Quarter, this elegantly furnished, spacious B&B provides a private, intimate setting with quick access to French Quarter attractions. You're served champagne upon arrival, and the smell of fresh French pastries fills the hallways every morning. Rooms are spacious, well-appointed, and homey; some face tree-lined Esplanade Avenue. This is one of the most comfortable inns in the city—and your host is as gracious as they come. **Pros:** residential neighborhood; private quarters. **Cons:** hard to get a reservation because there are few rooms. ✉*723 Esplanade Ave., French Quarter* ☎*504/949–2572 or 800/523–9091* *504/949–2572* *4 suites* *MC, V.*

$$$$ **W Hotel New Orleans French Quarter.** This sleekly renovated modern hotel has one of the best locations in the Quarter. Most rooms are in the main building, and many have balconies that overlook either the courtyard or Chartres Street. Some have French doors that open directly onto a sundeck. Two of the four carriage-house suites share a

cheery sundeck; others overlook the courtyard. The hotel is adjacent to Bacco, a contemporary Italian eatery operated by renowned restaurateur Ralph Brennan. The hotel also provides a "Whatever, whenever" policy—24-hour concierges will find those barbecued ribs you're craving at 3 AM, arrange a deep-tissue massage—even track down a last-minute gown for a Mardi Gras ball. **Pros:** well-kept rooms and public areas; great restaurant. **Cons:** a bit too hip for the French Quarter—the place feels more like SoHo than New Orleans. ✉ *316 Chartres St., French Quarter* ☎ *504/581–1200 or 800/448–4927* 🌐 *www.whotels.com* *98 rooms, 4 suites* *In-room: Wi-Fi. In-hotel: restaurant, bar, pool, parking (paid)* *AE, D, DC, MC, V.*

$$$$ **Westin Canal Place.** The Westin was designed with great views in mind. The huge, rose-Carrara-marble lobby, with European antiques, jardinieres, and grand piano, is on the 11th floor of the Canal Place shopping mall; tea is served daily in the lobby or the River 127 Restaurant, which has one of the few upscale bars in the city. Two-story arched lobby windows overlook the French Quarter and the great bend in the Mississippi River. Rooms have marble foyers and baths. Perks on the two executive floors include complimentary Continental breakfast and afternoon hors d'oeuvres. **Pros:** luxurious, sparkling rooms and suites; fabulous views of the Mississippi River and French Quarter. **Cons:** lobby is located on the 11th floor—and can be a bit cumbersome to access. ✉ *100 Iberville St., French Quarter* ☎ *504/566–7006 or 800/996–3426* 🌐 *www.starwoodhotels.com/westin* *438 rooms, 41 suites* *In-room: Wi-Fi. In-hotel: restaurant, room service, bar, pool* *AE, D, DC, MC, V.*

5

CBD AND WAREHOUSE DISTRICT

$$ **Ambassador Hotel.** Guest rooms at this hotel bordering the CBD and Warehouse District have real character, with hardwood floors, oversize windows, and high ceilings. Four-poster iron beds, armoires, and local jazz prints are among the furnishings. Exposed-brick walls and ceiling fans add to the ambience of the pre–Civil War building. This is a good alternative to the huge convention hotels; you're just steps from the major downtown attractions and the Convention Center, and Harrah's New Orleans Casino is a five-minute walk. **Pros:** distinctive decor; urban-chic atmosphere. **Cons:** some first-floor rooms let in too much noise from street and lobby area. ✉ *535 Tchoupitoulas St., CBD* ☎ *504/527–5271 or 800/455–3417* 🌐 *www.ambassadorneworleans.com* *165 rooms* *In-room: Wi-Fi. In-hotel: restaurant, bar, parking (paid)* *AE, D, DC, MC, V.*

¢ **Courtyard by Marriott.** The iron trellis balcony overlooking St. Charles Avenue is just one of many nods to the Verandah Hotel, which occupied this building from 1829 to 1855. Architectural elements from the original hotel have been artfully incorporated into the current design, and the centerpiece of this property is a stunning six-story atrium. Balcony rooms overlooking St. Charles Avenue are in high demand during Mardi Gras. The dining room is open for breakfast only, but the hotel is within walking distance of several moderately priced restaurants and other attractions, including the kid-friendly Aquarium of the Americas. **Pros:** central CBD location; close to the French Quarter. **Cons:** significant street noise at all hours. ✉ *124 St. Charles Ave., CBD* ☎ *504/581–9005 or 800/321–2211* 🌐 *www.marriott.com* *140 rooms* *In-room: Wi-Fi. In-hotel: restaurant, pool, gym, parking (paid)* 💳 *AE, D, DC, MC, V.*

¢ **Depot House at Madame Julia's.** What once was Madame Julia's Boarding House is now a charming, no-frills collection of Creole town houses dating from 1830. All rooms have shared baths, but most guests don't seem to mind. The atmosphere is family-like and friendly; Joanne, the proprietor, says it's like staying at grandmother's without a curfew. Near major attractions, this B&B is recommended for visitors on a budget who appreciate authentic local ambience. A complimentary bakery breakfast is served under the garden tent. **Pros:** charming; owners are hospitable and fun; room rates are among the lowest in town. **Cons:** shared bathrooms; street noise; small rooms. ✉ *748 O'Keefe St., CBD* ☎ *504/529–2952* 📠 *504/529–1908* *15 rooms* *In-room: no phone* 💳 *No credit cards.*

$ **Doubletree Hotel.** This chain hotel is close to the river, across the street from Canal Place mall, and a block from the French Quarter. The small, comfortable lobby is adorned with floral arrangements and bowls of potpourri, along with the hotel's trademark jar of freshly baked chocolate-chip cookies. The decor is country French, and rooms have an open, airy feeling, with pastel draperies and spreads and light-color furniture. Rooms ending in 05 are larger. The hotel is adjacent to the French Quarter, close to tourist attractions and the Convention Center. **Pros:** adjacent to French Quarter and Riverfront attractions, across the street from the upscale Canal Place shops and the recently opened Insectarium. **Cons:** some rooms could use refreshing or updating; restaurant quality is average at best. ✉ *300 Canal St., CBD* ☎ *504/581–1300 or 800/222–8733* 🌐 *www.doubletree.com* *363 rooms, 15 suites* *In-room: Internet. In-hotel: restaurant, bar, pool, gym, laundry service, Wi-Fi, parking (paid), no-smoking rooms* 💳 *AE, D, DC, MC, V.*

$ **Embassy Suites.** If your primary target is the Morial Convention Center or the Warehouse District's contemporary-art galleries and museum collection, this is a great choice. The balconied high-rise sits right on Gallery Row. All suites have a bedroom and separate parlor (with three phones and a TV in each room); most have balconies. Room service is available from the Sugar House restaurant. A large atrium area is a great gathering spot for families. The Lofts at Embassy Suites is in a separate building just around the corner. Both properties are close to Morial Convention Center, which is about three blocks away. The hotel is also

BED AND BREAKFASTS

Bed-and-breakfasts provide an intimate alternative to hotels and motels, and New Orleans has many charming accommodations of this kind.

Bed & Breakfast.com (☎ *512/322–2710 or 800/462–2632* 🌐 *www.bedandbreakfast.com*).

New Orleans Bed & Breakfast and Accommodations (☎ *504/524–9918 or 888/240–0070* 🌐 *www.neworleansbandb.com*).

within walking distance of some of the best Warehouse/Arts District restaurants, including Emeril's and Tommy's Cuisine. **Pros:** spacious, well-maintained rooms. **Cons:** mediocre restaurant and room service. ✉ *315 Julia St., CBD* ☎ *504/525–1993 or 800/362–2779* 🌐 *www.embassyneworleans.com* *347 suites* *In-room: refrigerator, Wi-Fi. In-hotel: restaurant, gym* *AE, D, MC, V* *BP.*

$ **Hampton Inn.** This moderately priced facility is one of several office buildings that have been converted into hotels. The lobby, with lavish furnishings and decor, is an oasis in the midst of the bustling CBD. Rooms are large and comfortable, and all bathrooms have hair dryers. Among the safety features are key-access elevators. Just a few blocks from Bourbon Street, the hotel is surrounded by great restaurants and attractions. A surprisingly lavish complimentary buffet breakfast is served daily, and complimentary beer, wine, and snacks are served in the evening Monday through Thursday. **Pros:** particularly nice Continental breakfast; convenient to French Quarter (but be careful when walking at night). **Cons:** rooms that face the street can be noisy. ✉ *226 Carondelet St., CBD* ☎ *504/529–9990 or 800/426–7866* 🌐 *www.neworleanshamptoninns.com* *187 rooms* *In-room: refrigerator, Wi-Fi. In-hotel: restaurant, gym, parking (paid)* *AE, D, DC, MC, V* *CP.*

5

$ **Hampton Inn and Suites–Convention Center.** Two century-old warehouses have been converted into a French colonial–style hotel that is comfortable, architecturally distinctive, and moderately priced. The grand lobby has original hardwood floors and exposed-brick walls, and the lobby bar overlooks a pool and a lush garden courtyard. Rooms are large and airy, with four-poster beds and wood floors; many overlook a small park. The hotel is on the edge of the Warehouse District, directly across the street from the Convention Center; it's within walking distance of several moderately priced restaurants, including Wolfe's in the Warehouse, Rio Mar, and 7 on Fulton. **Pros:** exquisite renovation; architecturally stunning; minutes from Convention Center. **Cons:** extremely high traffic area. ✉ *1201 Convention Center Blvd., Warehouse District* ☎ *504/566–9990 or 800/292–0653* 🌐 *www.neworleanshamptoninns.com* *288 rooms* *In-room: Wi-Fi. In-hotel: bar, pool, gym, parking (paid)* *AE, D, DC, MC, V* *CP.*

$ **Harrah's New Orleans Hotel.** Located directly across the street from Harrah's New Orleans Casino, this 26-story hotel is richly appointed with marble floors, exquisite chandeliers, plush furnishings, and artwork selected and installed by local gallery owner Arthur Roger. The lobby-level restaurant, Ruth's Chris Steak House, is considered by locals to be among the best steak restaurants in the city. Guest rooms are larger than the local norm and have extras like refrigerators, high-definition televisions, cordless phones, and Wi-Fi. The Fulton Street Corridor, a four-block promenade featuring shops, private party spaces, and live entertainment areas, is connected to the hotel. **Pros:** well-trained staff provides above-average service; guests without cars can easily walk to Riverfront, CBD, and French Quarter attractions. **Cons:** the hustle and bustle of this part of town might not suit travelers seeking peace and quiet. ✉ *Poydras St. at Fulton St., CBD* ☎ *504/533–6000*

Fodor's Choice ★

or 800/847–5299 www.harrahs.com 450 rooms, 81 suites In-room: refrigerator, Wi-Fi. In-hotel: restaurant, bar, pool, gym, spa, laundry service AE, D, DC, MC, V.

$$ **Homewood Suites by Hilton.** This is one of the city's most central and spacious hotels (suites are 625 square feet). Contemporary furnishings mix easily with traditional New Orleans ambience. High ceilings, big windows, and a kid-friendly atmosphere make this a perfect pick for families. A complimentary buffet breakfast is served every morning; the manager's evening reception has beer, wine, and snacks. **Pros:** casual atmosphere; huge apartment-size rooms. **Cons:** no in-hotel restaurant—and you'll need to travel some distance for good dining choices. *901 Poydras St., CBD 504/581–5599 www.homewoodsuites.com 166 suites In-room: kitchen, refrigerator, Internet. In-hotel: pool, gym, Wi-Fi AE, D, DC, MC, V.*

$$ **Hotel InterContinental.** One of the major convention hotels, the InterContinental is a modern rose-granite structure overlooking St. Charles Avenue. Public spaces include a spacious, inviting second-floor lobby and a peaceful sculpture garden. Guest rooms are large and well lighted, with matching draperies and quilted spreads; balcony rooms overlook an urban garden. The Club level contains some of the city's finest suites, featuring original artwork commissioned for the hotel and antique furnishings from around the globe. **Pros:** superior service; elegant lobby-level cocktail lounge; club-level rooms are among the best accommodations in the city. **Cons:** located on one of the city's busiest downtown streets which can be less pleasant at night. *444 St. Charles Ave., CBD 504/525–5566 or 800/445–6563 www.intercontinental.com 482 rooms, 20 suites In-room: Internet. In-hotel: 2 restaurants, bar, pool, gym, laundry service, Wi-Fi, parking (paid) AE, D, DC, MC, V.*

$$$ **Hotel New Orleans.** This eight-story property is across the street from the Convention Center. Built around a three-story atrium, it has a handsome lobby with marble floors and wood paneling. All rooms are soundproof and have irons and ironing boards, coffeemakers, and hair dryers; executive rooms and suites have two phone lines, call waiting, and speakerphones. Several noteworthy restaurants, the Riverwalk, and Harrah's New Orleans Casino are within walking distance. **Pros:** close to Convention Center and Riverwalk shopping center. **Cons:** typical chain hotel; no trace of New Orleans decor or ambience. *881 Convention Center Blvd., Warehouse District 504/524–1881 or 800/465–4329 www.hotelneworleansconventioncenter.com 168 rooms, 2 suites In-room: Internet. In-hotel: restaurant, bar, gym, laundry facilities, Wi-Fi, no-smoking rooms AE, D, DC, MC, V CP.*

$$ **International House.** The lobby of this boutique hotel is an architectural dream, with 23-foot-high ceilings, ornate pilasters, marble floors, and a seasonally changing decor. Fine linens and fabrics enhance the guest rooms, which, although small, are attractively decorated in a contemporary New Orleans style. All rooms feature complimentary wireless service, iHome docking stations, and black-and-white photographs of jazz greats; bathrooms, featuring either glass-enclosed showers or oversize bathtubs as well as Aveda amenities, are sleek and contemporary.

A recent lobby redesign by L.A. designer LM Pagano is simultaneously elegant, cutting-edge, and inviting. In loa, the hotel's trendy see-and-be seen candlelit cocktail spot, Pagano tapped her fascination with romantic decadence, forming an excerpt from *Tales from a Thousand and One Nights* Arabian fantasy. **Pros:** great downtown location, especially appropriate for those who like cool, sophisticated surroundings. **Cons:** hotel faces busy downtown street with heavy traffic. ⊠*221 Camp St., CBD* ☎*504/553–9550 or 800/633–5770* ⊕*www.ihhotel.com* *119 rooms, 3 suites* *In-room: Wi-Fi. In-hotel: bar, gym, Wi-Fi, parking (paid)* *AE, D, MC, V.*

¢ **Lafayette Hotel.** This small brick building has housed the Lafayette since it was built in 1916. Handsome millwork, brass fittings, and marble baths adorn the property throughout. The tiny lobby is chic, and guest rooms are spacious and sunny. Some rooms have four-poster beds; all have cushy easy chairs and ottomans. Some second-floor rooms have floor-length windows that open onto a balcony; a number overlook Lafayette Square. **Pros:** streetcar stops right outside the front door; within walking distance of Riverfront and French Quarter attractions; pet friendly. **Cons:** not a great area for walking late at night. ⊠*600 St. Charles Ave., CBD* ☎*504/524–4441 or 800/733–4754* ⊕*www.thelafayettehotel.com* *24 rooms, 20 suites* *In-room: Wi-Fi. In-hotel: restaurant, laundry service, parking (paid), no-smoking rooms* *AE, D, DC, MC, V.*

$$$$ **Le Pavillon Hotel.** Magnificent chandeliers adorn the European-style lobby of this historic 1907 hotel, and a handsome collection of artwork lines the corridors; the marble railing in the clubby Gallery Lounge is originally from the Grand Hotel in Paris. Guest rooms have high ceilings and identical traditional decor; suites are particularly luxurious. The elegant Crystal Room has a huge weekday soup, salad, and pasta lunch buffet, as well as à la carte service. The opulent hotel bar has 30-foot ceilings, marble columns, and a magnificent mahogany bar. Locals consider it one of the most civilized spots in the city for an afternoon cocktail. **Pros:** elegant Old South ambience. **Cons:** guest rooms could use some updating and brightening. ⊠*833 Poydras St., CBD* ☎*504/581–3111 or 800/535–9095* ⊕*www.lepavillon.com* *219 rooms, 7 suites* *In-room: Wi-Fi. In-hotel: restaurant, bar, pool, gym, laundry service, parking (paid), no-smoking rooms* *AE, D, DC, MC, V.*

$$$ Fodor's Choice ★ **Loews New Orleans Hotel.** A refashioned bank building in the heart of downtown is home to this plush 21st-century hotel. The West Indies–style lobby provides a welcoming atmosphere, and bright, oversize rooms are enriched with local artwork and soothing colors. The guest rooms are among the largest and most well appointed in the city. Café Adelaide and the Swizzlestick Bar, both on the lobby level, are operated by the same family that owns the legendary Commander's Palace Restaurant. This may look like a typical chain hotel on the outside—but inside it's singular in its quality and consistency. **Pros:** well managed; accessible to everything that counts downtown; reliable service and product. **Cons:** located in one of the most high-traffic downtown areas. ⊠*300 Poydras St., CBD* ☎*504/595–5310 or 800/235–6397* ⊕*www.loewshotels.com* *273 rooms, 12 suites* *In-room: Wi-Fi.*

In-hotel: restaurant, bar, pool, gym, spa, laundry service ▭*AE, D, DC, MC, V.*

$$ **Loft 523.** This sleek, seductive loft hotel is so subtle from the outside, you may have trouble finding it among the surrounding buildings. Once inside, the atmosphere is strictly contemporary and chic—think Frank Lloyd Wright mixed with a SoHo loft. Cavernous limestone bathrooms with Aveda amenities, stone vanity tables, Frette linens, Fortuny lamps, and DVD surround-sound systems make this an adult playground. A personal assistant is assigned to you at check-in for your entire stay. **Pros:** sexiest environment of any hotel in the city. **Cons:** some guests may find the experience a bit too trendy. ✉*523 Gravier St., CBD* ☎*504/200–6523* 🌐*www.loft523.com* *16 rooms* *In-room: Internet, Wi-Fi. In-hotel: room service, bar, gym* ▭*AE, D, DC, MC, V.*

$$$ **New Orleans Hilton Riverside.** The sprawling multilevel Hilton complex sits right on the Mississippi, with superb views. Guest rooms have French provincial furnishings, and the 180 rooms that share a concierge have fax machines. The lavish Sunday brunch is consistently outstanding. Adjacent to Riverwalk Shopping Center, the hotel is directly across the street from Harrah's New Orleans Casino; the Riverfront streetcar stops out front. The health club is among the best in town, and the hotel has a resident golf pro and a four-hole putting green. Designed for large convention groups, this hotel is also a great choice for independent travelers. **Pros:** well-maintained facilities; hotel runs like a well-oiled machine. **Cons:** the city's biggest hotel; typical chain service and surroundings; garage needs better lighting and security. ✉*Poydras St. at the Mississippi River, CBD* ☎*504/561–0500 or 800/445–8667* 🌐*www.hilton.com* *1,600 rooms, 67 suites* *In-room: Wi-Fi. In-hotel: 3 restaurants, tennis courts, pools, gym, parking (paid), no-smoking rooms* ▭*AE, D, DC, MC, V.*

¢ **Parc St. Charles.** This property is on one of the Big Easy's best Carnival corners, at the intersection of Poydras Street and St. Charles Avenue. Rooms in the intimate hotel are decorated with contemporary furniture, and large plate-glass windows provide lots of light and wide views of the CBD. The hotel's restaurant, Panasia, serves Thai cuisine. **Pros:** possibly the best location for Mardi Gras parade viewing in the city; pet friendly. **Cons:** room decor is lackluster and needs updating or refreshing; street noise can be a problem at night. ✉*500 St. Charles Ave., CBD* ☎*504/522–9000 or 888/211–3447* 🌐*www.parcstcharles.com* *120 rooms, 2 suites* *In-room: safe, Wi-Fi. In-hotel: restaurant, bar, pool, gym, parking (paid), no-smoking rooms* ▭*AE, D, DC, MC, V.*

$ **Pelham Hotel.** A restored four-story office building houses the charming Pelham, an ideal place for those who want to be in the center of the CBD—near the Riverwalk, Harrah's New Orleans Casino, and the Convention Center—but who seek a quiet alternative to the bustling convention hotels. The small lobby has a green-marble floor and fresh flowers. Rooms are small; some have four-poster beds, and all have marble baths with terry robes and English soaps. Inside rooms, though attractively furnished, have no windows. You can use the fitness center and pool at the nearby Sheraton for $10 per day. **Pros:** centrally located, but far enough away from heavily traveled tourist streets; pet friendly. **Cons:**

guest rooms can be noisy from downtown traffic. ✉444 *Common St., CBD* ☎*504/522–4444 or 800/659–5621* 🌐*www.thepelhamhotel.com* *60 rooms* *In-room: safe, Wi-Fi. In-hotel: restaurant, room service, laundry service, parking (paid)* 💳*AE, D, DC, MC, V.*

¢ **Queen and Crescent Hotel.** Intimate and tasteful, this hotel two blocks outside the French Quarter is a good alternative to the mega-hotels that surround it. The 1913 building retains many of its original architectural elements. Guest rooms are small, but come with in-room coffeemakers, hair dryers, and ironing boards. The hotel is a good choice for business travelers who don't want to stay in the large convention properties. **Pros:** feels like a smaller, more intimate property. **Cons:** no in-hotel restaurant; not advisable to walk around the nearby neighborhood late at night. ✉*344 Camp St., CBD* ☎*504/587–9700 or 800/975–6652* 🌐*www.queenandcrescenthotel.com* *196 rooms* *In-room: safe, Wi-Fi. In-hotel: gym, parking (paid), no-smoking rooms* 💳*AE, D, DC, MC, V.*

HOTEL OR GALLERY?

Some of the best galleries in New Orleans are located in the Warehouse/Arts District, but guests at the Renaissance Arts Hotel don't even have to leave the property to see fine works of art. The Arthur Roger Project is located lobby level at the hotel, and fine art, all selected and installed by the renowned gallery owner, adorns the hotel's public spaces, guest rooms, and sculpture garden. Most of the art is local, although internationally known artists are represented as well.

$$ **Renaissance Arts Hotel.** Art lovers looking to stay close to downtown but not in the CBD should check out this circa-1910 warehouse-turned-hotel; the huge windows now make for great views from the guest rooms. Local gallery owner Arthur Roger—who opened a second location of his nationally acclaimed gallery on the lobby level—hand-selected every piece of art in the hotel. The comfortable, spacious, well-designed rooms are furnished with a minimalist bent. La Cote Brasserie, the hotel's restaurant, has an upscale, urban feel, with an open kitchen and rotating art displays. **Pros:** modern, well-appointed facilities; beautiful artwork. **Cons:** odd location—especially for those who want to walk downtown or to the French Quarter. ✉*700 Tchoupitoulas St., Warehouse District* ☎*504/613–2330 or 800/431–8634* 🌐*www.marriott.com* *208 rooms, 9 suites* *In-room: safe, Internet, Wi-Fi. In-hotel: restaurant, bar, pool* 💳*AE, D, DC, MC, V.*

$$ **Renaissance Pere Marquette Hotel.** Rooms at this historic downtown urban-chic property are generously sized and surprisingly quiet, even though the hotel sits in the middle of the CBD. Each has soothing colors, comfortable fabrics, and an oversize marble bathroom. A jazz theme is carried throughout the hotel, with each floor named after a renowned musician. **Pros:** lobby-level MiLa Restaurant is outstanding. **Cons:** chain property. ✉*817 Common St., CBD* ☎*504/525–1111 or 800/372–0482* 🌐*www.renaissancehotels.com* *275 rooms, 5 suites* *In-room: safe, Internet. In-hotel: restaurant, room service, bar, pool, gym, laundry service* 💳*AE, D, DC, MC, V.*

5

$$$ **Roosevelt Hotel New Orleans.** For more than a century the Roosevelt was an anchor in downtown New Orleans, until Hurricane Katrina decimated the storied property. Now, after a $145 million restoration and as part of the Waldorf-Astoria collection, the Roosevelt is back. The property features 500 rooms, including 135 luxury suites (some named for celebrities who once visited the hotel), and a 12,000-square-foot, world-class spa and fitness center. The legendary Sazerac Bar has reopened, and the Blue Room is back for Sunday brunch. Local chef John Besh helms the Italian-inspired Domenica Restaurant. **Pros:** exquisite lobby; central location near downtown and French Quarter. **Cons:** guests should exercise caution when walking in the area late at night. ✉ *123 Baronne St., CBD* ☎ *504/648–1200* 🌐 *www.therooseveltneworleans.com* *504 rooms, 135 suites* *In-room: Wi-Fi. In-hotel: 2 restaurants, bars, spa, Wi-Fi, parking (paid)* *AE, D, DC, MC, V.*

$ **St. James Hotel.** The St. James defines privacy in the CBD. Rooms, decorated West Indies–style with tropical accents, are set far enough from busy Magazine Street to ensure quiet and solitude. Restaurant Cuvée sits adjacent to the hotel lobby. This hotel is one of the best-kept secrets in the local hotel collection; it's a great choice for business travelers looking for proximity to the CBD and leisure travelers who want to avoid the high-energy atmosphere of the French Quarter. **Pros:** the epitome of privacy; pet friendly. **Cons:** room quality is inconsistent. ✉ *330 Magazine St., CBD* ☎ *504/304–4000* 🌐 *www.saintjameshotel.com* *86 rooms, 6 suites* *In-room: Wi-Fi. In-hotel: restaurant, pool, laundry service* *AE, D, MC, V.*

$$$ **Sheraton New Orleans.** The oversize lobby of this hotel is usually bustling with conventioneers. A tropical atmosphere permeates the Pelican Bar, which presents nightly jazz and sells a fine assortment of cigars. The hotel offers a nice balance of Creole and Cajun-style dishes in the airy second-floor Roux Bistro. Executive rooms come with many special amenities, but even regular guest rooms are spacious and well appointed. Expect top-quality service, but keep in mind that the hotel caters primarily to big convention groups. One of the great downtown eateries, the Palace Café, is right across Canal Street. **Pros:** large hotel with lots of availability; well-established staff; great service. **Cons:** typical corporate convention property; lacks the warmth of some of its competitors. ✉ *500 Canal St., CBD* ☎ *504/525–2500 or 800/253–6156* 🌐 *www.sheratonneworleans.com* *1,100 rooms, 72 suites* *In-room: Wi-Fi. In-hotel: 3 restaurants, bar, pool, gym, parking (paid), no-smoking rooms* *AE, D, DC, MC, V.*

$$ **Staybridge Suites New Orleans.** The emergence of the utilitarian all-suites hotel in the early 1990s has spawned numerous versions, but this one is exceptionally comfortable. Spacious guest rooms have full kitchenettes, a business work area, free Wi-Fi, and nice city views. The hotel has limited housekeeping service, on-site laundry facilities, and a good-size pool. The best feature here is the location—right across from Harrah's Casino, within walking distance of riverfront attractions and the Convention Center. **Pros:** located directly across from Harrah's Casino; within walking distance of riverfront attractions; spacious all-suites accommodations. **Cons:** a bit generic; no in-hotel restaurant;

located on one of the busiest corners in the downtown area. ✉*502 Tchoupitoulas St., CBD* ☎*504/571–1818 or 800/541–4998* 🌐*www.staybridge.com* *182 suites* *In-room: Wi-Fi. In-hotel: bar, gym, Wi-Fi, parking (paid)* *AE, D, MC, V.*

$$$$ **W Hotel New Orleans.** A sleek, contemporary blend of East Coast sophistication and Southern charm gives way to inspired accommodations at the W. Rooms are decorated in red and black, with first-rate amenities such as Bliss bath products and beds with goose-down pillows and comforters; 100 are designated as home-office rooms. The lobby has a trendy upscale look, and the Rande Gerber–designed Whiskey Blue lounge is on the lobby level. **Pros:** great for those looking for contemporary, hip quarters. **Cons:** beautifully designed, but lacking the warmth of comparable properties in the city. ✉*333 Poydras St., CBD* ☎*504/525–9444 or 800/777–7372* 🌐*www.whotels.com* *423 rooms, 23 suites* *In-room: Wi-Fi. In-hotel: restaurant, gym, Wi-Fi, parking (paid)* *AE, D, DC, MC, V.*

5

$ **The Whitney, A Wyndham Historic Hotel.** The historic Whitney Bank Building has been classically restyled into a true European-style hotel. Listed on the National Register of Historic Places, this elegant property is in the middle of downtown. Rooms include comfy pillow-top mattresses, upscale toiletries and amenities, and ergonomic chairs. **Pros:** L'il Dizzy's Café—known for authentic soul food—is located on the lobby level. **Cons:** located at one of the busiest downtown intersections in the city; restaurant is breakfast only. ✉*610 Poydras St., CBD* ☎*504/581–4222 or 800/996–3426* 🌐*www.wyndham.com* *70 rooms, 23 suites* *In-room: Internet, Wi-Fi. In-hotel: restaurant, bar, gym, no-smoking rooms* *AE, D, MC, V.*

$$$ **Windsor Court Hotel.** Exquisite, gracious, elegant, eminently civilized—
Fodor's Choice ★ these words are frequently used to describe Windsor Court, but all fail to capture the wonderful essence of this hotel. From Le Salon's delightful afternoon tea—the city's only authentic European presentation, served daily in the lobby—to the unbelievably large rooms, this is one of *the* places to stay in New Orleans. Plush carpeting, canopy and four-poster beds, fully stocked wet bars, marble vanities, and mirrored dressing areas are just a few of the many amenities. The Grill Room is considered the premiere fine-dining room in the city, and the Polo Lounge has one of the best martini presentations to be found anywhere, as well as a highly imaginative appetizer menu. The hotel is four blocks from the French Quarter and easy walking distance to the Riverfront and fabulous shopping options. **Pros:** old-world elegance; superior service. **Cons:**. lobby is on the 11th floor; only two elevators from ground level to lobby. ✉*300 Gravier St., CBD* ☎*504/523–6000 or 800/262–2662* 🌐*www.windsorcourthotel.com* *58 rooms, 266 suites, 1 penthouse* *In-room: Wi-Fi. In-hotel: 2 restaurants, bar, pool, gym, laundry service, parking (paid)* *AE, D, DC, MC, V.*

GARDEN DISTRICT/UPTOWN

$ **Avenue Plaza Resort.** A spartan lobby belies the many amenities here. Public areas include a romantic lounge with dark-wood panels from a French chalet. Spacious rooms have generous dressing areas; decor is

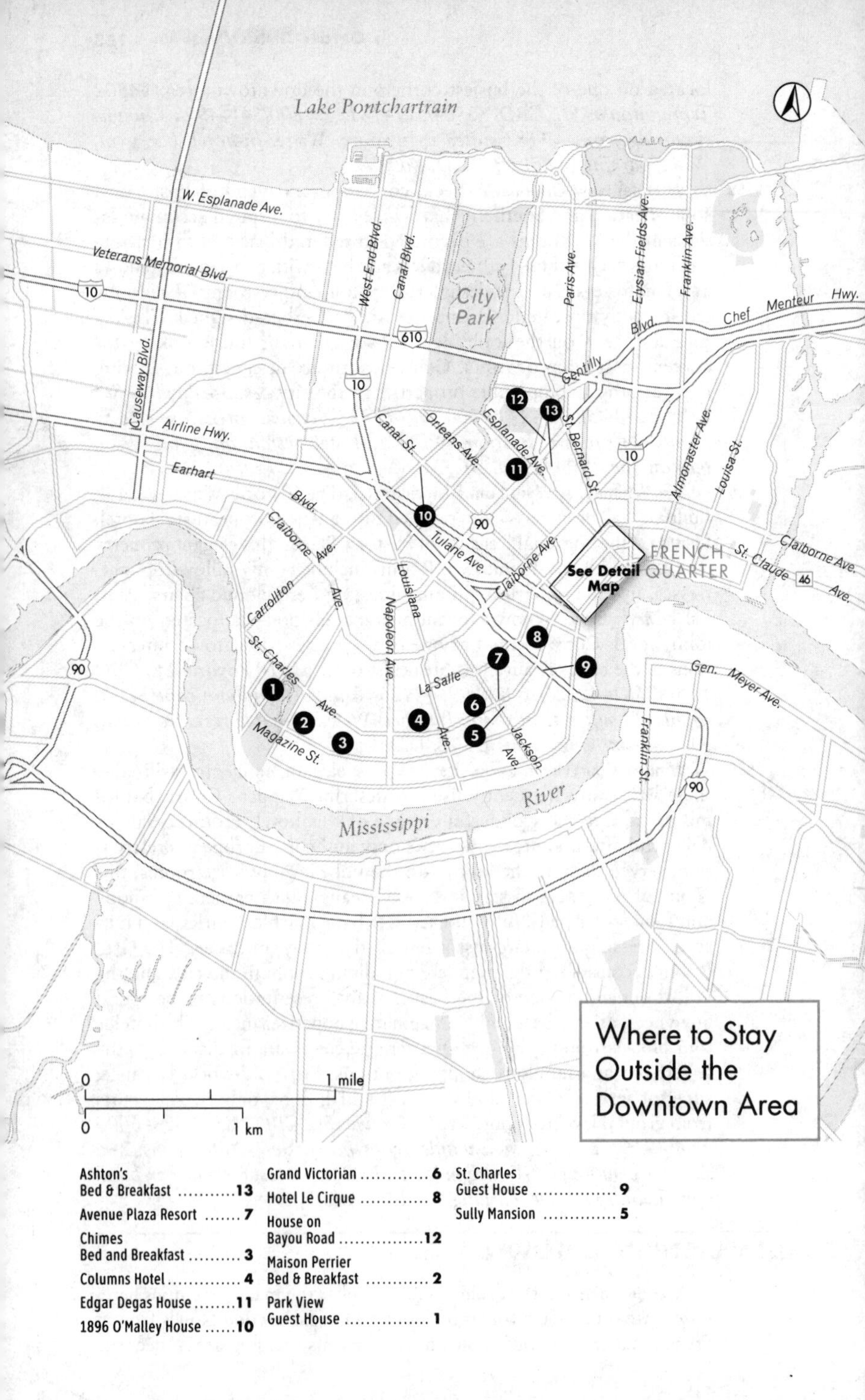

Lake Pontchartrain
W. Esplanade Ave.
Veterans Memorial Blvd.
10
Causeway Blvd.
West End Blvd.
Canal Blvd.
City Park
610
10
Paris Ave.
Elysian Fields Ave.
Franklin Ave.
Chef Menteur Hwy.
Blvd.
Gentilly
Airline Hwy.
Earhart
Blvd.
Canal St.
Orleans Ave.
Esplanade Ave.
St. Bernard St.
10
Almonaster Ave.
Louisa St.
Claiborne Ave.
90
Tulane Ave.
Claiborne Ave.
See Detail Map
FRENCH QUARTER
St. Claude Ave.
Claiborne Ave.
46
Carrollton Ave.
Louisiana
Napoleon Ave.
St. Charles Ave.
La Salle
Ave.
Magazine St.
Jackson Ave.
Gen. Meyer Ave.
90
Franklin St.
90
Mississippi River
0 1 mile
0 1 km
Where to Stay Outside the Downtown Area
Ashton's Bed & Breakfast 13
Avenue Plaza Resort 7
Chimes Bed and Breakfast 3
Columns Hotel 4
Edgar Degas House 11
1896 O'Malley House 10
Grand Victorian 6
Hotel Le Cirque 8
House on Bayou Road 12
Maison Perrier Bed & Breakfast 2
Park View Guest House 1
St. Charles Guest House 9
Sully Mansion 5

either traditional or art deco—both are equally appealing. The health club has a Turkish steam bath, Swiss showers, and a Scandinavian sauna. The pool is in a pleasant courtyard, and a sundeck and hot tub are on the roof. If you're looking for real local charm, this is the place. Mr. John's Steakhouse, located on the lobby level, is great for a moderately priced steak. **Pros:** picturesque location; delightful private pool and patio area. **Cons:** room decor is a bit dated. ✉*2111 St. Charles Ave., Garden District* ☎*504/566–1212 or 800/439–6493* 🌐*www.avenueplazahotel.com* *256 suites* *In-room: kitchen, refrigerator, Wi-Fi. In-hotel: restaurant, bar, pool, gym, spa, laundry facilities, parking (paid)* 💳*AE, D, DC, MC, V.*

$ **Chimes Bed and Breakfast.** Jill and Charles Abbyad's charming Uptown residence has rooms in the main house and a converted carriage house, with hardwood or slate floors. The Abbyads maintain a homey environment with all the conveniences of a large hotel: hair dryers, irons, stereos, coffeemakers, and private entrances. A Continental breakfast is served in the airy dining room; afterward, you can relax in the butterfly garden in the courtyard. English, French, Arabic, and Spanish are spoken in the house, and children are welcome. All rooms have private entrances onto the courtyard. **Pros:** premises and guest rooms are extremely well kept and clean. **Cons:** noise carries easily from room to room. ✉*1146 Constantinople St., Uptown* ☎*504/899–2621* 🌐*www.chimesneworleans.com* *5 rooms* *In-room: Internet, Wi-Fi. In-hotel: some pets allowed, no-smoking rooms* 💳*AE, MC, V* *CP.*

Fodor's Choice ★

$ **Columns Hotel.** This impressive, white-columned 1883 Victorian hotel is listed on the National Register of Historic Places. The wide veranda, set with cloth-covered tables for outdoor dining or cocktails, is very inviting, as are the two parlors furnished with period pieces. Dark and intimate, the lounge is a favorite with locals and has excellent live progressive jazz Monday through Thursday; there's also a Sunday jazz brunch. One of the most impressive staircases you may ever climb leads to the large—though somewhat sparsely furnished—rooms. If you can wangle a weekend Mardi Gras reservation here, you'll have one of the best seats on St. Charles Avenue for the nightly parades. **Pros:** exquisite architecture; having a cocktail on the veranda is one of the city's great pleasures; perfect parade-watching spot. **Cons:** second-floor rooms feel a bit stale (try to book on the third floor). ✉*3811 St. Charles Ave., Uptown* ☎*504/899–9308 or 800/445–9308* 🌐*www.thecolumns.com* *20 rooms* *In-room: Wi-Fi. In-hotel: restaurant, bar* 💳*AE, MC, V* *CP.*

¢ **1896 O'Malley House.** This house is sheer elegance. Rooms are furnished with beautiful antiques, with heavy cypress doors, hardwood floors, granite bathroom counters, and oversize windows with plush draperies. The owners have paid attention to every detail, down to the chocolates delivered with the evening turndown service—on a silver tray. Step outside and board the Canal Street streetcar for a quick ride downtown. This place is a true find. **Pros:** surprisingly low rates; steps away from the Canal Street streetcar line. **Cons:** some distance from downtown and French Quarter attractions. ✉*120 S. Pierce St., Uptown*

5

☎504/488–5896 or 866/226–1896 🌐www.1896omalleyhouse.com ⇨8 rooms ⚐In-room: Wi-Fi ▭AE, MC, V ¶CP.

$$ **Grand Victorian Bed & Breakfast.** Just a block and a half from Commander's Palace Restaurant, the Grand Victorian more than lives up to its lofty name. Each lavishly appointed room evokes old Louisiana with period pieces and distinctive private baths. The Greenwood Suite includes a hot tub, stained-glass windows, and a private balcony that extends across the front of the house and overlooks historic St. Charles Avenue. An oak-shaded common balcony on the second floor stands atop a traditional New Orleans garden. A Continental breakfast is served in either the dining room or on the balcony. **Pros:** true elegance; rooms are exquisitely appointed; possibly the best B&B value in the area. **Cons:** located on a high-traffic street. *✉2727 St. Charles Ave., Garden District ☎504/895–1104 or 800/977–0008 🌐www.gvbb.com ⇨8 rooms ⚐In-room: Wi-Fi. In-hotel: restaurant ▭AE, D, MC, V.*

Fodor's Choice ★

¢ **Hotel Le Cirque.** This former YMCA has been artfully transformed into a stylish, contemporary boutique hotel. Rooms are extremely small but elegant, with chic minimalist decor. The hotel's extensive art collection includes Herb Ritts's black-and-white photos in public areas and Philippe Starck benches in the courtyard. It's located somewhat off the beaten path, between downtown and the Garden District. **Pros:** streetcar stop right outside the front door; urban-chic decor. **Cons:** exercise caution in this area if you go out after dark; limited lobby space and public areas; small rooms. *✉2 Lee Circle, CBD ☎504/962–0900 🌐www.hotellecirqueneworleans.com ⇨137 rooms, 2 suites ⚐In-room: Wi-Fi. In-hotel: restaurant, bar, spa ▭AE, D, MC, V.*

$ **Maison Perrier Bed & Breakfast.** This 1890s Victorian mansion reportedly housed a gentlemen's club, and rooms have been named after the ladies of the evening who entertained here. Comfortable, spacious rooms have high ceilings and exceptionally large, well-appointed private baths; some have private balconies and sitting rooms. The daily homemade breakfast may include waffles and praline French toast. Fresh-baked brownies and tea are served in late afternoon; complimentary wine, beer, and cheese are served in the charming front parlor on Friday and Saturday evening. **Pros:** recent redecorating has truly brought the place up a notch; the lavender "Dolly's Room" is one of the most beautiful rooms in town; fantastic balconies for Mardi Gras parade watching. **Cons:** rooms that face St. Charles Avenue can be noisy. *✉4117 Perrier St., Uptown ☎504/897–1807 or 888/610–1807 🌐www.maisonperrier.com ⇨9 rooms ⚐In-room: Wi-Fi ▭AE, D, MC, V.*

$ **Park View Guest House.** Adjacent to beautiful Audubon Park, this Victorian guesthouse has graced St. Charles Avenue since 1884. Rooms on the east side have great views of the park. The general rule here is that you get either antiques or a view: brass beds and ceiling fans are found in the "view" rooms. There is a lounge with a fireplace, and breakfast is served in a bay-window dining room. **Pros:** incomparable views of Audubon Park; easy access to St. Charles streetcar line; great restaurants nearby. **Cons:** not convenient to downtown or French Quarter attractions. *✉7004 St. Charles Ave., Uptown ☎504/861–7564 or*

888/533–0746 @www.parkviewguesthouse.com 22 rooms, 16 with bath In-room: Wi-Fi AE, D, MC, V CP.

¢ **St. Charles Guest House.** Simple and affordable, this 125-year-old European-style B&B is located in the historic Garden District, convenient to the St. Charles Avenue streetcar line (stop 11) and an easy ride or walk to the French Quarter (just 17 blocks away). A complimentary bakery breakfast is served by the pool. Telephones are available in the lobby, but books replace TVs in this low-tech, high-character guesthouse (though Internet and fax service are available in the office). The peace and quiet is often interrupted by the musicians, artists, and educators discussing the *laissez les bons temps rouler* nature of the city. Tours can be arranged at the front desk. **Pros:** rates are among the lowest in town; within walking distance of the St. Charles streetcar line; well run by B&B veterans Joanne and Dennis Hilton. **Cons:** spartan furnishings and surroundings. *1748 Prytania St., Garden District 504/523–6556 @www.stcharlesguesthouse.com 30 rooms, 24 with bath In-room: no a/c (some), no TV, Wi-Fi. In-hotel: pool AE, MC, V CP.*

5

$ **Sully Mansion.** New Orleans architect Thomas Sully built this handsome, rambling Queen Anne–style house in 1890. In the foyer, light filters through stunning, pastel-color stained-glass windows that are original to the house. The guest rooms have high ceilings, oil paintings, tall windows with swagged floor-length drapes, and Victorian hand-me-downs. A neighbor to other grand mansions, the house is on a tree-lined street—just a block from St. Charles Avenue and close to Magazine Street shops. **Pros:** old-world charm; owners are experts at paying individual attention to guests. **Cons:** not located near major tourist attractions. *2631 Prytania St., Garden District 504/891–0457 or 800/364–2414 @www.sullymansion.com 5 rooms, 2 suites In-room: Wi-Fi AE, D, MC, V CP.*

MID-CITY

$ **Ashton's Bed & Breakfast.** Few details have been missed in re-creating this sumptuous 1861 mansion, nine blocks from the French Quarter. Eight distinctively appointed guest rooms have a range of beds, including iron, Shaker, and four-poster. The full breakfast includes such treats as *pain perdu* (French toast), eggs Benedict, and crab cakes. Fresh baked goods and snacks are constantly replenished in the house. The common parlor has a selection of great books, and the backyard is intimate and quiet. Concierge services are provided. **Pros:** exquisite, spacious room decor; nice location, not far from New Orleans City Park. **Cons:** no streetcar or easy public transportation nearby. *2023 Esplanade Ave., Mid-City 504/942–7048 or 800/725–4131 @www.ashtonsbb.com 8 rooms In-room: Wi-Fi AE, MC, V BP.*

¢ Fodor's Choice ★ **Edgar Degas House.** Once home to French impressionist Edgar Degas, this historic 1852 home retains its original floor plan and colors. Spacious second-floor rooms have chandeliers that hang from 14-foot ceilings; one has a whirlpool bath; another has a balcony. The owners are happy to give you a private tour of the house, which has become a favorite local spot for weddings and private parties. Parlors on the first floor display reproductions of the artist's works. You can have an authentic Creole breakfast in the large private rear courtyard. **Pros:** meticulously maintained and expertly operated; designated on the National Register of Historic Places. **Cons:** no streetcar or easy public transportation nearby. ✉*2306 Esplanade Ave., Mid-City* ☎*504/821–5009 or 800/755–6730* 🌐*www.degashouse.com* *9 rooms* *In-room: Wi-Fi* *AE, MC, V* *CP.*

$$ **House on Bayou Road.** This circa-1798 West Indies–style Creole plantation home, set on 2 acres of lawns and gardens, has rooms filled with Louisiana antiques, including handsome four-poster featherbeds. Accommodations are in the main house as well as in detached cottages. The grand suite in the private cottage has a skylight over the bed, bookshelves, and a whirlpool bath. A celebrity favorite, this inn has hosted Dan Aykroyd, Alfre Woodard, and Fran Drescher. A cooking school is conducted on the premises. **Pros:** quiet; private; a bit off the beaten path. **Cons:** be careful about walking in this area after dark; not really convenient to restaurants. ✉*2275 Bayou Rd., Bayou St. John* ☎*504/945–0992, 504/949–7711, or 800/882–2968* 🌐*www.houseonbayouroad.com* *8 rooms, 1 cottage* *In-room: Wi-Fi. In-hotel: pool* *AE, DC, MC, V* *BP.*

DELICIOUS DIGS

The luxurious House on Bayou Road has a truly unique amenity—a cooking school. The New Orleans Cooking Experience, which offers half-day and multiday classes, is located in the 1798 inn's state-of-the-art teaching kitchen. For total immersion, sign up for the cooking school vacation program, which focuses on traditional Creole and Cajun recipes; classes are taught by noted New Orleans chefs like James Beard Award–winning chef Frank Brigtsen and New Orleans's "food diva," Poppy Tooker.

Nightlife and the Arts

6

WORD OF MOUTH

"Many of the bars had live music and I have never heard such wonderful bands whether in a bar, a restaurant, or even the street. We hated to ever move along because there seems to be such talent. It was definitely an experience. The Hurricanes were very sweet, but after two I was wearing boas!!"

—writealiving

"I walked past the French Quarter through part of Marigny the residential area and Frenchmen's Reef, a street of jazz bars which my bartender last night told me to explore—much nicer than Bourbon Street."

—NeoPatrick

www.fodors.com/community

By David Parker Jr.

PEOPLE COME HERE TO EAT, LISTEN TO LIVE MUSIC, AND PARTY; and the city still delivers on all three counts. No American town places such a premium on pleasure as New Orleans. From swank hotel lounges to sweaty dance clubs, refined jazz clubs and raucous Bourbon Street bars, this city is serious about frivolity—and famous for it. Partying is more than an occasional indulgence in this city—it's a lifestyle.

New Orleans's fabled nightlife was one of the first things to rebound from Hurricane Katrina; indeed, one French Quarter bar, Johnny White's, never closed its doors throughout the entire disaster, serving warm beer by candlelight and keeping a 24-7 vigil until the rest of the city returned to join them. Sure enough, Bourbon Street is once again awash in neon and noise.

Many New Orleans artists, who found themselves in a limelight of national and international attention, have used the depth of their experiences to produce some of the most vibrant music, theater, literature, and creative work to come out of New Orleans in decades. From the colorful performances of the Wild Magnolia Mardi Gras Indians to the Pulitzer-nominated plays of John Biguenet, New Orleans music and culture has been infused with new inspirations, both uplifting and tragic, and is reaching wider audiences than ever. More than just jazz and blues, the city features rock, hip-hop, avant-garde fusion, Cajun and zydeco, folk, electronica, and homegrown New Orleans R&B.

Wherever you go you're sure to find a venue that suits your tastes. Quiet and charming or wild and raucous. New and chic or 1800s elegant. Whether you're looking for the simple pleasures of a local brew, or something entirely more decadent, this is a city that lives to accommodate. And while Bourbon Street, with its bright lights and beers-to-go, is usually one of the first stops for visitors, it's not truly representative of the city. The real soul of New Orleans nightlife lies in the out-of-the-way clubs, the impromptu street parties, and the music that wafts from rustic dives.

If you don't care for the club scene, or have kids in tow, you can always take to the streets. Throughout the French Quarter, and especially along Royal Street and Jackson Square, brass bands, gypsy bands, and blues performers play for tips and applause. Outdoor cafés along Decatur Street have live jazz bands most days of the week, and the National Park Service sponsors free live music shows at a couple of locations in the French Quarter: the patio of its headquarters at 419 Decatur Street, and on a stage at the French Market visitor center for the New Orleans Jazz National Historical Park (919 North Peters Street)—which also has a good selection of books and CDs. Call *504/589–4841* or visit *www.nps.gov/jazz* for a schedule. The Louisiana Music Factory (210 Decatur Street), which is the city's greatest record store for local music, hosts in-store appearances by artists. Call ahead for a schedule and information at ☎*504/586–1094* or visit 🌐*www.louisianamusicfactory.com*.

CLOSE UP

Practical Matters

Bars tend to open in the early afternoon and stay open well into the morning hours. Live music, while abundant, is a little less predictable. A handful of French Quarter clubs have sets beginning in the early afternoon, and many more venues will get going around 6. For the most part, however, gigs begin between 10 and 11 PM, and this is when you'll spot locals descending on their favorite night spots. Bear in mind that many venues operate on "New Orleans time," meaning that if a show is advertised for 10 PM then it might kick off closer to 11.

Dress codes are as rare as snow in this city. On any given night in the French Quarter, and especially during the Carnival season, you'll see everything from tuxedoes to tutus, from fairy wings and ball gowns to T-shirts and torn jeans.

Many bars on Bourbon Street entice visitors by presenting bands or strip shows with no cover charge. They make their money by imposing a one- or two-drink minimum, with draft beer or soft drinks costing $5 to $8 apiece. In general prices for beer, wine, and cocktails range from $4 to $9, unless you land in a good neighborhood dive bar, and then the prices can drop by as much as half. Music clubs generally charge a flat cover between $5 and $20, with the high-end prices usually reserved for national touring artists, holidays, and special occasions.

A great source of information and entertainment is WWOZ at 90.7 FM, the public radio station which showcases New Orleans music and announces a nightly calendar of concerts and events. For more detailed event listings, consult the Friday "Lagniappe" section of the *Times-Picayune,* or pick up a copy of *Gambit,* the alternative weekly that is carried free in many bars, cafés, and stores. The monthly *OffBeat* magazine has in-depth coverage of local music and venues and is available at many hotels, stores, and restaurants. All of these publications have up-to-date listings on their Web sites.

6

BARS AND LOUNGES

FRENCH QUARTER

Bar Tonique. Nestled in among the eclectic nightspots on North Rampart Street, this wine-and-cocktail bar harkens back to bygone eras, serving absinthe drinks and 19th-century Sazeracs in a brick-walled lounge with private nooks and crannies and a beautiful outdoor courtyard. A favorite among the theater crowd. ✉ *820 N. Rampart St., French Quarter* ☎ *504/324–6045.*

★ **Bombay Club.** A longtime favorite for the martini set, Bombay Club has become equally known for its upscale dinner menu. It's a rather swanky place for the French Quarter, with leather chairs and dark paneling, and one of the few places in the city that enforces a dress code, although it's not overly formal: no shorts, no jeans. Tucked away from the street, this bar in the Prince Conti Hotel hosts live music on many nights. ✉ *830 Conti St., French Quarter* ☎ *504/586–0972.*

★ **Carousel Revolving Bar.** The piano bar at the Hotel Monteleone comes with a literary pedigree: Tennessee Williams, Truman Capote, and

Ernest Hemingway all drank here. Grab a bar stool at the eponymous revolving carousel and mull over your own Great American Novel. ✉ *214 Royal St., French Quarter* ☎ *504/523–3341.*

Cat's Meow. There are many New Orleanians who rarely set foot in the French Quarter; when they do, they tend to gravitate toward this popular karaoke bar, where "American Idol" wannabes of all ages come to practice their chops. Even Louisiana export Britney Spears is said to have graced the stage at the Cat's Meow—long before she was tabloid fodder, of course. ✉ *701 Bourbon St., French Quarter* ☎ *504/523–1157.*

Chart Room. Unpretentious even by New Orleans standards, this little bar not far from Canal Street draws a good number of locals from the Quarter and beyond. Drinks are a better value here than at many places in the neighborhood. ✉ *300 Chartres St., French Quarter* ☎ *504/522–1708.*

Cosimo's. Few tourists make their way to this hip neighborhood bar tucked away in a far corner of the Lower Quarter. A short flight of stairs leads to a pool and dart room, and quirky chandeliers, ample windows, and a decent wine selection lend the street-level bar a touch of class. An adjacent restaurant serves Tex-Mex treats, including fish tacos and fat burritos; to order, you have to ring a bell and the chef pops his head out the kitchen door. ✉ *1201 Burgundy St., French Quarter* ☎ *504/522–9715.*

Crescent City Brewhouse. This convivial brewpub makes five specialty brews on the premises and one seasonal selection. The suds pair well with oysters on the half shell and other pub grub. Jazz combos set up near the entrance most afternoons, and seating on a second-floor balcony affords a nice view of the Mississippi River and busy Decatur Street. ✉ *527 Decatur St., French Quarter* ☎ *504/522–0571.*

The Dungeon. A narrow alley leads to this aptly named, skull-and-chain-theme bar, which doesn't open until 10:30 PM. Partying here is a rite of passage for many young locals, and the place has become a cult destination of sorts; the rich and famous might turn up, shaking it on the dance floor alongside the regulars. It's not to be confused with the Front of the Dungeon, a more-traditional bar next door. ✉ *738 Toulouse St., French Quarter* ☎ *504/523–5530.*

★ **French 75.** Sophistication awaits in the form of rich cigars and fine liquor served up in cozy French-style surroundings. The specialty here is the French 75, made with brandy and premium champagne. After a round or two, venture upstairs to the Germaine Wells Mardi Gras Museum, showcase for many ball gowns worn by the original owner's daughter. ✉ *813 Bienville St., French Quarter* ☎ *504/523–5433.*

Kerry Irish Pub. This comfortably well-worn Irish pub has a pool table, a jukebox stocked with the Pogues and Flogging Molly and, of course, Guinness on draft. A small stage at the back hosts singer-songwriters and R&B or jazz musicians most evenings, with no cover charge. ✉ *331 Decatur St., French Quarter* ☎ *504/527–5954.*

Fodor's Choice ★ **Lafitte's Blacksmith Shop.** Probably the most photographed building in the Quarter after St. Louis Cathedral, this 18th-century cottage was, according to legend, once a blacksmith shop that served as a front for

CLOSE UP

Nightlife Around Town

The **French Quarter** and the **Faubourg Marigny** are the easiest places to hear music. Dozens of quality bands play nightly at clubs that are within walking distance of one another, and the myriad dining options makes it convenient to spend a whole evening here. Frenchmen Street in the Marigny is currently the hottest music strip in town. Locals also flock to this area for the food and the street life. Much of Frenchmen's activity is within a three-block area. You can roam the streets, pub crawl, or simply people-watch outside on the sidewalk—a popular activity on weekend nights and during peak festival seasons. Some clubs along this strip charge a $5–$10 cover for music, but many charge none at all. Snug Harbor, the premiere modern-jazz venue in town, is pricier, with shows usually costing $10–$20, but a seat is always guaranteed.

Uptown is rich in clubs, although they are far less concentrated, tucked instead down various residential and commercial streets. A minor hub has formed around the Riverbend area, far uptown where St. Charles Avenue and Carrollton Avenue intersect. Cooter Brown's, right at the levee, is a good stop for imported beers and local grub, served all night. Some blocks away, near Carrollton and Oak streets, the Maple Leaf hosts live music every night of the week. Around the corner you will find Carrollton Station, which has bands on the weekends, although walking the few short blocks is not a good idea. Another hub is Magazine Street in the lower Garden District, where you can sit at an outdoor table at the Bulldog or drink on the balcony at the Balcony Bar. Although driving the two minutes from one spot to the next might seem silly, for safety's sake it's best to call a taxi at night.

The **Warehouse District** harbors a number of good bars and clubs, some of them in renovated 19th-century warehouses that hark back to the city's cotton exporting heyday. The enormous New Orleans Convention Center runs along the edge of this district, and many spots are often filled with dazed conventioneers. The Central Business District (CBD) is mostly quiet at night, but closer to the edge of Canal Street and the French Quarter are some terrific nightspots, like the Sazerac Bar in the newly renovated Roosevelt Hotel or the swanky dance club and lounge Ampersand in the converted Whitney Bank building.

Perhaps the edgiest local scene is in the **Bywater** District, home to a dozen low-key bars, straight, gay, and mixed. The corner of Royal and Franklin streets forms something of a hub, with a smattering of bars catering to a varied crowd. At the far end of the Bywater, you can be sure to find one of the hippest events of the week when Kermit Ruffins plays Vaughan's every Thursday. On Sunday a mini-party takes place in the courtyard of the wine retail shop, Bacchanal.

Mid-City, the area near City Park and Bayou St. John, is chock-full of neighborhood joints. There are some hidden treasures, from unique wine and cocktail bars like Clever Wine Bar in the renovated American Can Company building overlooking the bayou, to the ever-popular Rock 'n' Bowl, moved down the street to a new location in 2009. Venues are fairly spread out, so a car or taxi is recommended at night.

the eponymous pirate's less legitimate business ventures. Today, it's a popular and atmospheric piano bar with a rustic, candlelit interior and a small outdoor patio that has banana trees and a sculpture by the late Enrique Alferez (whose work also decorates City Park). ✉*941 Bourbon St., French Quarter* ☎*504/522–9397*.

LIGHTS OUT

In January 2007, Louisiana enacted a law that bans smoking in restaurants and in bars where food accounts for more than 50% of total sales. Check before you light up; just because it looks like a bar doesn't mean you can enjoy that cigar.

Molly's at the Market. This stretch of Decatur Street sports a number of hangouts where bartenders and waiters from other downtown spots wind down after their shifts. Molly's also draws a lot of writers and local media types with special happy hours for journalists; during campaign season, candidates for mayor and city council serve as guest bartenders, mixing drinks for and sparring with reporters. ✉*1107 Decatur St., French Quarter* ☎*504/525–5169*.

★ **Napoleon House Bar and Cafe.** This vintage watering hole has long been popular with writers, artists, and various other free spirits; even locals who don't venture often into the French Quarter will make it a special destination. It's a living shrine to the New Orleans school of decor: faded grandeur. Chipped wall paint, diffused light, and a tiny courtyard with a trickling fountain and lush banana trees create a timeless escapist mood. The house specialty is a Pimm's Cup (Pimm's No. 1, juice, and club soda—a sort of fizzy, spiked lemonade); a menu including sandwiches, soups, salads, and cheese boards is also available. This is the perfect place for late-afternoon people-watching. ✉*500 Chartres St., French Quarter* ☎*504/524–9752*.

Old Absinthe House. A low-key oasis in the middle of Bourbon Street's excess, the building that houses this popular watering hole has had some illustrious visitors over its 200-year history, including Oscar Wilde, Mark Twain, Franklin Roosevelt, and Frank Sinatra. Thousands of business cards stapled to the wall serve as interesting wallpaper. ✉*240 Bourbon St., French Quarter* ☎*504/523–3181*.

★ **Pat O'Brien's.** Sure, it's touristy, but there are reasons Pat O's has been a must-stop on the New Orleans cocktail trail for so long. For one thing, there's plenty of room to spread out, from the elegant side bar and piano bar that flank the carriageway entrance to the lush (and in winter, heated) patio. Friendly staff, an easy camaraderie among patrons, and a signature drink—the pink, cloying, and extremely potent Hurricane, which comes with a souvenir glass—make this French Quarter stalwart a pleasant afternoon diversion. ✉*718 St. Peter St., French Quarter* ☎*504/525–4823*.

Pravda. If there is a rule that every major city aspiring to some measure of cultural life must have at least one Soviet and/or Cold War communism-themed bar within its boundaries, then Pravda is an exceptionally skillful take on the form. A luxurious salon/boudoir/cabaret decor greets patrons, complete with plush red velvet and an impressive selection of absinthes from around the world. The beautiful back garden, surprising in its openness after the warmth and intimacy of the bar space, is said to be a reenactment of the primitivist spirit behind fantasies of collectivist social organization. ⊠*1113 Decatur St., French Quarter* ☎*504/525–1818.*

FAUBOURG MARIGNY AND BYWATER

★ **Bacchanal Fine Wine & Spirits.** Although technically a wineshop, Bacchanal, in the far reaches of Bywater, is also part tasting room, part neighborhood hangout. Among the wine racks in the old New Orleans building are two big round tables, as well as seating in the courtyard. You can have a bottle uncorked on the premises or order by the glass. High-end Scotches, bourbons, and rums are also on the menu. Sunday afternoons are especially fun, when a local band (and often a chef with a grill) sets up on the courtyard. ⊠*600 Poland Ave., Bywater* ☎*504/948–9111.*

Country Club New Orleans. If you're looking for a unique and out-of-the-way experience, check out this "restaurant, lounge, pool, Jacuzzi, cabana bar." Set in a handsome 19th-century Bywater mansion, this onetime gay club now offers an elegant retreat from the hustle and bustle of the city, with a lounge area, an up-and-coming restaurant, and large outdoor pool and deck bar hidden away behind lush vegetation and high walls. ⊠*634 Louisa St., Bywater* ☎*504/945–0742.*

6

Fodor'sChoice ★ **d.b.a.** A slice of Manhattan sophistication on Frenchmen Street, d.b.a. is the southern outpost of the East Village hot spot. The selection—including international beers on tap, aged Scotches, and obscure tequilas, all listed on chalkboards above the bar—is reason enough to visit. Live music most nights and the Marigny's best people-watching make it a neighborhood favorite. ⊠*616 Frenchmen St., Faubourg Marigny* ☎*504/942–3731.*

Mimi's. The big windows at this corner bar and café stay open most evenings, letting the atmosphere of the shabby-chic neighborhood drift in. Downstairs is a popular gathering spot, with bar stools and a few tables; there's more seating upstairs, along with a kitchen that turns out a respectable selection of tapas well into the early morning hours. ⊠*2601 Royal St., Faubourg Marigny* ☎*504/872–9868.*

R Bar. Just outside the French Quarter, this neighborhood corner bar turns into something of a hipster scene and social hub at night and during holiday weekends. Tinted windows and red vinyl provide a throwback ambience, and classic New Wave (and pitchers of local Abita Beer) are always on tap. The place likes to run some offbeat specials—on Monday night, for example, 10 bucks will get you a shot and a haircut—and it's the best place to catch the Krewe of St. Ann parade early Mardi Gras day, when the procession of outlandishly costumed revelers makes an extended pit stop here. ⊠*1431 Royal St., Faubourg Marigny* ☎*504/948–7499.*

CBD AND WAREHOUSE DISTRICT

Bridge Lounge. Formerly a showcase for gritty punk bands, Bridge Lounge had a radical makeover a few years back; now, instead of motorcycle jackets and wild hair, it's mostly youngish professionals kicking back, many with their dogs in tow. The drinks are good, the light flattering, and the owners' oenophilia is reflected in the bar's

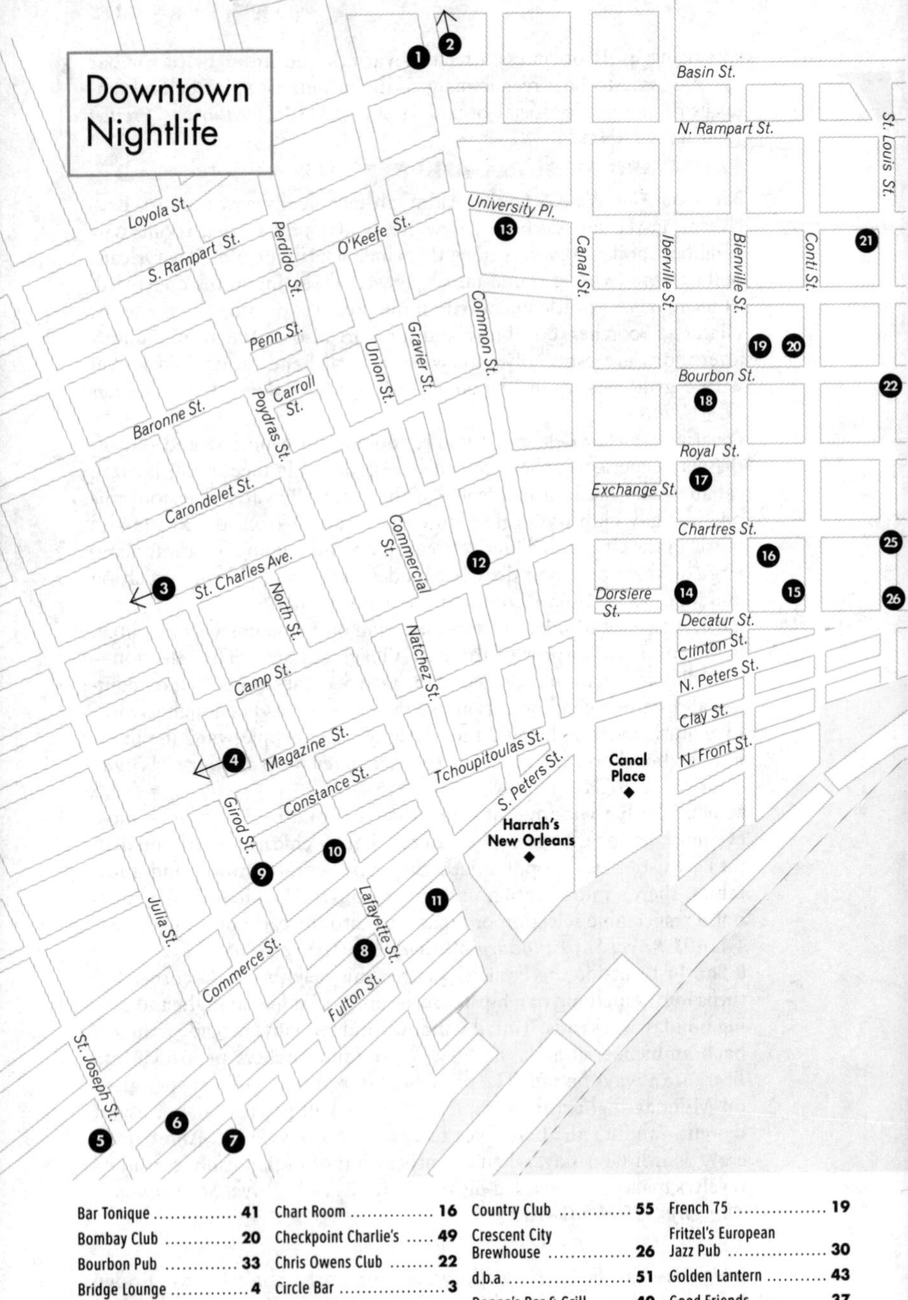

Bar Tonique **41**
Bombay Club **20**
Bourbon Pub **33**
Bridge Lounge **4**
Café Lafitte in Exile **35**
Carousel Revolving Bar .. **17**
Cat's Meow **29**
Chart Room **16**
Checkpoint Charlie's **49**
Chris Owens Club **22**
Circle Bar **3**
Club Ampersand **1**
Corner Pocket **21**
Cosimo's **42**
Country Club **55**
Crescent City Brewhouse **26**
d.b.a. **51**
Donna's Bar & Grill **40**
The Dungeon **23**
Ernst Cafe **8**
528 on Fulton **11**
French 75 .... **19**
Fritzel's European Jazz Pub **30**
Golden Lantern **43**
Good Friends **37**
Handsome Willy's **2**
House of Blues **14**
Howlin' Wolf **5**

Louis Armstrong Park
N. Rampart St.
Burgundy St.
Dauphine St.
Bourbon St.
Royal St.
Chartres St.
Decatur St.
French Market Pl.
N. Peters St.
Toulouse St.
St. Peter St.
Orleans St.
St. Ann St.
Dumaine St.
St. Philip St.
Ursulines St.
Gov. Nicholls St.
Barracks St.
Esplanade Ave.
Kerlerec St.
Touro St.
Frenchmen St.
Elysian Fields Ave.
Wilk Row
Madison St.
Jackson Square
Café du Monde
Moon Walk
Mississippi River
0 1/4 mi
0 1/4 km
Kerry Irish Pub 15
Lafitte's Blacksmith Shop 36
Loa 12
Lucy's Retired Surfer's Bar & Restaurant 9
Margaritaville Café 44
Mimi's 54
Molly's at the Market 45
Mulate's 7
Napoleon House Bar and Cafe 25
Napoleon's Itch 31
Ninth Circle 39
Old Absinthe House 18
One Eyed Jack's 24
Oz 32
Palm Court Jazz Café 48
Parade Disco 34
Pat O'Brien's 28
Pravda 46
Preservation Hall 27
R Bar 50
Rawhide 38
Republic 6
Ruby Fruit Jungle 47
Sazerac Bar 13
Snug Harbor 52
Spotted Cat 53
Vic's Kangaroo Cafe 10

CLOSE UP

Bright Lights, Big Easy

One legacy of New Orleans's Caribbean cultural climate that comes as a pleasant shock to many visitors is the city's tolerant attitude toward alcohol. Most bars stay open as long as a crowd is on hand: with 24-hour liquor licenses, closing time is strictly voluntary. Revelers can leave a bar and take their drinks along in a "go-cup." Whiskey, beer, or wine can be purchased anywhere, anytime, at such unlikely outlets as gas stations or drive-through daiquiri depots. And beware, liquor used to mix drinks is rarely measured. New Orleans bartenders are generous people.

Many bars advertise the Hurricane—a rum-and-fruit concoction that is the signature drink at **Pat O'Brien's,** the best place to order one. Less Hawaiian Punch-y than the Hurricane is the light-pink Monsoon, a specialty at **Snug Harbor.**

extensive list of wines by the glass. ✉*1201 Magazine St., Warehouse District* ☎*504/299–1888.*

Ernst Cafe. Ernst has been operating as a bar since the first years of the 20th century, and the classic interior and upstairs balcony provide a welcome respite to conventioneers, lawyers from nearby firms, and service-industry folks finishing shifts at surrounding hotels. The menu is classic, too, heavy on bar food staples like fried seafood, wraps, and burgers. ✉*600 S. Peters St., Warehouse District* ☎*504/525–8544.*

Handsome Willy's. Sandwiched between a forlorn stretch of the Interstate 10 overpass and the Medical District, Handsome Willy's—named for a dapper repeat customer of the notorious brothel that used to be on the site—dubs itself "a bar and hot dog bistro." The menu has daily specials to go with the dogs, and at night there's a rotating cast of DJs, frequent (and irreverent) literary events, and the occasional live band on the outdoor patio. It's not on any tourist map, but casually hip and worth seeking out. ✉*218 S. Robertson St., CBD* ☎*504/525–0377.*

Loa. In voodoo tradition, loa are the divine spirits, and this bar just off the lobby of the chic International House hotel certainly strives for an extraordinary experience. From the patterned fabrics to the elongated crystal chandeliers, the room sets a tone of chic elegance. Well-heeled downtown professionals mingle with international jet setters gathering for the evening and sipping on inventive, high-end cocktails. Try the Loatini, which comes garnished with edible flowers. ✉*221 Camp St., CBD* ☎*504/200–6514.*

Lucy's Retired Surfer Bar & Restaurant. Space can get tight in this out-of-its-element urban beach bar, especially when the young professionals arrive in search of happy-hour cold beer and cocktails. The other half of the place is a restaurant that serves tasty sandwiches, fish tacos, and brunch on weekends; upstairs, a secondary club hosts occasional open-mike comedy shows. ✉*701 Tchoupitoulas St., Warehouse District* ☎*504/523–8995.*

The Sazerac Bar. Located in the historic and newly renovated Roosevelt Hotel, this is one of the most famous bars in Louisiana, providing libations and inspiration since 1893. Drawn to the signature Sazerac cocktails and ramos gin fizzes, a famous and intriguing clientele has graced the bar over the years, including Governor Huey P. Long, who in the 1930s built a 90-mi highway between New Orleans and the state capital, so, many believe, he could get directly to the hotel lounge for his signature drink. ✉ *123 Baronne St., CBD* ☎ *504/648–1200.*

Vic's Kangaroo Café. This narrow Aussie pub has a dartboard, a good beer selection, and a menu sprinkled with Cajun-style dishes. It's especially lively on Friday afternoons when the downtown after-five crowd hits the bars. ✉ *636 Tchoupitoulas St., Warehouse District* ☎ *504/524–4329.*

UPTOWN AND THE GARDEN DISTRICT

The Bulldog. A beautiful new brick patio has become the main draw of this neighborhood institution, allowing patrons to gather in droves for happy hour and evening sessions overlooking the hustle and bustle of this lively stretch of Magazine Street. The dog-friendly venue calls itself "Uptown's International Beer Tavern," offering 50 different brews on tap and more than 100 selections in bottles. A surprisingly good pub-grub menu keeps patrons fueled for evenings out, and during crawfish season boiled mudbugs are a popular option from the corner seafood market across the street. ✉ *3236 Magazine St., Garden District* ☎ *504/891–1516.*

6

Fodor'sChoice ★ **Columns Hotel.** An evening cocktail on the expansive front porch of the Columns, shaded by centuries-old oak trees and overlooking the St. Charles Avenue streetcar route, is one of the more romantic New Orleans experiences. The Victorian Lounge, with period decor and a fireplace, and plenty of decaying elegance, draws a white-collar crowd of all ages. Live jazz combos play Monday through Wednesday evenings. ✉ *3811 St. Charles Ave., Uptown* ☎ *504/899–9308.*

Cure. Tucked away on a quiet Uptown intersection, this elegant nightspot drops a touch of urban chic into a historic rambling neighborhood. A well-heeled doorman welcomes guests into this custom-designed bar and restaurant complete with 20-foot ceilings, lovely patio, and doors salvaged from a 19th-century bank. The cocktail menu favors traditional classics, and the bartenders are masters of their art form. ✉ *4905 Freret St., Uptown* ☎ *504/302–2357.*

Delachaise. A charming sliver of a building on a busy stretch of St. Charles Avenue, Delachaise looks like it was air-dropped straight from Paris. Offering a carefully chosen (and reasonably priced) selection of beer, liquor, and wines by the glass, the menu also sports brasserie fare—mussels, pommes frites, cheese platters—in appetizer-size portions, and the long, slender room and plush banquettes make you feel like you've wandered into the lounge car of a particularly elegant train. ✉ *3442 St. Charles Ave., Uptown* ☎ *504/895–0858.*

F&M Patio Bar. For some people, an all-nighter in New Orleans isn't complete until they've danced on top of the pool table at this perpetually open hangout. There's a loud jukebox, a popular photo booth, and a late-night kitchen (it gets going around 8 PM and keeps serving until early in the morning). The tropical patio can actually be peaceful at times. You'll need a car or a taxi to get here. ✉ *4841 Tchoupitoulas St., Uptown* ☎ *504/895–6784.*

CLOSE UP

Cocktail Culture

In the early 1800s, Antoine Amadie Peychaud, a Creole apothecary, opened a shop in the French Quarter where he invented a drink for his friends, using French cognac, water, sugar, and his homemade bitters. It was the world's first Sazerac. According to legend, Peychaud served his invention in a traditional French egg cup called a coquetier, which was soon mispronounced by his American clients and turned into the word cocktail. In the 200 years since then, the landscape of New Orleans has changed, but the spirit remains the same as people pursue the sublime pleasure of drinking a chilled, perfectly made cocktail in the warmth of this subtropical city. From the world-renowned Hurricane to Peychaud's now-famous bitters, New Orleans is home to many of the greatest inventions and ingredients in cocktail history.

In recent years, a new generation of bar owners, bartenders, and "mixologists," as they're known, have reinvigorated the entire cocktail culture of New Orleans, bringing a new energy and zeal to the traditional world of bars and drinks. With top-shelf liquors, fresh ingredients, and inventive recipes, bartenders and mixologists are ushering in what some observers call a "cocktail revolution," by combining the traditional skills and history of New Orleans drink making with unparalleled inventiveness and access to uncommon ingredients. On any given night patrons can take a spin through history, ordering drinks like the Sazerac, the Ramos Gin Fizz, or the Obituary Cocktail at venues like the **Sazerac Bar**, the **Napoleon House**, or **Lafitte's Blacksmith Shop**. Or drop into trendy new bars like **Bar Tonique**, **Clever**, **Cure**, or **loa** for modern inventions such as the Oriole, the Window Box, the Tequila Old-Fashioned, or the loatini.

Celebrating its unique position in the history of cocktail culture, New Orleans boasts some of the most interesting museums dedicated to the art of drinking. **The Museum of the American Cocktail** (✉ *Southern Food & Beverage Museum, Riverwalk Marketplace, 1 Poydras St., Warehouse District* ☎ *504/569–0405* 🌐 *www.museumoftheamericancocktail.org*) hosts an extensive collection of rare spirits, books, Prohibition-era literature and music, vintage cocktail shakers, glassware, tools, gadgets, and all manner of cocktail memorabilia and photographs culled from the outstanding collections of museum founders and patrons.

The **Absinthe Museum of America** (✉ *823 Royal St., French Quarter* ☎ *504/523–0903* 🌐 *www.absinthemuseumofamerica.com*) is the first of its kind in the United States, showcasing a rare and extensive collection of antique items, including fountains, hundreds of spoons, glasses, saucers, drippers, labels, prints, and topettes.

Each July the annual Tales of the Cocktail, billed as "the most spirited event of the summer," brings thousands of experts and enthusiasts together for an internationally acclaimed, five-day celebration dedicated to the artistry and science of making drinks. In addition to enjoying some of "the best cocktails ever made," attendees participate in dinners, demonstrations, tastings, competitions, seminars, book signings, tours, and parties.

The Kingpin. Deep-red walls and a velvet Elvis lend this Uptown spot a touch of kitsch, but it's the friendly atmosphere, a jukebox stocked with vintage soul and modern rock, and a young, attractive crowd that draws people in nightly. Stop in on a Sunday during football season for barbecue and a chance to cheer on the beloved Saints. ✉*1307 Lyons St., Uptown* ☎*504/891–2373.*

ONE FOR THE ROAD

Although bottles and glasses are officially banned on the street, New Orleans is one of the few places where it's perfectly legal to carry a drink in public. Ready to move on? Ask the bartender for a "go-cup."

Parasol's Restaurant & Bar. Po'boy devotees practically genuflect at the mention of this hole-in-the-wall, which has been serving the sloppy sandwiches, along with Guinness on tap, for more than 50 years. The annual St. Patrick's Day party at Parasol's spills out into the surrounding neighborhood of the Lower Garden District; it's grown so large that police have to erect barricades to keep traffic out—or keep the revelers in. ✉*2533 Constance St., Garden District* ☎*504/897–5413.*

St. Joe's. This popular nightspot is known for its religious-themed decor and its mixed drinks. The narrow front bar draws inspiration from Latin American churches; the back patio, strung with Chinese lanterns and decorated with statues of Asian deities, is a "Caribbean Zen temple," in the owner's words. Drinks are made with real juice, and the mojitos are especially popular. ✉*5535 Magazine St., Uptown* ☎*504/899–3744.*

6

MID-CITY AND BEYOND

Clever Wine Bar. A spin-off of the popular Cork & Bottle wineshop, this new Mid-City hot spot draws a devoted crowd by offering a diverse menu of fine wines by the glass, vintage cocktails, and a lineup of local musical talent on the weekends. Plush sofas and chairs line the walls, and candlelit tables create great gathering places for groups both large and small. Drop in at the wineshop on Thursday for free wine tastings, and then move next door to the bar to keep the evening rolling. ✉*3700 Orleans Ave., Mid-City* ☎*504/281–4384.*

Finn McCool's Irish Pub. Run by devoted soccer fans, this popular and expansive neighborhood bar beams in European football games via live satellite feed for devout expats, who because of the time difference sometimes gather at 7 AM to hoist stouts and cheer on their team. Pool and darts tournaments are a regular feature as well, and a new kitchen serves delicious fish-and-chips. On Monday night, there's a popular and competitive trivia quiz; prizes include sacks of potatoes. ✉*3701 Banks St., Mid-City* ☎*504/486–9080.*

Pal's. Tucked away in a quiet Bayou St. John neighborhood, this little gem is a surprisingly hip hangout with a carefully crafted, Rat Pack–era louche vibe, right down to the pinup girl wallpaper in the men's room. Thursday is martini and manicure night, when one price gets you well groomed and well oiled. ✉*949 N. Rendon St., Bayou St. John* ☎*504/488–7257.*

COFFEEHOUSES

Fodor'sChoice ★ **Café du Monde.** It just wouldn't be a trip to New Orleans without a stop at the French Market mainstay, which has been dishing up chicory-laced café au lait and sugar-dusted beignets since 1862. The open-air seating area, with a view of Jackson Square, makes for prime people-watching. ✉*800 Decatur St., French Quarter* ☎*504/525–4544.*

Café Rose Nicaud. Named after a former slave who bought her freedom by selling coffee in Jackson Square, this comfortable Marigny coffee shop also has a respectable wine and beer selection, along with a café menu of soups, salads, and sandwiches. Nestled among the shops and jazz clubs on Frenchmen Street, it's a great place to take a break, and there's free Wi-Fi. ✉*632 Frenchmen St., Faubourg Marigny* ☎*504/949–3300.*

CC's Coffeehouse. The coffee shop–retail outlet for the local Community Coffee brand, CC's offers muffins, pastries, and croissants, along with a decent cup of java. Iced coffee drinks are popular, especially during the extended New Orleans summer. ✉*941 Royal St., French Quarter* ☎*504/581–6996* ✉*2800 Esplanade Ave., Mid-City* ☎*504/482–9865* ✉*900 Jefferson Ave., at Magazine St., Uptown* ☎*504/891–4969.*

P. J.'s Coffee & Tea Cafes. This chain of coffeehouses has locations throughout New Orleans. Though the decor favors a country-bumpkin shade of pink, the coffee is excellent, and the cold-brewed iced coffee—a New Orleans specialty—is the best in the city. Hours vary among locations, with the University District branch on Maple Street usually open latest. ✉*7624 Maple St., Uptown* ☎*504/866–7031* ✉*5432 Magazine St., Uptown* ☎*504/895–2202* ✉*644 Camp St., CBD* ☎*504/529–3658.*

Rue de la Course. When nearby universities are in session, students *camp* out here getting hopped up on caffeine while tapping out their theses on laptops. The comfortable surroundings and nice views of Magazine Street will make you want to linger. Both locations are open daily until midnight. ✉*3121 Magazine St., Uptown* ☎*504/899–0242* ✉*1140 S. Carrollton Ave., Uptown* ☎*504/861–4343.*

GAMBLING

Admission to all casinos is free, but you must be 21 or older to enter. Harrah's New Orleans, at the foot of Canal Street, is the only land-based casino and is by far the largest and nicest. The other casinos are on boats, which remain dockside. Harrah's and Boomtown Belle are open 24 hours daily, and feature live entertainment.

Boomtown Belle Casino. On the west bank of the Mississippi River, the *Boomtown Belle* is docked at the Harvey Canal, 10 mi from New Orleans. The vessel has 30,000 square feet of gaming space and accommodates 1,600 passengers. Besides the 1,500 slots and 46 gaming tables, the casino has a café, arcade, and lounge. ✉*4132 Peters Rd., Harvey* ☎*504/366–7711* ⊕*www.boomtownneworleans.com.*

Harrah's New Orleans. Commanding the foot of Canal Street, this beaux arts–style casino is the largest in the South. Its 100,000 square feet hold 2,900 slots and 120 gaming tables. There's an upscale steak restaurant run by local celebrity-chef John Besh and the French brasserie Riche.

Valet parking is available. ✉4 *Canal St., CBD* ☎*504/533–6000 or 800/427–7247* 🌐*www.harrahs.com.*

Treasure Chest Casino. Seven minutes from the airport on Lake Pontchartrain, the *Treasure Chest* has more than 900 slot machines, 40 gaming tables, and a no-smoking gaming area. The lunch and dinner buffet serves Louisiana specialties; a free shuttle operates to and from nearby hotels. It's open daily from 11 AM to 3 AM, and until 5 AM on Friday and Saturday. ✉*5050 Williams Blvd., Kenner* ☎*504/443–8000 or 800/443–8000* 🌐*www.treasurechestcasino.com.*

GAY AND LESBIAN

New Orleans has a sizable gay-and-lesbian community and has long been a popular destination for gay travelers. Mardi Gras and Southern Decadence, which takes place Labor Day weekend in early September, are the biggest draws. Crowds are also thick at Halloween and at Easter, when a gay Easter parade rolls through the Quarter. The city celebrates Gay Pride in October, but it's a fairly low-key affair.

Bars are concentrated in the French Quarter, especially near the intersection of Bourbon and St. Ann streets, and in the Faubourg Marigny, where they tend to be quieter and populated almost entirely by locals from the surrounding neighborhood. A few bars are clustered on North Rampart Street, on the Quarter's northern edge, but exercise caution when walking around here late at night. Women are welcome at most all of the establishments listed below, but there are few bars that cater exclusively to lesbians. A scene of sorts has developed around **Swirl** (✉*3143 Ponce de Leon, Mid-City* ☎*504/304–0635*), a wineshop just off Esplanade Avenue near City Park, where the Friday-evening wine tastings draw a throng of neighborhood denizens, including a good number of gay women.

6

A more complete list of nightlife and other services can be found in the free publication *Ambush* available at most bars or at **FAB—Faubourg Marigny Art and Books** (✉*600 Frenchmen St., Faubourg Marigny* ☎*504/947–3700*).

BARS

Bourbon Pub. You can't miss this 24-hour video bar at the corner of St. Ann and Bourbon, especially in early evenings, when the doors are open and the dance crowd spills into the street. There's usually a cover charge on Friday and Saturday nights after 10 PM; Sunday afternoon is devoted to vintage videos by assorted gay icons. ✉*801 Bourbon St., French Quarter* ☎*504/529–2107.*

Café Lafitte in Exile. A Bourbon Street stalwart, Lafitte attracts a somewhat older and very casual group of gay men. The bar has a second floor with a pool table and wraparound balcony with a bird's-eye view of the street scene below. Sunday afternoon, when the oldies spin and the paper-napkin confetti flies, is especially lively. ✉*901 Bourbon St., French Quarter* ☎*504/522–8397.*

Corner Pocket. Filmmaker John Waters reportedly counts the Pocket as a New Orleans favorite, and with skinny, tattooed strippers on the bar and an inebriated drag queen emceeing the show, it's easy to see why.

Sleazy fun on a good night, but keep your wits about you. ⊠*940 St. Louis St., French Quarter* ☎*504/568–9829.*

Golden Lantern. The Lower Quarter has become a lot more upscale since this neighborhood gay haunt's heyday, but the Lantern soldiers on. The bartender's whims determine the music, the drinks are strong, and the 4–9 PM happy hour is one of the city's longest. The bar is best known as ground zero for the annual Southern Decadence drag parade, when a throng gathers out front for the kickoff. ⊠*1239 Royal St., French Quarter* ☎*504/529–2860.*

Good Friends. With its tasteful decor and reasonable volume level, Good Friends provides a slightly more upscale, sedate alternative to the blasting disco bars down the street. The Queen's Head Pub on the second floor, open weekends, has darts, a wraparound balcony, and respectable martinis. Brush up on your show tunes at the popular Sunday afternoon piano sing-along. ⊠*740 Dauphine St., French Quarter* ☎*504/566–7191.*

Napoleon's Itch. The only no-smoking gay bar in New Orleans, this narrow space offers a tobacco-free alternative right in the heart of St. Ann-and-Bourbon gay central. The screeching diva dance music is pretty much the same as in the neighboring bars, but comfy sofas and handsome bartenders are a plus, and the crowd tends to be a bit dressier. ⊠*732 Bourbon St., French Quarter* ☎*504/371–5450.*

Ninth Circle. One of the more popular Rampart Street bars, this small joint gets jumping late with DJs and frequent drag shows. The sunrise happy hour caters to service-industry workers just coming off the night shift. ⊠*700 N. Rampart St., French Quarter* ☎*504/524–7654.*

Rawhide. As the name indicates, this is a rowdy—and sexually charged—leather-and-Levi's bar. It's two blocks from Bourbon Street and is open around the clock. ⊠*740 Burgundy St., French Quarter* ☎*504/525–8106.*

Rubyfruit Jungle. After shutting its doors nearly a decade ago, this landmark lesbian bar is back with most of its original staff and DJs in a new, three-story French Quarter location. Catering to a lesbian and mixed crowd, the club offers two dance floors, spiral staircases, and a balcony over Decatur Street, creating an ideal space for weekly parties such as Booty Bounce and Androgyny Night performances. ⊠*1135 Decatur St., French Quarter* ☎*504/373–5431.*

DANCE BARS

Oz. A spacious dance club with a demographic skewed to young gay men, Oz nevertheless draws a good number of straight men and women, largely because of the scarcity of good dance floors in the French Quarter. It's open around the clock and tends to peak very late. ⊠*800 Bourbon St., French Quarter* ☎*504/593–9491.*

Parade Disco. High-energy disco rules at this dance club above the Bourbon Pub. If it gets to be too much, a quieter back bar and a balcony offer retreat. The crowd is mostly male and young, but women are welcome. ⊠*801 Bourbon St., above Bourbon Pub, French Quarter* ☎*504/529–2107.*

MUSIC VENUES

First-time visitors to New Orleans are often bowled over by the amount of both musical talent the city contains and the opportunities to witness it live—in clubs, coffee shops, at festivals, even on the street. Use the following list as a starting point: the venues selected here host good bands on a regular basis, but represent just a fraction of the opportunities you'll have to hear live music.

> **FEED THE KITTY**
>
> Bring cash to live-music clubs; many bands play for tips alone. Expect the hat (or more often, an old coffee can) to be passed around once per set.

French Quarter and Faubourg Marigny jazz clubs usually get going around 8 PM, with sets going late into the night. Some clubs present music in the afternoon as well, usually on weekends. If you're heading out to a nightclub in other parts of town, it's advisable to call ahead or double-check the event listing in one of the city's periodicals. The opening sets at neighborhood bars and rock clubs usually don't start until 10 PM or later.

6

FRENCH QUARTER

Chris Owens Club. The owner and star of this eponymous nightclub is a reluctantly aging French Quarter dancer and entertainer, whose slightly risqué act includes gams, feathers, and conga drums. The kitsch factor is high in the black-and-white tile theater, but the ebullient Ms. Owens takes it all very seriously, and her energy and dedication are admirable. ✉*500 Bourbon St., French Quarter* ☎*504/523–6400.*

★ **Donna's Bar & Grill.** Donna's is a great place to hear traditional jazz, R&B, and the city's young brass bands in an informal neighborhood setting. On Monday night many of the city's top musicians stop by after their regular gigs to sit in for the diverse sets of drummer Bob French; free red beans and rice are served. ✉*800 N. Rampart St., French Quarter* ☎*504/596–6914.*

Fritzel's European Jazz Pub. Although much of the Bourbon Street scene can seem crass or tawdry, this modest club, with its tattered interior and picnic table seating, feels just right. Jazz and German beer are on tap daily, and the intimate setting erases the distance between audience and band, which invariably includes seasoned, accomplished musicians. ✉*733 Bourbon St., French Quarter* ☎*504/561–0432.*

★ **House of Blues.** Despite its name, blues is a relatively small component in the booking policy, which also embraces rock, jazz, country, soul, funk, world music, and more, performed by everyone from local artists to international touring acts. The adjoining restaurant has an eclectic menu, with classic Southern cuisine, served in ample portions at reasonable prices. The **Parish,** a smaller, more intimate offshoot upstairs from the main house, hosts local and touring groups. ✉*225 Decatur St., French Quarter* ☎*504/529–2583 concert line.*

Margaritaville Café. Yes, it's named after *that* song. Jimmy Buffett's devoted fans, called "parrotheads," flock to the shrine for local and regional blues, rock, and zydeco performers starting sets as early as 3 PM and going into the night. Menu items such as the "Cheeseburger in Paradise" derive from Buffett songs, and several varieties of the salt-rimmed signature drink are served. Decor consists mainly of Buffett photos, and the man himself has been known to drop in occasionally. ✉*1104 Decatur St., French Quarter* ☎*504/592–2565.*

One Eyed Jack's. This former Toulouse Street theater plays host to touring modern rock acts as well as local up-and-comers. The 19th-century saloon interior provides an appropriately decadent backdrop for Fleur de Tease, a resident burlesque troupe. ✉*615 Toulouse St., French Quarter* ☎*504/569–8361.*

Palm Court Jazz Café. Banjo player Danny Barker immortalized this restaurant in his song "Palm Court Strut." The best of traditional New Orleans jazz is presented in a classy setting with tile floors, exposed-brick walls, and a handsome mahogany bar. There are decent creature comforts here; regional cuisine is served, and you can sit at the bar and rub elbows with local musicians. There's a wide selection of records, tapes, and CDs on sale here. ✉*1204 Decatur St., French Quarter* ☎*504/525–0200.*

MINORS WELCOME

Bourbon Street's entertainment options are largely off-limits to children, but younger music fans need not feel excluded. Both Preservation Hall and Palm Court Jazz Café welcome underage patrons; other clubs, including Tipitina's and Howlin' Wolf, occasionally host all-ages shows. Kids are also welcome at the free shows staged by the National Park Service's New Orleans Jazz Historical Park, both at the park's visitor center (419 Decatur Street, 504/589–4841) and the Tuesday-through-Saturday afternoon shows at 916 North Peters Street, in the French Market.

★ **Preservation Hall.** The jazz tradition that flowered in the 1920s is enshrined in this cultural landmark by a cadre of distinguished New Orleans musicians, most of whom were schooled by an ever-dwindling group of elder statesmen. There is limited seating on benches—many patrons end up squatting on the floor or standing in back—and no beverages are served or allowed. Nonetheless, the legions of satisfied customers regard an evening here as an essential New Orleans experience. Cover charge is $10, but can run a bit higher for special appearances. Call ahead for performance times; sometimes the show ends before you even begin pre-partying. ✉*726 St. Peter St., French Quarter* ☎*504/522–2841 or 504/523–8939.*

FAUBOURG MARIGNY AND BYWATER

Checkpoint Charlie's. This bustling corner bar draws young locals who shoot pool and listen to blues and rock, whether live or from the jukebox—24 hours a day, seven days a week. There's also a paperback library and a fully functioning Laundromat. ✉*501 Esplanade Ave., Faubourg Marigny* ☎*504/947–0979.*

★ **Snug Harbor.** This intimate club is one of the city's best rooms for soaking up modern jazz, blues, and R&B. It is the home base of such esteemed talent as vocalist Charmaine Neville and pianist-patriarch Ellis Marsalis (father of Wynton and Branford). The dining room serves good local food but is best known for its burgers. Budget-conscious types can listen to the band through speakers in the bar without paying the rather high cover charge. ✉ *626 Frenchmen St., Faubourg Marigny* ☎ *504/949–0696.*

Fodor's Choice ★ **Jimbeaux's.** Jazz, funk, and blues bands perform nearly every night, with early-afternoon sets weekends, at this rustic club right in the thick of the Frenchmen Street action. A rattan seat near the front window makes for good people-watching. ✉ *623 Frenchmen St., Faubourg Marigny* ☎ *504/943–3887.*

Vaughan's. Jazz trumpeter Kermit Ruffins's Thursday-night sets (served up with free red beans and rice) are the big draw at this ramshackle place in Bywater's farthest reaches; at other times, it's a picturesque and exceptionally friendly neighborhood bar with live music two or three nights a week and boiled seafood or barbecue in the back. ✉ *800 Lesseps St., at Dauphine St., Bywater* ☎ *504/947–5562.*

CBD AND WAREHOUSE DISTRICT

Circle Bar. Around 10 PM, hipsters and scenesters descend on this underground rock club in an old Lee Circle town house; earlier in the evening, anything goes. If you can't squeeze into the room that holds what must be the world's tiniest stage, you can watch the action on a monitor over the bar. ✉ *1032 St. Charles Ave., Warehouse District* ☎ *504/588–2616.*

6

Club Ampersand. This converted bank building is now one of New Orleans's premier dance clubs and music venues, featuring two levels, a large dance floor, VIP Suite, a balcony, courtyard, and several cozy sitting rooms, one of which used to be the bank's vault. Regularly featuring local talent and DJs, the venue also boasts performances by many of the most famous names in electronic and hip-hop music. ✉ *1100 Tulane Ave., CBD* ☎ *504/587–3737.*

528 on Fulton. Across from its looming casino, Harrah's has created its own mini-entertainment district just off Poydras Street. This upscale jazz venue is part of it. The room is attractive, if a little sanitized, by New Orleans music-club standards, but the acoustics are good and the entertainment top-notch. Shows take place Wednesday through Saturday. ✉ *528 Fulton St., CBD* ☎ *504/533–6117.*

Howlin' Wolf. This longtime Warehouse District music club recently relocated to a larger space across the street, but the focus is still on touring rock bands and local hardcore, funk, Latin, and hip-hop acts. ✉ *907 S. Peters St., Warehouse District* ☎ *504/529–5844.*

Mulate's. Across the street from the Convention Center, this large restaurant seats 400, and the dance floor quickly fills with couples twirling and two-stepping to authentic Cajun bands from the countryside. Regulars love to drag first-timers to the floor for impromptu lessons. The home-style Cajun cuisine is quite good, and the bands play until 10:30 or 11 PM. ✉ *201 Julia St., Warehouse District* ☎ *504/522–1492.*

Republic. A newcomer to the Warehouse District music scene, this rock venue retains the rough-timbered feel of the cotton-and-grain warehouse it used to be. The club books touring indie rock bands as well as local acts; DJs take over the sound system late at night. ✉ *828 S. Peters St., Warehouse District* ☎ *504/528–8282.*

UPTOWN

Carrollton Station. This cozy little neighborhood bar showcases local roots rock acts on weekends. It's a few blocks off St. Charles Avenue, and worth a trip to see one of Susan Cowsill's frequent performances. ✉*8140 Willow St., Uptown* ☎*504/865–9190.*

Le Bon Temps Roulé. Local acts from a wide range of genres—rock, jazz, blues, or funk—take the stage nightly at this lovably ramshackle Magazine Street nightspot. The music gets started after 10 PM; pool tables and a limited pub-grub menu keep the crowd, which includes a lot of students from nearby Tulane and Loyola universities, entertained until then. ✉*4801 Magazine St., Uptown* ☎*504/897–3448.*

Fodor'sChoice ★ **Maple Leaf.** The phrase "New Orleans institution" gets thrown around a lot, but this place deserves the title. It's wonderfully atmospheric, with pressed-tin walls and a lush tropical patio, and one of the city's best venues for blues, New Orleans–style R&B, funk, zydeco, and jazz. On Sunday, the bar hosts the South's longest-running poetry reading. It's a long haul from the French Quarter, but worth the trip, especially if combined with a visit to one of the restaurants clustered near this commercial stretch of Oak Street. ✉*8316 Oak St., Uptown* ☎*504/866–9359.*

★ **Tipitina's.** A bust of legendary New Orleans pianist Professor Longhair, or "Fess," greets visitors at the door of this Uptown landmark, which takes its name from one of his most popular songs. As the concert posters pinned to the walls attest, Tip's hosts a wide variety of touring bands and local acts. The long-running Sunday-afternoon Cajun dance still packs the floor. The Tipitina's Foundation has an office and workshop upstairs, where local musicians affected by Hurricane Katrina can network, gain access to resources, and search for gigs. ✉*501 Napoleon Ave., Uptown* ☎*504/895–8477.*

MID-CITY

Banks Street Bar and Grill. Over the past few years, this Mid-City neighborhood nightspot has become one of the city's most reliable venues for local music, with live shows—sometimes two—every night of the week. The bill of fare tends to blues and funk, with Walter "Wolfman" Washington and the Roadmasters putting in regular appearances. ✉*4401 Banks St., Mid-City* ☎*504/486–0258.*

★ **Rock 'n' Bowl.** Down-home Louisiana music, New Orleans swing, and swamp pop in a bowling alley? Go ahead, try not to have fun. This iconic New Orleans music venue has moved to a new Carrollton location, offering the same terrific lineup of music Tuesday through Saturday, not to mention brand new, custom-built bowling lanes. Owner John Blancher loves the music, and in addition to his lineup of rockabilly and R&B, Thursday is Zydeco Night, when some of the best musicians from rural Louisiana take the stage. ✉*3000 S. Carrollton Ave., Mid-City* ☎*504/861–1700.*

THE ARTS

For a relatively small city, New Orleans has a remarkably active and varied performing-arts community. Although Hurricane Katrina shuttered many of the most prominent performance spaces, such as the renowned Orpheum and Saenger Theaters, arts organizations worked diligently with local universities, and with city, state, and federal organizations to keep the arts alive and bring major performance centers back online. One of the greatest accomplishments to date is the $27 million renovation and restoration of the Mahalia Jackson Center for the Performing Arts and the Louis Armstrong Park that surrounds it. The performance center provides an anchor for local organizations and a world-class venue for national and international touring acts and performers.

In addition, nationally recognized fine-arts programs at several local universities and high schools provide terrific performances. For current listings, check the daily calendar in the *Times-Picayune* and its Friday "Lagniappe" section. The free alternative weekly *Gambit* also runs an extensive weekly calendar of events.

Ticket prices for theater and for concerts vary widely, from $10 for performances at smaller venues to $70 for top acts at major halls. **Ticketmaster** (☎*504/522–5555* 🌐*www.ticketmaster.com*) sells tickets for performances at many venues.

6

CLASSICAL MUSIC

Philharmonic orchestral and chamber groups thrived in New Orleans during the 19th century, giving rise to many performers and composers, including the famed classical composer Louis Moreau Gottschalk. As jazz achieved society status during the 20th century, classical music took a backseat; however, many professional and amateur players ensure the scene stays active.

Friends of Music. This organization brings superior performers from all over the world to Tulane University's **Dixon Hall** (✉*Tulane University, Willow St. entrance, Uptown* ☎*504/865–5267*). Concerts take place approximately once a month, and tickets usually cost $10 to $20. ☎*504/895–0690* 🌐*www.friendsofmusic.org.*

Louisiana Philharmonic Orchestra. The always good, sometimes excellent LPO has regained a primary performing space with the return of the Mahalia Jackson Center for the Performing Arts, and continues to stage popular events and classical concerts at Tulane and Loyola university auditoriums and at local churches throughout the metro area. The orchestra also performs children's concerts and free concerts at parks and public spaces around the city, as well as a popular Casual Classics Series at the suburban **Pontchartrain Center** (✉*4545 Williams Blvd., Kenner*). Tickets for most events range from $25 to $65, with discounts for students and seniors. ✉*1010 Common St., Suite 2120, CBD* ☎*504/523–6530* 🌐*www.lpomusic.com.*

New Orleans Center for Creative Arts (NOCCA). Wynton Marsalis and Harry Connick Jr. are just two of the better-known alumni of this prestigious high school. NOCCA hosts some fine student and faculty shows at its modern Faubourg Marigny campus, and its Center Stage Series presents top-notch performances by visiting jazz, classical, dance, and theater artists. The focus is on emerging talent, and tickets usually sell out fast. ✉*2800 Chartres St., Bywater* ☎*504/940–2787* 🌐*www.nocca.com.*

DANCE

New Orleans Ballet Association. The city's prestigious dance organization has returned to the lavishly renovated Mahalia Jackson Theater with a full schedule of performances and events. Tickets run $30 to $80, with discounts for students and seniors. ✉ *1 Lee Circle, Warehouse District* ☎ *504/522–0996* 🌐 *www.nobadance.com.*

FILM

Generous state tax breaks and scenic architecture have made New Orleans a popular place to film movies. For film enthusiasts, however, the scene is pretty bleak. Despite the presence of a determined clique of local film buffs and filmmakers, the city does not offer many venues or outlets for either the creation or presentation of independent film. One notable exception is the **Zeitgeist Multidisciplinary Arts Center** (✉ *1618 Oretha Castle Haley Blvd., Uptown* ☎ *504/827–5858* 🌐 *www.zeitgeistinc.net*). Working with volunteer staff and a shoestring budget, Zeitgeist founder and filmmaker Rene Broussard has almost single-handedly preserved the spirit of independent film in New Orleans with this funky and eclectic art space.

The **New Orleans Film Festival** (☎ *504/309–6633* 🌐 *www.neworleansfilmfest.com*), held in October, also brings an influx of indie and film culture, commanding screens at Canal Place Cinemas and other venues throughout the city.

Landmark's Canal Place Cinemas. A southern branch of the art-house chain occupies a tight four-screen space in the upscale Canal Place shopping center, on the edge of the French Quarter. ✉ *Canal Place, 333 Canal St., French Quarter* ☎ *504/581–5400* 🌐 *www.landmarktheatres.com.*

Prytania Theatre. A visit to the city's last single-screen movie house, hidden in an Uptown residential area, is a reminder of the days when neighborhood movie houses offered entertainment as well as air-conditioned relief from the summer heat. The Prytania shows first-run crowd-pleasers and the occasional independent feature. ✉ *5339 Prytania St., Uptown* ☎ *504/891–2787.*

MUSIC VENUES

Free year-round musical events are held in the city's parks and universities. Jazz Fest, French Quarter Fest, and Satchmo Fest—to name just a few—fill the city with music, food, and crafts.

Most of the city's major concert facilities have reopened since Hurricane Katrina, taking advantage of the situation to conduct some major renovations. The **New Orleans Arena** (✉ *1501 Girod St., CBD* ☎ *504/587–3663* 🌐 *www.neworleansarena.com*) is the venue of choice for hip-hop and pop stars. It is also home to the New Orleans Hornets.

Kiefer UNO Lakefront Arena (✉ *6801 Franklin Ave., Lakefront* ☎ *504/280–7222* 🌐 *www.arena.uno.edu*) of the University of New Orleans has reopened its doors, and hosts a wide variety of events—everything from university sporting events to heavy-metal concerts to family-oriented Disney on Ice performances. Check the Web site for the most updated event information.

Fodor'sChoice ★ Three years after Hurricane Katrina nearly destroyed the **Mahalia Jackson Theater of the Performing Arts** (✉*801 N. Rampart St., in Armstrong Park, Tremé* ☎*504/218–0149*), a $27 million renovation has returned the lights to the stage once more and restored the park grounds. With a 21st-century sound system, a digital cinema screen, enhanced lighting, a new orchestra shell, and a cutting-edge ballet floor, the 2,100-seat theater once again plays hostess to the Louisiana Philharmonic Symphony, the New Orleans Opera Association, the New Orleans Ballet Association, the New Orleans Jazz Orchestra, Broadway shows, and much more.

OPERA

New Orleanians have had a long love affair with opera. The first grand opera staged in North America was performed here, and during the mid-19th century New Orleans had three full-time opera companies, including one specifically for Creoles of color. It was also here that the great European divas wanted to be heard in the United States. But those days came to an end with Reconstruction, and ever since the French Opera House burned down in 1919 the city has not had an aria arena per se. Still, through the 20th century the city continued to produce famous singers, including Norman Treigle, Phyllis Treigle, Ruth Falcon, and Jeanne-Michelle Charbonnet.

New Orleans Opera Association. Returning to the Mahalia Jackson Theater for the Performing Arts, and the newly dedicated Placido Domingo Stage, the October-through-March season generally showcases four operas, and a small handful of special events. Full details can be found on the Web site; tickets run $30 to $125 for premium seating. ✉*1010 Common St., Suite 1820, CBD* ☎*504/529–2278* 🌐*www.neworleansopera.org.*

THEATER

Bayou Playhouse. Theater buffs routinely take the hour's drive from downtown New Orleans to this unique theater that sits on the banks of Bayou Lafourche in the small Cajun town of Lockport, Louisiana. Theater director Perry Martin is a hometown hero there, having spent years working on Broadway and in Los Angeles, directing and producing more than 80 theatrical productions, many of them award winning. Returning home, he has brought an incredible artistic vision and world-class talent to this charming and unlikely location. ✉*101 Main St., Lockport* ☎*888/992–2968* 🌐*www.bayouplayhouse.com.*

★ **Le Chat Noir.** A classy tiled bar leads to a state-of-the-art performance space, where the night's entertainment might be a touring torch singer, a comedy revue, a campy movie spoof, or Varla Jean Merman, the gender-bending chanteuse and frequent Chat Noir guest. The Arts District cabaret is elegant and eclectic, and patrons, whether in their twenties

6

or fifties, are appropriately urbane. ✉ *715 St. Charles Ave., Warehouse District* ☎ *504/581–5812* 🌐 *www.cabaretlechatnoir.com.*

★ **Le Petit Théâtre.** The oldest continuously running community theater in the United States occupies a historic building in the French Quarter and puts on quality plays year-round. It has children's entertainment, in addition to its usual fare of classics, musicals, and dramas, often on local themes. Events in the Tennessee Williams Festival take place here in March. ✉ *616 St. Peter St., French Quarter* ☎ *504/522–2081* 🌐 *www.lepetittheatre.com.*

★ **Southern Repertory Theater.** This well-established theater company specializes in first-rate contemporary theater productions. Southern Rep stages premieres by regional and international playwrights; Edward Albee debuted one of his plays, The Goat, or Who is Sylvia? here in 2004. ✉ *Canal Place, 3rd level, 333 Canal St., French Quarter* ☎ *504/522–6545* 🌐 *www.southernrep.com.*

Tulane University. Best known for its summer bills of fare, the university has several theater groups that stage top-notch productions. **Summer Lyric Theatre** (☎ *504/865–5269* 🌐 *summerlyric.tulane.edu*) produces three crowd-pleasing musicals every summer; tickets run $25 to $32, and tend to sell out fast. Tulane's **Summer Shakespeare Festival** (☎ *504/865–5105* 🌐 *www.neworleansshakespeare.com*) interprets the Bard in imaginative, high-quality productions. ✉ *Tulane University Campus, Uptown* 🌐 *www2.tulane.edu.*

Shopping

7

WORD OF MOUTH

"Royal is a very cute street with lots of stores full of art and gifts. I had no idea of the quality of art and antiques in New Orleans! I was very impressed."

—shormk2

"Walk around the Riverfront area and see the local artists work. I bought several things."

—writealiving

"Magazine Street is about six miles long, with shops and restaurants dotting the area from the 1800 block on. You can rent a car and make several stops along the street as you see shops that interest you, or take a cab to the 1800 block and walk among the shops, then ride a bus to the next cluster of stores you want to visit."

—neworleansagogo

www.fodors.com/community

By Kandace Power Graves

SHOPPING IN NEW ORLEANS IS like opening a treasure chest in which everything you want is at your fingertips, from rare antiques to novelty T-shirts, artwork, jewelry, and packaged foods that represent the city's flavors and culture.

New Orleanians have a deep love and devotion for the Crescent City and the varied ethnic components that make up its unique cultural gumbo. For shoppers, this translates into merchandise that reflects that pride, including jewelry and clothing bearing city icons such as the fleur-de-lis—a French symbol associated with the city since its early days—Mardi Gras masks, tributes to its world-class food and culture, and unique and often humorous statements about Hurricane Katrina and its effects on New Orleans, political issues, and local personalities. New Orleanians also strongly support local entrepreneurs, which means shoppers can find many unique works by Crescent City artists and items produced in the city.

PRIDE IN BLOOM

The fleur-de-lis, historically an emblem of French royalty, has long been an icon of New Orleans. Since Hurricane Katrina, however, locals have fallen in love with it all over again, and artists have found creative and beautiful ways to use it to adorn a range of items including jewelry, T-shirts, artwork, candles, glassware, and even wrought-iron home decor. You can find many examples of the quintessential New Orleans symbol at stores all over the city.

Make sure you take home some of the city's local artwork, including the posters designed around New Orleans's special events such as Mardi Gras and the New Orleans Jazz & Heritage Festival (which often become collector's items). Favorite sons such as Tennessee Williams and William Faulkner are often depicted in local artwork, as are historic areas of the city. The special sounds of New Orleans—Dixieland and contemporary jazz, rhythm and blues, Cajun, and zydeco—are available in music stores like Louisiana Music Factory and Peaches Records, and at live-music venues such as Preservation Hall, Snug Harbor, and House of Blues. Independent bookstores and major chains stock a plethora of local cookbooks, photography, history, and local literature and lore. Clothing stores focus on items that wear well in the subtropical heat, with styles ranging from the latest runway fashions, European designer wear, and vintage items, as well as styles from local designers.

WHAT'S WHERE

The main shopping areas in the city are the French Quarter, with narrow, picturesque streets lined with specialty, gift, fashion, and antiques shops and art galleries; the Central Business District (CBD), populated mostly with specialty and department stores; the Warehouse District, best known for contemporary-arts galleries and cultural museums; Magazine Street, home to antiques shops, art galleries, home-furnishings stores, dining venues, fashion boutiques, and specialty shops; and the Riverbend/Maple Street area, which offers clothing, jewelry, and bookstores, as well as some specialty shops.

FRENCH QUARTER

The shops that line the French Quarter's streets are filled with an array of clothing, jewelry, novelties, works of art, and antique furniture and accessories, mostly from the 17th to 20th centuries. Browsing through the picturesque storefronts in this compact area is as much a cultural experience as a shopping excursion, and unique treasures are waiting everywhere to be discovered. If your energy lags, plenty of cafés, coffee shops, candy shops, and bistros will provide a boost.

DO YOU VOODOO?

Voodoo souvenirs are available all over the French Quarter, including voodoo dolls with pins, special hex or prayer candles, and gris-gris bags. Pick yours with care. Gris-gris bags, for example, are not created equal; they are prepared according to your needs—attracting love, bringing luck or ending bad luck, or protection from the evil eye. They are prepared with an even number of items, and you have to add something personal of your own. Follow the instructions that come with the bag for best results.

Jax Brewery. A historic building that once was a factory for Jax beer now holds an upscale mall filled with local shops and a few national chains such as Chico's, along with a food court and balcony that overlooks the Mississippi River. Shops in Jax provide souvenirs, fashions, books, and more, with an emphasis on New Orleans–theme items. The mall is open daily, and during hot days serves as an air-conditioned refuge. ✉ *600 Decatur St., French Quarter* ☎ *504/566–7245* 🌐 *www.jacksonbrewery.com.*

ANTIQUES

Brass Monkey. A small but charming shop, Brass Monkey's specialty is Limoges boxes ranging from small red beans—a favorite food in New Orleans—to baby carriages. It also has antique walking sticks, Venetian glass, and English Staffordshire porcelain. ✉ *407 Royal St., French Quarter* ☎ *504/561–0688.*

★ **French Antique Shop.** One of the largest collections of European crystal and bronze chandeliers in the country glitters over gilded mirrors, authentic 18th- and 19th-century hand-carved and marble mantels, French and Continental furniture, porcelain, and objets d'art in this shop, which originally opened in 1927 and is run by a third generation of the founding family. ✉ *225 Royal St., French Quarter* ☎ *504/524–9861* 🌐 *www.gofrenchantiques.com.*

Harris of Royal. Locals as well as visitors are drawn to this shop for its four floors of 19th-century paintings, 18th- and 19th-century French and English furniture, trumeau mirrors, estate jewelry, bronze sculptures, and chandeliers. ✉ *233 Royal St., French Quarter* ☎ *504/523–1605* 🌐 *www.harrisantiques.com.*

James H. Cohen & Sons Inc. Pick up a piece of history in this shop, opened in 1898, which sells many one-of-a-kind firearms, swords, and currency, including coins from as early as 319 BC. There also are obsolete bank notes, jewelry made from rare coins, and collectibles such as antique telescopes and opera glasses. ✉ *437 Royal St., French Quarter* ☎ *504/522–3305 or 800/535–1853* 🌐 *www.cohenantiques.com.*

7

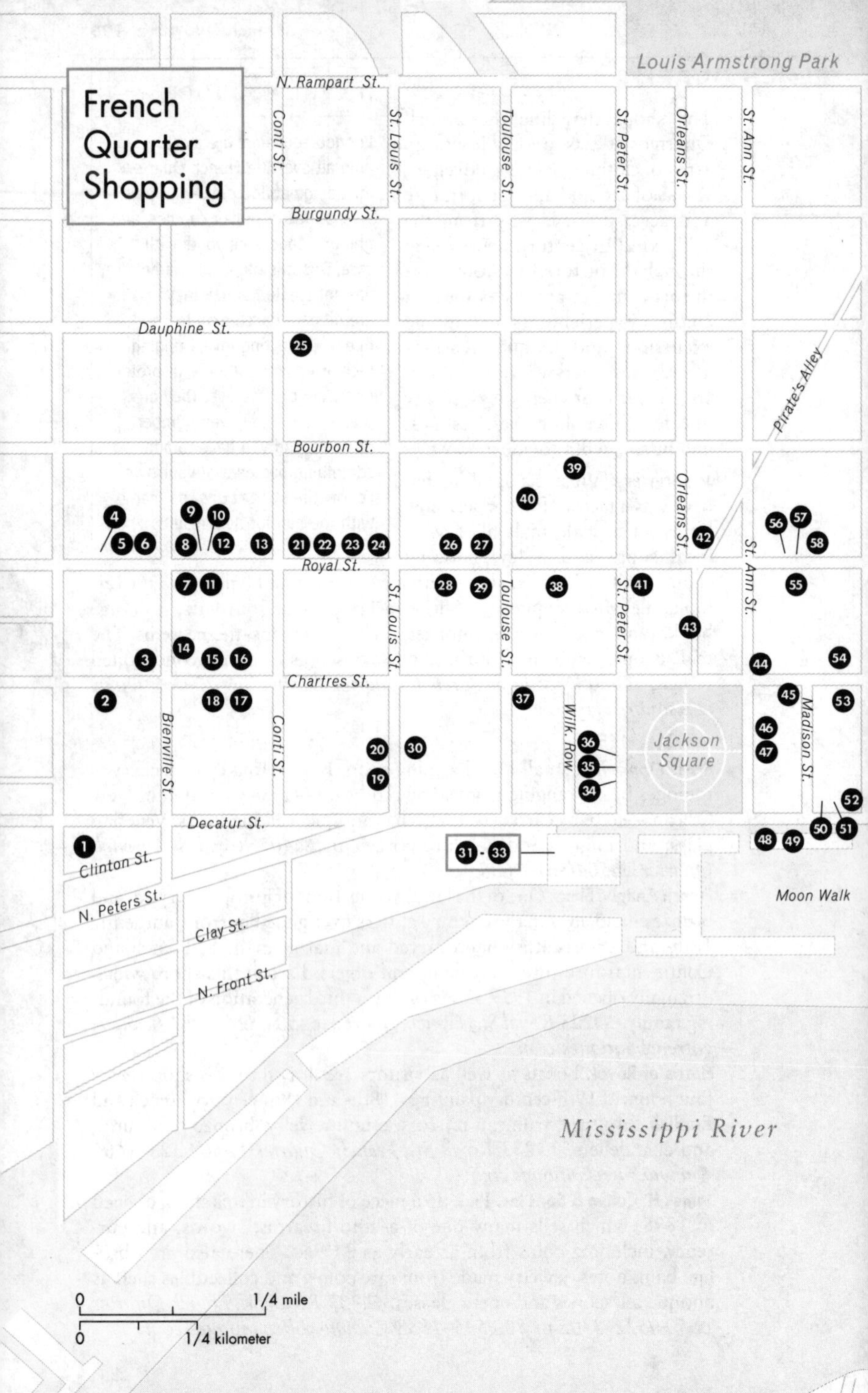
French Quarter Shopping
Louis Armstrong Park
N. Rampart St.
Burgundy St.
Dauphine St.
Bourbon St.
Royal St.
Chartres St.
Decatur St.
Clinton St.
N. Peters St.
Clay St.
N. Front St.
Conti St.
St. Louis St.
Toulouse St.
St. Peter St.
Orleans St.
St. Ann St.
Bienville St.
Wilk. Row
Madison St.
Pirate's Alley
Jackson Square
Moon Walk
Mississippi River
0
1/4 mile
0
1/4 kilometer

N. Rampart St.
Dumaine St.
St. Philip St.
Ursulines St.
Gov. Nicholls St.
Burgundy St.
Dauphine St.
Bourbon St.
Royal St.
Chartres St.
Decatur St.
N. Peters St.
French Market Pl.
59 60 61 62 63 64 65 66 67 68

Angela King Gallery **6**
Artist's Market **68**
Aunt Sally's Praline Shop **49**
Bourbon French Parfums **56**
Brass Monkey **21**
Café du Monde **48**
Cajun Clothing Co. **32**
Community Flea Market **65**
Currents Fine Jewelry **8**
Dashka Roth Contemporary Jewelry **17**
Dauphine Street Books **25**
Elliott Gallery **29**
Erzulie's Authentic Voudou **57**
Esoterica Occult Goods **62**
Evan's Creole Candy Factory **51**
The French Antique Shop ... **4**
French Market **66**
Faulkner House Books **43**
Fifi Mahony's **61**
Forever New Orleans **41**
Galerie Rive Gauche **7**
A Gallery for Fine Photography **3**
Great Artists' Collective ... **58**
Harouni Gallery **59**
Harris of Royal **5**
Hové Parfumeur, Ltd. **55**
The Idea Factory **53**
James H. Cohen & Sons Inc. **24**
Jax Brewery **31**
Keil's Antiques **12**
The Kite Shop **36**
Kurt E. Schon, Ltd. **19**
La Belle Galerie & the Black Art Collection **15**
Laura's Candies **16**
Librairie Book Shop **45**
Little Toy Shop **47, 63**
Louisiana Music Factory **1**
Lucullus **37**
M.S. Rau **38**
Mask Gallery **27**
Michalopoulos **14**
Moss Antiques **22**
New Orleans School of Cooking and Louisiana General Store **20**
Oh Susannah **34**
Peaches Records **33**
The Quarter Smith **30**
Rendezvous, Inc. **35**
Rodrigue Studios **42**
Rothschild's Antiques **10**
Royal Antiques **9**
Royal Cameo Glass **11**
Rumors **26**
Santa's Quarters **64**
Serendipitous Masks **52**
Sigle's Historic New Orleans Metal Craft **60**
Sterling Silvia **67**
Sword and Pen **28**
Tabasco Country Store **46**
Trashy Diva **54**
Victoria's Shoes **18**
Vintage 429 .... **23**
Violets **44**
Waldhorn & Adler **13**
Wehmeier's Belt Shop **40**
What's New **50**
Whisnant Galleries **2**
Yesteryear's **39**

Keil's Antiques. Leave yourself plenty of time to browse through the three floors of 18th- and 19th-century furniture, chandeliers, estate jewelry, art, statuary, and other furnishings at this business, run by the fourth generation of the family that started it in 1899. It's a favorite stop for interior designers looking for the perfect pieces for their clients. ✉*325 Royal St., French Quarter* ☎*504/522–4552 www.keilsantiques.com.*

SHOPPING TOUR

If you want a personal guide, local art and antiques shopping consultant **Macon Riddle** (☎*504/899–3027* 🌐*www.neworleansantiquing.com*) conducts half- and full-day personalized shopping expeditions by appointment; She can sometimes gain access to antiques warehouses that are not normally open to the public.

Fodor's Choice ★ **Lucullus.** The entire store is focused on the art of food—preparing it, serving it, and eating it—and is filled with French tables, English china, cooking and serving utensils, linens, lighting, food-related art, snuff boxes and more, including oddities like Lady Sarah Churchill's picnic set. Items are mainly from the 18th and 19th centuries. The shop is owned by Patrick Dunne, author of *Epicurean Collector*. ✉*610 Chartres St., French Quarter* ☎*504/528–9620* 🌐*www.lucullusantiques.com.*

Fodor's Choice ★ **M.S. Rau.** Historically significant items, such as furniture and other pieces from royal families, are spotlighted among 18th- and 19th-century French, American, and English furniture, sterling silver, cut glass, statuary, and jewelry in this 30,000-square-foot store, which opened in 1912. ✉*630 Royal St., French Quarter* ☎*504/523–5660 or 800/544–9440* 🌐*www.rauantiques.com.*

Moss Antiques. Specialties include French and English antiques from the early 19th century, including period jewelry, wooden boxes, furniture with inlaid woods, porcelain oyster plates, sculpture, objets d'art, walking sticks, and silver services. ✉*411 Royal St., French Quarter* ☎*504/522–3981* 🌐*www.mossantiques.com.*

Rothschild's Antiques. Signs that read PLEASE DO NOT TOUCH. THESE ITEMS CANNOT BE REPLACED emphasize the rarity of the 18th-, 19th-, and 20th-century French and English antique home furnishings available here. Most of the store's real business, however, is its jewelry, much of it one-of-a-kind pieces its artisans design and manufacture, as well as antique and estate pieces. ✉*321 Royal St., French Quarter* ☎*504/523–5816.*

Royal Antiques. French, English, and Continental antique furniture as well as Biedermeier pieces can be found in this 100-year-old shop, alongside chandeliers, sconces, mirrors, trumeau, accessories, estate jewelry, and art from the 18th and 19th centuries by artists such as John Bennett, G. Bohm, Hans von Stegmann, and others. ✉*309 Royal St., French Quarter* ☎*504/524–7033* 🌐*www.royalantiques.com.*

Waldhorn & Adler. Founded in 1881, the city's oldest antiques store specializes in French, Italian, and English furniture from the 18th, 19th, and early 20th centuries, but also has estate jewelry, and watches by Rolex, Cartier, and Patek Philippe. ✉*343 Royal St., French Quarter* ☎*504/581–6379* 🌐*www.waldhornadlers.com.*

CLOSE UP

Mardi Gras Shopping Blitz

New Orleans during Mardi Gras may seem chaotic, but it's actually very organized, and those locals who participate are focused on capturing their favorite prizes thrown from floats and showing off their city to visitors. Orient yourself by attending some evening parades before you jump into the all-day celebration on Fat Tuesday, and you'll soon find you can catch beads and other trinkets like a pro. Next, you'll want to find a suitable costume and mask to fully immerse yourself in the experience. You can assemble a costume easily if you keep your eyes open at such places as the **Community Flea Market** in the back part of the French Quarter. Then walk over to Royal Street for makeup, wigs, and costume jewelry at **Fifi Mahony's** before you continue on down Royal Street to the **Artist's Market**, where you'll find an assortment of masks you'll want to keep long after Mardi Gras has faded into Lent. For a one-stop costume experience, travel to Magazine Street and **Funky Monkey**, where you can find handmade costumes, stockings, wigs, and accessories in one place, or the **Encore Shop**, where you can choose from affordable ball gowns, suits, and more. The important thing to remember about Mardi Gras is that it is meant to be fun for all ages. So dress the part, enjoy the sardonic humor of Carnival krewes' floats, and have a ball.

★ **Whisnant Galleries.** Antique weapons and armor are the real eye-catchers and range from the Gothic to art-deco periods, but the shop also carries a large selection of antique gilded furniture, lighting, and mirrors; paintings from the 18th, 19th, and 20th centuries; African and ethnic art and jewelry; religious items; objets d'art; and statuary. ✉ *222 Chartres St., French Quarter* ☎ *504/524–9766* 🌐 *www.whisnantgalleries.com.*

ART AND CRAFTS GALLERIES

Angela King Gallery. Gallery owner Angela King renovated an 1850s jewelry store into a modern gallery that exhibits oil paintings, prints, and metal and cast-glass sculptures from about 25 contemporary artists including Leroy Neiman, Marlena Rose, Peter Max, Barbara Kline, and Frederick Hart. ✉ *241 Royal St., French Quarter* ☎ *504/524–8211* 🌐 *www.angelakinggallery.com.*

Artist's Market. This co-op of regional artists showcases a wide variety of works, including handmade masks, photography focusing on New Orleans personalities and scenes, ceramics, blown-glass, paintings, wrought-iron architectural accents, turned-wood bowls and vases, prints, jewelry, beads, and more. ✉ *1228 Decatur St.,French Quarter* ☎ *504/561–0046* 🌐 *www.artistsmarketnola.com.*

Elliott Gallery. Pioneers of modern and contemporary art are represented, with a large selection of prints and paintings by Theo Tobiasse, Max Papart, Nissan Engle, James Coignard, Garrick Yrondi, and others. ✉ *540 Royal St., French Quarter* ☎ *504/523–3554* 🌐 *www.elliottgallery.com.*

Galerie Rive Gauche. Dedicated to original European paintings by contemporary artists, the offerings here include colorful landscapes and vibrant and moody works in both abstract and realistic styles by emerging artists (including a few from outside Europe). ✉318 Royal St., French Quarter ☎504/524–5623.

Fodor's Choice ★ **A Gallery for Fine Photography.** The rare books and photographs here include works from emerging local artists like Josephine Sacabo and Jerry N. Uelsmann; luminaries such as E.J. Bellocq, Ansel Adams, and Henri Cartier-Bresson; and more-contemporary giants, including Annie Leibovitz, Walker Evans, Helmut Newton, and local Herman Leonard. ✉241 *Chartres St., French Quarter* ☎504/568–1313 🌐*www.agallery.com.*

Great Artists' Collective. More than 40 regional artists display their works in this double-shotgun house in the middle of the French Quarter. You'll find paintings, metalwork mirrors, a vast array of earrings, blown glass, ceramics, wood sculptures, handmade clothing, hats, ironwork, masks, vignettes in oyster shells, and more. ✉*815 Royal St., French Quarter* ☎*504/525–8190* 🌐*www.greatartistscollective.com.*

Harouni Gallery. David Harouni, a favored artist among locals and businesses who decorate their walls with fine art, displays his take on neo-Expressionism in his paintings of faces, figures, and streetscapes, created in this gallery-studio space. He also sells silk screens. ✉*900 Royal St., French Quarter* ☎*504/299–8900* 🌐*www.harouni.com.*

Kurt E. Schon, Ltd. In the hushed atmosphere of an art museum, and with a well-educated staff, this gallery showcases high-end European paintings from the 18th and 19th centuries. A sister gallery at 523 Royal Street displays contemporary art. ✉*510 St. Louis St., French Quarter* ☎*504/524–5462* 🌐*www.kurteschonltd.com.*

La Belle Galerie & the Black Art Collection. African-American experiences in music, history, contemporary life, and culture are portrayed through limited-edition graphics, photographs, posters, paintings, furniture, ceramics, textiles, and sculpture. ✉*309 Chartres St., French Quarter* ☎*504/529–5538.*

Michalopoulos. Local artist James Michalopoulos showcases his abstract visions of New Orleans's architecture, street scenes, and personalities in oil paintings, lithographs, prints, posters, and serigraphs. Recently he has added landscapes from the river Grosne to his offerings. ✉*617 Bienville St., French Quarter* ☎*504/558–0505* 🌐*www.michalopoulos.com.*

Rodrigue Studios. Louisiana artist George Rodrigue is best known for his vibrant Blue Dog series, which is collected by such celebrities as Whoopi Goldberg and Tom Brokaw. Images of the artist's Cajun ancestors in stylized, traditional Acadiana settings and his colorful impressions of hurricanes are available in original paintings and signed and numbered silk-screen prints. He also sells his iconic works in sculpture and jewelry. ✉*721 Royal St., French Quarter* ☎*504/581–4244* 🌐*www.georgerodrigue.com.*

Vintage 429. An essential stop for memorabilia collectors, the store carries items autographed by celebrities, including a framed photo signed by Gene Autry, a music sheet autographed by Fred Astaire and Ginger Rogers, a guitar signed by the Allman Brothers band, posters from performances; first-edition signed books; and more. New items arrive every week. ✉*429 Royal St., French Quarter* ☎*504/529–2288 or 866/846–8429* 🌐*www.vintage429.com.*

BOOKS

Dauphine Street Books. Stocking both new and used books, this store specializes in local history, the arts, modern fiction, and out-of-print titles. Bibliophiles will delight in its selection of antique books and rare titles. ✉*410 Dauphine St., French Quarter* ☎*504/529–2333.*

Faulkner House Books. Named for William Faulkner, who rented a room here in 1925, this bookstore is designated a National Literary Landmark. It specializes in first editions, rare and out-of-print books, mostly by Southern authors, but also carries new titles. The store, which keeps thousands of additional books at an off-site warehouse, hosts an annual Words & Music Festival that salutes Faulkner and new Southern writers and musicians. ✉*624 Pirate's Alley, French Quarter* ☎*504/524–2940* 🌐*www.faulknerhousebooks.net.*

> **DID YOU KNOW?**
>
> Literary legends like Tennessee Williams, William Faulkner, Truman Capote, and Anne Rice called New Orleans home for at least part of their lives, and a number of other modern writers work in and write about the city, its food, and its culture. Because of this heritage, bookstores give local authors optimum shelf space.

Fodor's Choice ★ **Librairie Book Shop.** Set up like a library with well-stocked shelves of old, new, and hard-to-find volumes, this spot carries the Quarter's largest selection of books, posters, and postcards of local lore. ✉*823 Chartres St., French Quarter* ☎*504/525–4837.*

CLOTHING AND ACCESSORIES

Cajun Clothing Co. A smaller version of the Perlis *(⇨Magazine Street)*, popular among locals, this shop carries clothing for men, women, and children, with a focus on Polo shirts, boxers, and ties with crawfish logos, as well as everything from Hawaiian shirts to boxers printed with images of Tabasco products. ✉*Jax Brewery, 600 Decatur St., Suite 104, French Quarter* ☎*504/523–6681* 🌐*www.perlis.com.*

Fifi Mahony's. Anyone with a passion for pretty things and a flair for the dramatic will love this place, with its custom wigs, wild accessories, cosmetics for costuming or everyday enhancement, hair-care products, and creative advice. ✉*934 Royal St., French Quarter* ☎*504/525–4343* 🌐*www.fifi-mahony.com.*

Fodor's Choice ★ **Trashy Diva Boutique.** Boutique owner/designer Candice Gwinn puts a retro-romantic spin inspired by the 1920s to 1950s on the women's fashions she creates. You'll find dresses, blouses, skirts, coats, jewelry, upscale shoes, and hats. The Trashy Diva Lingerie Boutique next door (831 Chartres St.) features corsets and romantic evening wear. ✉*829 Chartres St., French Quarter* ☎*504/581–4555* ✉*2048 Magazine St., Uptown* ☎ *504/299–8777* 🌐*www.trashydiva.com.*

Victoria's Shoes. Jimmy Choo, Giuseppe Zanotti, and Charles David are just a few of the names available at this upscale shoe emporium, which also carries handbags and jewelry. ✉*328 Chartres St., French Quarter* ☎*504/568–9990.*

Violets. Girly girls rule at this boutique, which caters to the softer side of females with dresses, skirts, sexy blouses, handbags, jewelry, and accessories—many that hark to the Edwardian and 1920s periods. ✉*808 Chartres St., French Quarter* ☎*504/569–0088.*

CLOSE UP

Crescent City to Go!

There are lots of treats to sample while you're in the Big Easy—but you don't have to eat them all while you're here, since many of the city's famous tastes come in easy-to-pack (or ship) forms. In the French Quarter you can pick up classic pralines at **Aunt Sally's Praline Shop** or **Laura's Candies,** which also sell other to-go items. Don't forget beignet mix and chicory coffee to re-create breakfast at **Café du Monde.** In the Warehouse District, **Riverwalk Marketplace** has candy shops that will make fudge and pralines while you watch, then package them for you to take home. Stores like **New Orleans School of Cooking and Louisiana General Store** not only provide the ingredients you need to create New Orleans dishes in your own kitchen, they'll even give you cooking classes to help you do it right. All the city's bookstores and many gift shops are stocked with a variety of cookbooks by local chefs and tomes about the area's foods. Uptown, stop in **Savvy Gourmet** for packaged gourmet mixes, cooking lessons, and samples of the foods you'll want to remember.

Wehmeier's Belt Shop. Exotic leathers—especially American alligator, lizard, and South African ostrich—become fashionable men's and women's belts, boots, shoes, handbags, wallets, briefcases, and even golf bags at this 50-year-old store. ✉ *719 Toulouse St., French Quarter* ☎ *504/525–2758 or 888/525–2758* ✉ *Canal Place, 333 Canal St., CBD* ☎ *504/681–2082* ⊕ *www.wehmeiers.com.*

FOOD AND GIFT PACKAGES

Aunt Sally's Praline Shop. Satisfy your sweet tooth with an array of pralines made while you watch. The traditional version is concocted from cane sugar spiked with pecans, but newer treatments include chocolate and other ingredients. You also can buy prepackaged tomato gravy, muffuletta mix, Bourbon Street glaze, and Italian salad dressing, as well as art and books about New Orleans, zydeco CDs, and logo cups and aprons. ✉ *810 Decatur St., in the French Market, French Quarter* ☎ *504/524–3373 or 800/642–7257* ⊕ *www.auntsallys.com.*

Café du Monde. This open-air café and New Orleans landmark serves café au lait (half coffee, half hot milk) and beignets (holeless doughnuts sprinkled liberally with powdered sugar). Take-home products from the café include prepackaged chicory coffee and beignet mix, coffee mugs, prints, and posters depicting the spot. The café's store across the street also sells logo T-shirts, aprons, and other souvenirs. ✉ *800 Decatur St., French Quarter* ☎ *504/525–4544 or 800/772–2927* ✉ *Riverwalk Marketplace, 1 Poydras St., Suite 27, CBD* ☎ *504/587–0841* ⊕ *www.cafedumonde.com.*

Evans Creole Candy Factory. The smell of candy being made on-site will draw you in to this shop, established in 1900. You'll find a variety of pralines, pecan logs, and New Orleans's own Cuccia Chocolates, as well as gift baskets. ✉ *848 Decatur St., French Quarter* ☎ *504/522–7111 or 800/637–6675* ⊕ *www.evanscreolecandy.com.*

French Market. New Orleans chefs snap up local farmers' produce for their restaurant kitchens at this covered, open-air emporium. Seasonal produce includes pecans, sugarcane, mirlitons (chayotes), Creole tomatoes, strawberries, okra, and more. ✉*1008 N. Peters St., French Quarter* ☎*504/522–2621* 🌐*www.frenchmarket.org.*

Laura's Candies. In the candy-making business since 1913, this shop sells sweet pralines as well as chocolate specialties—including its signature Mississippi mud, made with milk or dark chocolate laced with caramel. ✉*331 Chartres St., French Quarter* ☎*504/525–3880 or 800/992–9699* 🌐*www.laurascandies.com.*

New Orleans School of Cooking and Louisiana General Store. You can learn Louisiana cooking techniques at this school (located in a renovated 1800s molasses warehouse); lessons are spiced with history and tales about the state's famous cuisine. The store also stocks all kinds of regional spices, condiments, sauces, snacks, gift baskets, and cookbooks. ✉*524 St. Louis St., French Quarter* ☎*504/525–2665 or 800/237–4841* 🌐*www.neworleansschoolofcooking.com.*

HEALTHY JAVA

Made from the roasted root of *Cichorium pumilum*, or wild endive, chicory in the past was used to stretch supplies of scarce or expensive coffee. New Orleanians today, however, drink chicory in their coffee because they believe it adds richness and smoothness to the drink. Local manufacturers like Community, French Market, Luzianne, and Café Du Monde add up to 30% chicory to the coffee they sell. Chicory is also caffeine-free and reportedly is healthful for your liver, helps control blood sugar and reduce cholesterol, and boosts bone-mineral density.

Tabasco Country Store. Named for the famous Louisiana-produced hot sauce, the store also offers spices, cookbooks, Louisiana- and cooking-theme clothing and aprons, kitchen accoutrements, ties, posters, pewter items with New Orleans icons, and more. ✉*537 St. Ann St., French Quarter* ☎*504/539–7900* 🌐*countrystore.tabasco.com.*

JEWELRY

New Orleans is a place that revels in beauty both old and new, and that adoration is reflected in the jewelry offerings of local stores, where shoppers find meticulously collected estate and antique jewelry alongside new creations ranging from exquisite to edgy.

Currents Fine Jewelry. Owners Terry and Sylvia Weidert create a variety of chic, art-deco-inspired designs in 14- and 18-karat gold and platinum. ✉*305 Royal St., French Quarter* ☎*504/522–6099.*

Fodor's Choice ★ **Dashka Roth Contemporary Jewelry and Judaica.** The handmade contemporary jewelry on display is created by designer Dashka Roth and 75 other American artists. The eclectic pieces focus mainly on Judaica, including kiddush cups, mezuzahs, menorahs, and dreidels. The store is closed for all Jewish holidays. ✉*332 Chartres St., French Quarter* ☎*504/523–0805 or 877/327–4523* 🌐*www.dashkaroth.com.*

Quarter Smith. Gemologist and gold- and silversmith Ken Bowers will custom design a special piece of contemporary jewelry in gold, silver, or platinum for you, or you can choose from a selection of antique pieces. ✉ *535 St. Louis St., French Quarter* ☎ *504/524–9731* 🌐 *www.quartersmith.com.*

★ **Sterling Silvia.** Silvia and Juan Asturias operate this business near the French Market, where Silvia's fleur-de-lis and flower-inspired jewelry designs share space with other silver jewelry from Chile, Mexico, Indonesia, Russia, Thailand, and elsewhere. There's also jewelry made from coral beads, gift items, ceramic dolls, and more. ✉ *41 French Market Pl., French Quarter* ☎ *504/299–9225 or 504/299–9229* 🌐 *www.sterlingsilvia.com.*

MASKS

Masks traditionally created to wear during Mardi Gras are great to buy as souvenirs and gifts, but also are gaining popularity as decorative works of art. There are feather masks and mass-produced ceramic versions available for about $10, but better, handcrafted, locally made masks that bear the artist's insignia are more of an investment. Cost can run as high as several thousand dollars, depending on the materials used, the size, and craftsmanship.

Mask Gallery. One of the treats of visiting this shop is watching the artist Dalili fabricating the intricate but wearable masks out of leather at his workstation at the front of the store. There's also Venetian and feather masks, pewter sculptures, jewelry, and figurines. ✉ *537 Royal St., French Quarter* ☎ *504/525–0290 or 888/278–6672* 🌐 *www.neworleansmask.com.*

Rumors. Thirty-five artists from around the country create masks of all sizes from leather, ceramics, and feathers to wear on your face, as a lapel pin, as jewelry, or to hang on your wall as art. The shop also sells walking sticks with decorative handles and juju dolls to bring good fortune. ✉ *513 Royal St., French Quarter* ☎ *504/525–0292 or 888/278–6672* 🌐 *www.rumorsno.com.*

Serendipitous Masks. The layout of the shop, with masks mingled with elaborately dressed dolls, evokes the air of a ball or the playroom of royalty. The masks are made by local artists using exotic feathers, jewels, ceramics, and leather. ✉ *831 Decatur St., French Quarter* ☎ *504/522–9158.*

Yesteryear's. Elaborate feather masks made by owner Teresa Latshaw and other artists comprise most of the inventory, but voodoo dolls and folklore objects are also available. ✉ *626 Bourbon St., French Quarter* ☎ *504/523–6603.*

MUSIC

Though many of New Orleans's musicians haven't returned home permanently since Hurricane Katrina, those who are here keep the city's special brands of jazz, rhythm and blues, funk, and fusion alive in local clubs, on the streets, and through recordings. The latter is an easy way to take these special sounds home with you as a reminder of the city's special musical flavors.

★ **Louisiana Music Factory.** A favorite haunt for locals looking for New Orleans's and regional music—new and old—this retail store has records, tapes, CDs, DVDs, sheet music, and books as well as listening stations, music-oriented T-shirts, original art of musicians, and a stage for live concerts. ✉210 Decatur St., French Quarter ☎504/586–1094 🌐www.louisianamusicfactory.com.

Peaches Records. This locally owned shop specializes in vinyl records used by DJs and those who make remixes. Music selections are mainly rap, hip-hop, and bounce, but you'll also find jazz, gospel, classic soul and a few music accessories. Live music is sometimes presented in a café at the front of the store. Discounts are offered for cash sales. ✉*Jax Brewery, 408 N. Peters St., French Quarter* ☎*504/282–3322.*

NOVELTIES AND GIFTS

Community Flea Market. Dozens of vendors set up tables inside and outside this covered market, which has air-conditioning for the comfort of its patrons. Vendors sell new merchandise such as jewelry, handbags, T-shirts, and curios as well as vintage and used items, clothing, and collectibles at discount prices. The market generally is open daily from about 7 AM to 8 PM, but hours can vary depending on the weather. ✉*1200 block of N. Peters St., in the French Market, French Quarter* ☎*504/522–2621* 🌐*www.frenchmarket.org.*

Erzulie's Authentic Voudou. Stepping into this shop is like entering the mystical world of voodoo, with altars displaying good-luck charms and other ritual items, spell kits, elixirs and potions, body-care products, voodoo dolls, gris-gris bags, and gift items. Psychic, tarot, and palm readings are available. ✉*807 Royal St., French Quarter* ☎*504/525–2055 or 866/286–8368* 🌐*www.erzulies.com.*

Esoterica Occult Goods. For a hint of New Orleans's fabled past, head here to pick up potions, gris-gris, jewelry, spell kits, incense, altar and ritual items, and books on magic and the occult arts and sciences. You can make an appointment for a tarot reading, past-life regression, or an astrological consultation. ✉*541 Dumaine St., French Quarter* ☎*504/581–7711* 🌐*www.onewitch.com.*

Forever New Orleans. It's all about the Crescent City in this small shop filled with New Orleans–theme items including glassware adorned with pewter fleur-de-lis, affordable jewelry that boasts local icons, stationery, tiles, clocks, ceramics, framed crosses, charms, bottle stoppers, frames, candles, and more. ✉*700 Royal St., French Quarter* ☎*504/586–3536.*

★ **Idea Factory.** Wood becomes art at the hands of craftspeople who carve clocks; functional items such as clipboards, boxes, and company logos; as well as more whimsical items including toys, whirligigs, hand-carved board games, puzzle boxes, kaleidoscopes, and freestanding works of art. The shop is closed Tuesday. ✉*838 Chartres St., French Quarter* ☎*504/524–5195* 🌐*www.ideafactoryneworleans.com.*

Rendezvous Inc. A throwback to romantic old New Orleans, this shop on Jackson Square has linens and lace in forms ranging from christening outfits for babies to table runners, napkins, women's handkerchiefs, and more. It also offers a charming array of antiques and reproductions such as perfume bottles, tea sets, fleur-de-lis, and crosses. ✉*522 St. Peters St., French Quarter* ☎*504/522–0225.*

Royal Cameo Glass. Beautiful and unique items made of glass are the specialty here, with a spotlight on exclusive cameo glass and pieces by Ulla Darni and Afro Celotto, Lotton art glasses, ceiling light fixtures, lamps, vases, sculpture, jewelry, and artwork by American studio artists. ✉*322 Royal St., French Quarter* ☎*504/522–7840* 🌐*www.royalcameo.com.*

Santa's Quarters. It's Christmas year-round at this shop, which displays a diverse range of traditional and novelty ornaments and decorations, Santa Clauses of all kinds, and a host of Louisiana-theme items that make great souvenirs. ✉*1025 Decatur St., French Quarter* ☎*504/581–5820 or 888/599–9693* 🌐*www.santasquartersno.com.*

Sigle's Antiques and Metalcrafts. New Orleans's architectural elements, often used on French Quarter buildings, have been handcrafted here since 1938. The shop has a selection of metal accents and cast-iron planters; they can also custom design items. ✉*935 Royal St., French Quarter* ☎*504/522–7647.*

What's New. Everything in the store carries a New Orleans theme, making it a great place to buy souvenirs people will actually want to keep and use, including fleur-de-lis–clad flasks, decorative pillows, nightlights with shades made from photographs of city scenes, glassware, ceramics, jewelry, and other works by local artists. ✉*824 Decatur St., French Quarter* ☎*504/586–2095* 🌐*www.whatsnew-nola.com.*

A RELAXING SCENT

Take home the scents of New Orleans with soaps, room sprays, candles, and perfumes in sweet olive or vetivert. The latter was a staple in proper Creole households, where it was used to keep moths away from fabrics and add a pleasant scent to bed linens and clothing stored in armoires. Oil extracted from the roots of the grassy plant is popular among aromatherapy enthusiasts, who claim the scent relieves stress and increases energy.

PERFUMES

Bourbon French Parfums. Opened in 1843, the shop has about three dozen signature scents for men and women, including a 200-year-old formula for men's cologne. It will custom blend perfumes for individuals based on assessments of body chemistry, personality, and scent preferences. The shop also sells perfume bottles and toiletries. ✉*805 Royal St., French Quarter* ☎*504/522–4480 or 800/476–0303* 🌐*www.neworleansperfume.com.*

Fodor's Choice ★ **Hové Parfumeur, Ltd.** Scented oils, soaps, sachets, and potpourri have been made to order on-site for three generations and are sold all over the world. There are 52 fragrances for men and women, as well as bath salts, anti-aging treatments, massage and body oils, antique shaving and dressing-table accessories, new and antique perfume bottles, and bed and bath items. ✉*824 Royal St., French Quarter* ☎*504/525–7827* 🌐*www.hoveparfumeur.com.*

TOYS

Kite Shop. The ceiling is thick with hanging wind socks. Kites of all designs, including an assortment of stunt kites, line one wall; another is stocked with hand and finger puppets, marionettes, flying toys, and other fanciful playthings. ✉*542 St. Peter St., French Quarter* ☎*504/524–0028* 🌐*www.kiteshopneworleans.com.*

Little Toy Shop. There's a mix of New Orleans souvenirs, miniature die-cast metal cars from the Model T to the Hummer, character lunch boxes, puppets, plastic animals, costume hats, and collectible Madame Alexander dolls in a dozen different costumes at this 50-year-old business. ✉*900 Decatur St., French Quarter* ☎*504/522–6588* ✉*513 St. Ann St., French Quarter* ☎*504/523–1770.*

Oh Susannah. Many stores in the French Quarter carry collectible dolls, but this one has one of the largest and highest-quality selections, including dolls from Annette Hinestedt and Hildegard Gunzel. ✉*518 St. Peter St., French Quarter* ☎*504/586–8701.*

Sword and Pen. This store stocks beautifully crafted and hand-painted miniature armies, from sword- and spear-wielding ancient Roman and Greek soldiers to World War II troopers. It also has a selection of war memorabilia, including Civil War hats and uniform insignia from a variety of conflicts. ✉*528 Royal St., French Quarter* ☎*504/523–7741.*

CBD AND WAREHOUSE DISTRICT

This area between the French Quarter and the Magazine Street shopping district is filled with boutique hotels, upscale malls, locally owned and national chain department stores, and (in the Warehouse District) museums and art galleries displaying a variety of artworks and crafts from local, regional, and nationally known artists. Julia Street in particular is a cornucopia of small art galleries, many of them artist-owned.

Canal Place. This upscale shopping center focuses on national chains including Williams-Sonoma, Pottery Barn, Banana Republic, Coach, Saks Fifth Avenue, and Brooks Brothers, but also includes quality local stores like the artist co-op RHINO, Wehmeier's Belt Shop, Jack Sutton's Fine Jewelry, Saint Germain shoes featuring Donald Pliner, and a selection of jewelry and accessories. Mignon Faget is a jewelry store that carries the local designer's full line of Louisiana-inspired creations. ✉*333 Canal St., CBD* ☎*504/522–9200* 🌐*www.theshopsatcanalplace.com.*

Riverwalk Marketplace. Built in what once was the International Pavilion for the 1984 World's Fair, Riverwalk Marketplace offers respected national names as well as a plethora of shops filled with souvenirs, jewelry, clothing, shoes, and merchandise with local themes. There's a food court with local candies, a Café du Monde, and a variety of dining choices. An outside balcony that extends much of the length of the mall overlooks the Mississippi River and provides a place for a respite from shopping. Outside the mall is Spanish Plaza, the scene of frequent outdoor concerts and special events. ✉*1 Poydras St., Warehouse District* ☎*504/522–1555* 🌐*www.riverwalkmarketplace.com.*

ART AND CRAFTS GALLERIES

The local daily and weekly newspapers publish listings that detail openings of new exhibits, which generally are accompanied by wine, hors d'oeuvres, and sometimes music. Because many of the galleries are artist-owned and -operated, hours and days of operation can vary. It's best to call and confirm gallery hours; many owners are also happy to set up special appointments for you to view their art.

Ariodante. Mostly local and Gulf Coast artists are represented at this gallery, which has custom-made cases that display high-end but reasonably priced contemporary crafts and fine arts, including glass

7

items, sculpture, furniture, photography, paintings, ceramics, jewelry, and decorative accessories. ✉ *535 Julia St., Warehouse District* ☎ *504/524–3233* 🌐 *www.ariodantegallery.com.*

Art For The Soul. This small gallery features arts and crafts from 25 local and regional artists, including functional art, lamps, ceramics, masks, jewelry, purses, candles, and decorative arts. The gallery also sells custom furniture. ✉ *818 Howard Ave., Suite 101, Warehouse District* ☎ *504/558–7770.*

Fodor'sChoice ★ **Arthur Roger Gallery.** One of the most respected names among art aficionados, Arthur Roger has compiled a must-see collection of local contemporary artworks by Lin Emery, Jacqueline Bishop, and Willie Birch, as well as such national names as glass artist Dale Chihuly and filmmaker-photographer John Waters. ✉ *432 Julia St., Warehouse District* ☎ *504/522–1999* ✉ *730 Tchoupitoulas St., Warehouse District* ☎ *504/524–9393* 🌐 *www.arthurrogergallery.com.*

Contemporary Arts Center. Focusing on visual and performing arts by local and regional artists, the center curates innovative exhibits with all types of installations, ranging from the beautiful to the bizarre. The galleries are open Thursday through Sunday from 11 to 4. ✉ *900 Camp St., Warehouse District* ☎ *504/528–3805* 🌐 *www.cacno.org.*

George Schmidt Gallery. History, particularly New Orleans history, is the passion of artist George Schmidt. His gallery displays and sells paintings and narrative art, from small-scale monotypes to mural-size depictions of historic moments. He also sells signed and numbered prints of his work. The gallery is open Tuesday through Saturday. ✉ *626 Julia St., Warehouse District* ☎ *504/592–0206 or 504/524–8137* 🌐 *www.georgeschmidt.com.*

Heriard-Cimino Gallery. The front gallery holds a changing solo exhibit, and a second gallery displays abstract and figurative paintings, sculptures, drawings, photos, and prints from contemporary artists—most based in New York, Miami, or Louisiana. The gallery is open Tuesday through Saturday. ✉ *440 Julia St., Warehouse District* ☎ *504/525–7300* 🌐 *www.heriardcimino.com.*

Jean Bragg Gallery of Southern Art. Aficionados call it the city's best source for collectible pottery from Newcomb and George Ohr, but the gallery also carries 19th- and 20th-century Louisiana paintings. Contemporary artist exhibits are presented each month. ✉ *600 Julia St., Warehouse District* ☎ *504/895–7375* 🌐 *www.jeanbragg.com.*

Jonathan Ferrara Gallery. Cutting-edge art with a message is standard at this gallery's monthly exhibits. Contemporary paintings, photography, mixed-media artworks, sculpture, and glass and metalwork by local and international artists are displayed. ✉ *400-A Julia St., Warehouse District* ☎ *504/522–5471* 🌐 *www.jonathanferraragallery.com.*

Fodor'sChoice ★ **LeMieux Gallery.** Gulf Coast artists from Louisiana to Florida display art and crafts here alongside work by the late New Orleans abstract artist Paul Ninas. ✉ *332 Julia St., Warehouse District* ☎ *504/522–5988* 🌐 *www.lemieuxgalleries.com.*

New Orleans Art Works. The South's largest glassblowing and printmaking studio has a viewing room where visitors can watch glassblowers at work. The rest of the gallery displays and sells functional and decorative

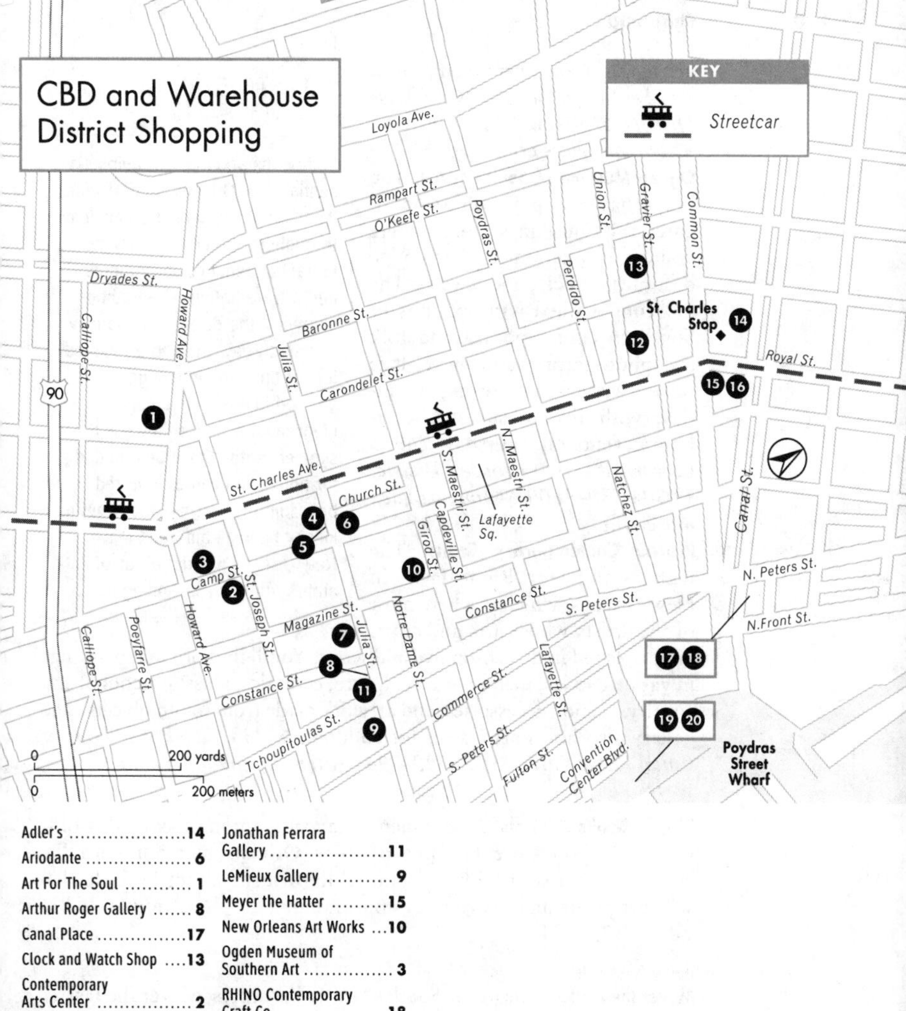

Adler's 14
Ariodante 6
Art For The Soul 1
Arthur Roger Gallery 8
Canal Place 17
Clock and Watch Shop 13
Contemporary Arts Center 2
Deville Books & Prints 12
George Schmidt Gallery 4
Heriard-Cimino Gallery 7
Jean Bragg Gallery of Southern Art 5
Jonathan Ferrara Gallery 11
LeMieux Gallery 9
Meyer the Hatter 15
New Orleans Art Works ...10
Ogden Museum of Southern Art 3
RHINO Contemporary Craft Co. 18
Riverwalk Marketplace 19
Rubensteins 16
The Walking Co. 20

art in glass and metal sculptures. ✉727 *Magazine St., Warehouse District* ☎*504/529–7277* 🌐*www.neworleansglassworks.org.*

Ogden Museum of Southern Art. You don't have to pay admission to enter this museum's store, where you can buy ceramics, glassworks, decorative pieces, and jewelry. The museum is filled with exhibits of Southern contemporary and folk art, photography, and more. It is open Wednesday through Sunday, with live music and after-hours events on Thursday. ✉*925 Camp St., Warehouse District* ☎*504/539–9600* 🌐*www.ogdenmuseum.org.*

Fodor's Choice ★ **RHINO Contemporary Crafts.** The name stands for Right Here In New Orleans, which is where most of the artists whose arts and crafts are displayed in this co-op live and work. You'll find original paintings in varying styles, metalwork, sculpture, ceramics, glass, functional art, jewelry, fashion accessories, and artwork made from found objects. The gallery also holds art classes for children. ✉*333 Canal St., Shops at Canal Place, CBD* ☎*504/523–7945* 🌐*www.rhinocrafts.com.*

A TASTE FOR PRACTICALITY

Red beans and rice is a quintessential New Orleans comfort food. It's traditionally served on Monday throughout the city at fancy restaurants, casual establishments, and private homes. The tradition started in the days when Monday was wash day. The chore required lots of time and elbow grease, and red beans were a convenient meal because they could simmer on the stove unattended for hours. You can pick up red beans in any grocery store (they're kidney beans)—but don't leave New Orleans without a box of Zatarain's red-bean seasoning mix.

BOOKS

Deville Books & Prints. A sentimental favorite among locals, this old-fashioned bookstore has lots of New Orleans and Southern literature, and a staff with exceptional knowledge about both. It also sells art prints and provides custom framing. ✉*736 Union St., CBD* ☎*504/525–1846.*

CLOTHING

Meyer the Hatter. One of the South's largest hat stores, Meyer the Hatter has been in operation for 113 years and is run by a third generation of the Meyer family. It's a favorite of locals seeking men's head wear and has a large selection of dress hats, fun Kangols, tweed caps, and women's fashion hats. Meyer has a faithful following of out-of-towners, too. ✉*120 St. Charles Ave., CBD* ☎*504/525–1048 or 800/882–4287* 🌐*www.meyerthehatter.com.*

Fodor's Choice ★ **Rubensteins.** Known as one of the city's premier men's stores, this locally owned clothier also has a large selection of contemporary fashions for women. Labels include Brioni, Zegna, Burberry, Prada, Bruno Magli, Valentino, and Missoni. ✉*102 St. Charles Ave., CBD* ☎*504/581–6666* 🌐*www.rubensteinsneworleans.com.*

Walking Co. New Orleans is a wonderful place to walk around, and it's imperative that you have comfortable shoes. Here's the place to find them, in stylish designs by makers like Birkenstock, Timberland, and Mephisto. There also are accessories such as canvas hats, folding canes, and hiking staffs. ⌧*Riverwalk Marketplace, 1 Poydras St., Suite 58, Warehouse District* ☎*504/522–9255* 🌐*www.walkingcompany.com.*

JEWELRY

Adler's. Locally owned and operated, Adler's carries respected name brands in watches, engagement rings, jewelry with gemstones, wedding gifts, top-of-the-line silver, and more. ⌧*722 Canal St., CBD* ☎*504/523–5292 or 800/925–7912* 🌐*www.adlersjewelry.com.*

Clock and Watch Shop. Master clock maker Josef Herzinger repairs and restores all types of new, vintage, and antique watches and clocks at his two-story shop. The store also sells more than 15 brands of new watches and clocks, ranging from miniature and mantle styles to large grandfather clocks. ⌧*824 Gravier St., CBD* ☎*504/523–0061 or 504/525–3961* 🌐*www.clockwatchshop.com or www.worldoftime.com.*

MAGAZINE STREET

Magazine Street has become a favorite shopping area for locals and university students as well as visitors, who are charmed by the historic area. Many of the stores are in shotgun houses and cottages that once served as residences. The 6-mi-long street that curves from Canal Street to Carrollton Avenue is one of the oldest and most diverse shopping districts in the city—second only to the French Quarter.

City buses provide transportation to and along Magazine Street, and streetcars travel along St. Charles Avenue, which runs parallel to Magazine Street. The easiest way to navigate this shopping district, however, is by car, which allows you to stop when you see something interesting and peruse clusters of shops within a block or two of each other at a time.

The **Magazine Street Merchants Association** (☎*866/679–4764 or 504/342–4435* 🌐*www.magazinestreet.com*) publishes a free brochure with maps and store descriptions; it's available in hotels and stores, or you can request one from the association's Web site. **Macon Riddle** (☎*504/899–3027* 🌐*www.neworleansantiquing.com*) shares her expertise in antiques and collectibles in half- or full-day shopping expeditions tailored to her clients' needs.

ANTIQUES

Antiques Magazine. Lighting is the specialty here, with nearly 200 lighting fixtures hanging from the ceiling, some dating back to the 1850s. The store also carries Victorian furniture, rare oyster plates, and accessories. The shop is closed Thursday and Sunday. ⌧*2028 Magazine St., Uptown* ☎*504/522–2043.*

★ **As You Like It Silver Shop.** Everything you'd want in silver is available here, with a bounty of discontinued, hard-to-find, and obsolete American sterling-silver tea services, trays, and flatware. Victorian pieces, art-nouveau and art-deco pieces, and engraved pillboxes round out the selection. ⌧*3033 Magazine St., Uptown* ☎*504/897–6915 or 800/828–2311* 🌐*www.asyoulikeitsilvershop.com.*

Fodor's Choice ★ **Bush Antiques.** Antique beds are the specialty, but you'll also find religious artifacts, Continental furniture, architectural elements, ironwork,

7

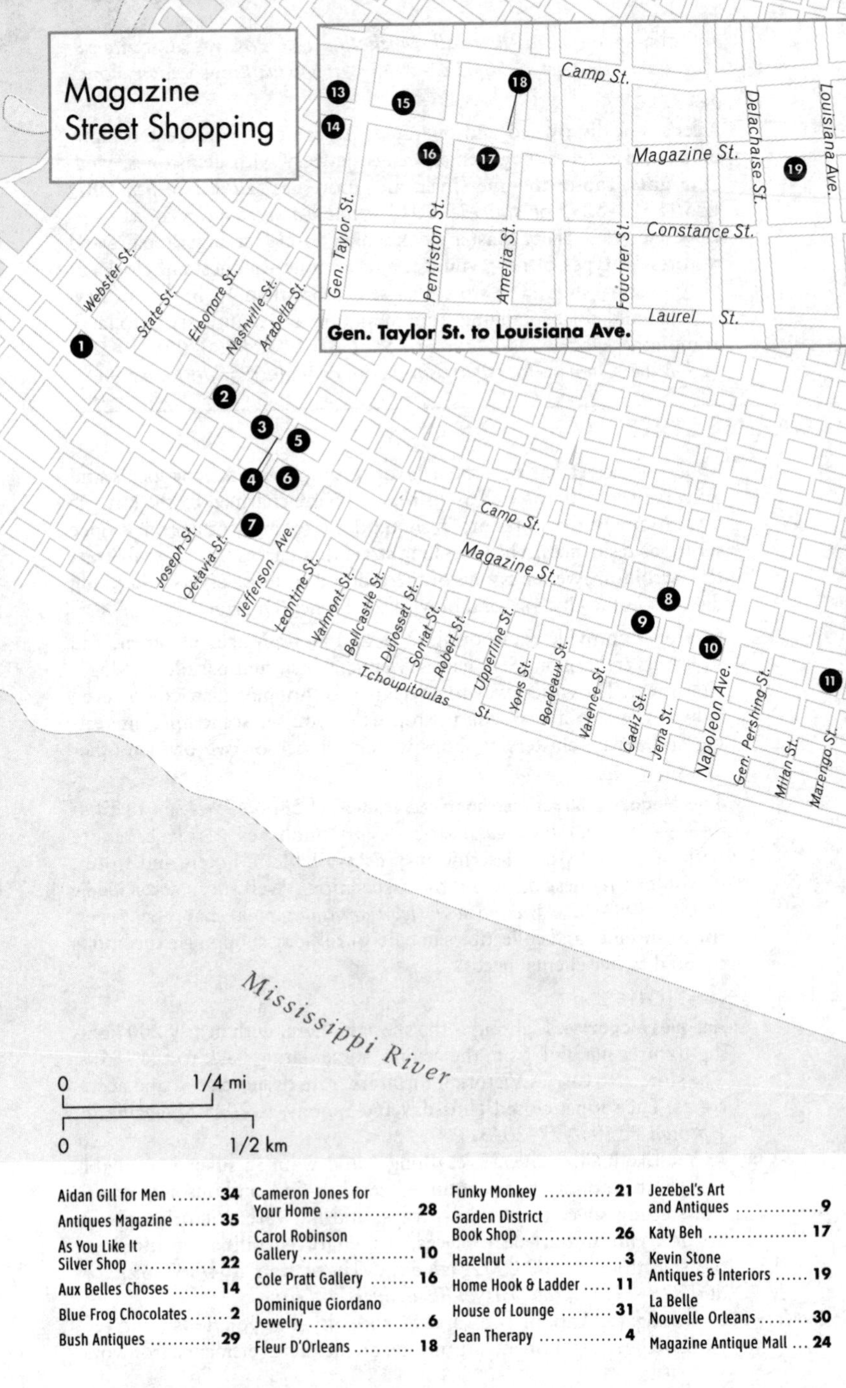
Magazine Street Shopping
Gen. Taylor St. to Louisiana Ave.
Camp St.
Magazine St.
Constance St.
Laurel St.
Gen. Taylor St.
Pentiston St.
Amelia St.
Foucher St.
Delachaise St.
Louisiana Ave.
Webster St.
State St.
Eleonore St.
Nashville St.
Arabella St.
Joseph St.
Octavia St.
Jefferson Ave.
Leontine St.
Valmont St.
Bellcastle St.
Dufossat St.
Soniat St.
Robert St.
Upperline St.
Tchoupitoulas St.
Yons St.
Bordeaux St.
Valence St.
Cadiz St.
Jena St.
Napoleon Ave.
Gen. Pershing St.
Milan St.
Marengo St.
Mississippi River
0 1/4 mi
0 1/2 km
Aidan Gill for Men 34
Antiques Magazine 35
As You Like It Silver Shop 22
Aux Belles Choses 14
Blue Frog Chocolates 2
Bush Antiques 29
Cameron Jones for Your Home 28
Carol Robinson Gallery 10
Cole Pratt Gallery 16
Dominique Giordano Jewelry 6
Fleur D'Orleans 18
Funky Monkey 21
Garden District Book Shop 26
Hazelnut 3
Home Hook & Ladder 11
House of Lounge 31
Jean Therapy 4
Jezebel's Art and Antiques 9
Katy Beh 17
Kevin Stone Antiques & Interiors 19
La Belle Nouvelle Orleans 30
Magazine Antique Mall ... 24

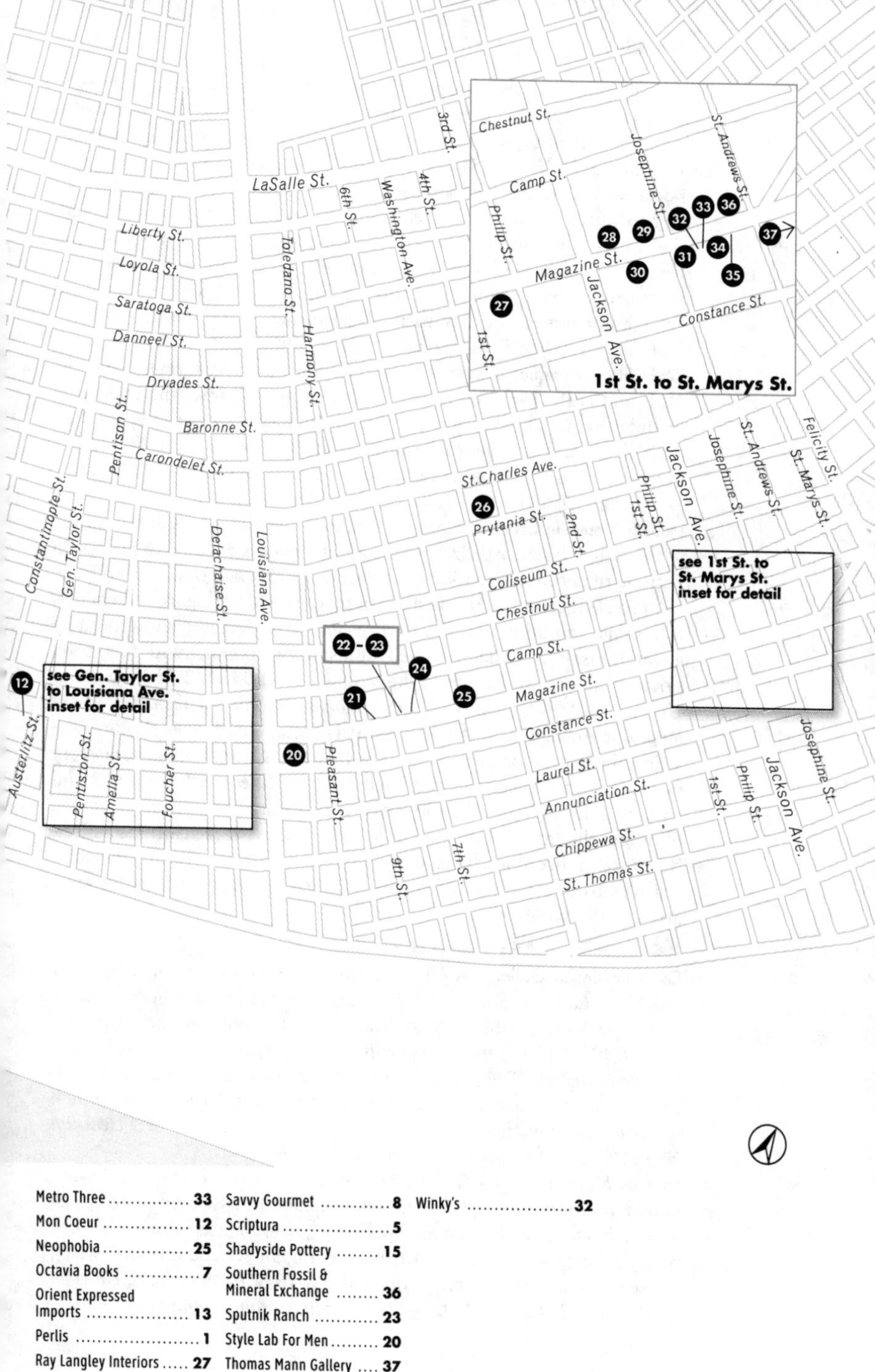

Metro Three 33
Mon Coeur 12
Neophobia 25
Octavia Books 7
Orient Expressed Imports 13
Perlis 1
Ray Langley Interiors 27
Savvy Gourmet 8
Scriptura 5
Shadyside Pottery 15
Southern Fossil & Mineral Exchange 36
Sputnik Ranch 23
Style Lab For Men 20
Thomas Mann Gallery 37
Winky's 32

and lighting. The shop displays its beds, furniture, and accessories in vignettes in 12 rooms on two floors. A courtyard in the back holds a bounty of antique garden accoutrements. ✉ *2109 Magazine St., Uptown* ☎ *504/581–3518* 🌐 *www.bushantiques.com.*

Home Hook & Ladder. The almost cavernous layout of this fire station–turned–antiques shop provides plenty of room for browsing through the shop's collection of 18th- and 19th-century French, English, and Continental antique furniture, accessories, garden art, and curios. The store is open by appointment only on Sunday and Monday, but there are regular hours Tuesday through Saturday. ✉ *4100 Magazine St., Uptown* ☎ *504/895–4480 or 877/792–6169.*

Kevin Stone Antiques & Interiors. Unusual antique pieces, most from the 18th and early 19th centuries, fill this shotgun house; the collection includes many large, very ornate furniture pieces from the Louis XIV and XV eras. The inventory ranges from small decorative bowls and ornate sconces to a large grand piano and armoires. ✉ *3420 Magazine St., Uptown* ☎ *504/891–8282* 🌐 *www.ksantiquer.com.*

La Belle Nouvelle Orleans. Elaborate stained-glass windows are mounted to the ceiling because the rest of the ample space is devoted to European antique furniture, artwork, porcelain, sculpture, and oddities from the 18th to 20th century. An open-air patio outfitted with garden benches, fountains, and other outdoor decor is linked to the main showroom by a warehouse-type gallery stacked almost floor to ceiling with furniture, salvaged doors, and other architectural items. ✉ *2112 Magazine St., Uptown* ☎ *504/581–3733* 🌐 *www.labellenouvelleorleans.com.*

Magazine Antique Mall. If you are easily intimidated, you should take a deep breath before you walk into this expansive shop, where every possible inch of counter and shelf space is filled with antiques and vintage goods. You find an array of costume and fine jewelry, vintage photographs, antique clocks, home decor, glassware, clothing, silver, furniture, collectible china and ceramics, and a variety of other collectibles from a number of vendors. ✉ *3017 Magazine St., Magazine Street* ☎ *504/896–9994.*

ART AND CRAFTS GALLERIES

Fodor's Choice ★ **Carol Robinson Gallery.** A Victorian house is home to contemporary paintings and sculpture by U.S. artists, with a special nod to those from the South. ✉ *840 Napoleon Ave., at Magazine St., Uptown* ☎ *504/895–6130* 🌐 *www.carolrobinsongallery.com.*

Cole Pratt Gallery. The contemporary paintings and sculptures of mid-career Southern artists are displayed at this modern gallery, which is open Tuesday through Saturday. ✉ *3800 Magazine St., Uptown* ☎ *504/891–6789* 🌐 *www.coleprattgallery.com.*

Thomas Mann Gallery I/O. The handmade jewelry of Thomas Mann, known for his unique style of "techno-romantic" pins, earrings, bracelets, and necklaces (which often feature hearts), is showcased alongside work by a changing slate of other artists, creating an eclectic mix of jewelry, housewares, sculpture, and unique gifts. ✉ *1812 Magazine St., Uptown* ☎ *504/581–2113 or 800/923–2284* 🌐 *www.thomasmann.com.*

BOOKS

Garden District Book Shop. This small, one-room bookstore at the Rink shopping center is packed with works of history, fiction, and cookbooks by local, regional, and national authors; it was the first stop in novelist Anne Rice's book tours when she lived in New Orleans. Autographed copies and limited editions of her titles are usually in stock. ✉*2727 Prytania St., Uptown* ☎*504/895–2266* 🌐*www.gardendistrictbookshop.com.*

Octavia Books. The building itself gets attention because of its contemporary architecture, and an attractive layout inside invites leisurely browsing. The collection includes a strong selection of architecture, art, and fiction. ✉*513 Octavia St., Uptown* ☎*504/899–7323* 🌐*www.octaviabooks.com.*

CLOTHING AND ACCESSORIES

Funky Monkey. Popular among local college students, the clothing exchange mixes new, used, and vintage clothing for men and women with hipster couture, custom-made T-shirts, handmade costumes, and lots of quirky accessories, all at affordable prices. ✉*3127 Magazine St., Uptown* ☎*504/899–5587.*

Fodor's Choice ★ **House of Lounge.** Opened by two women with backgrounds in film and costuming, the boutique is theatrical in its plush furnishings and fun, decadent special events. Merchandise includes high-quality bustiers, bras, slips, panties, hosiery, gowns, and sexy accessories. ✉*2044 Magazine St., Uptown* ☎*504/671–8300* 🌐*www.houseoflounge.com.*

Jean Therapy. Popular among locals because of its diverse range of jeans—the shop carries more than 100 styles for men and women to fit all body types—Jean Therapy also offers T-shirts, tops, lingerie, hats, jackets, handbags, and body products. ✉*5505 Magazine St., Uptown* ☎*504/897–5535* ✉*Canal Place, 333 Canal St., CBD* ☎*504/558–3966* 🌐*www.jeantherapy.com.*

Metro Three. This is the place New Orleanians come to when they want to wear their civic pride. The shop is dedicated to T-shirts that reflect the various personalities of the city, its neighborhoods, and its cultures, as well as Hurricane Katrina themes. Other fashions available include shorts, skirts, and casual shirts and blouses. ✉*2032 Magazine St., Uptown* ☎*504/558–0212* 🌐*www.metrothree.com.*

Perlis. The bottom floor of this New Orleans institution is devoted to outfitting men with classic suits, sportswear, shoes, ties, and accessories, as well as the store's signature crawfish-logo polo shirts. Upstairs, there's a children's section and dressy, casual, and formal apparel for women. ✉*6070 Magazine St., Uptown* ☎*504/895–8661 or 800/725–6070* 🌐*www.perlis.com.*

Sputnik Ranch. Inspired by the fashions of yesteryear, this shop puts a contemporary spin on Western attire in clothing and boots for men and women. It also sells designer toys, lowbrow art, books, collectibles, and gifts. ✉*3029 Magazine St., Uptown* ☎*504/897–5446* 🌐*www.sputnikranch.com.*

Fodor's Choice ★ **Style Lab for Men.** With a pool table in the back, this shop aims to dress the city's men well and make their shopping experience enjoyable and stress-free. The store stocks racks of fashions more commonly found in

New York or Los Angeles, with an eye toward not-too-dressy business apparel and casual wear, as well as shoes, skin-care products, belts, and wallets. ✉*3326 Magazine St., Uptown* ☎*504/304–5072* 🌐*www.stylelabformen.com.*

Winky's. This shop's fashions for men, women, and children have a decidedly retro influence, with a heavy dose of spunky New Orleans attitude. There's also a variety of toys and novelty gifts. Upstairs is Unique Products, an art gallery that specializes in lamps, clocks, jewelry, and decorative accessories made from recycled items such as cookie tins, melted Mardi Gras beads, and even laundry detergent bottles and vinyl records. ✉*2038 Magazine St., Uptown* ☎*504/568–1020.*

HOME FURNISHINGS

Fodor's Choice ★ **Cameron Jones for Your Home.** Furniture, local art, home accessories, custom rugs, art glass, lighting, and a cadre of gift items here have a distinctly West Coast attitude melded with New Orleans flair. ✉*2127 Magazine St., Uptown* ☎*504/524–3119.*

Neophobia. Retro furniture and accessories for the home are the specialties at this shop, which carries furniture, clocks, lamps, tableware, glasses, jewelry, and vintage clothes from the 1920s to the 1970s. ✉*2855 Magazine St., Uptown* ☎*504/899–2444* 🌐*www.neophobia-nola.com.*

Ray Langley Interiors. Contemporary, eclectic, and elegant home furnishings include oversize sofas, colorful finishes, and uncommon accessories with a modern European sensibility. ✉*2302 Magazine St., Uptown* ☎*504/522–2284* 🌐*www.raylangley.com.*

The Savvy Gourmet. Innovative kitchenware, equipment, and utensils from more than 50 vendors are available at this shop, which also houses a demonstration kitchen for cooking classes and serves lunch Tuesday through Saturday, brunch on Sunday. ✉*4519 Magazine St., Uptown* ☎*504/895–2665* 🌐*www.savvygourmet.com.*

JEWELRY

Dominique Giordano Jewelry. Local designer Dominique Giordano creates handmade contemporary jewelry designs in sterling silver and 18-karat gold with semiprecious and precious stones, pearls, and resin inlay. Styles range from casual to elegant. ✉*5420 Magazine St., Magazine Street* ☎*504/895–3909* 🌐*www.dgiordano.com.*

Fleur D'Orleans. Silver jewelry adorned with the fleur-de-lis is the main attraction here, but you'll also find items that carry other New Orleans icons such as architecture, crowns, masks, hearts, and more. In addition to jewelry, the store sells handbags, art, glassware, wood and ceramic boxes, batik scarves, ironwork, and more. ✉*3701-A Magazine St., Magazine Street* ☎*504/899–5585* 🌐*www.fleurdorleans.com.*

Jezebel's Art and Antiques. Past the shop's almost cartoonish mural and the cottage garden leading up to the entrance is an impressive collection of antique and estate jewelry by famous designers as well as more-affordable reproductions and new pieces by local artists. The store also carries new and vintage fashion furs, coats, and hats. ✉*4610 Magazine St., Uptown* ☎*504/895–7784* 🌐*www.jezebelscloset.com.*

Fodor's Choice ★ **Katy Beh Contemporary Jewelry.** The owner's penchant for unusual, finely crafted contemporary jewelry is evident in the display cases that hold national and emerging artists' delicate and sometimes bold pins, bracelets, earrings, rings, and pendants. ✉*3708 Magazine St., Uptown* ☎*504/896–9600 or 877/528–9234* 🌐*www.katybeh.com.*

Mon Coeur by Janet Bruno-Small. Handmade jewelry crafted by Janet Bruno-Small from antique and vintage pieces is a specialty, but the showroom also has an assortment of distinctive jewelry by contemporary designers as well as antique and estate jewelry. ✉*3952 Magazine St., Uptown* ☎*504/899–0064* 🌐*www.moncoeurfinejewelry.com.*

LOOKING FOR LAGNIAPPE

Lagniappe (pronounced lan-yap), or a little something extra, is a tradition in New Orleans, whether it is getting a free taste of fudge at the candy store, free whipping cream on your coffee drink, or a balloon animal from the clowns that often entertain visitors on Jackson Square.

NOVELTIES AND GIFTS

Fodor'sChoice ★ **Aidan Gill for Men.** Relax in an old-fashioned barber chair while getting a contemporary cut by Aidan Gill, who also brings old and new together in his shaves, which feature the application of a number of hot towels. The front of the store is devoted to manly diversions, with new and reproduction shaving sets, contemporary and New Orleans–theme cuff links, cutting-edge pocket knives, wallets, bow ties (a specialty), grooming products for face and hair, and gifts. ✉*2026 Magazine St., Uptown* ☎*504/587–9090* ✉*550 Fulton St., CBD* ☎ *504/566–4903* 🌐*www.aidangillformen.com.*

Aux Belles Choses. This dreamy cottage of French and English delights has richly scented soaps, vintage and new linens, antique enamelware, collectible plates, and decorative accessories. It's open Tuesday through Saturday. ✉*3912 Magazine St., Uptown* ☎*504/891–1009* 🌐*www.abcneworleans.com.*

Blue Frog Chocolates. Chocolates and other confections from all over the world are sold individually from an old-fashioned display case in the front of the store. Pack the goodies in gift boxes, arrangements, or on trays. Many of the candies are molded into novel shapes; candy-covered almonds form the petals of flowers gathered into sweet bouquets. ✉*5707 Magazine St., Uptown* ☎*504/269–5707* 🌐*www.bluefrogchocolates.com.*

Hazelnut. Founded by local actor Bryan Batt and his partner Tom Cianfichi, this shop sells eclectic accessories and gifts, including New Orleans toile pillows, decorative accessories and bags, stemware, tableware, accent furniture, frames, and more. ✉*5515 Magazine St, Uptown* ☎*504/891–2424* 🌐*www.hazelnutneworleans.com.*

Orient Expressed Imports. Imported porcelain, vases, ceramics, jewelry, and the store's own line of smocked children's clothing are popular gift items. The store also has a showroom of home furnishings, including accent furniture, lamps, and antique accessories. ✉*3905 Magazine St., Uptown* ☎*504/899–3060* 🌐*www.orientexpressed.com.*

Scriptura. Fitting tributes to the arts of writing and communication are evident in the Italian leather address books and journals, hand-decorated photo albums, specialty papers and stationery, handmade invitations, and a varied selection of glass and high-quality fountain pens sold here. ✉5423 *Magazine St., Uptown* ☎*504/897–1555* 🌐*www.scriptura.com.*

Shadyside Pottery. Master potter Charles Bohn's studio and shop is filled with the functional and decorative stoneware, raku, and pottery he creates on-site as well as his custom wood tables and male and female torso sculptures. ✉*3823 Magazine St., Uptown* ☎*504/897–1710* 🌐*www.shadysidepottery.com.*

Southern Fossil & Mineral Exchange. A wonderland for geologists or anyone enamored with natural history, this shop carries everything from inexpensive tumbled rocks to a table-size slab covered with fish fossils. In between you'll find crystals, bowls, vases, and other home decor fashioned from beautiful rocks, many with fossils, as well as alligator-skin knife sheaths, jewelry, mounted butterflies, and more. ✉*2049 Magazine St., Magazine Street* ☎*504/523–5525.*

MAPLE STREET/RIVERBEND

Most of the shops and restaurants here are housed in turn-of-the-20th-century cottages, which lend an old-fashioned, small-town feeling to your shopping excursion. Once you're inside the shops, though, most of the wares are contemporary and modern. On Maple Street, the shops run about six blocks, from Carrollton Avenue to Cherokee Street, and in the Riverbend they dot the streets behind a shopping center on Carrollton Avenue. St. Charles Avenue streetcars provide an easy way to get to the area.

ART AND CRAFTS GALLERIES

Nuance/Louisiana Artisans Gallery. Mostly local and regional handblown-glass artists are represented in the studio, which also carries jewelry, pewter, ceramics, lamps, T-shirts, and more. ✉*728 Dublin St., Uptown* ☎*504/865–8463* 🌐*www.nuanceglass.com.*

BOOKS

Maple Street Book Shop. Local authors and touring ones stop here to catch up on literary trade news, perform readings, and autograph their work for readers. The store's focus is New Orleans and Louisiana, but you'll find most new titles in its maze of well-stocked small rooms. ✉*7523 Maple St., Uptown* ☎*504/866–4916 or 504/862–0008* 🌐*www.maplestreetbookshop.com.*

Maple Street Children's Book Shop. Children find a comfortable introduction to literature here with shelves of books divided into age groups, stuffed animals tucked onto bookshelves, and toys to divert young non-readers while their parents and siblings shop. The store frequently hosts storytellers. ✉*7529 Maple St., Uptown* ☎*504/861–2105* 🌐*www.maplestreetbookshop.com.*

CLOTHING

Angelique & Victoria's Shoes. It's two stores in one, and both are trend-setters. Angelique provides apparel by designers such as Diane von Furstenberg, Nanette Lepore, and BCBG, and Victoria's covers the soles with shoes from top designers like Jimmy Choo, Chaplier, and Jack Gomme, as well as jewelry and accessories from local and

national artists. ✉7725 *Maple St., Uptown* ☎*504/866–1092* 🌐*www.angeliqueboutiques.com.*

C. Collection. Geared toward young adults, this store resembles a sorority-house closet jammed with hip, flirty women's clothes, shoes, handbags, and accessories ranging from casual to dressy by makers such as XOXO and ToTheMax. ✉*8141 Maple St., Uptown* ☎*504/861–5002* 🌐*www.ccollectionnola.com.*

Encore Shop. This fund-raising resale shop for the local symphony orchestra is stuffed with previously owned designer clothes, from casual to formal, for men and women, as well as shoes, handbags, and jewelry, all at yard-sale prices. The shop, which takes consignment as well as donated items, is open Tuesday through Saturday. ✉*7814 Maple St., Uptown* ☎*504/861–9028* 🌐*www.symphonyvolunteers.org/encore-shop.asp.*

Gae-Tana's. Natural fabrics and stylish-but-comfortable clothing and hip designs make this a favorite stop for fashion-conscious mature women as well as college students looking for skirts, jeans, shorts, dressy skirts, blouses, fun shoes, handbags, and jewelry. ✉*7732 Maple St., Uptown* ☎*504/865–9625.*

N.O. Surf Shop. There are no rolling waves in New Orleans, but this shop caters to the Crescent City's street surfers and sun lovers with a range of skateboards, hip beachwear, swimsuits, sunglasses, fashion accessories, and its own line of T-shirts that combine city icons such as fleur-de-lis and king-cake babies with surfer themes. ✉7722 *Maple St., Uptown* ☎*504/866–6030* 🌐*www.nosurfshop.com.*

Yvonne LaFleur. Romantic fashions for women include lingerie, casual blouses, flirty dresses, ball gowns, tiaras, jewelry, handbags, and a whole room filled with wedding dresses in a variety of styles. Owner Yvonne LaFleur also custom designs hats for all occasions, and her store is always infused with the sweet scent of her signature perfume line. ✉*8131 Hampson St., Uptown* ☎*504/866–9666* 🌐*www.yvonnelafleur.com.*

HISTORY AND COMMERCE

Get all you can out of a shopping trip to the Riverbend area by taking a St. Charles Avenue streetcar, which runs all the way from Canal Street to the Riverbend area. The leisurely ride along St. Charles Avenue takes you through the renowned Garden District neighborhood, with its historic mansions, Audubon Park, and Tulane and Loyola universities. At the corner where St. Charles meets Carrollton, step off the streetcar to eat at the famous Camellia Grill or grab a cup of coffee and a croissant at La Madeleine to give you energy for your shopping trip.

Side Trips from New Orleans

8

WORD OF MOUTH

"I suggest you try to visit some of the smaller towns right around Lafayette. As for driving around, your best bet is probably to head southeast from Lafayette toward Houma—lots of great towns to visit in between. And while you are there, eat lots of crawfish and shrimp."

—Wayne

"We used Cypress Swamp Tour and were very pleased with it. Whichever tour group you pick, just go on a half day tour—once you've seen a heron, nutria, and gator you've seen them all. There's too much to do in New Orleans to spend much time out of the city."

—ccolor

www.fodors.com/community

By Sue Strachan

NEW ORLEANS HAS NEVER BEEN A TYPICAL OLD SOUTH city. But look away to the west of town, and you can find the antebellum world conjured by the term Dixieland, which was coined here in the early 19th century. Between New Orleans and Baton Rouge, the romantic ruins of plantation homes alternate with the occasional restored manor, often open to visitors. Anyone with an interest in the history of the Old South or a penchant for a picturesque drive along country roads should spend at least half a day along the antebellum grand route, the Great River Road.

Popular day trips include tours of the swamps and bayous that surround New Orleans. *Bayou* comes from a Native American word that means "creek." The brackish, slow-moving waters of south Louisiana were once the highways and byways of the Choctaw, Chickasaw, and Chitimacha. Two centuries ago Jean Lafitte and his freebooters easily hid in murky reaches of swamp, which were covered with thick canopies of subtropical vegetation; pirate gold is said still to be buried here. The state has an alligator population of about 500,000, and most of them laze around in the meandering tributaries and secluded sloughs of south Louisiana. Wild boars, snow-white egrets, bald eagles, and all manner of other exotic creatures inhabit the swamps and marshlands. A variety of tour companies, large and small, take groups to swampy sites a half-hour to two hours away from the city center. Guides steer you by boat through still waters, past ancient gnarled cypresses with gray shawls of Spanish moss, explaining the state's flora and fauna and the swamp traditions of the trappers who settled here. *(For swamp tour operators, ⇨ Alligators Up Close: Swamp Tours.)*

South Louisiana, cradle of the Cajun population, is decidedly French in flavor. In small communities along the coast and in the upland prairie, Cajun French is still spoken, although just about everyone also speaks English. After a hard day's work fishing or working crawfish ponds, rural residents of Cajun Country often live up to the motto *Laissez les bons temps rouler!,* which means "Let the good times roll!"

ABOUT THE RESTAURANTS

Part of the considerable charm of the region west of New Orleans is the Cajun food, popularized by Cajun chef Paul Prudhomme, a native of Opelousas. This is jambalaya, crawfish pie, and filé gumbo country, and nowhere else on Earth is Cajun food done better than where it originated. Cajun food is often described as the robust, hot-peppery country kin of Creole cuisine. It is a cuisine built upon economy—heavy on the rice and the sauces, lighter on the meats—and heavily reliant upon African cooking traditions. Indigenous sea creatures turn up in étouffées, bisques, and pies, and on almost every Acadian menu are jambalaya, gumbo, and blackened fish. Alligator meat is a great favorite, as are sausages like andouille and boudin (stuffed with pork and rice). Cajun food is very rich, and portions tend to be ample. Biscuits and grits are breakfast staples, and many an evening meal ends with bread pudding.

Cajun cuisine extends beyond Cajun Country itself, and into many of the restaurants along River Road. North of Baton Rouge, however, in

IF YOU LIKE

MUSIC

Music beats at the heart of Cajun life. Ensembles of fiddles, accordions, and guitars produce eminently danceable folk music, with songs sung in a mélange of English and Cajun French. Zydeco, closely related to Cajun music, adds washboard and drums to the mix and has more of a blues-rock feel to it. Saturday morning and afternoon are devoted to Cajun music, played in small gatherings and in bars beginning at 8 AM. Zydeco music rocks back-road barns and country clubs on Friday and Saturday nights. Many Cajun clubs and restaurants host Sunday-afternoon jams.

HISTORIC HOMES

The sweeping artistry of the grand plantation houses stands in the eerie shadow of massive chemical plants that operate on the Mississippi today, and plantation ruins sometimes appear in the middle of a cow field or alongside a bayou, directly testifying to this clash between old and new. Some are low-slung, West Indies–style structures that are relatively humble, whereas others are grandly columned mansions.

St. Francisville, more-typical Southern fare prevails. Here you will still find po'boys and sometimes gumbo, but barbecue is more common than boudin. (⇨*For explanations of many Cajun foods, see Chapter 3.)*

ABOUT THE HOTELS

Some of the handsome antebellum mansions along River Road are also B&Bs in which you may roam the high-ceiling rooms before bedding down in a big four-poster or canopied bed. The greatest concentration of accommodations in Cajun Country is in Lafayette, which has an abundance of chain properties as well as some B&Bs. In nearby towns are charming B&Bs, where friendly hosts can give you insider tips about touring the region. St. Francisville is valued as one of the best B&B towns in the South.

8

WHAT IT COSTS

	¢	$	$$	$$$	$$$$
RESTAURANTS	under $10	$10–$15	$16–$22	$23–$30	over $30
HOTELS	under $50	$50–$89	$90–$120	$121–$150	over $150

Restaurant prices are for a main course at dinner. Hotel prices are for two people in a standard double room in high season, excluding 8% sales tax.

PLANTATION COUNTRY

The area designated Plantation Country envelops a cascade of plantations along the Great River Road leading west from New Orleans, plus a reservoir of fine old homes north of Baton Rouge, around the town of St. Francisville. Louisiana plantation homes range from the grandiose Nottoway on River Road to the humble, owner-occupied Butler Green-

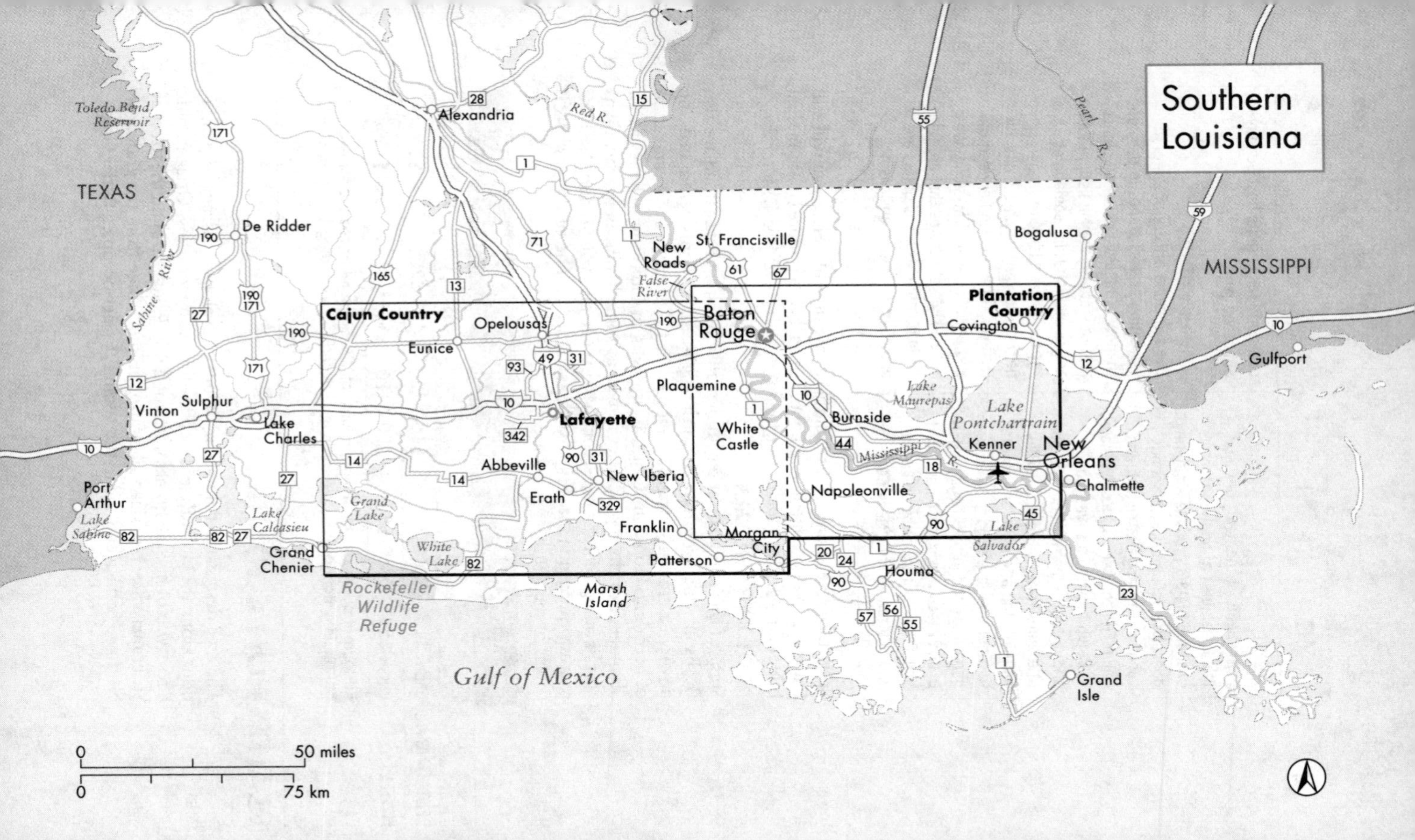

Southern Louisiana
TEXAS
MISSISSIPPI
Toledo Bend Reservoir
Sabine River
Red R.
Pearl R.
Alexandria
De Ridder
St. Francisville
New Roads
False River
Bogalusa
Cajun Country
Plantation Country
Opelousas
Eunice
Baton Rouge
Covington
Gulfport
Plaquemine
White Castle
Burnside
Lake Maurepas
Lake Pontchartrain
Kenner
New Orleans
Chalmette
Mississippi R.
Napoleonville
Vinton
Sulphur
Lake Charles
Lafayette
Abbeville
Erath
New Iberia
Franklin
Morgan City
Patterson
Houma
Lake Salvador
Port Arthur
Lake Sabine
Lake Calcasieu
Grand Lake
White Lake
Grand Chenier
Rockefeller Wildlife Refuge
Marsh Island
Grand Isle
Gulf of Mexico
0
50 miles
0
75 km

wood near St. Francisville. Some sit upon an acre or two; others, such as Rosedown, are surrounded by extensive, lush grounds.

The River Road plantations are closely tied to New Orleans's culture and society: it was here that many of the city's most prominent families made their fortunes generations ago, and the language and tastes here are historically French. The St. Francisville area, on the other hand, received a heartier injection of British-American colonial culture during the antebellum era, evidenced in the landscaped grounds of homes such as Rosedown and the restrained interior of Oakley House, where John James Audubon lived while in the area. Baton Rouge, the state capital, provides a midpoint between the River Road plantations and St. Francisville and has some interesting sights of its own.

THE GREAT RIVER ROAD

The Old South is suspended in an uneasy state of grace along the Great River Road, where the culture that thrived here during the 18th and 19th centuries, both elegant and disturbing, meets the blunt ugliness of the industrial age. Between New Orleans and Baton Rouge, beautifully restored antebellum plantations along the Mississippi are filled with period antiques, ghosts of former residents, and tales of Yankee gunboats. Yet industrial plants mar the scenery, and the man-made levee, constructed in the early 20th century in a desperate ploy to keep the mighty Mississippi on a set course, obstructs the river views that plantation residents once enjoyed. Still, you can always park your car and climb up on the levee for a look at Ol' Man River.

Between the Destrehan and San Francisco plantations you will drive through what amounts to a deep bow before the might of the Mississippi: the Bonnie Carre Spillway is a huge swath of land set aside specifically to receive the river's periodic overflow, thus protecting New Orleans, 30 mi downriver.

The Great River Road is also called, variously, Route or LA 44 and 75 on the east bank of the river and Route or LA 18 on the west bank. "LA" and "Route" are interchangeable; we use Route throughout this chapter. Alternatives to the Great River Road are Interstate 10 and U.S. 61; both have signs marking exits for various plantations. All the plantations described are listed on the National Register of Historic Places, and some of them are B&Bs. Plantation touring can take anywhere from an hour to two days, depending upon how many houses you want to see.

DESTREHAN PLANTATION

23 mi west (upriver) of New Orleans.

The oldest plantation left intact in the lower Mississippi Valley, this simple West Indies–style house, built in 1787 by a free man of color, is typical of the homes built by the earliest planters in the region. The plantation is notable for the hand-hewn cypress timbers that were used in its construction and for the insulation in its walls, made of *bousillage,* a mixture of horsehair, Spanish moss, and mud. Some days bring period demonstrations of indigo dying, candle making, or open-hearth

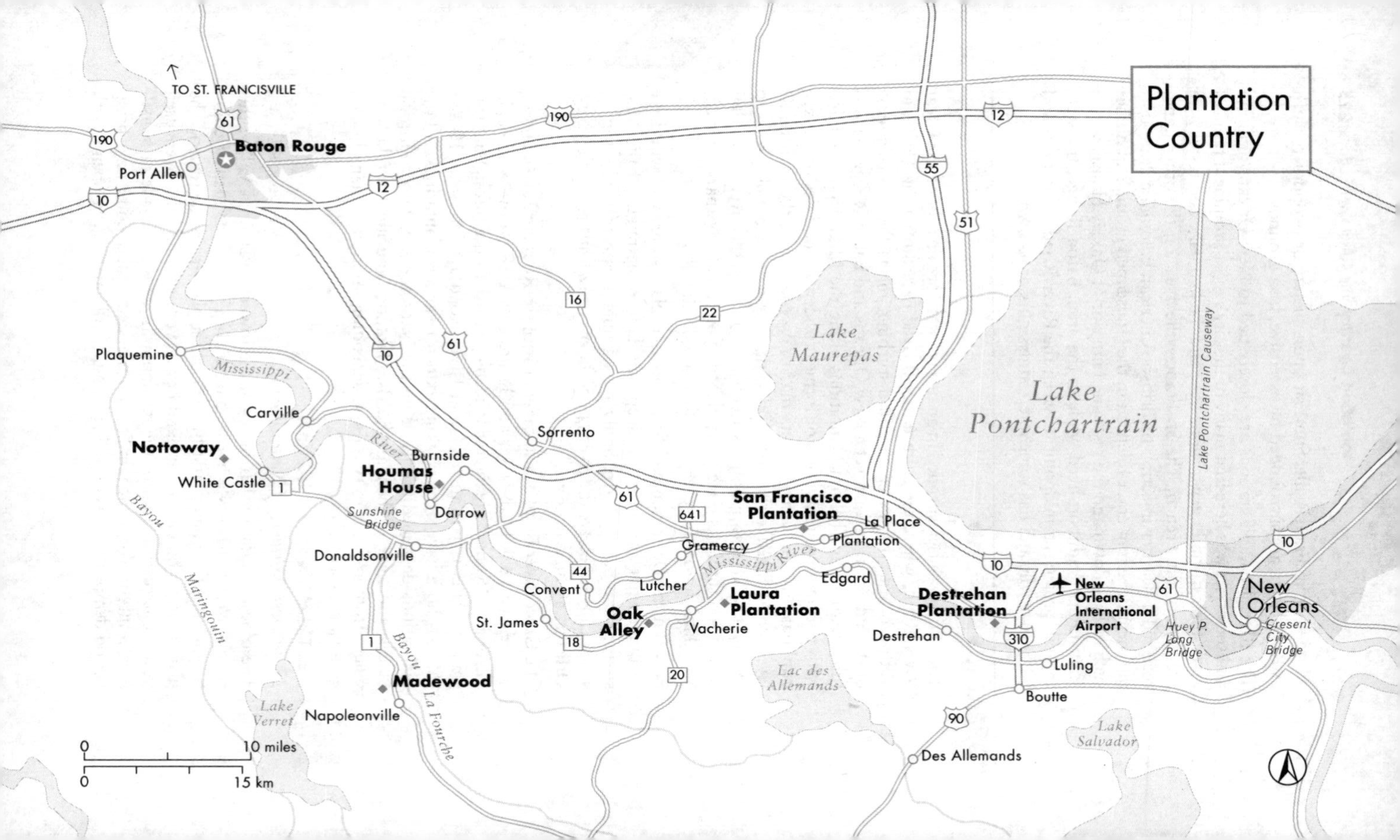
Plantation Country
TO ST. FRANCISVILLE
Baton Rouge
Port Allen
Plaquemine
Carville
Nottoway
White Castle
Houmas House
Burnside
Darrow
Sunshine Bridge
Donaldsonville
Sorrento
Convent
St. James
Lutcher
Gramercy
Oak Alley
Vacherie
Laura Plantation
San Francisco Plantation
La Place
Plantation
Edgard
Destrehan Plantation
Destrehan
Luling
Boutte
Des Allemands
Madewood
Napoleonville
New Orleans International Airport
Huey P. Long Bridge
New Orleans
Cresent City Bridge
Lake Maurepas
Lake Pontchartrain
Lake Pontchartrain Causeway
Lac des Allemands
Lake Salvador
Lake Verret
Mississippi River
Bayou La Fourche
Bayou Maringouin
0
10 miles
0
15 km

cooking; an annual fall festival with music, crafts, and food is held during the second weekend in November. A costumed guide leads you on a 45-minute tour through the house, which is furnished with period antiques and some reproductions. You are free to explore the grounds, including several smaller structures and massive oak trees borne down by their weighty old branches. ⊠*13034 River Rd., Destrehan* ☎*985/764–9315 or 877/453–2095* 🌐*www.destrehanplantation.org* 🎫*$10* 🕒*Daily 9–4.*

PACE YOURSELF

Don't try to visit every plantation listed here—your trip will turn into a blur of columns. If you can, spend the night at one of the plantations, such as Oak Alley or Madewood, and then tour the region. Oak Alley and Laura plantations are just a few miles from each other and provide a nice contrast in architectural styles. St. Francisville is a weekend trip in its own right. If you're visiting from New Orleans and are strapped for time, Destrehan, one of the state's oldest plantations, might fit the bill; it's just 23 mi from the city.

SAN FRANCISCO PLANTATION

18 mi west of Destrehan Plantation, 35 mi west of New Orleans.

An elaborate Steamboat Gothic house completed in 1856, San Francisco presents an intriguing variation on the standard plantation styles, with galleries resembling the decks of a ship. The house was once called St. Frusquin, a name derived from a French slang term, *sans fruscins,* which means "without a penny in my pocket"—the condition its owner, Valsin Marmillion, found himself in after paying exorbitant construction costs. Valsin's father, Edmond Bozonier Marmillion, had begun the project. Upon his father's death, Valsin and his German bride, Louise von Seybold, found themselves with a plantation on their hands. Unable to return to Germany, Louise brought German influence to south Louisiana instead. The result was an opulence rarely encountered in these parts: ceilings painted in trompe l'oeil, hand-painted "toilets" with primitive flushing systems, and cypress painstakingly rendered as marble. Tour guides impart the full fascinating story on the 45-minute tour through the main house. An authentic one-room schoolhouse and a slave cabin have been installed on the grounds, which you can tour at your leisure. Louisiana novelist Frances Parkinson Keyes used the site as the model for her book *Steamboat Gothic.* ⊠*2646 River Rd., Garyville* ☎*985/535–2341 or 888/322–1756* 🌐*www.sanfranciscoplantation.org* 🎫*$15* 🕒*Nov.–Mar., daily 9–4; Apr.–Oct., daily 9:30–4:30.*

LAURA PLANTATION

10 mi west of San Francisco Plantation, 57 mi west of New Orleans.

Laura Plantation provides a more intimate, well-documented presentation of Creole plantation life than any other property on River Road. The narrative of the guides is built on first-person accounts, estate records, and original artifacts from the Locoul family, who built the simple, Creole-style house in 1805. Laura Locoul, whose grandmother founded the estate, kept a detailed diary of plantation life, family fights, and the management of slaves. The information from Laura's

8

diary and the original slave cabins and other outbuildings (workers on the plantation grounds lived in the cabins into the 1980s) provide rare insights into slavery under the French. The plantation gift shop stocks a large selection of literature by and about slaves and slavery in southern Louisiana and the United States. Senegalese slaves at Laura are believed to have first told folklorist Alcee Fortier the tales of Br'er Rabbit; his friend Joel Chandler Harris used the stories in his Uncle Remus tales. ✉*2247 River Rd. (Rte. 18), Vacherie* ☎*225/265–7690 or 888/799–7690* 🌐*www.lauraplantation.com* *$15* ⏲*Daily 10–4.*

WHERE TO EAT

¢ SOUTHERN ✕**B&C Seafood.** This small shop and deli serves the tastiest seafood gumbo ever ladled into a Styrofoam bowl. Try it with a dash of hot sauce and a sprinkle of filé, or sample the alligator and garfish po'boys. Finish with a scoop of soft and chewy bread pudding. The deli has fresh and frozen catfish, crawfish, alligator, and turtle meat harvested from the nearby swamps. You can buy seafood packed to travel. ✉*2155 Rte. 18, beside Laura Plantation, Vacherie* ☎*225/265–8356 www.bandcseafood.com* *AE, D, MC, V* ⏲*Closed Sun.*

OAK ALLEY

3 mi west of Laura Plantation, 60 mi west of New Orleans.

Built between 1837 and 1839 by Jacques T. Roman, a French-Creole sugar planter from New Orleans, Oak Alley is the most famous of all the antebellum homes in Louisiana and an outstanding example of Greek Revival architecture. The 28 gnarled oak trees that line the drive and give the columned plantation its name were planted in the early 1700s by an earlier settler, and the oaks proved more resilient than the dwelling he must have built here. A guided tour introduces you to the grand interior of the manor, furnished with period antiques. Be sure to take in the view from the upper gallery of the house and to spend time exploring the expansive grounds. A number of late-19th-century cottages behind the main house provide simple overnight accommodations and a restaurant is open daily for breakfast (8:30–10:30) and lunch (11–3). ✉*3645 River Rd. (Rte. 18), Vacherie* ☎*225/265–2151 or 888/279–9802* 🌐*www.oakalleyplantation.com* *$15* ⏲*Weekdays 10–4, weekends 10–5.*

HOUMAS HOUSE

29 mi northwest from San Francisco Plantation, 58 mi west of New Orleans.

Surrounded by majestic 200-year-old oaks, Houmas House is a classic Louisiana plantation home—grand white pillars and all. The house here is actually two buildings, of quite different styles, joined together. In 1790 Alexander Latil built the smaller rear house in the French–Spanish Creole style that was becoming popular in New Orleans. The Greek Revival mansion was added to the grounds in 1840 by John and Caroline Preston, who eventually connected the two structures with an arched carriageway. ✉*40136 Hwy. 942, ½ mi off Rte. 44, Darrow* ☎*225/473–7841 or 225/473–9380* 🌐*www.houmashouse.com* *Guided home and garden tour $20, self-guided garden tour $10* ⏲*Mon. and Tues. 9–5, Wed.–Sun. 9–7.*

WHERE TO EAT

$ SOUTHERN **The Cabin.** Yellowed newspapers and antique farm implements hang from the walls of this 150-year-old slave cabin, which was part of the Monroe Plantation. Crawfish étouffée and other Cajun seafood dishes are the specialties here, but you can also choose po'boys, burgers, or steaks. *5404 Rte. 44, at the corner of Rte. 22, Burnside 225/473–3007 www.thecabinrestaurant.com AE, D, MC, V No dinner Mon.*

$–$$ CREOLE **Latil's Landing Restaurant and Café Burnside.** Set in the rear wing of Houmas House Plantation, Latil's Landing Restaurant is furnished with period antiques and reproductions that put you in the mood for the "nouvelle Louisiana" food, a mélange of traditional ingredients with more contemporary cooking techniques and flavors. Try the bisque of curried pumpkin, crawfish and corn, rack of lamb, and the chocolate napoleon. Café Burnside is open for a lunch with a menu of salads and sandwiches. *40146 Hwy. 942, Darrow 225/473–9380 or 888/323–8314 AE, D, MC, V No dinner Mon. and Tues.*

MADEWOOD

20 mi south of Houmas House, 74 mi west of New Orleans.

This galleried, 21-room Greek Revival mansion with its massive white columns was designed by architect Henry Howard and completed in 1854. The house, across the road from Bayou Lafourche, has an enormous freestanding staircase and 25-foot-high ceilings, and is best experienced overnight in the B&B. Guests can arrange a tour with the owners; call for appointments. *4250 Rte. 308, 2 mi south of town, Napoleonville 985/369–7151 or 800/375–7151 www.madewood.com $10 Daily 10–4.*

River Road African American Museum. This museum explores the contributions of African-Americans in Louisiana's rural Mississippi River communities through exhibits that explore their cuisine, the Underground Railroad, free people of color, jazz, and other topics. *406 Charles St., Donaldsonville 225/474–5553 www.africanamericanmuseum.org $4 Wed.–Sat. 10–5, Sun. 1–5.*

WHERE TO STAY

$$$$ ★ **Madewood.** Expect gracious hospitality, lovely antiques, and canopied beds in both the 21-room main house and Charlet House, a smaller structure on the plantation grounds. Guests come here for the social experience as well as the elegant accommodations: a Southern dinner is shared in the formal dining room at 7 PM, preceded by a cocktail hour in the library. The cost of a room includes breakfast, dinner, and a tour of the house. **Pros:** quiet; beautiful; staying here is like stepping back in time—though with modern amenities. **Cons:** some may find it too quiet; no TV; dinner is a group affair. *4250 Rte. 308, Napoleonville 985/369–7151 or 800/375–7151 www.madewood.com 5 rooms, 3 suites In-room: Wi-Fi AE, D, MC, V MAP.*

$$$$ **Oak Alley.** Stay in 100-year-old cottages on Oak Alley Plantation's grounds. The furnishings have country charm, with brass beds and antiques or reproductions. **Pros:** spectacular sunrise views from the levee in front of the plantation; serene quiet; charming rooms with comfortable Tempur-Pedic beds. **Cons:** few nearby options for supplies

and food. ✉3645 River Rd. (Rte. 18), Vacherie ☎225/265–2151 or 800/442–5539 🌐www.oakalleyplantation.com *6 cottages* *In-room: no phone, kitchen (some), Wi-Fi (some). In-hotel: no-smoking rooms* *AE, D, MC, V* *MAP.*

NOTTOWAY

Fodor's Choice ★

33 mi northwest of Madewood, 70 mi west of New Orleans.

The South's largest plantation house, Nottoway, should not be missed. Built in 1857, the mansion is a gem of Italianate style. With 64 rooms, 22 columns, and 200 windows, this white castle (the town of White Castle was named for it) was the crowning achievement of architect Henry Howard. It was saved from destruction during the Civil War by a Northern officer (a former guest of the owners, Mr. and Mrs. John Randolph). An idiosyncratic layout reflects the individual tastes of the original owners and includes a grand ballroom, famed in these parts for its crystal chandeliers and hand-carved columns. You can stay here overnight, and a formal restaurant serves lunch and dinner daily. ✉*31025 Hwy. 1, 2 mi north of White Castle* ☎*225/545–8632 or 866/527–6884* 🌐*www.nottoway.com* *$15* *Daily 9–5.*

WHERE TO STAY

$$$$ **Nottoway.** The largest antebellum plantation in the South, this recently renovated stunner is fun to wander around at night. You can sit on the upstairs balcony and watch the ships go by on the river. The antiques-filled plantation home has three suites and rooms in its wings and surrounding cottages. A delicious Southern breakfast awaits in the morning, and you can dine at the plantation for lunch and dinner. **Pros:** sleeping in history. **Cons:** if you book one of the suites in the main house, your room is on the tour. ✉*31025 Hwy. 1, White Castle* ☎*225/545–8632 or 866/428–4748* 🌐*www.nottoway.com* *11 rooms, 3 suites* *In-room: Wi-Fi. In-hotel: restaurant, pool* *AE, D, MC, V* *BP.*

BATON ROUGE

80 mi northwest of New Orleans via I–10.

Hemmed in as it is by endless industrial plants, Baton Rouge does not look like much from the road. Yet government-history enthusiasts will want to stop here on their way through the south Louisiana countryside. Baton Rouge, the state capital, has several interesting and readily accessible sights, including the attractive capitol grounds and an educational planetarium. This is the city from which colorful, cunning Huey P. Long ruled the state; it is also the site of his assassination. Even today, more than half a century after Long's death, legends about the controversial governor and U.S. senator abound.

The parishes to the north of Baton Rouge are quiet and bucolic, with gently rolling hills, high bluffs, and historic districts. John James Audubon lived in West Feliciana Parish in 1821, tutoring local children and painting 80 of his famous bird studies. In both terrain and traits, this region is more akin to north Louisiana than to south Louisiana—which is to say, the area is very Southern.

Louisiana Arts & Science Museum and Irene W. Pennington Planetarium. Housed in a 1925 Illinois Central railroad station near the Old State Capitol, this idiosyncratic but high-quality museum brings together a contemporary art gallery, an Egyptian tomb exhibit, a children's museum and discovery zone, and a state-of-the-art planetarium, which is also kid-friendly. The planetarium presents regular shows, as does the ExxonMobil Space Theater. The museum also hosts traveling exhibits, and houses the nation's second-largest collection of sculptures by 20th-century Croatian artist Ivan Mestrovic, many of which adorn the entrance hall. *✉100 S. River Rd. ☎225/344–5272 🌐www.lasm.org 🎫$6, $8 including planetarium show ⏲Tues.–Fri. 10–4, Sat. 10–5 (planetarium 10–8), Sun. 1–5.*

Louisiana State Museum—Baton Rouge. This museum showcases the history of Louisiana through two exhibits: "Grounds for Greatness: Louisiana and the Nation," which relates Louisiana history to the nation and the world, from the Louisiana Purchase to World War II; and the "Louisiana Experience: Discovering the Soul of America," a road-trip-like exhibit that courses through the different regions of the state. There is also a gallery for changing exhibits. *✉660 N. 4th St. ☎800/568–6968 🎫$6 ⏲Tues.–Sat. 9–5, Sun. noon–5.*

Old Governor's Mansion. This Georgian-style home was constructed for Governor Huey P. Long in 1939, and nine governors have since lived there. The story goes that Long instructed the architect to design it to resemble the White House, representing Long's unrealized ambition to live in the real one. Notable features on the guided tour include Long's bedroom and a secret staircase. *✉502 North Blvd.70802 ☎225/387–2464 🌐www.oldgovernorsmansion.org 🎫$6 ⏲Tues.–Fri. 10–3, or by appointment.*

Old State Capitol. When this Gothic Victorian fantasia was completed in 1850, it was declared by some to be a masterpiece, by others a monstrosity. No one can deny that the restored building is colorful and dramatic. In the entrance hall a stunning purple, gold, and green spiral staircase winds toward a stained-glass atrium. The building now holds the **Louisiana Center for Political and Governmental History,** an education and research facility with audiovisual exhibits. The "assassination room," an exhibit covering Huey Long's final moments, is a major draw. *✉100 North Blvd., at River Rd. 🌐www.sec.state.la.us/osc 🎫$4 ⏲Tues.–Sat. 10–4, Sun. noon–4.*

Rural Life Museum & Windrush Gardens. This 5-acre complex, run by Louisiana State University (LSU), is an outdoor teaching and research facility. Three major areas—the Barn, the Working Plantation, and Folk Architecture—with 25 or so rustic 19th-century structures represent the rural life of early Louisianians. The Barn holds an eclectic collection of items including old farm tools, quilts, 19th-century horse-drawn carriages, slave items, and much more. The working plantation's several buildings include a gristmill, a blacksmith's shop, and several outbuildings. The gardens cover 25 acres and were created by landscape designer Steele Burden. It's a truly unique place. *✉4650 Essen La., off I–10 ☎225/765–2437 🌐rurallife.lsu.edu 🎫$7 ⏲Daily 8:30–5.*

8

Shaw Center for the Arts. This multicultural center houses the LSU Museum of Art, the Brunner Gallery, the Manship Theatre, the LSUMOA museum store, the LSU School of Art Gallery, two sculpture gardens, and a rooftop terrace with great views of the Mississippi River. River views can also be appreciated from the on-site restaurant, Tsunami, a nightlife hot spot with Asian-fusion cuisine. ✉*100 Lafayette St.70802* ☎*225/346–5001* 🌐*www.shawcenter.org* 🎟*$8* ⏲*Tues.–Sat. 9* AM*–11* AM*, Sun. 11–5*

> **HUEY'S "DEDUCT" BOX**
>
> One of the biggest mysteries about Huey P. Long is what happened to his "deduct box." The deduct box was where Long kept his political contributions—cash—from individuals and corporations. State employees—no matter how high or low—also gave a portion of their salary to Long. The box had a number of homes, and the best known was at the Roosevelt Hotel (which reopened in July 2009). But when Long was assassinated in 1935, the location of the deduct box went to the grave with him. Many still think it's behind the walls of the hotel.

State Capitol Building. Still called the "New State Capitol," this building has housed the offices of the governor and Congress since 1932. It is a testament to the personal influence of legendary Governor Huey Long that the funding for this massive building was approved during the Great Depression, and that the building itself was completed in a mere 14 months. You can tour the first floor, richly decked with murals and mosaics, and peer into the halls of the Louisiana legislature. Huey Long's colorful personality eventually caught up with him: he was assassinated in 1935, and the spot where he was shot (near the rear elevators) is marked with a plaque. At 34 stories, this is America's tallest state capitol; an observation deck on the 27th floor affords an expansive view of the Mississippi River, the city, and the industrial outskirts. ✉*900 N. 3rd St.70802* ☎*225/342–7317* 🎟*Free* ⏲*Daily 8–4:30 (tower until 4).*

USS Kidd & Veterans Memorial Museum. A Fletcher-class destroyer, the USS *Kidd* is a World War II survivor restored to its V-J Day configuration. A self-guided tour takes in more than 50 inner spaces of this ship and also the separate **Nautical Center** museum. Among the museum's exhibits are articles from the 175 Fletcher-class ships that sailed for the United States, a collection of ship models, and a restored P-40 fighter plane hanging from the ceiling. The Louisiana Memorial Plaza lists more than 7,000 Louisiana citizens killed during combat. ✉*305 S. River Rd. (Government St. at the levee)* ☎*225/342–1942* 🌐*www.usskidd.com* 🎟*$7* ⏲*Daily 9–5.*

WHERE TO EAT

$$$ SOUTHERN ★ ✕ **Juban's.** An upscale bistro with a lush courtyard and walls adorned with art, Juban's is a family-owned and -operated restaurant not far from the LSU campus. Tempting main courses of seafood, beef, and veal dishes, as well as roasted duck, rabbit, and quail, highlight the sophisticated menu. The Hallelujah Crab (soft-shell stuffed with seafood and topped with "creolaise" sauce) is a specialty, and Juban's own mango tea is delicious. The warm bread pudding is something to

write home about. ✉3739 *Perkins Rd. (Acadiana Shopping Center)* ☎*225/346–8422* 🌐*www.jubans.com* 💳*AE, D, DC, MC, V* ⊗*Closed Sun. No lunch Mon. and Sat.*

$$ SOUTHERN ✕ **Mike Anderson's.** This lively seafood spot manages to be a lot of things to a lot of people: first-daters, families, groups of friends, and solo diners all find a warm welcome here. Locals of every stripe praise the seafood, and it is true that the food is good, fresh, served in large portions, and consistent. The South Louisiana Combo—fried shrimp, oysters, crawfish tails, catfish, and stuffed crab served with french fries, hush puppies, and a choice of salad or coleslaw (pick the coleslaw!)—is a best bet. ✉*1031 W. Lee Dr.70820* ☎*225/766–7823* 🌐*www.mikeandersonsbr.com* 💳*AE, D, MC, V.*

$$ ITALIAN ✕ **Ruffino's.** A broad, clubby dining room invites lingering over the best Italian cuisine in town. Local ingredients find their way into hearty Italian preparations, such as eggplant Parmesan and shrimp scampi. A romantic bar area includes some smoking tables just off the main dining areas. The restaurant is a few minutes east from downtown along Interstate 10. ✉*18811 Highland Rd., Exit 166 off I–10* ☎*225/753–3458* 🌐*www.ruffinosrestaurant.com* 💳*AE, D, DC, MC, V* ⊗*No lunch Mon.–Sat.*

WHERE TO STAY

$$$$ **Embassy Suites.** This centrally located property has two-room suites with mahogany furniture and a wet-bar area with microwave, coffeemaker, and mini-refrigerator. A two-hour cocktail happy hour and a full breakfast, cooked to order, are included in the room rate, and the service is quite good across the board. **Pros:** great location if you're going to an LSU football game; comfortable rooms; lots of services. **Cons:** chain property; downtown sights are not within walking distance; occasionally packed with conventioneers—or high-spirited LSU fans. ✉*4914 Constitution Ave.* ☎*225/924–6566 or 800/362–2779* 🌐*www.embassysuites.com* *223 suites* *In-room: refrigerator, Wi-Fi. In-hotel: restaurant, room service, bar, pool, gym, laundry service* 💳*AE, D, DC, MC, V* *BP.*

$$$$ **Hilton Baton Rouge Capitol Center.** The former Heidelberg Hotel is centrally located in downtown Baton Rouge and boasts a fitness center, full-service spa and salon, and other amenities. Of note is the infamous tunnel from Huey P. Long's days that connected the hotel to the King Hotel (no longer open) across the street. It is now a private dining room. **Pros:** spectacular view of the river; near all the downtown sites. **Cons:** downtown Baton Rouge can sometimes feel like a ghost town at night. ✉*201 Lafayette St.* ☎*225/344–5866* 🌐*www.hiltoncapitolcenter.com* *291 rooms, 7 suites* *In-room: safe, Wi-Fi. In-hotel: restaurant, room service, bar, gym, spa, laundry service, no-smoking rooms* 💳*AE, D, DC, MC, V.*

$$$ **Marriott Baton Rouge.** This high-rise hotel has somewhat formal rooms and public spaces with traditional furnishings. The top four floors offer VIP perks such as Continental breakfast and afternoon hors d'oeuvres and cocktails. **Pros:** accommodating to large groups; full-service hotel; lots of comforts. **Cons:** not centrally located. ✉*5500 Hilton Ave.* ☎*225/924–5000 or 800/228–9290* 🌐*www.marriott.com* *300 rooms* *In-room: safe, Wi-Fi. In-hotel: restaurant, room service, bar, gym, laundry service, no-smoking rooms* 💳*AE, D, DC, MC, V.*

ST. FRANCISVILLE

25 mi north of Baton Rouge on U.S. 61.

A cluster of plantation homes all within a half-hour drive, a lovely, walkable historic district, renowned antiques shopping, and a wealth of comfortable B&Bs draw visitors and locals from New Orleans to overnight stays in St. Francisville. The town is a two-hour drive from New Orleans, so it is also possible to make this a day trip.

St. Francisville's historic district, particularly along Royal Street, is dotted with markers identifying basic histories of various structures, most of them dating to the late 18th or early 19th century. The region's Anglo-Protestant edge, in contrast to the staunchly French-Catholic tenor of the River Road plantations, is evident in the prominent **Grace Episcopal Church,** sitting proudly atop a hill in the center of town and surrounded by a peaceful, Spanish moss–shaded cemetery. The smaller (though older) Catholic cemetery is directly across a small fence from the Episcopal complex.

Butler Greenwood Plantation. This home has been occupied by the same family since its construction in the 1790s, and with much of the same furniture. This renders the house a bit musty and quirky compared to other, more showpiece-oriented plantations in the area, providing an intimate picture of day-to-day living in such a home. Butler Greenwood is relatively modest in size, and the tour focuses on details such as dress (several items of clothing worn by the family's ancestors are on display) and china (a beautiful set has been in the family for generations). A complete set of coveted rosewood furniture, still with the original upholstery, is of particular interest. The property is also a six-cottage B&B. ✉ *8345 U.S. 6170775* ☎ *225/635–6312* 🌐 *www.butlergreenwood.com* 🎫 *$5* ⏲ *Daily 9–5.*

OFF THE BEATEN PATH

Louisiana State Penitentiary Museum at Angola. The notorious Angola prison is a half-hour drive from St. Francisville, at the dead end of Route 66. With a prison population of about 5,000 inmates, this is one of the largest prisons in the United States. Wryly nicknamed "The Farm," Angola was once a working plantation, with prisoners for field hands. The prison has been immortalized in countless songs and several films and documentaries, including *Dead Man Walking* and *Angola Prison Rodeo—the Wildest Show in the South.* A small museum outside the prison's front gate houses a fascinating, eerie, and often moving collection of photographs documenting the people and events that have been a part of Angola. Items such as makeshift prisoner weapons and the electric chair used for executions until 1991 are also on display. ✉ *Hwy. 66* ☎ *225/655–2592* 🌐 *www.angolamuseum.org* 🎫 *Free* ⏲ *Weekdays 8–4:30, Sat. 9–5, Sun. 10–5.*

The Myrtles. A 110-foot gallery with Wedgwood-blue cast-iron grillwork makes a lovely setting for the weddings and receptions frequently held at the Myrtles. The house was built around 1796 and has elegant formal parlors with rich molding and faux-marble paneling. The upper floor is a B&B, thus limiting the scope of the daytime guided tour. The house is reputedly haunted, and the fun Friday- and Saturday-night mystery tours (offered at 6, 7, and 8) are perhaps more of a draw than the daytime tours. The Carriage House Restaurant, beside the house, is a fine place for lunch or dinner. ✉ *7747 U.S. 61, about 1 mi north of downtown St. Francisville* ☎ *225/635–6277 or 800/809–0565* 🌐 *www.myrtlesplantation.com* 🎟 *$8, mystery tours $10* ⏲ *Daily 9–5; mystery tours Fri. and Sat. nights at 6, 7, and 8.*

OFF THE BEATEN PATH

Oakley House and Audubon State Historic Site. John James Audubon did a major portion of his *Birds of America* studies in this 100-acre park. The three-story Oakley Plantation House on the grounds is where Audubon tutored the young Eliza Pirrie, daughter of Mr. and Mrs. James Pirrie, owners of Oakley. The simple, even spartan, interior contrasts sharply with the extravagances of the River Road plantations and demonstrates the Puritan influence in this region. The grounds, too, are reminiscent of the English penchant for a blending of order and wilderness in their gardens. You must follow a short path to reach the house from the parking lot. A state-run museum at the start of the path provides an informative look at plantation life as it was lived in this region 200 years ago. ✉ *11788 Rte. 965, 2 mi south of St. Francisville off U.S. 61* ☎ *225/635–3739 or 888/677–2838* 🌐 *www.lastateparks.com* 🎟 *Park and plantation $2* ⏲ *Daily 9–5.*

Fodor's Choice ★ **Rosedown Plantation and Gardens.** The opulent house at Rosedown dates from 1835, is beautifully restored, and nestles in 28 acres of exquisite formal gardens. The original owners, Martha and Daniel Turnbull, spent their honeymoon in Europe and Mrs. Turnbull fell in love with the formal gardens she saw there. She had the gardens at Rosedown laid out even as the house was under construction, and she spent the rest of her life lovingly maintaining them. The state of Louisiana owns Rosedown, and the beauties of the restored manor, including 90% of the original furniture, can be appreciated during a thorough one-hour tour led by park rangers. Be sure to allow ample time for roaming the grounds after the tour. ✉ *12501 I–10, off U.S. 61* ☎ *225/635–3332 or 888/376–1867* 🌐 *www.lastateparks.com* 🎟 *$10, grounds only $5* ⏲ *Daily 9–5.*

WHERE TO EAT AND STAY

$–$$ CREOLE ✕ **Carriage House Restaurant.** A fine-dining establishment in the shadow of the Myrtles Plantation, the Carriage House is a boon to overnighters in the St. Francisville area. The dining room is elegant yet intimate. The contemporary cuisine draws from a wealth of culinary traditions, with a mix of classic Southern cuisine and a dash of Creole. Sunday brunch is a favorite. Reservations are accepted for large parties only; it's best to arrive early to claim a table—and your share of specials. ✉ *7747 U.S. 61, at the Myrtles Plantation* ☎ *225/635–6278* 🌐 *www.myrtlesplantation.com* 💳 *AE, D, MC, V* ⏲ *Closed Tues. No dinner Sun.*

$ SOUTHERN ✕ **The Magnolia.** This low-key and unassuming dining establishment is a St. Francisville hot spot on weekend nights. During the day, locals and tourists flock here for Southern specialties and pizza. At night, go for cocktails or dinner; on Friday evening there's always a live band. ✉ *5689 Commerce St., St. Francisville* ☎ *225/635–6528* 💳 *MC, V* ⏲ *No dinner Sun.–Wed.*

$ SOUTHERN ★ ✕ **Roadside BBQ & Grill.** Looking for Southern barbecue? Here it is—ribs, pork, and chicken grilled to perfection. If you're not in the mood for 'cue, they also have hamburgers, salads, and fried seafood po'boys.

Most astonishing, though, are the sophisticated specials that hit the chalkboard on weekends, such as crab cakes topped with sautéed shrimp, and rib eye topped with lump crabmeat. A children's menu is also available. ✉ *Colonial Dr. and U.S. 61, 9 mi south of St. Francisville* ☎ *225/658–9669* ▭ *AE, D, DC, MC, V* ⏲ *Closed Mon. No dinner Tues., Wed., and Sun.*

$$$ **Barrow House & Printer's Cottage.** Along St. Francisville's historic Royal Street, these two old houses hold some of the most comfortable B&B accommodations in the area, with antique furnishings in most of the rooms. Breakfast is Continental; full breakfast is available for a small surcharge. A cassette walking tour of town is included. **Pros:** good location in downtown St. Francisville; B&B ambience; friendly staff. **Cons:** if you don't like antiques, you may feel like you're in a museum or your grandmother's home. ✉ *9779 Royal St.* ☎ *225/635–4791* 🌐 *www.topteninn.com* *3 rooms, 3 suites* *In-room: DVD* ▭ *AE, D, MC, V* *CP.*

$$$ **The Myrtles.** If you don't mind a deep legacy of hauntings, the Myrtles is a pleasant and convenient place to stay, just a few miles beyond the center of St. Francisville. The guest rooms fill the second floor of the plantation house and a couple of outlying buildings. A tour of the home is included in your stay, as is a Continental breakfast served beside the gift shop. In nice weather, many guests opt for the outdoor tables behind the house. The fine Carriage House Restaurant serves excellent lunches and dinners and is another good reason to stay here. **Pros:** historical property oozes atmosphere; ghost hunters' paradise; next door to Carriage House Restaurant. **Cons:** feels like it's in the middle of nowhere; easily frightened travelers might want to stay elsewhere. ✉ *7747 U.S. 61* ☎ *225/635–6277 or 800/809–0565* 🌐 *www.myrtlesplantation.com* *10 rooms, 1 suite* *In-room: DVD* ▭ *AE, D, MC, V* *CP.*

PLANTATION COUNTRY ESSENTIALS

To research prices, get advice from other travelers, and book travel arrangements, visit 🌐 *www.fodors.com.*

AIR TRAVEL

Baton Rouge Metropolitan Airport, 7 mi north of downtown, is served by American, Continental, Delta, and Northwest. New Orleans International Airport is off Interstate 10, just 20 minutes from Destrehan Plantation.

Airport Information Baton Rouge Metropolitan Airport *(BTR)* (✉ *9430 Jackie Cochran Dr.* ☎ *225/355–0333* 🌐 *www.flybtr.com*).

BUS TRAVEL

Greyhound Southeast Lines has frequent daily service from New Orleans to Baton Rouge, and limited service to surrounding areas.

Bus Information Greyhound Southeast Lines (☎ *800/231–2222* 🌐 *www.greyhound.com*).

CAR TRAVEL

From New Orleans, the fastest route to the River Road plantations is Interstate 10 west to Interstate 310 to Exit 6, River Road. Alternatives to the Great River Road are to continue on either Interstate 10 or U.S. 61 west; both have signs marking exits for various plantations. Route 18 runs along the west bank of the river, Route 44 on the east.

Interstate 10 and U.S. 190 run east–west through Baton Rouge. Interstate 12 heads east, connecting with north–south Interstate 55 and Interstate 59. U.S. 61 leads from New Orleans to Baton Rouge and north. Ferries across the Mississippi cost $1 per car; most bridges are free. Route 1 travels along False River, which is a blue oxbow lake created ages ago when the mischievous, muddy Mississippi changed its course. The route wanders past gracious homes and small lakeside houses.

EMERGENCIES

Dial 911 for assistance. Hospital emergency rooms are open 24 hours a day at Baton Rouge General Medical Center and Our Lady of the Lake Medical Center. Walgreens has a 24-hour pharmacy.

Hospitals **Baton Rouge General** Medical Center Mid-City (✉ *3600 Florida Blvd.* ☎ *225/387–7000* 🌐 *www.generalhealth.org*). **Our Lady of the Lake Regional Medical Center** (✉ *5000 Hennessy Blvd.* ☎ *225/765–6565* 🌐 *www.ololrmc.com*).

24-Hour Pharmacy **Walgreens** (✉ *3550 Government St.* ☎ *225/343–8878*).

VISITOR INFORMATION

Tourist Information **Baton Rouge Visitors & Conventions Bureau** (✉ *730 North Blvd., Baton Rouge* ☎ *225/383–1825 or 800/527–6843* 🌐 *www.visitbatonrouge.com*). **Louisiana Visitor Information Center** (✉ *900 N. 3rd St., Baton Rouge* ☎ *225/342–7317* 🌐 *www.louisianatravel.com*). **West Feliciana Tourist & Convention Information Center** (✉ *1157 Ferdinand St., St. Francisville 70775* ☎ *225/635–4224 or 800/789–4221* 🌐 *www.stfrancisville.us*).

CAJUN COUNTRY

French Louisiana, lying amid the bayous, rice paddies, and canebrakes to the west of New Orleans, has become famous in the rest of the country for its food (jambalaya and blackened fish) and music (both Cajun and zydeco). The Cajun culture has its roots far from these parts in the present-day Canadian provinces of Nova Scotia and New Brunswick, where French settlers colonized a region they called l'Acadie at the start of the 17th century. The British seized control of the region in the early 18th century and the French were expelled. Their exile was described by Henry Wadsworth Longfellow in his epic poem "Evangeline." Many Acadians eventually settled in 22 parishes of southwestern Louisiana. Their descendants are called "Cajun," a corruption of "Acadian"; some continue the traditions of the early French settlers, living by fishing and fur trapping.

Cajun culture is decidedly rural, rooted in a smattering of tiny towns and in the swamps and bayous that wind among them. Driving from one village to the next, antiques shoppers and nature lovers alike will find bliss. Live oaks with ragged gray buntings of Spanish moss form canopies over the bottle-green bayous. Country roads follow the contortions of the Teche (pronounced *tesh*), the state's longest bayou, and meander through villages where cypress cabins rise up out of the water on stilts and moored fishing boats and pirogues scarcely bob on the sluggish waters. At the centers of these same villages are wonderful bakeries, historic churches, fresh oyster bars, and regional antiques for sale in small, weathered shops.

Many visitors to this region are surprised to hear the dialect for the first time. Cajun French is an oral tradition in which French vocabulary and approximate grammar encounter the American accent, and it differs significantly from what is spoken in France. English is also spoken throughout Cajun Country, but you will hear Gallic accents and see many signs that read ICI ON PARLE FRANÇAIS (French spoken here).

LAFAYETTE

Lafayette (pronounced lah-fay-*ette*), 136 mi west of New Orleans and the largest city in Cajun Country, is a major center of Cajun life and lore, the "big city" in the middle of the countryside. It's an interesting and enjoyable town, with some worthwhile historical and artistic sights. The simulated Cajun villages at **Vermilionville** and **Acadian Village** provide evocative introductions to the traditional Cajun way of life. Excellent restaurants and B&Bs make Lafayette a good jumping-off point for exploring the region. The city has also had an infusion of new restaurants and nightclubs—particularly downtown, which is lively even on weekend nights.

Numbers in the margin correspond to numbers on the Lafayette map.

WHAT TO SEE

3 **Alexander Mouton House and Lafayette Museum.** Built in 1800 as the *maison dimanche,* or "Sunday house," of town founder Jean Mouton, this galleried town house with a mid-19th-century addition now preserves local history. The older section is an excellent example of early Acadian architecture and contains artifacts used by settlers. The main museum contains Civil War–era furnishings and memorabilia and a Mardi Gras exhibit. *✉1122 Lafayette St. ☎337/234–2208 $3 Tues.–Sat. 9–4:30, Sun. 1–4.*

6 **Children's Museum of Acadiana.** Good on a rainy day or to soak up extra energy in the kids, this museum is basically a large indoor playground, with educational games and interactive exhibits such as a grocery store, a kid's-size TV news studio, a bubble exhibit, and more. *✉201 E. Congress St. ☎337/232–8500 $5 Tues.–Sat. 10–5.*

4 **Jefferson Street Market.** A collective of artists, artisans, and dealers fills the deep hall of this market. Antiques and mod kitsch, refined gifts and quirky artwork—this market has it all. Changing contemporary art exhibits claim the central gallery space. *✉538 Jefferson St. ☎337/233–2589 Mon.–Sat. 10–5.*

2 **Lafayette Courthouse.** The courthouse contains an impressive collection of more than 2,000 historical photographs of life in the Lafayette area.

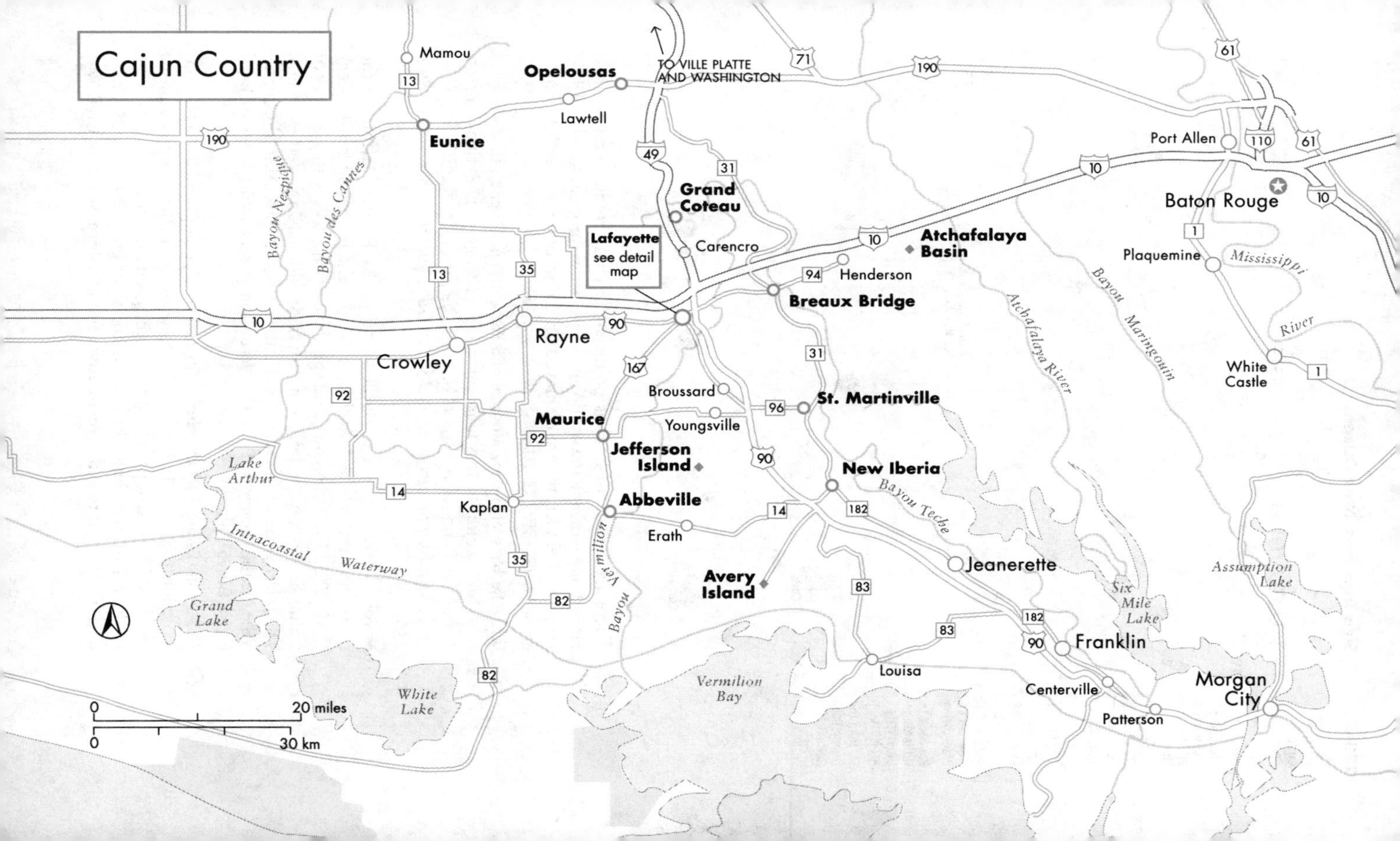

Cajun Country
Mamou
Opelousas
TO VILLE PLATTE AND WASHINGTON
Lawtell
Eunice
Port Allen
Baton Rouge
Grand Coteau
Carencro
Lafayette see detail map
Atchafalaya Basin
Plaquemine
Mississippi River
Henderson
Breaux Bridge
Bayou Nezpique
Bayou des Cannes
Bayou Maringouin
Atchafalaya River
Rayne
Crowley
White Castle
Broussard
St. Martinville
Maurice
Youngsville
Jefferson Island
New Iberia
Bayou Teche
Lake Arthur
Kaplan
Abbeville
Erath
Intracoastal Waterway
Bayou Vermilion
Jeanerette
Avery Island
Assumption Lake
Six Mile Lake
Grand Lake
Franklin
Louisa
Morgan City
Vermilion Bay
Centerville
White Lake
Patterson
0 20 miles
0 30 km

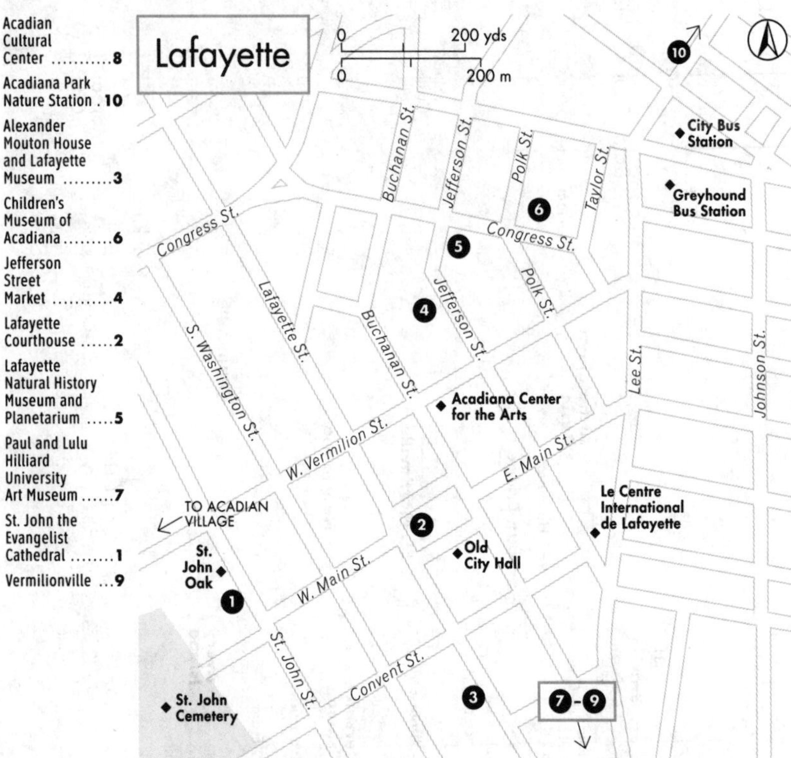

There are images of famous politicians such as Dudley LeBlanc and Huey Long working the stump and scenes from the great flood of 1927. Many of the pictures are displayed on the second floor. ✉ *800 Buchanan St.* ☎ *337/233–0150* ⏲ *Weekdays 8:30–4:30.*

5 **Lafayette Natural History Museum and Planetarium.** Opened in 2003, this sparkling natural-history museum includes changing exhibitions and lots of fun hands-on science for kids. ✉ *433 Jefferson St.* ☎ *337/291–5544* 🌐 *www.lnhmpmuseum.org* 🎟 *$5* ⏲ *Tues.–Fri. 9–5, Sat. 10–6, Sun. 1–6.*

Murals. There are several outdoor murals by Robert Dafford in the center of Lafayette. A Louisiana swamp scene is across from **Dwyer's Café** (✉ *323 Jefferson St.*), and splashy cars and TVs with vignettes of Cajun life are on the **Jefferson Tower Building** (✉ *556 Jefferson St.*). The microcosm of Lafayette inside the garage at **Parc Auto du Centre Ville,** at the corner of Polk and Vermilion streets, is the work of local artist Tanya Falgout.

1 **St. John the Evangelist Cathedral.** This cathedral, completed in 1916 (construction began in 1913), is a Romanesque structure with Byzantine touches. Union troops encamped on the grounds during the Civil War. In the cemetery behind the church are aboveground tombs that date back to 1820; interred here are town founder Jean Mouton, Civil War

hero General Alfred Mouton, and Cidalese Arceneaux. Arceneaux is believed to be the daughter of Gabriel, the lost love of Longfellow's Evangeline. Next to the cathedral is the 400-year-old St. John Oak, one of the charter members of the silent but leafy Louisiana Live Oak Society. ✉ *914 St. John St.* ☎ *337/232–1322.*

OUTSIDE DOWNTOWN

8 **Acadian Cultural Center.** A unit of the Jean Lafitte National Historical Park and Preserve, the center traces the history of the area through numerous audiovisual exhibits of food, music, and folklore. Be sure to watch the introductory film, which is a dramatization of the Acadian exile. Black-and-white clips from the 1929 movie *The Romance of Evangeline* are incorporated in the film; aficionados of early motion pictures will love it. Ranger-guided boat tours of Bayou Vermilion take place March through June in a traditional Louisiana boat. ✉ *501 Fisher Rd.* ☎ *337/232–0789* *Free* *Daily 8–5.*

OFF THE BEATEN PATH

Acadian Village. A re-creation of an early-19th-century bayou settlement, this park is on 10 wooded acres with a meandering bayou crisscrossed by wooden footbridges. Most structures here were constructed during the early 19th century; they were moved here to create this representative "village," though they actually represent a broad range of Acadian architectural styles. Each house is decorated with antique furnishings. The rustic general store, blacksmith shop, and chapel are replicas of 19th-century buildings. ✉ *200 Greenleaf Dr., south of downtown* ☎ *337/981–2364 or 800/962–9133* *www.acadianvillage.org* *$7* *Jan.–Oct. daily 10–4, first three weeks of Dec. 5:30–9* PM.

Acadiana Center for the Arts. This multicultural arts center hosts art exhibits, musical performances, lectures, and children's programs. ✉ *101 W. Vermilion St.* ☎ *337/233–7060* *www.acadianacenterforthearts.org* *Tues.–Fri. 10–5, Sat. 10–6.*

8

10 **Acadiana Park Nature Station.** Naturalists are on hand in the interpretive center at this three-story cypress structure, which overlooks a 42-acre park of natural forest. Discovery boxes help children get to know the wildflowers, birds, and other outdoorsy things they'll see on the 3.5-mi nature trail. Free guided trail tours take place every Saturday and Sunday at 1 PM. There is a guided evening hike on the last Saturday of the month ($2 per person). ✉ *1205 E. Alexander St.* ☎ *337/291–8448* *www.naturestation.org* *Free* *Weekdays 8–5, weekends 11–3.*

7 **Paul and Lulu Hilliard University Art Museum.** A gleaming contemporary architectural gem, this museum features world-class exhibits—including works by Deborah Butterfield and Robert Rauschenberg—and a bookstore. ✉ *710 E. St. Mary Blvd.* ☎ *337/482–2278* *www.louisiana.edu/uam* *$5* *Tues.–Sat. 10–5.*

9 **Vermilionville.** Directly behind the Acadian Cultural Center, a living-history village re-creates the early life of the region's Creoles and Cajuns, focusing on the late 1800s to early 1900s. On select days visitors can see a blacksmith demonstration or weavers. There are exhibits in 19 Acadian-style structures, including a music hall where live Cajun or zydeco music is played every Sunday afternoon. A large rustic restaurant serves Cajun classics, and cooking demonstrations are held on weekends.

⊠300 Fisher Rd., off Surrey St. ☎337/233–4077 or 866/992–2968 ⊕www.vermilionville.org $8 ⊙Tues.–Sun. 10–4.

> **CREOLE VS. CAJUN**
>
> Cajun cuisine relies on locally available ingredients, such as rabbit, mirliton, and rice. Most dishes have the "holy trinity" of celery, bell pepper, and garlic as a base; traditional examples include boudin and *maque choux* (a corn stew, usually served with crawfish tails). Creole cuisine is more cosmopolitan, incorporating French, Spanish, Italian, African, and French Caribbean influences. While many dishes use the same holy trinity, Creole dishes, like their French counterparts, are defined by their sauces. Examples include shrimp Creole, crawfish bisque, and oysters Rockefeller.

WHERE TO EAT

$$$ CAJUN ✕ **Café Vermilionville.** This 19th-century inn with crisp white napery and old-brick fireplaces serves French and Cajun fare to a well-dressed crowd. Among the specialties are Gulf fish Acadien and grilled duck breast. This is a favorite spot for special occasions among Lafayette residents. *⊠1304 W. Pinhook Rd. ☎337/237–0100 ⊕www.cafev.com ▭AE, D, DC, MC, V ⊙Closed Sun. No lunch Sat.*

$ SOUTHERN ✕ **Dwyer's Café.** People jam this diner as early as 6 AM for hot biscuits and grits. Dwyer's serves red beans and rice, jambalaya, pot roast, burgers, and omelets. Be sure to try the hearty plate lunches which include an entrée, two sides, and bread. *⊠323 Jefferson St. ☎337/235–9364 ▭AE, MC, V ⊙ No dinner Sun. and Mon.*

$ SPANISH ✕ **Pamplona Tapas Bar.** Tapas have arrived in Lafayette—and with great success. An authentic interior (one wall is covered with bullfighting posters) creates just the right mood for chef William Annesley's sophisticated dishes and one of the best wine lists in the area. *⊠631 Jefferson St. ☎337/232–0070 ▭AE, MC, V ⊙Closed Sun. and Mon.*

$$ CAJUN ★ ✕ **Prejean's.** Oyster shuckers work in a cozy bar at this local favorite along Interstate 49, north of central Lafayette. Three meals are served in this cypress house with a wide front porch. People gather at tables with red-and-white-check cloths to partake of Prejean's seafood platter (gumbo, fried shrimp, oysters, catfish, crab cakes and maque choux), and some of its legendary gumbo (you can pick from four varieties). There's a Black Angus steak for meat lovers, too. There's live Cajun music, and usually dancing, nightly. *⊠3480 U.S. I–49 N ☎337/896–3247 ⊕www.prejeans.com ▭AE, D, DC, MC, V.*

¢ CAJUN ✕ **T-Coon's Café.** This lively diner serves hearty Cajun breakfast and lunches, which include daily specials such as smothered rabbit or stuffed pork chops with two vegetables, rice, and gravy. More Southern fare includes fried chicken and fried seafood. *⊠1900 W. Pinhook Rd. ☎337/232–0422 www.tcoons.com AE, MC, V ⊙No dinner.*

WHERE TO STAY

$$–$$$ ★ **Bois des Chênes Inn.** This B&B is housed in the 19th-century Mouton Plantation, in a quiet residential area of Lafayette. An upstairs suite can accommodate five, and has early Acadian antiques; downstairs, the Louisiana Empire Suite has a queen-size bed, and the Victorian Suite a double bed. Breakfast is prepared by owner Marjorie Voorhies, and her

husband, Coerte Voorhies, conducts unusually informative boat tours through the surrounding swamps. A complimentary glass of wine and a tour through the home are included in the room rate. **Pros:** nice owners; pretty grounds. **Cons:** rooms feel like they could benefit from a good airing out. ✉*338 N. Sterling St.* ☎*337/233–7816* *5 rooms* *In-hotel: some pets allowed, no-smoking rooms* *AE, MC, V* *BP.*

$$$ **Juliet Boutique Hotel.** This new hotel (opened in late 2007) is the only boutique property in downtown Lafayette. All 20 rooms have fine bed linens and full baths; there's also a pool, and Wi-Fi and room service are available. **Pros:** great location; extremely comfortable beds; you'll feel like you're staying in your own private hotel. **Cons:** some rooms have structural poles; bathrooms have shuttered windows (and don't feel very private); checkout can take a while (since there's only one person at the front desk). ✉*800 Jefferson St.* ☎*337/261–2225* *www.juliethotel.com* *20 rooms* *In-room: Wi-Fi. In-hotel: pool, gym* *AE, D, MC, V.*

$$ **Lafayette Hilton & Towers.** Traditional furnishings outfit the standard rooms; some rooms on concierge floors come with hot tubs and wet bars. Riverside rooms of this high-rise overlook the Bayou Vermilion, though the hotel is on a heavily commercialized strip. **Pros:** typical Hilton amenities; good location is convenient for sightseeing; comfy beds. **Cons:** reservations are hard to come by if there's a wedding or event; halls can be loud when the hotel is full; chain property. ✉*1521 W. Pinhook Rd.* ☎*337/235–6111 or 800/332–2586* *www.hilton.com* *327 rooms* *In-room: Wi-Fi. In-hotel: restaurant, bar, pool, gym* *AE, D, DC, MC, V.*

$$ **T'Frere's House.** Built in 1880 of native cypress and handmade bricks, "little brother's house" has been a B&B since 1985. About 2 mi south of the Oil Center, the Acadian-style house with Victorian trim is furnished with French and Louisiana antiques. Additional accommodations are in an Acadian-style cottage behind the main house. You are greeted with a complimentary "T'julep" and "Cajun canapés," hors d'oeuvres made with boudin. The Cajun breakfast combines regional ingredients with traditional Southern cuisine. **Pros:** charming decor; owners like to feed their guests well; great if you are looking to get away from it all but still want to be near 21st-century amenities. **Cons:** it feels a bit far from everything; not a good option if you're on a diet. ✉*1905 Verot School Rd.* ☎*337/984–9347 or 800/984–9347* *www.tfreres.com* *9 rooms* *AE, D, MC, V* *BP.*

8

NIGHTLIFE AND THE ARTS

NIGHTLIFE Pick up a copy of the *Times of Acadiana* or the trendier *Independent* to find listings for *fais-do-dos,* zydeco dances, and other events. These free weeklies are available in hotels, restaurants, and shops.

Major concerts are held at the **Cajundome** (✉*444 Cajundome Blvd.* ☎*337/265–2100* *www.cajundome.com*). The **Heymann Performing Arts Center** (✉*1373 S. College Rd.* ☎*337/291–5540* *www.heymann-center.com*) hosts concerts and theatrical productions of all types.

Downtown galleries are open and the streets are hopping during the popular **ArtWalks,** which are held on the second Saturday of each month.

On Friday evening from mid-March through June and September through November, **Downtown Alive!** (✉*Jefferson St. at Main St.* ☎*337/291–5566* 🌐*www.downtownalive.org*) draws dancing crowds to downtown Lafayette, where bands play on an open-air stage. **El Sid–o's** (✉*1523 N. St. Antoine* ☎*337/235–0647*) is a family-run zydeco club with music on weekends. Sid Williams manages the club while his brother's band, Nathan and the Zydeco Cha-Chas, performs frequently, as does Nathan's son's band—Lil Nathan and the Zydeco Big Timers. **Randol's** (✉*2320 Kaliste Saloom Rd.* ☎*337/981–7080 or 800/962–2586* 🌐*www.randols.com*), a good Cajun restaurant, also has music and dancing nightly.

FESTIVALS The biggest bash in this neck of the woods is the **Courir de Mardi Gras** (February or March, depending on when Lent occurs), which showcases colorful parades and King Gabriel and Queen Evangeline. For information, contact the Lafayette Convention and Visitors Commission (☎*337/232–3737 or 800/346–1958*).

★ Lafayette's **Festival International de Louisiane** (☎*337/232–8086* 🌐*www.festivalinternational.com*), which takes place on the last weekend of April, is a free music festival, rivaling the New Orleans Jazz and Heritage Festival, that fills the streets with entertainers, artisans, and chefs from French-speaking nations and communities. The annual **Festival Acadiens** is a huge music-and-food fest in Lafayette, held in late September or early October. For information, contact the **Lafayette Convention and Visitors Commission** (☎*337/232–3737 or 800/346–1958*).

SHOPPING

ANTIQUES A cooperative of vendors sells antiques, as well as works by local artists and craftspeople in **Jefferson Street Market** (✉*538 Jefferson St.* ☎*337/233–2589* ⏲*Mon.–Sat. 10–5:30*). Look for beautiful cypress pieces and handwoven textiles.

If you are looking for authentic Louisiana crafts, then **Sans Souci Gallery** (✉*219 E. Vermilion St.* ☎ *337/266–7999 Closed Sun. and Mon.*) should be on your list. Pottery; furniture; items made out of gourds, metal, and wood; as well as cornhusk dolls and jewelry are created by members of the Louisiana Crafts Guild, of which this is its home.

FOOD The fresh French bread and pastries baked at **Poupart's Bakery** (✉*1902 Pinhook Rd.* ☎*337/232–7921* ⏲*Closed Mon.*) rival Paris's best. It also sells specialty sauces and preserves.

Looking to bring home some authentic Cajun goodies? Then a stop at **Don's Specialty Meats & Grocery** (✉*730 I–10 S. Frontage Rd., Scott* ☎*337/234–2528* ✉*104 Hwy. 726, Carencro* ☎*337/896–6370* 🌐*www.donsspecialtymeats.com*) is a must. You can fill your cooler with boudin, cracklin's, stuffed pork chops, quail, and a variety of sausages at Don's two locations—both just outside Lafayette.

GRAND COTEAU

11 mi north of Lafayette.

The tiny village of Grand Coteau may be the most serene place in south Louisiana. Nestled against a sweeping ridge that was a natural levee of the Mississippi River centuries ago ("grand coteau" means big hill), the town is oriented around a core of grand and beautiful religious institutions. Covering the hill itself is a peaceful cemetery, behind the stately St. Charles College, a Jesuit seminary. When the Mississippi overflowed its banks during the cataclysmic flood of 1927, the water stopped shy at the base of Grand Coteau's ridge, and the town was preserved. Today the entire town center is listed on the National Register of Historic Places, with dozens of historical structures including Creole cottages, early Acadian-style homes, and the grand Academy and Convent of the Sacred Heart. Martin Luther King Drive (Route 93) is the main thoroughfare. Antiques stores line the main street.

A magnificent avenue of pines and moss-hung oaks leads to the entrance of the **Academy and Convent of the Sacred Heart,** founded in 1821 as the first of the international network of Sacred Heart schools, and the site of the only Vatican-certified miracle to occur in the United States. The miracle occurred when nuns at the convent said novenas to St. John Berchmans, a 15th-century Jesuit priest, on behalf of Mary Wilson, a very ill novice. St. John Berchmans subsequently appeared to Mary twice, and she was suddenly and unexpectedly cured. St. John Berchmans was canonized in 1888. You may enter a shrine on the exact site of the miracle and (by appointment only) tour a museum with artifacts dating from the school's occupation by Union troops during the Civil War. ☒*1821 Academy Rd., end of Church St.* ☎*337/662–5275* 🌐*www.ashcoteau.org* 🎟*$5* ⏲*Weekdays 9–2.*

In one of Grand Coteau's historic cottages, the **Kitchen Shop** specializes in regional cookbooks and cooking supplies, in addition to a wide range of gifts and other merchandise. It also has prints and greeting cards by famed local photographer John Slaughter. In a tearoom, scones, cookies, and a rich pecan torte called gateau-na-na are served. ☒*296 Martin Luther King Dr., at Cherry St.* ☎*337/662–3500* ⏲*Tues.–Sat. 10–5, Sun. 1–5.*

St. Charles College was the first Jesuit seminary in the South. You can drive or walk through the grounds and cemetery, though you can only visit the beautiful interior of the **Church of St. Charles Borromeo** by appointment. ☒*313 E. Martin Luther King Hwy., at Church St.* ☎*337/662–5251, 337/662–5279 to visit church.*

WHERE TO EAT

$$$ ECLECTIC ✕**Catahoula's.** This stylish yet simple restaurant in a renovated former dry-goods store serves ambitious contemporary cuisine prepared with Mediterranean flair, yet with Cajun roots ever in evidence. The menu changes seasonally, ensuring the freshest ingredients and preparations. Depending on the time of year, the menu includes such inventions as firm gulf shrimp wrapped in a flour tortilla with grilled onions, poblano peppers, and feta cheese, or smoked-seafood-stuffed soft-shell crab with strawberry-fig butter. The decor is spare, and highlights artistic representations of the Catahoula Hound, Louisiana's state dog. ☒*234 Martin Luther King Dr.* ☎*337/662–2275* 🌐*www.catahoulasrest.com* 💳*AE, D, MC, V* ⏲*Closed Mon. No dinner Sun.*

OPELOUSAS

15 mi north of Grand Coteau.

In the heart of St. Landry Parish, Opelousas is the third-oldest town in the state—Poste de Opelousas was founded in 1720 by the French as a trading post. It is a sleepy spot with a historic central square, a provincial museum, and several excellent zydeco clubs within spitting distance. Look for two murals located in a pocket park–parking lot adjacent to the St. Landry Bank & Trust Co. building. One depicts the history of the area and historical monuments in St. Landry Parish and the other depicts the legend of the Seven Brothers Oak, which is located south of Washington, a charming nearby town. Contact the **St. Landry Parish Tourist Commission** (☎*337/948–8004* 🌐*www.cajuntravel.com*) for information about the entire area.

WEEKEND ANTIQUES HUNTING

Antiques lovers will want to stop in Washington, located north of Opelousas. It is a short, 2-mi diversion from the main route if you are traveling from Opelousas to Ville Platte. Founded in 1770, Washington has many buildings on its main street that are on the National Register of Historic Places. More than 10 antiques stores cluster within walking distance of one another. Most of these stores are open only Friday to Sunday. For more information, contact the town's **museum and tourist information center** (☎*337/826–3626*).

The **Opelousas Museum and Interpretive Center** (✉*315 N. Main St.* ☎*337/948–2589* 🎫*Free* ⏲*Mon.–Sat. 9–5*) traces the history of Opelousas from prehistoric times to the present and includes an exhibit on the town's brief stint as state capital, during the Civil War, and a collection of more than 400 dolls. The museum is also home to the Louisiana Video Library and the Southwest Louisiana Zydeco Festival archives.

Traveling exhibits from major museums and private art collections make up the **Opelousas Museum of Art** (✉*106 N. Union St.* ☎*337/942–4991* 🎫*Suggested donation $3* ⏲*Feb.–Dec., Tues.–Fri. 1–5, Sat. 9–5*) inside the Wier House, a rare Southern example of classic Federal architecture.

★ On the town square, you can step back in time at the **Palace Cafe** (✉*135 W. Landry St.* ☎*337/942–2142* ⏲*Closed Sun.*), an old-style diner serving breakfast, lunch, and dinner. Try one or all of the six different types of gumbo on the menu.

At the intersection of Interstate 49 and U.S. 190, look for the **Opelousas Tourist Information Center** (☎*337/948–6263* ⏲*Weekends 8–4*), where you can get plenty of information, arrange for tours of historic homes, and see memorabilia pertaining to Jim Bowie, the Alamo hero who spent his early years in Opelousas.

NIGHTLIFE AND THE ARTS

The roads surrounding Opelousas are *the* place to catch authentic, sweaty zydeco music.

Beloved **Richard's** (✉*U.S. 190, Lawtell* ☎*337/543–6596*) is a rural, wood-frame zydeco club west of Opelousas with music most weekends.

Plaisance, on the outskirts of Opelousas, holds a **Southwest Louisiana Zydeco Music Festival** (☎*337/942–2392* 🌐*www.zydeco.org*) the Saturday before Labor Day.

SHOPPING

For Cajun, zydeco, and Swamp pop-music recordings and related products, **Floyd's Record Shop** (✉*434 E. Main St., Ville Platte* ☎*337/363–2185* 🌐*www.floydsrecordshop.com*) is well worth the drive.

EUNICE

20 mi southwest of Opelousas.

As home to some of Cajun music's most prominent proponents and establishments, tiny Eunice lays claim to some heft within the Cajun music world. Saturday is the best time to visit: spend the morning at a jam at the **Savoy Music Center;** at midday move on to see Tante Sue de Mamou at Fred's Lounge; end the day at the variety show *Rendez-Vous des Cajuns,* in Eunice's Liberty Theatre.

The area surrounding Eunice is the major stomping ground for an annual event, **Courir de Mardi Gras,** which takes place on Mardi Gras Day. Costumed horseback riders dash through the countryside, stopping at farmhouses along the way to shout, "*Voulez-vous recevoir cette bande de Mardi Gras* (Do you wish to receive the Mardi Gras krewe)?" The answer is always Yes, and the group enlarges and continues, gathering food for the street festivals that wind things up.

The **Eunice Depot Museum** is in a former railroad depot and contains modest displays on Cajun culture, including Cajun music and Cajun Mardi Gras. ✉*220 S. C. C. Duson Dr.* ☎*337/457–6540 or 337/457–2565* 🎫*Free* ⏲*Tues.–Sat. 9–noon and 1–5.*

8

The impressive **Prairie Acadian Cultural Center,** part of the Jean Lafitte National Historical Park, has well-executed exhibits tracing the history and culture of the Prairie Acadians, whose lore and customs differ from those of the Bayou Acadians south of Lafayette. Food, crafts, and music demonstrations are held on Saturday. ✉*250 W. Park Ave.* ☎*337/457–8490* 🎫*Free* ⏲*Tues.–Fri. 8–5, Sat. 8–6.*

Fodor'sChoice ★ **Savoy Music Center and Accordion Factory** includes a music store and, in back, a Cajun accordion workshop. Proprietor Marc Savoy's factory turns out about five specialty accordions a month for people around the world. On Saturday morning, accordion players and other instrumentalists tune up during jam sessions in the shop. Musicians from all over the area drop in. ✉*U.S. 190, 3 mi east of town* ☎*337/457–9563* 🎫*Free* ⏲*Tues.–Fri. 9–noon and 1:30–5.*

NIGHTLIFE AND THE ARTS

★ **Fred's Lounge** (✉*420 6th St., Mamou* ☎*337/468–5411* 🎫*Free*) hops on Saturday from about 8 AM until about 2 PM, or for as long as the Cajun band jams and dancers crowd the tiny dance floor. A regular radio broadcast (on KVPI 1050 AM) captures the event. Drive north from Eunice on Route 13 to Mamou, a town so small you can drive around it in five minutes.

CLOSE UP

Cajun and Zydeco Music

It's 9 AM on a typical Saturday morning in the Cajun prairie town of Mamou, and Fred's Lounge (⇨ *Nightlife and the Arts in Eunice)* is already so full that people are spilling out the door. Inside, Cajun singer Donald Thibodeaux gets a nod from the radio announcer, squeezes his accordion, and launches into a bluesy rendition of "Pine Grove Blues." Oblivious to the posted warning, THIS IS NOT A DANCEHALL, the packed bar begins to roll. Fred's Lounge may not be a "formal" dance hall, but plenty of dancing is done here; it gets especially lively during Mamou's Mardi Gras and Fourth of July celebrations. And every Saturday morning for more than 40 years, live Cajun radio shows have been broadcast from the late Fred Tate's lounge. Things get revved up at 8 AM and keep going till 1 PM, and the show is aired on Ville Platte's KVPI radio (1050 AM).

Music has been an integral expression of Cajun culture since early Acadian immigrants unpacked stringed instruments and gathered in homes for singing and socializing. With the growth of towns, these house parties—called *fais-do-dos* (pronounced *fay*-doh-doh, from "go to sleep" in French. The term fais-do-do comes from words mothers murmured to put their babies to sleep while the fiddlers tuned up before a dance.)—were supplanted by dance halls. Accordions, steel guitars, and drums were added and amplified to be heard over the noise of crowded barrooms.

Cajun music went through some lean years in the 1940s and '50s when the state attempted to eradicate the use of the Cajun-French language, but today Cajun music is enjoyed at street festivals and restaurants such as Randol's and Prejean's, which serve equal portions of seafood and song. These places not only keep the music and dance tradition alive but also serve as magnets for Cajun dance enthusiasts from around the world.

Zydeco, the dance music of rural African-Americans of south Louisiana, is closely related to Cajun music, but with a slightly harder, rock-influenced edge. The best place to find the music is in one of the roadside dance halls on weekends. Modern zydeco and Cajun music are both accordion-based, but zydeco tends to be faster and uses heavy percussion and electric instruments; electric guitars and washboards (called a *frottoir*), largely absent from Cajun music, are staples of zydeco. Zydeco bands often play soul- and rhythm and blues–inflected tunes sung in Creole French.

Dance is the universal language of Cajun Country, but don't worry if you're not fluent—there's always someone happy to lead you around the floor and leave you feeling like a local.

In addition to showcasing the best Cajun and zydeco bands, **Rendez-Vous des Cajuns** (✉ *Liberty Center for the Performing Arts, 200 W. Park Ave., at 2nd St.* ☎ *337/457–7389* 💵 *$5*), a two-hour variety program, presents local comedians and storytellers and even a "Living Recipe Corner." The show, mostly in French, has been dubbed the Cajun Grand Ole Opry; it's held every Saturday at 6 PM in a 1924 movie house and is broadcast on local radio and TV.

BREAUX BRIDGE

★ *10 mi northeast of Lafayette, 20 mi southeast of Grand Coteau.*

A dyed-in-the-wool Cajun town, Breaux Bridge is known as the Crawfish Capital of the World. During the first full weekend in May, the Crawfish Festival draws more than 100,000 visitors to this little village on Bayou Teche. Once a wild place, old Breaux Bridge has attracted a small arts community that includes renowned Louisiana photographer Debbie Fleming Caffery and has traded its honky-tonks for B&Bs, antiques shops, and restaurants.

You can pick up a city map and information at the **Chamber of Commerce** (*⊠314 E. Bridge St. ☎337/332–5406 🌐www.breauxbridgelive.com*), at the foot of the bridge that gives Breaux Bridge its name, about ½ mi south of Interstate 10.

WHERE TO EAT AND STAY

$$ CAJUN ★ ✕**Café des Amis.** The culinary heart and soul of downtown Breaux Bridge rests in this large, renovated storefront just a block from Bayou Teche where locals and visitors gather to enjoy hospitality that is second only to the food. Sample the ambience over cocktails or coffee at the bar, or take a table and try the extraordinary turtle soup or the crawfish corn bread. Breakfast here should be savored, from the fresh-squeezed orange juice to the *oreille de cochon* (pastry-wrapped boudin), *couche-couche* (corn-bread-based cereal), and black java. Saturday mornings bring the popular Zydeco Breakfast, featuring a band and dancing. *⊠140 E. Bridge St. ☎337/332–5273 🌐www.cafedesamis.com 💳AE, D, MC, V ⊗Closed Mon. and Tues. No dinner Sun.*

¢ CAJUN ✕**Poche's.** At this no-frills operation, order your authentic Cajun cooking at the counter, then eat in or take away. Daily specials are stick-to-your ribs Cajun food. Boudin, sausage, cracklings, and stuffed chicken are just a few of the items to take out. *⊠33015-A Main Hwy., 2 mi from center of Breaux Bridge ☎337/332–2108 💳 MC, V.*

$$$ Fodor'sChoice ★ 🏨**Maison des Amis.** The owners of Café des Amis renovated this 19th-century house on the bank of Bayou Teche with comfort and relaxation in mind. Each room has a private entrance and a queen-size bed covered with luxurious linens and pillows. A pier and gazebo are perfect for watching moonlight over the bayou. The complimentary Cajun breakfast at Café des Amis is not to be missed. **Pros:** just steps from Cafe des Amis and its famous brunch; located in downtown Breaux Bridge. **Cons:** not all rooms have private bathrooms. *⊠111 Washington St. ☎337/507–3399 🌐www.maisondesamis.com ⇨3 rooms, 1 suite 💳AE, D, MC, V 🍽BP.*

NIGHTLIFE

La Poussière (*⊠1215 Grand Point Rd. ☎337/332–1721*) is an ancient Cajun honky-tonk with live music on Saturday and Sunday.

8

ATCHAFALAYA BASIN

5 mi northeast of Breaux Bridge, 12 mi east of Lafayette.

The Atchafalaya Basin is an eerily beautiful 800,000-plus-acre swamp wilderness, the storybook version of mystical south Louisiana wetlands.

CLOSE UP

Alligators Up Close: Swamp Tours

The bayous, swamps, and rivers of south Louisiana's wetlands present a tantalizingly unfamiliar landscape to many visitors, and the best way to get better acquainted is by boat. Tour operators offer convenient departure times and hotel pickups in New Orleans. Most tour operators use pontoon boats, but—depending on the size of the group—a bass boat might be used. Anticipate from one to two hours on the water and 45 minutes to two hours' commute time to and from New Orleans. Prices generally range from \$10 to \$20 per person. Expect to see nutria, a member of the rodent family that resembles a beaver in appearance and size; egrets (a white, long-necked heron with flowing feathers); turtles; and the occasional snake. During the warmer months, alligator sightings are common. Many of the guides use either chicken or marshmallows to attract them. Plant life includes Spanish moss, cypress, water oaks, and water hyacinths (a member of the lily family). In the summer months, be prepared for the heat and humidity—and don't forget the insect repellent.

Pontoon boats at **McGee's Landing** take passengers daily for 1½-hour tours of the Atchafalaya Basin. McGee's is a 25-minute drive east of Lafayette. Tour times are contingent upon the presence of at least four passengers. ✉*1337 Henderson Levee Rd., Henderson (from I–10, Exit 115 at Henderson; 1 block south of the highway turn left on Rte. 352 and follow it more than 2 mi east over Bayou Amy; turn right atop the levee onto Levee Rd.)* ☎*337/228–2384* 🌐*www.mcgeeslanding.com* *Tour \$18* *Tours daily 10, 1, and 3. Additional tour at 5 during daylight saving time.*

Cajun Country Swamp Tours (✉*1226 N. Berard, Breaux Bridge* ☎*337/319–0010* 🌐*www.cajuncountryswamptours.com* *Tours daily*) are led by guide Walter "Butch" Guchereau, who was born, raised, and still lives on the banks of Bayou Teche in Breaux Bridge. An experienced outdoorsman with a degree in zoology and biology, his ecotours use Cajun crawfish skiffs to be environmentally unobtrusive.

Boating enthusiasts, bird-watchers, photographers, and nature lovers are drawn by vast expanses of still water, cypresses standing knee-deep in marsh and dripping with Spanish moss, and blue herons taking flight. The basin is best viewed from one of the tour boats that ply its waters, but it is possible to explore around its edges on the 7 mi of Henderson's Levee Road (also known as Route 5; off Interstate 10, Exit 115), which provides several opportunities to cross the levee and access swamp tours, bars, and restaurants on the other side.

McGee's Cafe and Bar offers Cajun cuisine and is known for its boiled crawfish. For a rustic touch, rent one of the floating "Cajun Cabins" for a night on the swamp. ✉*1337 Henderson Levee Rd., Henderson (from I–10, Exit 115 at Henderson; 1 block south of the highway turn left on Rte. 352 and follow it just over 2 mi east over Bayou Amy; turn right atop the levee onto Levee Rd.)* ☎*337/228–2384* 🌐*www.mcgeeslanding.com.*

WHERE TO EAT

$$ CAJUN Fodor'sChoice ★ ✕ **Pat's Fishermans Wharf Restaurant.** Adjacent to Bayou Amy, Pat's is the real deal, with heaping platters of seafood. On a cool night, get a table on the porch overlooking the bayou. The Atchafalaya Club, which is the area hot spot for Cajun dancing on Saturday nights, is nearby. ✉*1008 Henderson Levee Rd.70157* ☎*337/228–7512* ▭*AE, D, MC, V.*

ST. MARTINVILLE

15 mi south of Breaux Bridge.

St. Martinville, along winding Bayou Teche, is the heart of Evangeline country. It was founded in 1761 and became a refuge for both Acadians kicked out of Nova Scotia and royalists who escaped the guillotine during the French Revolution. Known as Petit Paris, this little town was once the scene of lavish balls and operas, and you can still roam through the original old opera house on the central square. St. Martinville is tucked away from the state's major highways and misses much of the tourist traffic. It is a tranquil and historically interesting stop, although neighboring towns are better for dining and nightlife. The St. Martinville Tourist Information Center is located across the street from the Acadian Memorial and African American Museum.

In all of Acadiana, St. Martinville is the spot where you can sense most vividly the tragic aspect of the Cajun story, whether in the tiny cemetery behind the main church, or at the bayou-side Evangeline Oak. Henry Wadsworth Longfellow's classic poem "Evangeline," about the star-crossed lovers Evangeline and Gabriel, is based on a true story. According to the oft-told tale, the real-life lovers, Emmeline Labiche and Louis Arceneaux, met for the last time under the **Evangeline Oak.** Louis arrived in St. Martinville, a major debarkation port for the refugees, but it was many years before Emmeline came. Legend has it that the two saw each other by chance just as she stepped ashore. He turned deathly pale with shock and told her that, having despaired of ever seeing her again, he was betrothed to another. *The Romance of Evangeline* was filmed in St. Martinville in 1929. The privately owned movie was never distributed, but clips from it are incorporated in the film presentation at the Jean Lafitte National Historical Park Acadian Cultural Center *(⇨Acadian Cultural Center in Lafayette)*. Its star, Dolores Del Rio, posed for the bronze statue of Evangeline that the cast and crew donated to St. Martinville; it is in the cemetery behind the church of St. Martin de Tours, near the final resting place of Emmeline Labiche. ✉*Evangeline Blvd. at Bayou Teche.*

Shaded by giant live oaks draped with Spanish moss, the 157-acre **Longfellow-Evangeline State Historic Site** has picnic tables and pavilions and early Acadian structures. A small museum traces the history of the Acadians. The Evangeline legend claims that Louis Arceneaux, on whom Gabriel was based, lived in the **Maison Olivier,** a plantation house on the park's grounds, but there is no evidence that he did. The modest house was built in the early 18th century of handmade bricks, and it contains Louisiana antiques. A lively one-hour tour includes many interesting details about life on the indigo plantation. ✉*1200 N. Main St. (Rte.*

8

CLOSE UP

Gone Fishin'

Legend has it that somewhere in the Atchafalaya swamp lives a catfish more than 6 feet long. Although that "whopper" may or may not be true, what can't be disputed is Louisiana's claim to be a sportsmen's paradise. Ever since chef Paul Prudhomme blackened his first redfish caught in local waters, the secret has been out—there are plenty of fish to be had almost everywhere in Louisiana.

The **Gulf of Mexico** and its brackish-water coastal marsh region have made Louisiana famous for shrimp, blue crab, oysters, and fish. And folks are looking for much more than just oil out at the rigs in the gulf. Whether you choose to troll around the rigs or to anchor for some casting, you'll find brag-size lemonfish, cobia, snapper, yellowfin tuna, speckled trout, Spanish and king mackerel, sailfish, wahoo, and even pompano. Many of the marinas in Grand Isle, Cocodrie, and Venice (due south of New Orleans) offer charter-fishing trips that include all fishing tackle, fuel, soft drinks, ice, and someone to bait your hook during the trip and clean your fish when it's over. Prices range from $200 to $500 a day depending on where you fish, the length of the trip, and the number of passengers. Trips range from four to eight hours or overnight. If you're not inclined to pay for a charter, there are plenty of piers, wharves, bridges, and jetties like those at Grand Isle State Park to give you easy access to the open water.

If saltwater fishing isn't your thing, don't worry: there's plenty of fresh-water to go around. Top spots include the **Atchafalaya Basin,** Louisiana's magnificent 800,000-plus-acre natural swampland with facilities at Lake Fausse Point State Park; and **Toledo Bend Reservoir,** a 186,000-acre bass-fishing paradise lined with camp-grounds, marinas, and North Toledo Bend State Park. There are numerous oxbow lakes such as **False River,** north of Baton Rouge, and **Lake Bruin,** where you can find scads of bream, goggle-eye, and perch.

The New Orleans Convention and Visitors Bureau *(⇨ Visitor Information in New Orleans Travel Smart)* can provide a list of charter-fishing companies.

31), ½ mi north of St. Martinville ☎337/394–3754 or 888/677–2900 🌐www.crt.state.la.us/parks 🎟$2 ⏲Daily 9–5.

The **Petit Paris Museum** on the church (St. Martin de Tours) square contains historical records, Carnival costumes, a video history of Mardi Gras, and a chariot exhibit. The chariots are from an annual one-of-a-kind event, the Chariot Parade—a colorful procession of wagons, made by children, which depict anything from a streetcar to a castle. The children and their fanciful chariots circle the church square beginning at dusk on the third Sunday of August. *✉103 S. Main St. ☎337/394–7334 🎟$1 ⏲Call ahead for hrs.*

St. Martin de Tours is the mother church of the Acadians and one of the country's oldest Catholic churches; the 1836 building was erected on the site of an earlier church. Inside is a replica of the Lourdes grotto and a baptismal font said to have been a gift from Louis XVI. Emmeline

EVANGELINE

Henry Wadsworth Longellow's epic poem "Evangeline" (1847) is based on historic documents that chronicle a couple's tragic separation, a result of the British expelling Acadians from Nova Scotia in 1755. Evangeline Bellefontaine and Gabriel Lajeneusse were taken from each other on their wedding day. Once Evangeline arrives in Louisiana, she finds out Gabriel has been there, but has left to live in the Ozarks. After years of searching for him, Evangeline finds Gabriel on his deathbed in Philadelphia. Many believe the two represent real-life counterparts Emmeline Labiche and Louis Arceneaux, though those names themselves are based on another fictional version of the legend. The story shows how the Cajuns faced oppression, separation, and adversity and made a new life for themselves in south Louisiana.

A video introduction, a wall of names of Acadian Louisiana refugees, and a huge mural relate the odyssey of the Acadians at the **Acadian Memorial.** Behind the small heritage center containing these memorials, an eternal flame and the coats of arms of Acadian families pay symbolic tribute to their cultural and physical stamina. ✉ *121 S. New Market St.70582* ☎ *337/394–2258* 🌐 *www.acadianmemorial.org* 🎫 *$2* 🕒 *Daily 10–4.*

The **African American Museum** traces the African and African-American experience in southern Louisiana in riveting detail. Videos, artifacts, and text panels combine to create a vivid, disturbing, and inspiring portrait of a people. It is an ambitious and refreshing balance to the often sidelined or romanticized references to slavery customary in this region. ✉ *121 New Market St.70582* ☎ *337/394–2250* 🎫 *$2* 🕒 *Daily 10–4.*

8

Labiche is buried in the small cemetery behind the church. ✉ *123 S. Main St.* ☎ *337/394–4203.*

WHERE TO STAY

$$ **Old Castillo Bed & Breakfast.** In the late 19th century the Castillo Hotel, a two-story redbrick building next to the Evangeline Oak and Bayou Teche, was an inn for steamboat passengers and a gathering place for French royalists. Rooms are comfortable, with hardwood floors and the odd early Louisiana antique. Some look over the bayou, and all have access to a downstairs parlor and breakfast room. **Pros:** there's no better place to stay in St. Martinville, as its right by a number of attractions; friendly staff; delicious breakfast. **Cons:** if you have a downstairs room, you hear everything that happens downstairs; decor is a little dated. ✉ *220 Evangeline Blvd.* ☎ *337/394–4010 or 800/621–3017* 🌐 *www.oldcastillo.com* *7 rooms* *In-hotel: Wi-Fi, no-smoking rooms* *AE, MC, V* *BP.*

NEW IBERIA

★ *14 mi south of St. Martinville.*

The town of New Iberia is the hub of lower Cajun Country, second only to Lafayette as an arts-and-culture draw. The grand homes of sugarcane planters dominate the residential section of Main Street, just off Bayou Teche, pointing to a glorious past at the center of a booming sugar industry and anchoring the current cultural revival taking place here. Park downtown or stay in one of the numerous B&Bs here and you can easily walk to the bayou, restaurants, art galleries, and shops in the historic business district. Downtown stretches eight blocks east and west on Main Street (Route 182) from the intersection of Center Street (Route 14). The Shadows-on-the-Teche plantation home is at this intersection and is a good place to park.

Check with the **Acadiana Arts Council** (☎*337/233–7060* 🌐*www.acadianaartscouncil.org*) for the latest information on performances at the intimate **Sliman Theater for the Performing Arts** (☎*337/369–2337*), on Main Street. It is the site for the "Louisiana Crossroads" concert series, which features mainly Louisiana musicians, but also showcases musicians from out of state who are influenced by the region.

The **Conrad Rice Mill** is the country's oldest rice mill still in operation, dating from 1912, and it produces a distinctive wild pecan rice. Tours are conducted on the hour between 10 AM and 3 PM. The adjacent **Konriko Company Store** sells Cajun crafts and foods. ✉*307–309 Ann St.* ☎*337/367–6163 or 800/551–3245* 🌐*www.conradricemill.com* *Mill $4* *Mon.–Sat. 9–5.*

★ **Shadows-on-the-Teche,** one of the South's best-known plantation homes, was built on the bank of the bayou for wealthy sugar planter David Weeks in 1834. In 1917 his descendant William Weeks Hall conducted one of the first history-conscious restorations of a plantation home. Truckloads of original documents were deliberately preserved. The result is one of the most fascinating tours in Louisiana. Weeks Hall willed the property to the National Trust for Historic Preservation in 1958, and each year the trust selects a different historical topic to emphasize. Surrounded by 2 acres of lush gardens and moss-draped oaks, the two-story rose-hue house has white columns, exterior staircases sheltered in cabinet-like enclosures, and a pitched roof pierced by dormer windows. The furnishings are 85% original to the house. ✉*317 E. Main St.* ☎*337/369–6446* 🌐*www.shadowsontheteche.org* *$7* *Mon.–Sat. 9–4:30, Sun. noon–4:30.*

WHERE TO EAT AND STAY

$$ CAJUN ✕ **Clementine.** Named for folk artist Clementine Hunter, with an insignia based on her signature, Clementine favors cuisine that might be called nouveau-Cajun: inspired by local ingredients and traditions, but subtly seasoned and artfully presented. Changing art exhibits by locals are introduced at bimonthly openings featuring wine and hors d'oeuvres. Clementine hosts live music on Friday and Saturday nights. ✉*113 E. Main St.* ☎*337/560–1007* 🌐*www.clementinedowntown.com* *AE, D, MC, V* *Closed Sun. No lunch Sat. No dinner Mon.*

$ **Bayou Teche Guest Cottage.** There could scarcely be a better way to appreciate the Queen City of the Teche than to spend a night in this simple, two-room, 18th-century cottage on the bank of the bayou, down the road from downtown attractions. Guests are left on their own, with self-service breakfast items provided in the refrigerator. You can explore the 3 acres of quiet grounds or sit in the front-porch rocking chairs and watch towboats ply the waters. The house canoe is also at your disposal. **Pros:** pretty views; good location to explore New Iberia; if you want to be alone, this is the place. **Cons:** depending on what you expect from a B&B, you'll either find it charming—or a bit worn around the edges. ✉*100 Teche St.* ☎*337/364–1933* *1 cottage* *In-room: refrigerator* *No credit cards.*

$$ **Le Rosier.** A gracious reception awaits at this 19th-century house across from Shadows-on-the-Teche plantation. Guest rooms, in the renovated service wing behind the main house, are small and simple, but the king-size beds are supremely comfortable. A delicious breakfast is served in the main house. **Pros:** walking into town is easy; beautiful courtyard; good for groups who want to get away and be near each other. **Cons:** rooms can seem like you know everything your neighbor is doing. ✉*314 E. Main St.* ☎*337/367–5306 or 888/804–7673* *www.lerosier.com* *6 rooms* *In-room: refrigerator* *AE, MC, V* *BP.*

AVERY ISLAND

9 mi southwest of New Iberia.

The Louisiana coastline is dotted with "hills" or "domes" that sit atop salt mines, and Avery Island is one of these. They are covered with lush vegetation, and because they rise above the surface of the flatlands, they are referred to as islands.

Avery Island is the birthplace of Tabasco sauce, which pleases the Cajun palate and flavors many a Bloody Mary.

The 250-acre **Jungle Gardens,** on Avery Island, has trails through stands of wisteria, palms, lilies, irises, and ferns and offers a lovely perspective on southern Louisiana wilderness. Birdlife includes ducks and geese, and there's also a 1,000-year-old statue of the Buddha. These gardens belonged to Edward Avery McIlhenny, who brought back flora from his travels: lotus and papyrus from Egypt, bamboo from China. **Bird City,** a bird sanctuary on the southeast edge of Jungle Gardens, is sometimes so thick with egrets that it appears to be blanketed with snow. The largest egret colony in the world (20,000) begins nesting here in February or March, and offspring remain until the following winter. Herons and other birds find refuge here as well. You can park your car at the beginning of the trails and strike out on foot, or drive through the gardens and stop at will. ✉*Rte. 329* ☎*337/369–6243* *junglegardens.org* *Jungle Gardens and Bird City $6.25, toll onto Avery Island $1* *Daily 9–5.*

Tabasco was invented by Edmund McIlhenny in the mid-1800s, and the **Tabasco Factory** is presided over by the fourth generation of the McIlhenny family. Tabasco is sold all over the world, but it is produced and bottled only here, on Avery Island. You can take a factory tour, which lasts about 20 minutes and highlights the bottling process. The Jungle Gardens and Bird City are adjacent. ✉*Rte. 329* ☎*337/365–8173 or 800/634–9599* *www.tabasco.com* *Tour free; $1 toll to enter Avery Island* *Daily 9–4.*

8

JEFFERSON ISLAND

4 mi from Avery Island, 9 mi from New Iberia.

Like Avery Island, Jefferson Island is actually a salt dome. The highlight of a visit here is the magnificent 20-acre **Rip Van Winkle Gardens,** filled with semitropical vegetation and the sort of vistas that only a salt dome can offer in southern Louisiana. A café looks over Lake Peigneur and provides a restful and picturesque spot for refreshments following exploration of the gardens. Be on the lookout for the peacocks—if you're lucky, one of the males will open his feathers for you. Also on the grounds is the **Joseph Jefferson Home,** a highly personalized mansion that combines Steamboat Gothic, Moorish, and French-plantation styles. It was built as a country home for stage actor Joseph Jefferson in the mid-19th century and is open for 40-minute tours. There is also a bed-and-breakfast on the grounds should you like it so much you want to stay. ✉ *5505 Rip Van Winkle Rd.* ☎ *337/359–8525* 🌐 *www.ripvanwinklegardens.com* 🎫 *Garden access and house tour $10, garden only $5* ⏲ *Daily 9–4.*

ABBEVILLE

15 mi south of Lafayette.

Abbeville has a number of historic buildings and two pretty village squares anchoring the center of downtown. It is a good stop for pleasant town walks and for oysters on the half shell, a local fetish. The town sponsors the annual Giant Omelet Festival each November, when some 5,000 eggs go into the concoction. At other times, oysters are the culinary draw. It is also the base for Steen's Cane Syrup.

You can pick up a self-guided walking-tour brochure at the **Abbeville Tourist Office** (✉ *1905 Veterans Memorial Hwy.* ☎ *337/898–4264*). Many buildings in the 20-block Main Street district are on the National Register of Historic Places.

St. Mary Magdalen Catholic Church (✉ *N. Main and Père Megret Sts.* ☎ *337/893–0244* ⏲ *Mon.–Sat. 8–5; Sun. mass 6:30* AM) is a fine Romanesque Revival building with stunning stained-glass windows.

WHERE TO EAT

$ SEAFOOD ✕ **Dupuy's Oyster Shop.** This small restaurant has been serving family-harvested oysters in the same location since 1869. Seafood platters feature seasonal specials. ✉ *108 S. Main St.* ☎ *337/893–2336* 🌐 *www.dupuysoystershop.com* 💳 *MC, V* ⏲ *Closed Sun. and Mon.*

MAURICE

10 mi north of Abbeville, almost 11 mi south of Lafayette.

Maurice is considered the gateway to Vermilion Parish, and lies between Lafayette and Abbeville. Many overlook this small town but it's well worth the stop for Hebert's Specialty Meats' world-famous "turducken" and the Maurice Flea Market.

PARLEZ-VOUS CAJUN FRANÇAIS?

It's not uncommon while traveling through Cajun country to still hear French—the Cajun version. Here are a few words that might help you enjoy and understand the lingo.

Allons: Let's go!

Bayou: A sluggish body of water, larger than a creek, but smaller than a river.

C'est la vie: Such is life.

Cher: Dear

Cochon de lait: A pig roast.

Étouffée: A stew mainly made with seafood, in which the "holy trinity" (celery, garlic, and bell pepper) is used.

Fais-do-do: A dance. French for "Go to sleep," which was what parents would whisper to their children so they could go dancing.

Lagniappe: A little something extra.

Laissez les bons temps rouler: Let the good times roll.

Roux: Flour browned in fat and used as a thickener in many Cajun dishes such as gumbo.

WHERE TO EAT

$ CAJUN ✕ **Hebert's Specialty Meats.** A visit to Cajun country is not complete without stopping at Hebert's, rumored to be the spot where turducken was invented. A turducken is a turkey stuffed with a duck, stuffed with a chicken. Other to-go specialties include boudin, deboned chicken, and other regional delicacies. ✉ *8212 Maurice Ave. (Rte. 167)* ☎ *337/893–5062* ▭ *AE, D, MC, V.*

8

SHOPPING

ANTIQUES From fine antiques to slightly rusted kitchen utensils, the **Maurice Flea Market** (✉ *9004 Maurice Ave. [Rte. 167]* ☎ *337/898–2282* ⏲ *Thurs.–Sat. 10–5*) is a treasure-hunter's paradise. Be prepared to spend more than an hour here.

CAJUN COUNTRY ESSENTIALS

To research prices, get advice from other travelers, and book travel arrangements, visit 🌐 *www.fodors.com.*

BUS TRAVEL

Greyhound has numerous daily departures from New Orleans to Lafayette. The trip takes 3–3½ hours.

Bus Information Greyhound (☎ *800/231–2222* 🌐 *www.greyhound.com*).

CAR TRAVEL

Interstate 10 runs east–west across the state and through New Orleans. Take Interstate 10 west to the Lafayette exit, 128 mi from New Orleans. The interstate route takes about two hours. Return to New Orleans via U.S. 90, down through Houma, for scenic stopovers. This route also takes two hours.

TRAIN TRAVEL

Amtrak connects New Orleans and Lafayette via the *Sunset Limited*. Trains make the three- to four-hour scenic trip each way three times a week.

Train **Amtrak** (☎ *800/872–7245* 🌐 *www.amtrak.com*).

EMERGENCIES

Hospital **Medical Center of Southwest Louisiana** (✉ *2810 Ambassador Caffery Pkwy., Lafayette* ☎ *337/981–2949*).

24-Hour Pharmacy **CVS** (✉ *1920 Kaliste Saloom Rd., Lafayette* ☎ *337/984–1092*).

VISITOR INFORMATION

The Lafayette Convention and Visitors Commission is open weekdays 8:30 to 5 and weekends 9 to 5. La Remise, the St. Martinville visitor center, is across the street from the Evangeline Oak park, just behind the church square. It's open daily 10 to 4.

Contacts **Lafayette Convention and Visitors Commission** (✉ *1400 N. W. Evangeline Thruway (Box 52066), Lafayette* ☎ *337/232–3737 or 800/346–1958* 🌐 *www.lafayettetravel.com*). **La Remise** (✉ *215 Evangeline Blvd., St. Martinville* ☎ *337/394–2233* 🌐 *www.cajuncountry.org*).

Travel Smart New Orleans

WORD OF MOUTH

"Before we left, I printed out a little map of the French Quarter and marked the bars or restaurants that had been recommended by Fodorites or friends. That way, if we ever found ourselves in need of refreshment, I would be able to find a good place nearby. This map really came in handy."

—shormk2

"If you don't mind the heat and humidity, August is by far the cheapest month in New Orleans. If you can't stand heat and humidity and want cheap rates, December is your only option, as November is still high season. January after the Sugar Bowl is usually quiet as well, but it can get quite cold in January in New Orleans."

—bkluvsNola

www.fodors.com/community

GETTING HERE AND AROUND

New Orleans fills an 8-mi stretch between the Mississippi River and Lake Pontchartrain. Downtown includes the French Quarter, the Central Business District (CBD), Warehouse District, Tremé, and the Faubourg Marigny. Uptown includes the Garden District, Audubon Park, Tulane and Loyola universities, as well as the Carrollton and Riverbend neighborhoods.

It's best to know your location relative to the following thoroughfares: Canal Street (runs from the river toward the lake), St. Charles Avenue (runs uptown from Canal), Interstate 10 (runs west to the airport, east to Slidell), and LA Highway 90 (takes you across the river to the West Bank). To get to the CBD from Interstate 10, exit at Poydras Street near the Louisiana Superdome. For the French Quarter, look for the Orleans Avenue/Vieux Carré exit.

Canal Street divides the city roughly into the uptown and downtown sections (though the CBD and Warehouse District, considered part of downtown, actually lie just upriver from Canal). Keeping a visual on the Superdome is the surest way to know where the Central Business District is; the French Quarter lies just to the northeast of it over Canal Street.

Streets that start in the French Quarter and cross over Canal Street change names as they go upriver. For example, Decatur Street becomes Magazine Street and Royal Street becomes St. Charles Avenue. Addresses begin at 100 on either side of Canal Street, and begin at 400 in the French Quarter at the river.

AIR TRAVEL

Flying time is 2½ hours from New York, 2¼ hours from Chicago, 1¼ hours from Dallas, and 4½ hours from Los Angeles. Flights to the city have not fully returned to pre-Katrina levels, so book early to ensure that you have as many options as possible. This is especially true for popular weekends like Mardi Gras and Jazz Fest.

Airline Security Issues **Transportation Security Administration** (*www.tsa.gov*) has answers for almost every question that might come up. Airports

The major gateway to New Orleans is Louis Armstrong New Orleans International Airport (MSY), 15 mi west of the city in Kenner. There's an Airport Exit off Interstate 10. Plan for about 30–45 minutes of travel time from downtown New Orleans to the airport (more at rush hour). An alternative route is Airline Drive, which will take you directly to the airport from Tulane Avenue or the Earhart Expressway. Be prepared for stoplights and possible congestion.

Airport Information **Louis Armstrong New Orleans International Airport** (*900 Airline Dr., Kenner* *504/464–0831* *www.flymsy.com*.

FLIGHTS

Airline Contacts **AirTran** (*800/247–8726 or 678/254–7999*). **American Airlines** (*800/433–7300*). **Continental Airlines** (*800/523–3273*). **Delta Airlines** (*800/221–1212*). **jetBlue** (*800/538–2583*). **Northwest Airlines** (*800/225–2525*). **Southwest Airlines** (*800/435–9792*). **United Airlines** *800/864–8331*). **USAirways** (*800/428–4322*).

GROUND TRANSPORTATION

SHUTTLE BUSES

Shuttle-bus service to and from the airport and downtown hotels is available through Airport Shuttle New Orleans, the official ground transportation of Louis Armstrong International Airport. You can purchase shuttle tickets at the Airport Shuttle desk, located across from baggage claim areas 3, 6, and 12. To return to the airport, call 24 hours in advance of flight time. The cost one way is $15 per person, and the trip takes about 40 minutes.

Jefferson Transit also runs a bus between the airport, the CBD, and Mid-City, although it only goes to the CBD on weekdays. The trip costs $1.60 in exact change ($1.10 from Carrollton and Tulane avenues) and takes about 45 minutes. From the airport, you can catch the E-2 line on the second level near the Delta counter. Departures for the airport are every 10 to 20 minutes from Elks Place and Tulane Avenue across from the main branch of the New Orleans Public Library, and from the corner of Tulane and Carrollton avenues. The last bus leaves at 7:40 PM from Tulane and Elks Place, 11:45 PM from Tulane and Carrollton.

Contacts **Airport Shuttle New Orleans** (☎ *504/522–3500* 🌐 *www.airportshuttleneworleans.com*). **Jefferson Transit** (☎ *504/818–1077* 🌐 *www.jeffersontransit.org/busroutes.htm*).

TAXIS

A cab ride to or from the airport from uptown or downtown costs $28 for up to two passengers. For groups of three or more, the rate is $12 per person. Pickup is on the lower level, outside the baggage-claim area. There may be an additional charge for extra baggage.

Taxi Companies **American** (☎ *504/299–0386*). **United Cabs** (☎ *504/522–9771*). **White Fleet-Rollins Cab Co.** (☎ *504/822–3800*). **Yellow-Checker Cab** (☎ *504/525–3311*).

BOAT TRAVEL

By FerryThe ferry ride across the river to Algiers is an experience in itself, offering great views of the river and the New Orleans skyline as well as the heady feeling of being on one of the largest and most powerful rivers in the world. Pedestrians climb the stairs there is a ramp for wheelchair access) near the Spanish Plaza and the Riverwalk shopping area and board the Canal Street Ferry from above. Bicycles and cars board from below on the left of the terminal. The trip takes about 10 minutes; ferries leave on the hour and half hour from the east bank and on the quarter and three-quarter hour from the west bank—they run from 6 AM to midnight. Hours at night may vary, so be sure to check with the attendants if you are crossing in the evening—it is no fun to be stranded on the other side. There are wheelchair-accessible restrooms on the ferry.

Information **Canal Street Ferry** (✉ *Foot of Canal at Convention Center Blvd.* ☎ *504/376–8180*) 🎫 *1 cash round-trip per car, free for pedestrians.*

CRUISES

The Delta Queen Steamboat Company offers 3- to 11-night excursions up the Big Muddy and environs aboard the *Delta Queen*, a National Historic Landmark built in the 1920s; the *Mississippi Queen*, built in 1976; or the *American Queen*, the largest paddle wheeler ever built. Cruises up the Mississippi focus on the river's effect on history and historic onshore sites such as antebellum plantation houses, Vicksburg, and Natchez. Founded in 1890, the company operates from March to December out of an enormous and efficient waterfront terminal complex adjacent to the Ernest N. Morial Convention Center. Carnival Cruise Line, Norwegian Cruise Line, and Royal Caribbean International also depart from New Orleans.

For more information, visit the Port of New Orleans Web site at 🌐 *www.portno.com* or call ☎ *504/522–2551*.

Cruise Lines **Carnival Cruise Line** (☎ *800/227–6482 or 305/599–2600*). **Delta Queen Steamboat Company** (☎ *800/768–8946 or 504/586–0631*). **Norwegian Cruise Line** (☎ *800/327–7030 or 305/436–4000*). **Royal Caribbean International** (☎ *866/562–7625 or 305/539–6000*).

BUS AND STREETCAR TRAVEL

ARRIVING BY BUS

Greyhound has one terminal in the city, in the Union Passenger Terminal in the CBD. Ask about special travel passes. Check with your local Greyhound ticket office for prices and schedules.

GETTING AROUND BY BUS AND STREETCAR

Within New Orleans, the Regional Transit Authority (RTA) operates a public bus and streetcar (not "trolley") transportation system with interconnecting lines throughout the city. The buses are generally clean and on time. Buses run on a regular schedule from about 6 AM to 6 PM. Smoking, eating, and drinking are not permitted on RTA vehicles. Buses are wheelchair accessible; streetcars are not.

ROUTES

The riverfront streetcar covers a 2-mi route along the Mississippi River, connecting major sights from the end of the French Quarter (Esplanade Avenue) to the New Orleans Convention Center (Julia Street). Nine stops en route include the French Market, Jackson Brewery, Canal Place, the World Trade Center, the Riverwalk, and the Hilton Hotel. This streetcar operates daily 7 AM until 10:30 PM, passing each stop every 30 minutes.

The historic streetcars of St. Charles Avenue run from St. Charles Avenue at Common Street to the Riverbend at Carrollton Avenue roughly every 10 minutes on weekdays and every 15 minutes on weekends. This line continues on along Carrollton Avenue and stops at Claiborne Avenue in Mid-City. Streetcar service on St. Charles Avenue runs 24 hours a day, though wait times can be as long as 45 minutes to an hour between midnight and 5 AM.

A third streetcar line runs along Canal Street from the river near Harrah's Casino to either City Park or the Cemeteries. It passes every 12 minutes. The Canal Street line operates from 5 AM to about 3 AM, with longer waits after midnight.

COSTS

Bus and streetcar fare is $1.25 exact change plus 25¢ for transfers. Visiting senior citizens 65 or over who have a valid RTA ID card (available through RTA ID centers) may ride public transit for only 40¢. Children under 2 years of age ride for free. Unlimited passes, valid on both buses and streetcars, cost $5 for one day, $12 for three days, and $55 for a month. The daily passes are available from streetcar and bus operators; three-day passes are available at many hotels; monthly passes must be purchased from official vendors, including all local Whitney Banks.

Bus and Streetcar Information **Greyhound** (Union Passenger Terminal ✉ *1001 Loyola Ave.* ☎ *800/231–2222 or 504/525–6075* 🌐 *www.greyhound.com*). **RTA** ☎ *504/248–3900, 504/242–2600 automated information* 🌐 *www.norta.com*).

CAR TRAVEL

CAR RENTALS

Renting a car in New Orleans is a good idea if you plan to travel beyond the French Quarter and the Garden District. However, if you plan to stick to the highly touristed areas, you may want to keep it simple and use taxis, streetcars, and an airport shuttle.

If you do decide to rent a car, rates in New Orleans begin at around $40 per day ($250 per week) for an economy car with air-conditioning, automatic transmission, and unlimited mileage. Prices do not include local tax on car rentals, which is 13.75%, or other surcharges, which can add another 10%–15% to your cost.

Automobile Associations **American Automobile Association** (AAA) (☎ *315/797–5000* 🌐 *www.aaa.com*). **National Automobile Club** (☎ *650/294–7000* 🌐 *www.thenac.com*); membership is open to California residents only.

Major Agencies **Alamo** ☎ 877/222-9075. **Avis** (☎ *800/331–1212*). **Budget** (☎ *800/527–0700*). **Hertz** (☎ *800/654–3131*). **National Car Rental** (☎ *877/222–9058*).

GASOLINE

Gas stations are not plentiful within the city of New Orleans. The downtown area is particularly short on stations. Head for Lee Circle if you need gas while in the downtown area. If you are in Uptown, there are stations along Carrollton Avenue.

PARKING

Finding a parking space is fairly easy in most of the city, except for the French Quarter, where meter maids are plentiful and tow trucks eager. If in doubt about a space, pass it up and pay to use a parking lot. Avoid spaces at unmarked corners: less than 15 feet between your car and the corner will result in a ticket. Watch for temporary no parking signs, which pop up along parade routes and film shoots.

Garages Central Parking (*111 Iberville St., French Quarter* *504/529–3327* *www.parking.com.* *202 N. Peters St., French Quarter* *504/299–9786*). **Standard Parking** (*911 Iberville St., French Quarter* *504/524–5996* *www.standardparking.com*). **Towne Park** (*530 Natchez St., CBD* *504/525–8359* *www.townepark.com*).

ROAD CONDITIONS

Surface roads in New Orleans are generally bumpy and potholes are common. Many were damaged in post-Katrina flooding. Pay attention to the drivers in front of you who may need to slow down or swerve to avoid damaged patches. Along St. Charles Avenue, use caution when crossing over the neutral ground (median); drivers must yield to streetcars and pedestrians along this route. Afternoon rush hour affects New Orleans daily and backups on Interstate 10 can start as early as 3 PM. Ongoing construction on Interstate 10—also a positive sign—may cause delays.

FROM NEW ORLEANS TO	ROUTE	DISTANCE
Atchafalaya Basin	I-10	124 mi
Avery Island	I-10, U.S. 90	168 mi
Baton Rouge	I-10	80 mi
Breaux Bridge	I-10, U.S. 31	130 mi
Lafayette	I-10	136 mi
St. Francisville	I-10, U.S. 61	105 mi
Oak Alley	U.S. 44	60 mi
Opelousas	I-10, U.S. 49	162 mi
San Francisco Plantation	U.S. 44	35 mi

TAXI TRAVEL

Cabs are metered at $2.50 minimum for one passenger, plus $1 for each additional passenger, and $1.60 per mile. If you're trying to hail a cab in New Orleans, try Decatur Street, Canal Street, or outside major hotels in the Quarter or the CBD. Otherwise, call.

If you need a cab from a crowded major event, call and have one pick you up a block or two away on a less congested street. During Mardi Gras, it can be extremely difficult to get a cab; plan an alternate way home (or enjoy the party until public transportation starts up again in the morning).

Taxi Companies American *504/299–0386*. **United Cabs** (*504/522–9771*). **White Fleet-Rollins Cab Co.** *504/822–3800*). **Yellow-Checker Cab** (*504/525–3311*).

TRAIN TRAVEL

Three major Amtrak lines run at New Orleanss Union Passenger Terminal. The Crescent makes daily runs from New York to New Orleans by way of Washington, D.C. The City of New Orleans runs daily between New Orleans and Chicago. The Sunset Limited makes the two-day trip from Los Angeles to New Orleans en route to Orlando. It departs from New Orleans traveling westward on Monday, Wednesday, and Friday and leaves Los Angeles on Sunday, Wednesday, and Friday.

Information Amtrak (*800/872–7245* *www.amtrak.com*). **Union Passenger Terminal** (*1001 Loyola Ave.* *800/872–7245*).

TRAIN ROUTE	SERVES	COSTS (APPROX.)
City of New Orleans	Chicago	$200
Crescent	New York	$300
Sunset Limited	Los Angeles	$130

ESSENTIALS

CHILDREN IN NEW ORLEANS

Be sure to plan ahead and involve your youngsters as you outline your trip. When packing, include things to keep them busy en route. On sightseeing days try to schedule activities of special interest to your children. The *Times-Picayune*, the city's daily, publishes a "Kidstuff" column every Monday that lists upcoming events for families and kids. The Louisiana Children's Museum is an excellent resource for activities that are both educational and fun.

Be sure to plan activities for kids in the French Quarter with an aim to avoiding Bourbon Street. Things are out in the open, whether you plan to see them or not. In the evening, Bourbon Street quickly becomes overloaded with large, noisy, and inebriated crowds. With kids in tow, it's best to steer clear.

If you are renting a car, don't forget to arrange for a car seat when you reserve.

Local Information **Louisiana Children's Museum** (*✉420 Julia St., Warehouse District ☎504/586–0725 🌐www.lcm.org*). **New Orleans Convention & Visitors Bureau** (*✉2020 St. Charles Ave., Garden District ☎800/672–6124 or 504/566–5011 🌐www.neworleanscvb.com*).

DAY TOURS AND GUIDES

Given the variety of perspectives available in the city of New Orleans, a package tour can be a good option, especially for first-time visitors. Highlights will likely include the French Quarter and Riverwalk, with daytime visits to spots like Audubon Zoo, the Garden District, and possibly a plantation or swamp tour.

Bus ToursSeveral local tour companies give two- to four-hour city bus tours that include the French Quarter, the Garden District, Uptown New Orleans, and the lakefront. Prices range from $25 to $50 per person. Both Gray Line and New Orleans Tours offer a longer tour that combines a two-hour city tour by bus with a two-hour steamboat ride on the Mississippi River.

New Orleans Tours leads city, swamp, and plantation tours and combination city–paddle wheeler outings, and runs a Magazine Street Shopping Shuttle. Tours by Isabelle (now in its 30th year and the oldest tour company in New Orleans) runs city, swamp, plantation, and combination swamp-and-plantation tours.

Gray Line and Tours by Isabelle both offer tours of Hurricane Katrina damage and recovery. For those visitors interested in seeing the scope of the impact of the 2005 storm and keeping the local economy in motion, these tours offer perspective on the area's geography, ecology, and recovery. For the more personal experience, choose Tours by Isabelle.

PLANTATION TOURS

Full-day plantation tours by bus from New Orleans, which include guided tours through two antebellum plantation homes along the Mississippi River and a stop for lunch in a Cajun-Creole restaurant outside the city, are offered by Gray Line and New Orleans Tours.

Tours by Isabelle includes lunch in its full-day plantation package that traces the history of the Cajun people. Also available is the Grand Tour: a full-day minibus tour that includes a visit to one plantation, lunch in a Cajun restaurant, and a 1½-hour boat tour in the swamps with a Cajun trapper.

Tour Contacts **Gray Line** (*☎800/535–7786 or 504/569–1401 🌐www.graylineneworleans.com*). **New Orleans Tours** (*☎504/592–1991 🌐www.notours.com*). **Tours by Isabelle** (*☎877/665–8687 or 504/398–0365 🌐www.toursbyisabelle.co)m.*

RIVERBOAT CRUISES

The New Orleans Steamboat Company offers narrated riverboat cruises and evening jazz cruises up and down the Mississippi on the steamboat *Natchez*, an authentic paddle wheeler. Ticket sales and departures for the *Natchez* are at the Toulouse Street Wharf behind Jackson Brewery.

The same company operates the *John James Audubon* riverboat, a ship that can accommodate 600. It makes several trips daily between the Aquarium of the Americas and the Audubon Zoo. A visit to the zoo or aquarium can be combined with a 7-mi ride between the two that takes 30 to 45 minutes depending on river conditions. Tickets for such package tours are available in kiosks at both the zoo and the aquarium. Prices vary depending on whether you choose only the cruise or combine it with zoo and aquarium admissions.

New Orleans Paddle Wheel has a Mississippi River cruise aboard the *Creole Queen*, highlighting the port and French Quarter twice daily departing from the Riverwalk. There is also an evening jazz dinner cruise from 8 to 10 (boarding at 7 PM); tickets are available for the dinner and cruise, or just the cruise and live music. The ticket office is at the Poydras Street Wharf near the Riverwalk.

Cruise Operators **New Orleans Paddle Wheel** (☎ *800/445–4109 or 504/529–4567*). **New Orleans Steamboat Company** (☎ *800/233–2628 or 504/586–8777* 🌐 *www.steamboatnatchez.com*).

SPECIAL-INTEREST TOURS

For highlights of African-American history and culture, contact Le'Ob's Tours. It runs prearranged group tours (20–30 people) of the city, swamps, and plantations, as well as large-group jazz history tours, complete with club recommendations for the week of your visit. One of our favorites is the Louis Armstrong tour. Based in Houston since Hurricane Katrina, Le'Ob's runs specialty tours primarily during conventions and festivals. Call Lucille for reservations.

Macon Riddle's Let's Go Antiquing offers personalized shopping itineraries to the city's antiques stores, galleries, or boutiques based on your interests and preferences (not all tours are about antiques). The number for appointments is her residence; don't be afraid to leave a message. New Orleans School of Cooking, located in the heart of the French Quarter, offers classes on Cajun and Creole cuisine. Visit its Web site for details about class schedules, rates, and products. Savvy Gourmet offers a wide range of classes from local to international cuisine in its Magazine Street location. Its schedule is posted on the Web site. Savvy Gourmet recommends reserving a space in the class one to two weeks in advance. If you're feeling spontaneous, go ahead and call—you might get lucky.

Limousine services make arrangements for personal interests and private guides; rentals vary. Southern Seaplane will fly you over the city and its surrounding areas.

African-American Tours **Le'Ob's Tours** (☎ *281/751–7524 or 713/540–9399*).

Cooking Classes **New Orleans School of Cooking** (☎ *800/237–4841 or 504/525–2665* 🌐 *www.neworleansschoolofcooking.com*). **Savvy Gourmet School of Cooking** (☎ *504/895–2665* 🌐 *www.savvygourmet.com*).

Limousine Contact **Bonomolo Limousines** (☎ *800/451–9258*).

Seaplane Contact **Southern Seaplane** (☎ *504/394–5633* 🌐 *www.southernseaplane.com*).

Shopping **Let's Go Antiquing** (☎ *504/899–3027* 🌐 *www.neworleansantiquing.com*).

SWAMP TOURS

Exploring an exotic Louisiana swamp and traveling into Cajun country is an adventure not to be missed. Dozens of swamp-tour companies are available. You can check at your hotel or the visitor center for a complete listing. Many do not provide transportation from downtown hotels; those listed below do. Full-day tours often include visiting a plantation home.

Swamp Tours **Gray Line** (☎ *800/535–7786 or 504/569–1401* 🌐 *www.graylineneworleans.com*). **Honey Island Swamp Tours** (☎ *985/641–1769* 🌐 *www.honeyislandswamp.com*. **Jean Lafitte Swamp and Airboat Tours** (☎ *800/445–4109 or 504/529–4567* 🌐 *www.jeanlafitteswamptour.com*). **Tours by Isabelle** (☎ *877/665–8687 or 504/398–0365* 🌐 *www.toursbyisabelle.com*). **Westwego Swamp Tours** (☎ *800/633–0503 or 504/592–1991* 🌐 *www.westwegoswampadventures.com*).

WALKING TOURS

Free 1½-hour, general history tours of the French Quarter are given daily at 9:30 AM by rangers of the Jean Lafitte National Historical Park and Preserve. Each visitor may procure a ticket for the tour at the Park Service office at the National Park Visitor Center after 9 AM on the morning of the tour. Check the National Park Visitor Center for details. Tickets are free, but tours are limited to 25 people. Two-hour general history tours, beginning at the 1850 House on Jackson Square, are given Tuesday through Sunday at 10 and 1:30 by Friends of the Cabildo.

Several specialized walking tours conducted by knowledgeable guides on specific aspects of the French Quarter are also available. Because some of these tours accommodate as few as two people, be sure to make advance reservations. Heritage Tours leads a general literary tour as well as others focusing on either William Faulkner or Tennessee Williams.

The cemeteries of New Orleans fascinate many people because of their unique aboveground tombs. Save Our Cemeteries conducts guided walking tours of St. Louis No. 1 as well as Lafayette No. 1. Reservations are generally required.

French Quarter **Friends of the Cabildo** (☎ *504/523–3939* 🌐 *www.friendsofthecabildo.org*).

French Quarter and Garden District **Haunted History Tours** (☎ *888/644–6787 or 504/861–2727* 🌐 *www.hauntedhistorytours.com*). **Jean Lafitte National Historical Park and Preserve** (☎ *504/589–2636*).

Literary **Heritage Tours** (☎ *504/949–9805*).

Voodoo, Ghosts, Vampires, and Cemeteries **Haunted History Tours** (☎ *888/644–6787 or 504/861–2727* 🌐 *www.hauntedhistorytours.com*). **Historic New Orleans Walking Tours** (☎ *504/947–2120* 🌐 *www.tourneworleans.com*). **New Orleans Spirit Tours** (☎ *504/314–0806* 🌐 *www.neworleanstours.net*). **Save Our Cemeteries** (☎ *888/721–7493 or 504/525–3377* 🌐 *www.saveourcemeteries.org*).

EMERGENCIES

Doctors and Dentists **Touro Infirmary** (✉ *1401 Foucher St., Garden District* ☎ *504/897–7777*), physician-referral service available weekdays 8–5.

Hospitals and Clinics **Touro Infirmary** (✉ *1401 Foucher St., Garden District* ☎ *504/897–7011 (main desk) or 504/897–8250 (ER)*). **Tulane University Medical Center** (✉ *1415 Tulane Ave.* ☎ *800/588–5800 or 504/588–5800* 🌐 *www.tuhc.com*).

Pharmacies **Rite-Aid** (✉ *2669 Canal St., Mid-City* ☎ *504/827–1400* ✉ *3401 St. Charles Ave. Garden District* ☎ *504/896–4575*). **Walgreens** (✉ *900 Canal St., French Quarter* ☎ *504/568–1271* ✉ *134 Royal St., French Quarter* ☎ *504/525–2180* ✉ *3311 Canal St., Mid-City* ☎ *504/568–1271* ✉ *1801 St. Charles Ave.* (24-hr pharmacy), *Garden District* ☎ *504/561–8458*).

GAY AND LESBIAN TRAVEL

New Orleans has a large gay and lesbian population spread throughout the metropolitan area. The most gay-friendly neighborhood is the French Quarter, followed by the Faubourg Marigny, just outside the Quarter. Most bars for gay men are within these neighborhoods; lesbians may have to venture farther.

Robert Spatzen leads a 2½-hour Gay Heritage Tour through the French Quarter and environs on Wednesday at 4 PM and Saturday at 1 PM. Call ahead for a reservation; he needs at least four people signed up an hour before starting time to guarantee a tour.

Throughout the year a number of festivals celebrate gay culture. The biggest festival of the year is the Decadence Festival. The city also has gay-friendly guesthouses and B&Bs, particularly along Esplanade Avenue.

Faubourg Marigny Art and Books is open until 10 PM. It's the last independent gay-focused bookstore in New Orleans.

The Whiz and *Ambush*, local biweekly newspapers, provide lists of current events in addition to news and reviews. *Southern Voice* also publishes a newspaper with nightlife coverage of New Orleans, Atlanta, and the Gulf South. These publications are found in many gay bars and in the Faubourg Marigny Bookstore.

Gay and Lesbian-Friendly Travel Agencies **Different Roads Travel** (☎ *760/327-7212 or 323/350-9172*). **Skylink Travel and Tour/ Flying Dutchmen Travel** (☎ *800/225-5759 or 707/546-9888* 🌐 *skylinktravel.com*).

Local Sources **Faubourg Marigny Art and Books** (☎ *504/947-3700*). **Robert Spatzen** (☎ *504/945-6789*).

HEALTH

The intense heat and humidity of New Orleans in the height of summer can be a concern for anyone unused to a semitropical climate. Pace yourself to avoid problems such as dehydration. Pollen levels can be extremely high, especially in April and May. Know your own limits and select indoor activities in the middle of the day; youll find the locals doing the same thing.

INTERNATIONAL TRAVELERS

CURRENCY

The dollar is the basic unit of U.S. currency. It has 100 cents. Coins are the penny (1¢), the nickel (5¢), dime (10¢), quarter (25¢), half-dollar (50¢), and the rare golden $1 coin and rarer silver $1. Bills are denominated $1, $5, $10, $20, $50, and $100, all mostly green and identical in size; designs and background tints vary. A $2 bill exists but is extremely rare.

CUSTOMS

Information **U.S. Customs and Border Protection** 🌐 *www.cbp.gov.*

DRIVING

Driving in the United States is on the right. Speed limits are posted in miles per hour (usually between 55 MPH and 70 MPH). In small towns and on back roads limits are usually 30 MPH to 40 MPH. Most states require front-seat passengers to wear seat belts; also, children should be in the back seat and buckled up. In major cities rush hour is 7 to 10 AM; afternoon rush hour is 4 to 7 PM. Some freeways have special lanes, ordinarily marked with a diamond, for high-occupancy vehicles (HOV)—cars carrying two people or more.

Highways are well paved. Interstates—limited-access, multilane highways designated with an "I–" before the number—are fastest. Interstates with three-digit numbers circle urban areas, which may also have other expressways, freeways, and parkways. Limited-access highways sometimes have tolls.

Gas stations are plentiful. Most stay open late (some 24 hours) except in rural areas, where Sunday hours are limited and stations are very far apart. Along larger highways, roadside stops with restrooms, fast-food restaurants, and sundries stores are well spaced. State police and tow trucks patrol major highways. If your car breaks down, pull onto the shoulder and wait, or have your passengers wait while you walk to an emergency phone (available in most states). On a cell phone, dial *55.

ELECTRICITY

The U.S. standard is AC, 110 volts/60 cycles. Plugs have two flat pins set parallel to each other.

EMBASSIES

Contacts **Australia** (☎ *202/797-3000* 🌐 *www.austemb.org*). **Canada** (☎ *202/682-1740* 🌐 *www.canadianembassy.org*). **UK** (☎ *202/588-7800* 🌐 *www.britainusa.com*).

EMERGENCIES

For police, fire, or ambulance, dial 911 (0 in rural areas).

HOLIDAYS

New Year's Day (Jan. 1); Martin Luther King Day (3rd Mon. in Jan.); Presidents' Day (3rd Mon. in Feb.); Memorial Day (last Mon. in May); Independence Day (July 4); Labor Day (1st Mon. in Sept.); Columbus Day (2nd Mon. in Oct.); Thanksgiving Day (4th Thurs. in Nov.); Christmas Eve and Christmas Day (Dec. 24 and 25); and New Year's Eve (Dec. 31).

MAIL

You can buy stamps and aerograms and send letters and parcels in post offices. Stamp-dispensing machines can occasionally be found in airports, bus and train stations, office buildings, drugstores, convenience stores, and in ATMs. U.S. mailboxes are stout, dark-blue steel bins; pickup schedules are posted inside the bin (pull the handle). Mail parcels over a pound at a post office.

A first-class letter weighing 1 ounce or less costs 44¢; each additional ounce costs 17¢. Postcards cost 27¢. Postcards or 1-ounce airmail letters to most countries cost 94¢; postcards or 1-ounce letters to Canada or Mexico cost 72¢.

To receive mail on the road, have it sent c/o General Delivery to your destination's main post office. You must pick up mail in person within 30 days with a driver's license or passport for identification.

Contacts **DHL** (☎ *800/225-5345* 🌐 *www.dhl.com*). **FedEx** (☎ *800/463-3339* 🌐 *www.fedex.com*). **Mail Boxes, Etc./The UPS Store** (☎ *800/789-4623* 🌐 *www.mbe.com*). **USPS** (🌐 *www.usps.com*).

PASSPORTS AND VISAS

Visitor visas aren't necessary for citizens of Australia, Canada, the United Kingdom, or most citizens of EU countries coming for tourism and staying for under 90 days. A visa is $100, and waiting time can be substantial. Apply for a visa at the U.S. consulate in your place of residence.

Visa Information **Destination USA** (🌐 *www.unitedstatesvisas.gov*).

PHONES

Numbers consist of a three-digit area code and a seven-digit local number. In New Orleans, the area code is 504; surrounding areas use 225 or 985. Within many local calling areas, dial just seven digits. In others, dial "1" first and all 10 digits; this is true for calling toll-free numbers—prefixed by "800," "888," "866," and "877." Dial "1" before "900" numbers, too, but know they're very expensive.

For international calls, dial "011," the country code, and the number. For help, dial "0" and ask for an overseas operator. Most phone books list country codes and U.S. area codes. The country code for Australia is 61, for New Zealand 64, for the United Kingdom 44. Calling Canada is the same as calling within the United States (country code: 1).

For operator assistance, dial "0." For directory assistance, call 555–1212 or 411 (free at many public phones). To call "collect" (reverse charges), dial "0" instead of "1" before the 10-digit number.

Instructions are generally posted on pay phones. Usually you insert coins in a slot (usually 25¢–50¢ for local calls) and wait for a steady tone before dialing. On long-distance calls the operator tells you how much to insert; prepaid phone cards, widely available, can be used from any phone. Follow the directions to activate the card, then dial your number.

CELL PHONES

The United States has several GSM (Global System for Mobile Communications) networks, so multiband mobiles from most countries (except for Japan) work here. It's almost impossible to buy just a pay-as-you-go mobile SIM card in the United States—needed to avoid roaming charges—but cell phones with pay-as-you-go plans are available for well under $100. AT&T (GoPhone) and Virgin Mobile have the cheapest with national coverage.

Contacts **AT&T** (☎ *888/333-6651* ⊕ *www.att.com*). **Virgin Mobile** (⊕ *www.virginmobileusa.com*).

MONEY

Prices throughout this guide are given for adults. Substantially reduced fees are almost always available for children, students, and senior citizens.

ATMs can easily be found on Decatur Street, at most gift shops, and in most bars in the French Quarter. These machines generally have high fees, but there are some who advertise fees as low as 99¢. Bank ATMs are harder to find in the French Quarter, but are more prevalent along St. Charles Avenue. As always, use common sense when withdrawing cash and be aware of your surroundings. If getting cash at night, try to use machines in more populated areas.

ITEM	AVERAGE COST
Cup of Coffee	$1.50
Glass of Wine	$5–$7
Glass of Beer	$3–$5
Po'boy	$6–$8
One-Mile Taxi Ride	$2.50 plus $1.60 per mile
Museum Admission	$6–$12

PACKING

New Orleans is casual during the day and casual to slightly dressy at night. A few restaurants in the French Quarter require men to wear a jacket and tie. For sightseeing, pack walking shorts, sundresses, cotton slacks or jeans, T-shirts, and a light sweater.

In winter you'll want a coat or warm jacket, especially for evenings, which can be downright cold. In summer pack for hot, sticky weather, but be prepared for air-conditioning bordering on glacial, and bring an umbrella in case of sudden thunderstorms. Leave the plastic raincoats behind (they're extremely uncomfortable in the high humidity). In addition, pack a sun hat and sunscreen lotion, even for strolls in the city, because the sun can be fierce.

Insect repellent will also come in handy if you plan to be outdoors on a swamp cruise or in the city dining alfresco; mosquitoes come out in full force after sunset in warm weather.

SAFETY

New Orleans has long drawn unwelcome attention for its high crime rate. Tourists are seldom the target of major crimes but can, like other citizens, be the target of pickpockets and purse-snatchers. The New Orleans Police Department regularly patrols the French Quarter. Still, common sense is invaluable.

Know where you're going or ask the concierge at your hotel about the best route. In the French Quarter, particularly if you are on foot, stay on streets that are heavily populated. After dark, walk with a sense of purpose; night is not the time for obvious sightseeing.

In other areas of the city it is always advisable to drive. High-end neighborhoods and derelict properties back up to one another throughout New Orleans, making aimless strolling a bad idea outside the Quarter. Try to stick to the recommended walks and areas in this book, and be aware of your surroundings.

Call a taxi late at night or when the distance is too great to walk; this is even more important if you've been drinking.

TAXES

A local sales tax of 9% applies to all goods and services purchased in Orleans Parish, including food. Taxes outside Orleans Parish vary and are slightly lower.

Louisiana is the only state that grants a sales-tax rebate to shoppers from other countries who are in the country for no more than 90 days. Look for shops, restaurants, and hotels that display the distinctive tax-free sign and ask for a voucher for the 9% sales tax tacked on to the price of many products and services. Present the vouchers with your plane ticket and passport at the tax rebate office at the Louis Armstrong New Orleans International Airport, near the American Airlines ticket counter, and receive up to $500 in cash back. If the amount redeemable is more than $500, a check for the difference will be mailed to your home address. Call the airport refund office for complete information.

Contact **Airport Refund Office** (☎ *504/467-0723* 🌐 *www.louisianataxfree.com*).

TIPPING

A standard restaurant tip is 15%; if you truly enjoyed your meal and had no complaints, 20% is more appropriate. If you use the services of the concierge, a tip of $5 to $10 is appropriate, with an additional gratuity for special services or favors. Always keep a few dollar bills on hand—they'll come in handy for tipping bellhops, doormen, and valet parking attendants. As always, use your discretion when tipping.

WORD OF MOUTH

After your trip, be sure to rate the places you visited and share your experiences and travel tips with us and other Fodorites in Travel Ratings and Talk on 🌐 *www.fodors.com.*

VISITOR INFORMATION

For general information and brochures, contact the city and state tourism bureaus below. The New Orleans Convention & Visitors Bureau's Web site is a comprehensive source for trip planning, hotel and tour booking, and shopping in the city; you can also download brochures, coupons, walking tours, and event schedules, as well as find links to other helpful Web sites. The Louisiana Office of Tourism offers the same with a focus on the entire state.

Contacts **Louisiana Office of Tourism** (☎ *800/633-6970* 🌐 *www.louisianatravel.com*). **New Orleans Convention & Visitors Bureau** (☎ *800/672-6124 or 504/566-5011* 🌐 *www.neworleanscvb.com*).

ONLINE RESOURCES

The Louisiana Department of Culture, Recreation and Tourism's Web page gives a general overview of tourism in Louisiana, especially recovery efforts after Hurricanes Katrina and Rita.

New Orleans Online provides basic trip planning and travel tools. The New Orleans Multicultural Tourism Network produces a variety of multicultural heritage directories. The city's official site, *cityofneworleans.com*, has updates on local issues and government affairs, as well as a neat "City Stories" section that profiles residents of note. *Frenchquarter.com* is the place to go for great links to event, accommodations, and parking information, as well as an interactive French Quarter map. And for that something extra, *experienceneworleans.com* has links to a blog, podcast, and a fun video, in addition to the standard tourist sites.

Neworleans.com has general information about events, hotels, and restaurants. For Louisiana music coverage (plus other entertainment news), *OffBeat* magazine's Web site is a good bet. Everything you need to know about The New Orleans Jazz & Heritage Festival can be found at its Web site. Devoted entirely to Mardi Gras, *mardigrasneworleans.com* includes histories, parade schedules, and other specific Mardi Gras information.

Head to *Nola.com* for everything New Orleans; it includes links to the *Times-Picayune*, New Orleans's daily newspaper, with news stories, nightlife, and more. The Web site of *Gambit Weekly* magazine does a good job of representing varying perspectives on life in the city.

All About Louisiana The Louisiana Department of Culture, Recreation and Tourism (*www.crt.state.la.us*).

All About New Orleans City of New Orleans (*www.cityofno.com*). **Experience New Orleans** (*www.experienceneworleans.com*). **Frenchquarter.com** (*www.frenchquarter.com*). **New Orleans Multicultural Tourism Network** (*www.soulofneworleans.com*). **New Orleans Online** (*www.neworleansonline.com*).

Music, Festivals, and Events Mardi Gras New Orleans (*www.mardigrasneworleans.com*). **Neworleans.com** (*www.neworleans.com*). **New Orleans Jazz & Heritage Festival** (*www.nojazzfest.com*). **OffBeat Magazine** (*www.offbeat.com*).

Periodicals The Times-Picayune (*www.nola.com*). **Gambit Weekly** (*www.bestofneworleans.com*).

INSPIRATION

To prepare for your trip to New Orleans, rent *A Streetcar Named Desire*, starring Marlon Brando and Vivien Leigh. Seedy, steamy, and emotionally charged, this is the quintessential New Orleans film. Also check out Elvis in *King Creole,* a music-filled noir tale set in the French Quarter. Other New Orleans classics are *Jezebel, The Buccaneer*, and *Easy Rider.* You may also enjoy *Interview With A Vampire, Blaze*, or the *Pelican Brief*. More contemporary New Orleans films include *Double Jeopardy* with Ashley Judd, *Runaway Jury* starring John Cusack, *Déjà Vu* with Denzel Washington, and *The Curious Case of Benjamin Button*, set in the Garden District.

A necessary read for any New Orleans visitor is John Kennedy Toole's *A Confederacy of Dunces*. Ingatius J. Reilly, the book's bumbling protagonist, is as quirky as the city itself. Andrei Codrescu's *New Orleans, Mon Amour*, a collection of memoirs written over the last 20 years, is a humorous and touching read. For a look into life in old New Orleans, pick up anything by George Washington Cable. Since Hurricane Katrina, numerous books about the city have been published. Visit any locally owned bookstore for the insider's perspective on the New Orleans literary scene.

INDEX

T

U

V

W

Photo Credits: 5, *Russell McCulley*. 9 (left), *David Richmond/neworleansonline.com*. 9 (right), Inggita Notosusanto/Shutterstock. 13 (left), Corbis. 13 (right), Richard Nowitz/New Orleans CVB. 14 (left), Corbis. 14 (top center), Jose Gil/Shutterstock. 14 (top right), Natalia Bratslavsky/Shutterstock. 14 (bottom right), Harry Costner/New Orleans CVB. 15 (left), Richard Nowitz/New Orleans CVB. 15 (top right), Carl Purcell/New Orleans CVB. 15 (bottom right), Richard Nowitz/New Orleans CVB. 18, Kevin O'Hara/age fotostock. 19, John S. Sfondilias/Shutterstock. 20, Ray Laskowitz/Alamy. 21 and 23 (left), San Rostro/age fotostock. 23 (right), Doug Scott/age fotostock. 24, Simon Reddy/Alamy. 25 (top), *Jeff Schmaltz/MODIS Land Rapid Response Team/NASA*. 25 (bottom), *illinoisphoto.com*. 27, *Rick Wilking/Reuters*. 28-29, *Russell McCulley*. 30, George H. Long.

NOTES

NOTES

NOTES

NOTES

NOTES

NOTES

NOTES

NOTES

ABOUT OUR WRITERS

Michelle Delio, who updated our Experience chapter and the French Quarter, Faubourg Marigny, Bywater, and Tremè coverage in Exploring New Orleans, splits her time living in Miami, New York City, and the Big Easy. A freelance editor who covers art, pop culture, photography, travel, and technology, Michelle also contributes to *Fodor's New York City, Essential USA*, and *Florida*.

Jeanne Faucheux is the daughter of New Orleans natives. She has resided in Virginia, Georgia, Tennessee, Maryland, and New Jersey, but recently came to her senses and moved back to Louisiana. Jeanne teaches history to middle school students and travels as often as she can, making her a knowledgeable writer for our Travel Smart section.

Paul A. Greenberg, who revised the Where to Eat and Where to Stay chapters, is a New Orleans-based writer and the Program Director for Journalism and Media Arts at Tulane University. Greenberg writes for local, regional, and national publications, and has been part of the Fodor's team for ten years.

Molly Jahncke updated the CBD, Warehouse District, Garden District, Uptown, Bayou St. John, Mid-City, and Metairie and the Lakefront sections for the Exploring chapter. She's lived and worked as a writer and teacher in such exotic locales as France, Indonesia, Japan, Korea, Thailand, Australia, and even New Jersey. Thrilled to be back in hometown New Orleans and doing public affairs work for Delgado Community College, Molly still has a passion for freelance travel writing and globetrotting.

David Parker Jr., who updated the Nightlife and the Arts section, is a fiction writer and journalist who contributes regularly to *NOLAFugees.com*. In his ten years living in New Orleans he has been a bartender, bellhop, sailor, sorter, surfer, courier, carpenter, festival organizer, and warehouse manager. He currently lives, writes, and juggles employment opportunities in and around the French Quarter.

As Managing Editor at *Gambit Weekly* newspaper in New Orleans, **Kandace Power Graves** keeps her finger on the pulse of the city's ever-changing retail and business landscape. With her passion for local shops and boutiques, Kandace is the perfect person to update our shopping chapter.

Sue Strachan is a freelance writer, as well as the public relations director for the Ogden Museum of Southern Art in New Orleans. She loves to travel, and she journeyed to Louisiana's Cajun and Plantation regions to revise the Sidetrips chapter. She also partied at Mardi Gras and Jazz Fest to make sure our festival coverage is just right. *Laissez les bon temps roulez!*